W9-BVC-200

WITHDRAWN

Tribal Library
Saginaw Chippewa Indian Tribe
7070 E. Broadway
Mt. Pleasant MI 48858

the Weekend Woodworker

the Weekend Woodworker

101 EASY-TO-BUILD PROJECTS

By

John A. Nelson

Rodale Press, Emmaus, Pennsylvania

The authors and editors who compiled this book have tried to make all of the contents as accurate and as correct as possible. Plans, illustrations, photographs, and text have all been carefully checked and cross-checked. However, due to the variability of local conditions, construction materials, personal skill, and so on, neither the author nor Rodale Press assumes any responsibility for any injuries suffered or for damages and other losses incurred that result from the material presented herein. All instructions and plans should be carefully studied and clearly understood before beginning construction.

Copyright © 1990 by John A. Nelson

All rights reserved. No part of this publication may be reproduced or transmitted in any form or by any means, electronic or mechanical, including photocopy, recording, or any other information storage and retrieval system, without the written permission of the publisher.

Printed in the United States of America on acid-free, recycled paper

Editor in Chief: William Gottlieb
Senior Managing Editor: Margaret Lydic Balitas
Editor: Jeff Day
Contributing Editor: Roger Yepsen, Jr.
Editorial Assistance: Stacy Brobst
Book Designer: Darlene Schneck
Copy Editor: Nancy King-Bennink
Cover Design: Darlene Schneck
Cover Photograph: Mitch Mandel

If you have any questions or comments concerning this book, please write:
 Rodale Press
 Book Reader Service
 33 East Minor Street
 Emmaus, PA 18098

Library of Congress Cataloging-in-Publication Data

Nelson, John A., 1935–
 The weekend woodworker : 101 easy-to-build projects / John A. Nelson.
  p. cm.
  ISBN 0-87857-894-3 hardcover
  ISBN 0-87857-904-4 paperback
  1. Woodwork. I. Title.
 TT180.N44 1990
 684′.08—dc20   89-70250
                CIP

Distributed in the book trade by St. Martin's Press

2 4 6 8 10 9 7 5 3 1 hardcover
2 4 6 8 10 9 7 5 3 1 paperback

Contents

Acknowledgments vii
Introduction ix

Mallet 1
Wooden Hammer 2
Wooden Basket 3
Tie Rack 5
Cedar Jewelry Box 7
Eight-Sided Jewelry Box 9
Cranberry Scoop 12
Elephant Table Lamp 14
Shoeshine Box 17
In/Out Mail Basket 20
Wall Barometer 22
Fireboard 26
Box for Forstner Bits 29
Jelly Cupboard 33
Chest of Drawers 37
Toaster Tongs 42
Pasta and Salad Forks 43
Key Rack 45
Napkin Holder 46
Wooden Trivet 48
Scoop 50
Serving Tray 52
Candy Dish 54
Grocery List Holder 56
Small Jelly Cupboard 58
Bathroom Shelf 61
Cookbook Holder and Trivet 63
Wall Spice Box 65
Adjustable Corner Shelves 68

Rooster and Turkey on Sticks 70
Swan Cutting Board 72
Cat on a Stand 74
Tulips on a Stand 76
Duck Basket 78
Pull Toys 80
Office Bird 82
Knickknack Shelf 84
Miniature Rocking Horse 86
Chip-Carved Jewelry Box 88
Folk-Art Birdhouse 91
Weather Vane 93
Sailboat Half Model 95
Candle Box 99
Toy Blocks 102
Jigsaw Puzzle 104
Elephant Pull Toy 106
Toy Top 108
Chinese Checkers 110
Elephant Bank 114
Pyramid Puzzle 116
Dog Pull Toy 118
Toy Train 120
Model T Runabout 123
Jeep 127
Dump Truck 131
Tractor Trailer 136
Merry-Go-Round 140
Circus Toy 143
Flying Elephant Toy 150
Skittles 154
English Rocking Horse 158

Bootjack 163
Footstool 164
Silver Tray 166
Early American Candlestick 168
Wall Candle Box 170
Colonial Shelf 173
Pipe Box with Two Drawers 175
Colonial Pipe Box 178
Courting Mirror 182
Miniature Blanket Chest 185
Victorian Nightstand 190
Large Blanket Chest 193
Wall Shelf 197
Wall Cupboard 200
Shaker Table 204
Country Desk 207
Tambour Clock 216
Mission Wall Clock 218
Square Wall Clock 220
Child's Clock 222
Rooster Wall Clock 224

Terry Shelf Clock 226
Banjo Clock 230
Schoolhouse Clock 234
Trellis 240
Rail Planter 242
Bluebird Nesting Box 244
Artist's Easel 247
Mailbox Post 250
Wind Chimes 254
Whirligig 257
Coasting Sled 262
Child's Sleigh 265
Adirondack Chair and Child's
    Adirondack Chair 270
Victorian Garden Bench 274
Card Holder 277
Child's Wheelbarrow 279
Four-Tiered Plant Stand 284
Picnic Table 287

Appendix: Suppliers 290

Acknowledgments

I wish to thank the following people for their help in developing this book: Mitch Mandel and Deborah Porter, for taking the photographs; Bill Bigelow, teacher of woodworking at Conval Regional High School, for being my mentor as I developed many of these projects; David Sloan and his staff at *American Woodworker,* for their help in readying several projects for publication; Bill Hylton and Jeff Day of Rodale Press, for the hours and hours they put into conceiving this book and getting it under way; Darlene Schneck, also of Rodale, for her design work; Roger Yepsen, Jr., for helping to make sense of my writing; Judy Vaillancourt, of Vaillancourt Folk Art and Friends of Sutton, Massachusetts, for painting the Television Jelly Cabinet; Nancy Van Campen of Dublin, New Hampshire, for painting the Fireboard and the Pull Toys; and last but not least, my wife, Joyce, for painting the various toy projects throughout the book. Without them, I wouldn't have made it.

Introduction

This book is for woodworkers who find that their time often seems as rare as certain exotic woods. It offers dozens of pieces that can be built in a weekend. A few projects may be stretching that time frame a bit; the Country Desk, for example (pages 207 to 214), is presented as several subassemblies, each of which can be made in a weekend. But most projects are quite simple, involving straightforward joinery and the more common hand and power tools.

You'll find that some pieces demand more of your skills and your shop than others. I've tried for a mix, to interest both beginners and the experienced woodworker. Before tackling a project, read through it and study the drawings to make sure you know what will be required.

Like many woodworkers, I justify the expense of tools and materials by pointing out that the handy things I've made have more than paid for themselves. But I suspect that the real incentive for most of us is to get involved with wood—especially in a day when much of our surroundings is made of synthetic materials.

How to Use the Drawings

I've done my best to make sure that all the drawings and measurements are correct. Still, I suggest that you double-check the instructions before cutting any wood. When possible, dry-assemble the parts before gluing them together for good.

Each project is illustrated with a front view and either a right view or top view. In some cases I've included a section view; this reveals what a part would look like if cut through at a certain point. All but the simplest projects are illustrated with an exploded view, which shows how the various parts come together.

Parts of a project are identified by number in the drawings. The text and the Materials List identify the parts by name and number. In most cases, the parts are numbered in the order that I suggest you make and assemble them.

Materials Lists

All but the simplest projects include a Materials List to help you organize your work.

The first column of the Materials List gives each part by name and number. The second column lists the size of each part. I've followed woodworking convention in giving dimensions: Thickness is listed first, followed by stock width, followed by stock length. When a piece is something other than a rectangle, the Materials List gives you the size rectangle required to make the appropriate shape. The third column of the list tells you the number of each piece required.

A few hardware and mechanical items will have to be ordered, and I give addresses for a limited number of mail-order suppliers. You'll find a list of suppliers at the back of the book.

When the instructions tell you to make multiples of a certain part, take care that they are as nearly the same size and shape as possible. As I caution repeatedly in the text, don't routinely round edges; keep them sharp, so that parts meet squarely and securely. Edges can be rounded as necessary once the piece is assembled.

Mallet

Unless the handles of your wood chisels have metal-reinforced ends, a hammer will batter them. The mallet in this simple turning project will save the handles and is a pleasure to use.

You might want to turn a thinner mallet for lighter work. Make it the same length but reduce the diameter to about 2 in.

1. Select the stock. Mallets can be made out of any number of hardwoods. Maple and oak are two popular choices. The mallet in the photograph was made from oak only because I happened to have oak on hand when I needed a mallet. The blank should be 4 in. square and about 12 in. long. The finished mallet is only 9¾ in. long, but you will need the extra length in order to mount the blank on the lathe.

2. Mount the blank. Locate the *exact* center of each end by drawing diagonal lines between opposite corners. Mark the center point with an awl. To make the first stage of the turning go more easily, trim ¾ to 1 in. off the corners of the blank by running it through a table saw with the blade set at 45 degrees. The result will be an octagonal piece of wood. Mount it on the lathe.

3. Turn the blank. Turn the blank to a diameter of 3¾ in. along the entire length. Lay out the diameters given in the drawing. Turn each diameter to the size called for in the drawing. Trim both ends down until you have a ⅜-in. nib holding the mallet in place.

4. Apply finish. While the piece is still on the lathe, sand it and apply a coat of oil finish. (A hard finish such as polyurethane is a bad choice because it will chip off in use.) Remove the mallet from the lathe and cut off the nibs with a hand saw. Sand the ends smooth and apply a coat of finish to these spots.

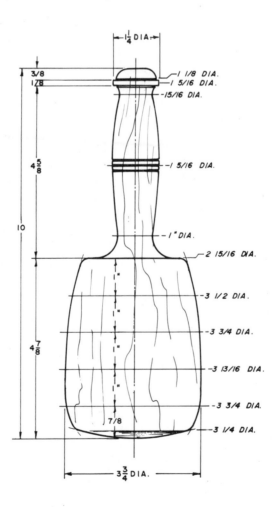

Wooden Hammer

A wooden hammer comes in handy when you want to persuade a tight joint to come together. A standard metal hammer will work, but it can damage the piece.

1. Select the stock. Both the handle and the head are lathe-turned from hardwood. Allow at least an extra inch on each piece so that they can be mounted on the lathe.

2. Turn the pieces. Locate the *exact* center on the end of each piece. Mark the centers with an awl. Trim the corners off the pieces with a table saw, setting the blade at 45 degrees; take about ¾ in. off each corner of the head and ¼ in. off each corner of the handle. You'll end up with two eight-sided blocks.

Both the handle and head are made the same way. Mount a blank on the lathe. Turn the entire length to the piece's maximum diameter. Lay out the finished length of the piece with a parting tool, but don't cut through the stock. Mark off locations of the various diameters along the length, as shown in the drawing. Turn to the final size.

Sand the pieces while they are still turning on the lathe. Sanding will change the diameters slightly, so don't sand the section of the handle that fits into the hammer head. Cut off the pieces with a saw.

3. Assemble the hammer. Drill a ¾-in.-diameter hole 1 in. deep into the center of one side of the hammer head. To keep the head steady while drilling, hold it with a clamp, vise, or a piece of wood with a V-shaped notch cut into it. The handle should fit snugly in the hole. If it is loose, cut a slot into the end of the handle and tighten it by inserting a thin wedge in the slot. Cut the slot into the center of the end with a backsaw. It should be no wider than the kerf created by the saw and ⅝ in. to ¾ in. deep. The wedge should be long enough and thick enough

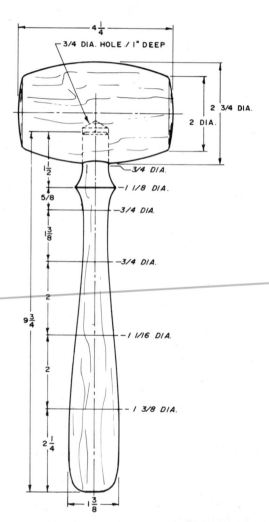

to open the the kerf two or three times its original width.

Spread glue inside the hole and on the ¾-in. section of the handle. If you have cut a slot in the handle, position it perpendicular to the grain of the hammer head. Tap the wedge gently until it will go no farther and allow the glue to dry before trimming off any excess.

4. Apply finish. Apply oil finish to the assembled hammer.

Wooden Basket

Baskets don't come much simpler than this, and yet its lines are pleasing. I've found that these baskets sell well at craft shows.

1. *Select the stock and cut the parts.* You can make this basket out of workshop scraps. Cut the parts to the sizes given in the Materials List.

2. *Cut the parts to shape.* Make two 45-degree cuts in both ends (part 1). Drill a ⅜-in.-diameter handle hole in the handle supports (part 3). Trim the top ends of the supports, as shown in the end view, by making 45-degree cuts that begin about ³⁄₁₆ in. from the corners. Chamfer the ends of the handle (part 4) slightly with sandpaper.

3. *Assemble the basket.* I recommend gluing the pieces together and then nailing them with roundhead brass nails (part 5), but any ½-in.-long nail will do.

Start assembly by putting the ends upside down on the bench and attaching the two bottom slats (part 2). Leave ¾ in. between the slats; the handle support fits into this space, as shown in the end view.

Turn the basket on one side and attach the three slats to the opposite side. Turn the basket over to attach the remaining slats.

Attach the handle supports. When attaching the second support, align it with the first support by temporarily putting the handle in

MATERIALS LIST

Part	Dimensions	Quantity
1. Ends	½″ × 3⅞″ × 5½″	2
2. Slats	⅛″ × ¾″ × 8″	8
3. Handle supports	¼″ × ¾″ × 8″	2
4. Handle	⅜″ dia. × 8¾″	1
5. Roundhead brass nails	½″	as needed

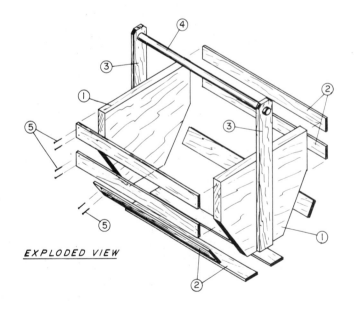

EXPLODED VIEW

3

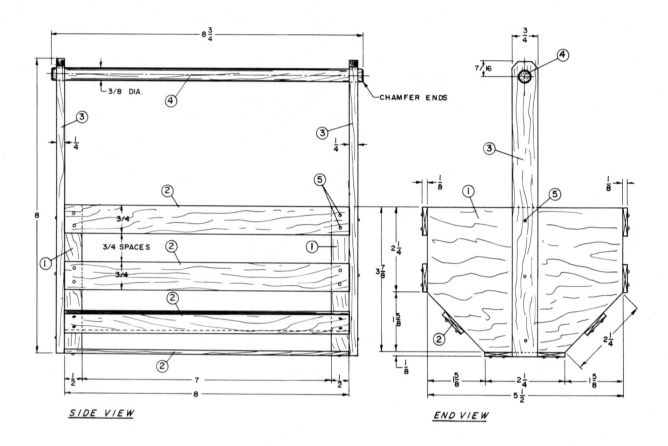

SIDE VIEW

END VIEW

place. After you've attached the supports, glue the handle in place.

4. *Apply finish.* You can leave the basket unfinished or stain and varnish it. If you will be storing food in the basket, finish it with salad bowl finish.

Tie Rack

This handy project could be a good one to try if you are interested in selling your work at craft shows.

1. *Select the stock.* Use any kind of wood for the base. The pegs (part 2) can be purchased locally or from the source given in the Materials List.

2. *Cut the base.* Before cutting out the base (part 1), drill the detail at each corner with a ¾-in.-drill bit. Then cut the base to its overall dimensions. Rout a cove around the edge of the base with a ¼-in.-radius cove bit with a ball-bearing guide.

3. *Lay out the peg positions.* With a soft pencil, draw two lines parallel to the long sides of the base and ⅝ in. from these sides. Along each line, lay out the centers of the peg holes. Mark the centers by dimpling the wood with an awl; this will keep the bit from wandering when you drill the holes. Start 1½ in. from either end on the top line and make a mark every ⅞ in. Make 16 marks, leaving a margin of 1½ in. at the far end. Next, mark 15 marks along the lower line. The two rows of pegs are staggered, so start this row 1¹⁵⁄₁₆ in. from either end. Make a mark every ⅞ in. If you've done everything correctly, you'll have 1¹⁵⁄₁₆ in. left when you reach the other end.

Lay out the centers of the two holes that will be used to hang the rack.

MATERIALS LIST

Part	Dimensions	Quantity
1. Base	¾″ × 2″ × 16⅛″	1
2. Pegs*	³⁄₁₆″ dia. (tenon) × 2⅜″	31

*Pegs are available from Meisel Hardware Specialties, P.O. Box 70, Mound, MN 55364; order #7459.

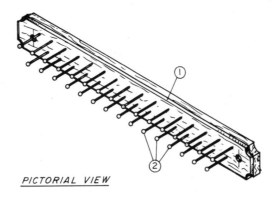

PICTORIAL VIEW

4. *Drill the holes.* Drill a ³⁄₁₆-in.-diameter hole ⅝ in. deep at each peg mark. Set the depth gauge on the drill press to make sure that the holes will be exactly the same depth. If you're using a hand drill, buy a commercially available drill-bit stop.

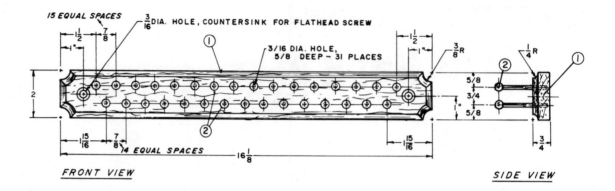

FRONT VIEW

SIDE VIEW

Drill the two 3/16-in.-diameter hanging holes and countersink them to take flathead screws.

Sand the face of the rack with a flat-sanding block or an electric palm sander. Sand the edges by hand.

5. *Assemble the rack.* Place a small amount of glue in each peg hole. (Be careful to keep glue off the surface of the rack.) Put the pegs in the holes. To drive them all the same depth, press down on them simultaneously with a piece of wood. Tap the wood lightly to drive the pegs home. Make a final check to see that all of the pegs extend the same distance. Let the glue dry.

6. *Apply finish.* Apply a coat of stain, if you wish, and follow with two or three coats of a high-gloss varnish. If you are like me, you'll have to go out and buy some ties to justify making the rack.

Cedar Jewelry Box

This is a copy of a jewelry box I first made for my wife in 1954. Its simple lines are quite attractive, and the box has held up well over the years. The box shown in the photograph was made some years later for my daughter.

Here is a wrinkle that you may not have encountered before. To ensure a lid that matches the box, build a sealed box and then cut the lid free. Note the sides are larger than the finished size of the box. The extra width is removed when cutting the lid free.

1. *Select the stock and cut the parts.* I made the original box from cedar and left it unfinished. You can order the hardware from the source given in the Materials List.

Cut the parts to the dimensions given in the Materials List. Rabbet the front and back to accept the sides. Sand the surfaces that will be inside the box.

2. *Assemble the box.* Glue the front and back (part 2) to the ends (part 3). Make sure that

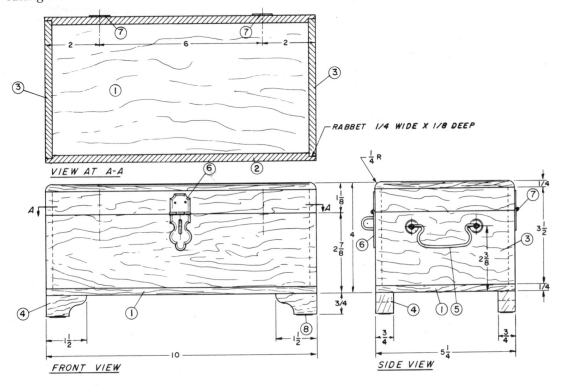

VIEW AT A-A

RABBET 1/4 WIDE X 1/8 DEEP

FRONT VIEW

SIDE VIEW

MATERIALS LIST

Part	Dimensions	Quantity
1. Top/bottom	¼″ × 5¼″ × 10″	1 each
2. Front/back	¼″ × 3⅝″ × 10″	1 each
3. Ends	¼″ × 3⅝″ × 5¼″	2
4. Feet	¾″ × ¾″ × 1½″	4
5. Bails*	2½″ size	1 pair
6. Hasp*		1
7. Hinges*		1 pair
8. Felt dots	½″ dia.	4

Hardware is available from The Woodworkers' Store, 21801 Industrial Boulevard, Rogers, MN 55374. Bail is #E1804, hasp is #D1265, and hinges are #D1267.

everything is square and then glue the top and bottom (part 1) in place. Use thick rubber bands to hold the box together until the glue sets. Check again for squareness before letting the glue dry.

Round-over the top edges, as shown, with a router and a ¼-in.-radius roundover bit with a ball-bearing guide.

3. Cut the lid. Set the blade of a table saw slightly more than a ¼ in. above the table and set the fence to make a 2⅞-in. cut. Put the bottom against the fence and carefully run the two *ends* of the box across the blade, making sure that you hold the box snugly against the fence. Next, insert a piece of scrap wood into both of the kerfs to keep the lid from wobbling as you make the next cut. The scraps should be the same thickness as the kerfs. Tape them in place.

Make the cut along the two *sides* to separate the lid from the box. Again be careful to hold the box against the fence as you make the cuts.

Glue the feet (part 4) in place.

4. Add the hardware. Temporarily attach the bails (part 5), hasp (part 6), and hinges (part 7) and check that everything functions as it should. Remove the hardware if you will be applying a finish.

5. Apply finish. Sand thoroughly. Although I didn't use a finish, you may wish to apply varnish. After the finish dries, reattach the hardware and glue on the four felt dots (part 8).

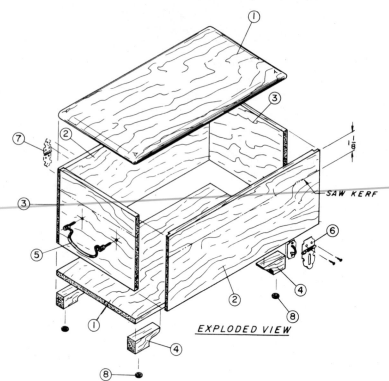

EXPLODED VIEW

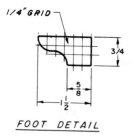

1/4″ GRID

FOOT DETAIL

Eight-Sided Jewelry Box

This box makes an excellent gift. It can be used for anything from a clock case to a music box.

Like other projects in this book, I make a lid that matches the box perfectly by first making a sealed box. Then I cut the box open to form the lid. Unlike most other projects, this box has a dust lip: A lip on the box fits inside a rabbet in the lid.

A friend of mine, Jerry Ernce, showed me how to cut the lip and rabbet in the process of cutting the box apart. I call it the Jerry Joint in his honor and now use this lid on nearly all the boxes I make.

Before jumping into this project, take the time to study how the box fits together and how the Jerry Joint is made.

1. *Select the wood and cut the board for the sides.* I suggest using a hardwood. If you choose to make it out of an undistinguished wood, you can make it resemble rosewood with the directions at the end of the project.

Begin the box by cutting a ½-in.-thick board to a width of 4¾ in. and a length of at least 24 in. In Step 2, you will cut the eight sides (part 1) from this board.

Cutting the Jerry Joint involves cutting a groove on what will be the *inside* of the box before assembly. Later, an adjoining groove on the *outside* will create the dust lip. For now, cut a groove ¼ in. wide and ³/₁₆ in. deep on the inside, as shown in Fig. 1.

2. *Cut the sides.* Set the blade of a table saw at 22½ degrees. Cut some sample joints to make sure the pieces will come together in an octagon without leaving gaps at the joints. Adjust as nec-

essary and then cut the 24-in.-long piece into the eight sides, each exactly 2⅝ in. long, as shown in Fig. 2. Dry-fit the eight sides to make sure they come together as they should.

Glue the octagon with the help of masking tape. Here's how: Put a long strip of tape on the bench, sticky side up. Place the outside face of one side on the tape with the top edge parallel to the tape. Put an adjoining side on the tape next to the first side. The toes of the miters—the long narrow edge that you will see from the outside of the assembled box—must touch along their entire lengths. Position the sides so that the grooves are in line with each other. Continue the process, side by side, until you've taped all eight pieces to form a long line.

Put glue in the miters, fold the pieces together to form an octagon, and clamp with a band clamp or heavy rubber band.

3. *Cut the top and bottom.* Cut the octagonal top and bottom (part 2) slightly oversized. Sand the edges flush with the box after you've assembled it. Glue the top and bottom to the box, as shown in Fig. 3.

4. *Measure for the lid cut.* The sealed box should now look as shown in the drawing for Fig. 4. When the glue has dried, sand the top and bottom edges flush with the sides. Draw a line

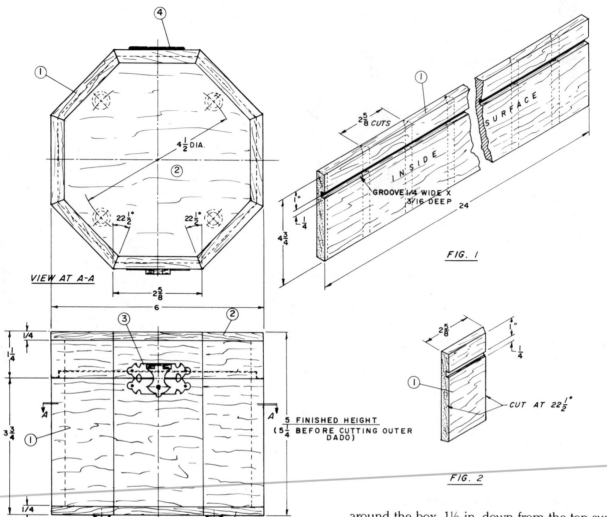

VIEW AT A-A

FRONT VIEW

GROOVE 1/4 WIDE X 3/16 DEEP

INSIDE

SURFACE

FIG. 1

CUT AT 22½°

FIG. 2

4½ DIA.

5 FINISHED HEIGHT
(5¼ BEFORE CUTTING OUTER DADO)

MATERIALS LIST

Part	Dimensions	Quantity
1. Side	½″ × 4¾″ × 2⅝″	8
2. Top/bottom	¼″ × 6″ × 6″	1 each
3. Hinged catch*		1
4. Hinge*		1
5. Rubber feet*	½″	4

*Hardware is available from The Woodworkers' Store, 21801 Industrial Boulevard, Rogers, MN 55374. Catch is #D3030, hinge is #D3025, and rubber feet are #D1290.

around the box, 1½ in. down from the top surface and parallel to it. This will be the top of a groove that separates the lid from the box.

5. *Cut the lid.* To free the lid, cut a groove along the line, ¼ in. wide and ³⁄₁₆ in. deep, as shown in Fig. 5. It should meet the inside groove to form a lipped lid. Follow a sequence of cuts as indicated by the letters *A* through *H*. If the lid fits too tightly, sand the lower of the two lips.

6. *Attach the hardware.* Temporarily add the hardware (parts 3, 4, and 5), as shown in the drawing for Fig. 6. Remove it to apply the finish.

7. *Apply finish.* Varnish the piece if you like the look of the wood as is. Or, use the following method to suggest the appearance of rosewood.

Apply two coats of oil-based orange or red paint, sanding between coats. Next apply two coats of varnish or shellac, rubbing with steel wool between coats.

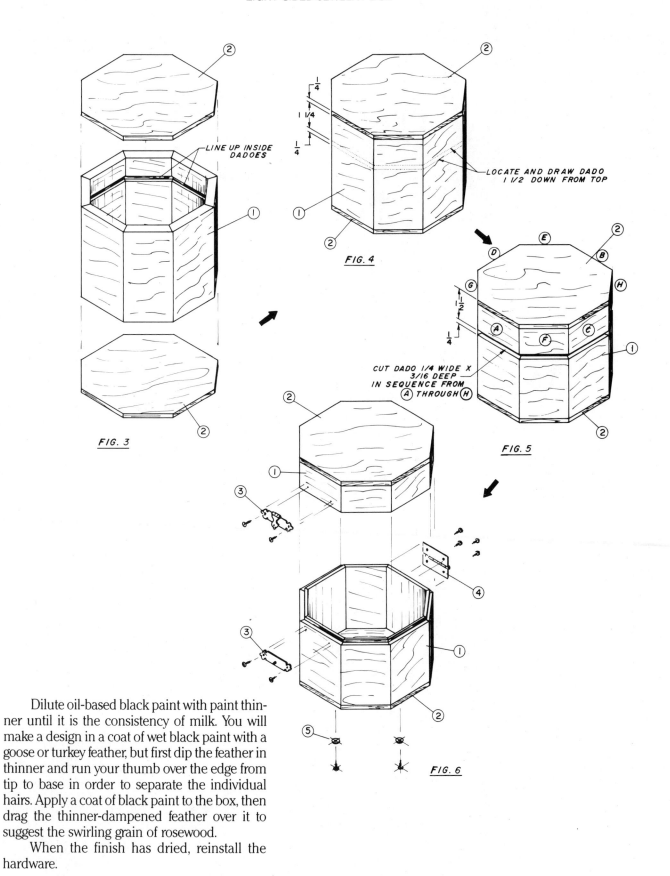

LINE UP INSIDE DADOES

FIG. 3

LOCATE AND DRAW DADO
1 1/2 DOWN FROM TOP

FIG. 4

CUT DADO 1/4 WIDE X
3/16 DEEP
IN SEQUENCE FROM
(A) THROUGH (H)

FIG. 5

FIG. 6

Dilute oil-based black paint with paint thinner until it is the consistency of milk. You will make a design in a coat of wet black paint with a goose or turkey feather, but first dip the feather in thinner and run your thumb over the edge from tip to base in order to separate the individual hairs. Apply a coat of black paint to the box, then drag the thinner-dampened feather over it to suggest the swirling grain of rosewood.

When the finish has dried, reinstall the hardware.

Cranberry Scoop

Massachusetts is known for its cranberries—and its cranberry scoops. When an old one turns up at an auction, it typically sells for a high price. Here is a reproduction that can serve as a good magazine rack.

1. *Select the stock and cut the parts.* Except for the tangs (part 6) that are made of dowels, this piece is made entirely from ¾-in. boards. The front and back (parts 4 and 2) are glued up from scrap. Before gluing up parts for the front, round-over the edges slightly with sandpaper. Glue up two pieces of stock to form the feet. Cut the parts to the overall sizes given in the Materials List. Cut a 60-degree bevel on one end of each tang.

2. *Make a paper pattern and cut the parts to shape.* Draw a grid with ½-in. squares and enlarge the outline of the sides (part 1), the feet (part 5), and the handle (part 7) onto it. Transfer the enlargements to the wood and cut the wood to shape. Sand the cut edges and round-over the top and front edges of the handle where it would have been gripped by hands.

Along the top edge of the back, lay out and drill the holes for the tangs.

3. *Assemble the scoop.* Dry-assemble all the parts to make sure they fit. Nail the bottom (part 3) to the back. Nail the sides in place and then nail the front to the sides and bottom. Glue the tangs in place; arrange them with the highest point of the tips at the rear of the scoop and check that all are the same height above the back. Position the handle. Predrill for screws and attach the handle. Screw the feet in place 1½ in. from the ends.

4. *Apply finish.* Sand the scoop thoroughly and paint or stain it.

MATERIALS LIST

Part	Dimensions	Quantity
1. Sides	¾″ × 5½″ × 19″	2
2. Back	¾″ × 10½″ × 14½″	1
3. Bottom	¾″ × 5½″ × 14½″	1
4. Front	¾″ × 9½″ × 16″	1
5. Feet	¾″ × 1½″ × 11″	4
6. Tangs	⅜″ dia. × 10″	14
7. Handle	¾″ × 3″ × 14½″	1
8. Flathead screws	#8 × 2″	6
9. Square-cut nails	6d	as needed

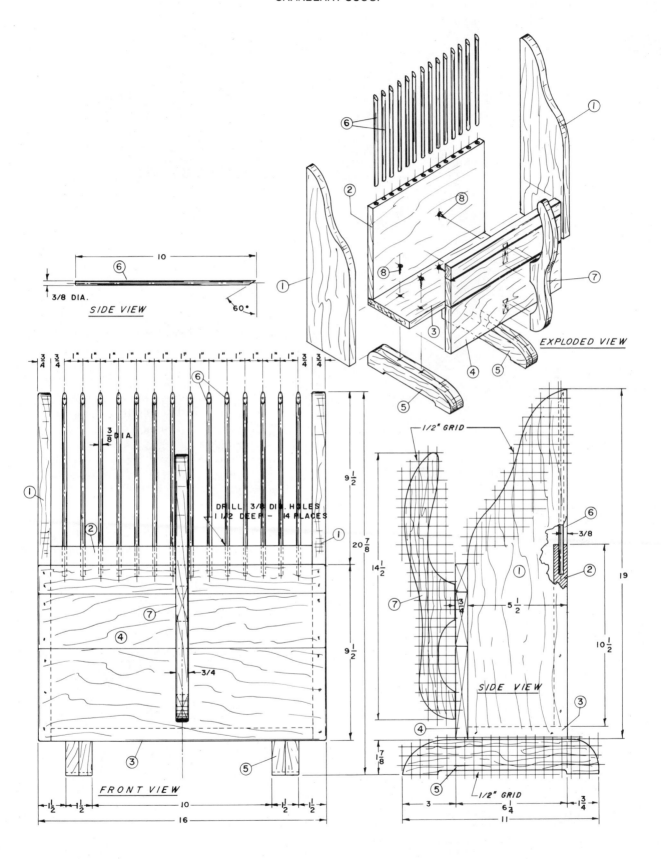

SIDE VIEW

3/8 DIA.

10

6

60°

EXPLODED VIEW

DRILL 3/8 DIA. HOLES
1 1/2 DEEP - 14 PLACES

3/8 DIA.

9 1/2

20 7/8

9 1/2

3/4

FRONT VIEW

1/2 1/2   10   1/2 1/2

16

1/2" GRID

14 1/2

SIDE VIEW

3/8

5 1/2

19

10 1/2

1 7/8

1/2" GRID

3

6 1/4

1 3/4

11

Elephant Table Lamp

There are several elephant projects in the book, all sharing the same pattern, so you may want to save the one you draw for this lamp.

1. Select the stock and cut the parts. Because this piece will be painted, use any wood that is easy to work. You'll need several different thicknesses. You can plane or resaw standard ¾-in. stock for the thinner pieces. If you can't find wood a full 1 in. thick for the base, glue up two thinner pieces. The optional items in this project, the lamp hardware, eyes, and feet, can be ordered from the sources given in the Materials List.

Cut the parts to the sizes given in the Materials List.

2. Make a paper pattern. Draw a grid with ½-in. squares and enlarge the body (part 1) and the hat onto it. Make a separate pattern for the ears (part 2). Transfer the patterns to the wood.

3. Cut the body and ears to shape. Cut the parts to shape. Cut a notch for the ears, as shown in the drawing, with a band saw, jigsaw, or coping saw. Glue the ears in place.

Carefully drill a ⅜-in.-diameter hole through the body and ears for the lamp hardware, as shown in the front view. Drill the ¼-in.-diameter hole for the tail (part 3) and glue the tail in place. Drill a ⅞-in.-diameter hole for the rider (part 4), about ¾ in. deep.

4. Cut the base to shape. Draw an 8-in.-diameter circle on the wood for the base (part 6) with a compass. Cut the circle out and drill a ⁷⁄₁₆-in.-deep hole in the exact center with a 1½-in. Forstner bit. Drill a ⅜-in.-diameter hole on the same center through the base, as illustrated in the detail of the center hole. Drill a ¼-in. hole for the lamp cord from the edge of the base to the center hole, as shown.

MATERIALS LIST

Part	Dimensions	Quantity
1. Body	1″ × 7½″ × 7½″	1
2. Ear	½″ × 3¾″ × 5½″	1
3. Tail	¼″ dia. × 1¼″	1
4. Rider	1″ dia. × 2″	1
5. Jiggle eyes*		1 pair
6. Base	¾″ × 8″ × 8″	1
7. Star	⁵⁄₁₆″ × 4″ × 4″	1
8. Main pipe**	⅛″ IP × 10⅛″ all-thread pipe	1
9. Brass tubing**	½″ OD	1
10. Brass tubing**	½″ OD	1
11. Check ring**	½″ dia., slip ⅛″ IP	1
12. Flat washer**	1″ dia.	1
13. Lock washer**	⅛″ IP, slip	1
14. Lock nut**	⅛″ IPF	1
15. Socket with switch**		1
16. Cord with plug**	8′, or as needed	1
17. Clip-on shade**	To suit	1
18. Rubber feet*	¼″ × ½″ dia.	4

*Hardware is available from Meisel Hardware Specialties, P.O. Box 70, Mound, MN 55364. Eyes are #7647, and feet are #421.

**Hardware is available from Paxton Hardware Ltd., 7818 Bradshaw Road, Dept. R.P., Upper Falls, MD 21156. Kit without shade is #8720, and kit with shade is #8721.

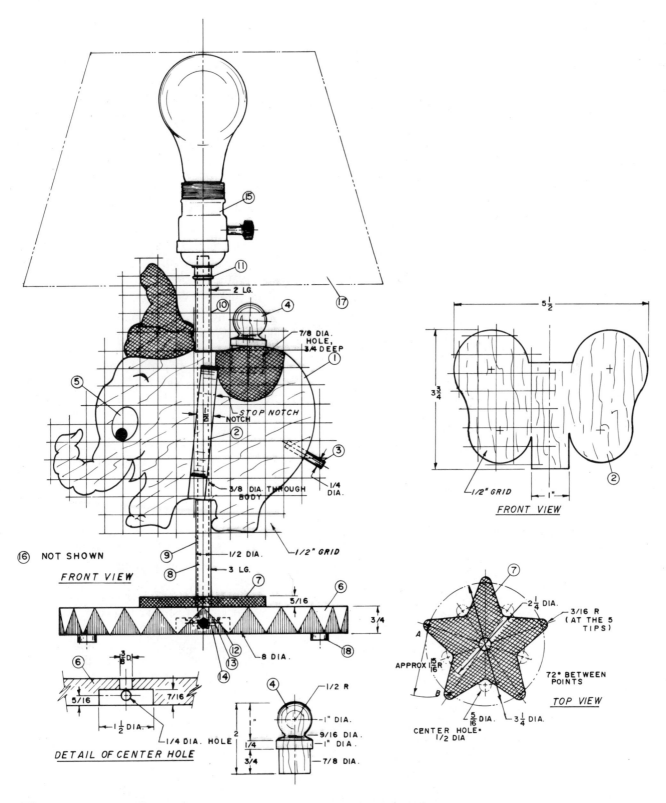

5. *Cut the star to shape.* Study the top view of the star (part 7). I lay the star out with a compass. Center a 3¼-in.-diameter circle on a piece of wood. Then set the compass to a 1⁵/₁₆-in. radius, place the point anywhere on the circle

you just drew, and swing an arc that intersects the circle, as shown in point B in the top view of the star. Place the compass point at B and swing an arc to make a second intersection farther along the circle, as shown. Continue until around

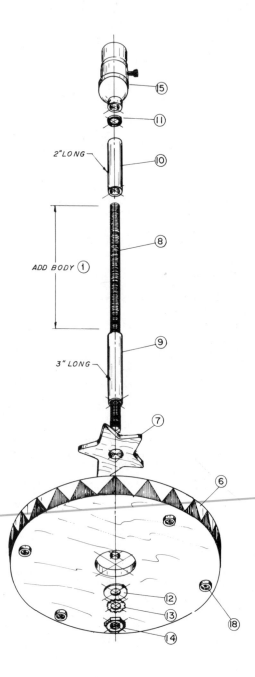

2" LONG

ADD BODY ①

3" LONG

the five points on the larger circle through the center of the star and to the far side of the 2¼-in.-diameter circle. This establishes five equally spaced points around the smaller circle. Set the compass at ⁵/₃₂ in. and swing arcs from these points to define the bases of the star's arms. Connect the bases of the arcs, as shown, to complete the star.

To cut out the star, drill a ⁵/₁₆-in.-diameter hole along the base of each arm and cut along the layout lines. Drill a ⅜-in.-diameter hole in the center of the star. Sand the star.

6. *Turn the rider.* Turn the rider on a lathe. If you don't have a lathe, carve a 2-in. length of ⅞-in.-diameter dowel to an approximation of the shape shown in the detail of the rider.

7. *Dry-assemble the lamp.* Put the lamp together temporarily to make sure that all the parts fit. Don't bother with the cord at this point. Slip the main pipe (part 8) through the body of the elephant and slide the brass tubing (parts 9 and 10) over it. Screw the check ring (part 11) and socket (part 15) to the top end, making things snug.

Slip the lower end of the main pipe down through the star and the base. Add the flat washer, lock washer, and nut (parts 12, 13, and 14) and tighten them. Add the shade (part 17) and the four feet (part 18).

8. *Apply finish.* Disassemble the lamp and paint the wooden parts with bright, nontoxic colors. The eyes can be painted on, rather than purchased.

Here is a tip for painting the triangles around the base: First, brush on a first coat of paint and allow it to dry completely. Run a piece of ¾-in. masking tape around the base and mark off twenty 1¼-in. spaces, starting at the cord hole. Draw the triangles on the tape, as shown, and cut them out with a sharp knife. Peel off every other triangle and paint the spaces with a contrasting color. When the paint has dried, peel off the remaining tape.

Glue on the jiggle eyes (part 5) if you choose to use them. Reassemble the lamp. Run the cord (part 16) into the cord hole and up through the main pipe. Attach the wires to the socket, add a light bulb, and check that the lamp works as it should.

the circle. After marking five even spaces, you should end up on the point at which you started.

The "points" of the star are slightly rounded. To draw them, set the compass to ³/₁₆ in. and swing an arc at each of the five points you marked on the circle.

Now lay out the bases of the star's arms. Draw a 2¼-in.-diameter circle, concentric with the first circle. Draw a straight line from each of

Shoeshine Box

A while ago my wife bought a shoeshine box in which to store shoe polish and brushes, but it was too small to contain half of our stuff. I suggested that if she returned the box to the store, I would make a better one. Here is my version. It is a bit higher than the typical store-bought box so that you don't have to bend over quite so far to shine your shoes. Note that I have used only simple butt joints throughout.

1. Select the stock. The box is made entirely from ¾-in. stock. I made mine out of ash. The hinges, hasp, and feet can be ordered from the source given in the Materials List.

2. Build the box. Rather than build a lid to match an open box, I built a closed box and cut it open to create a perfectly matching lid. Dimensions for building a box with this technique are given in the Materials List. Make sure that all cuts are exactly 90 degrees: Butt joints that do not meet squarely are weak. Dry-fit the two sides (part 1), the two ends (part 2), and the top and bottom (part 3). If necessary, trim the parts to fit and then glue up the box, keeping everything square.

3. Cut the lid. Draw a line 8 in. from the bottom all the way around the box. Set the table saw fence to make an 8-in.-wide cut and set the blade slightly more than ¾ in. above the table. Run the box through the saw to cut the two ends, keeping the box firmly against the fence. To keep the kerfs open when running the remaining two sides through the saw, place scraps of wood the width of the kerf into each cut and tape them in place. Cut the sides, again keeping the box firmly against the fence. Reinforce the butt joints with 6d finishing nails (part 9) and fill the holes. Sand the box well.

4. Cut the shoe rest and support. Band saw the shoe rest (part 5) to the shape shown in the illustration and sand off the saw marks. Rout a cove with a ¼-in.-radius cove bit around the perimeter except at the end which meets the heel.

Glue up three pieces of ¾-in. stock to make the 2¼-in.-thick support (part 4). After the glue sets, band saw the support to the shape, as shown.

5. Assemble the box. Glue the support to the shoe rest. Center the support and shoe rest

SHOESHINE BOX

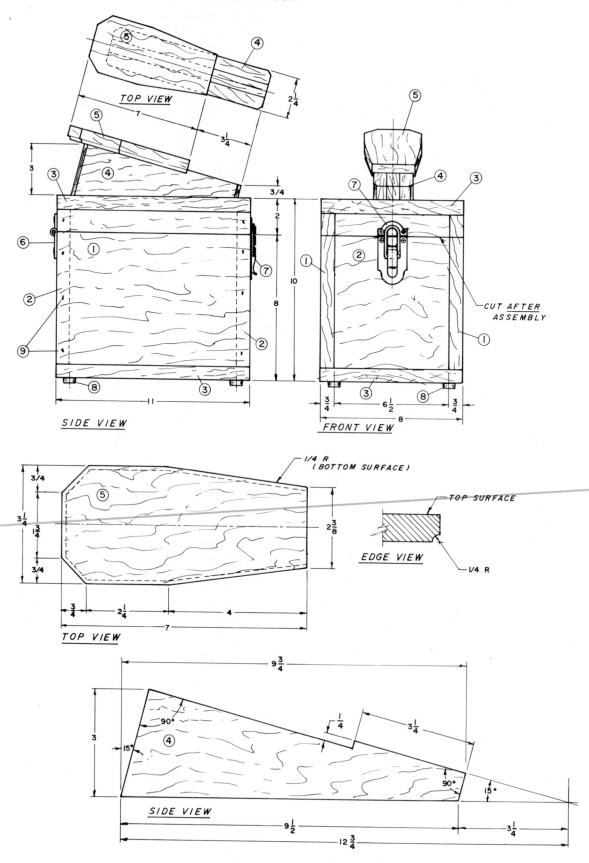

TOP VIEW

SIDE VIEW

FRONT VIEW

CUT AFTER ASSEMBLY

1/4 R (BOTTOM SURFACE)

TOP SURFACE

TOP VIEW

EDGE VIEW

1/4 R

SIDE VIEW

90°

15°

90°

15°

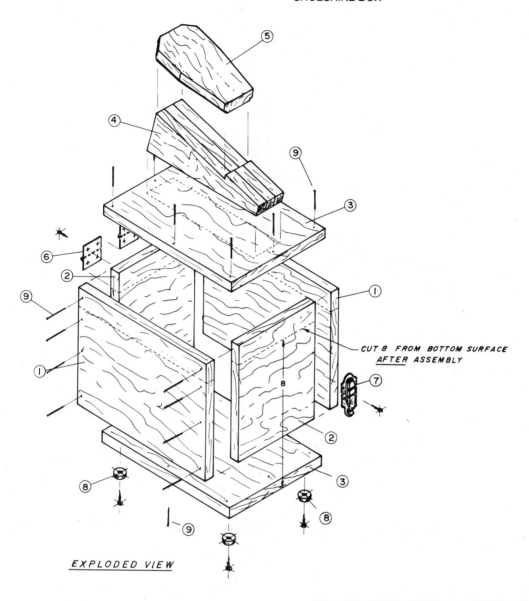

CUT 8 FROM BOTTOM SURFACE
AFTER ASSEMBLY

EXPLODED VIEW

assembly on the top of the lid and glue it in place. Temporarily attach the two hinges (part 6), hasp (part 7), and four rubber feet (part 8). If everything works as it should, remove them and proceed to the next step.

6. *Finish the box.* Brush on two coats of varnish. Reattach the hardware.

MATERIALS LIST

Part	Dimensions	Quantity
1. Sides	¾" × 8⅝" × 11"	2
2. Ends	¾" × 8⅝" × 6½"	2
3. Top/bottom	¾" × 8" × 11"	1 each
4. Supports	¾" × 3" × 9¾"	3
5. Shoe rest	¾" × 3¼" × 7"	1
6. Hinges*	1½" × 1½"	2
7. Hasp*		1
8. Feet*		4
9. Finishing nails	6d	as needed

Hardware is available from Meisel Hardware Specialties, P.O. Box 70, Mound, MN 55364. Hinges are #928, hasp is #312, and feet are #421.

In/Out Mail Basket

This is a good-looking replacement for the standard office supply in-out mail basket.

1. ***Select the stock and cut the parts.*** Any hardwood will do, but oak and ash strike me as appropriate for an office. I chose ash for the basket in the photo. The entire piece is made from ¼-in. stock.

Decide how many units the basket will have. The Materials List gives the number of parts required to make one unit. With a couple of simple spacers, you can stack two units on top of each other; four spacers will let you stack three units, as shown here.

Cut all pieces to the sizes listed in the Materials List. Lay out the notch in the front (part 1) and cut it out on a band saw or jigsaw. If you are making more than one basket, tape the fronts together in a pile and cut out all the notches at once. Sand the edges of the notches while the fronts are still together.

Rabbet the front and back to accept the sides (part 2). Cut a groove for the bottom in the front, back, and sides, as shown in the side view.

Cut a piece of ⅝-in. stock for the spacers (part 4), making it about an inch longer than the combined lengths of the individual spacers you'll need. Rout or cut grooves along both the top and bottom edges of this piece, as shown in the spacer detail. Cut the piece into the individual 4-in.-long spacers.

2. ***Assemble the basket.*** Dry-fit the parts. Trim as necessary and glue up the parts, keeping everything square. Do *not* glue the bottom (part 3) in place so that it can expand and contract with the weather. Sand the basket and spacers.

3. ***Finish the basket.*** I gave the basket in the photo a coat of light stain and two coats of varnish, but the distinctive grains of ash and oak look equally good without stain.

MATERIALS LIST

Part	Dimensions	Quantity
1. Fronts/backs	¼″ × 2½″ × 10″	1 each
2. Sides	¼″ × 2½″ × 11¾″	2
3. Bottom	¼″ × 9¹¹/₁₆″ × 11¾″	1
4. Spacers	⅝″ × 1⅛″ × 4″	2 for each additional unit

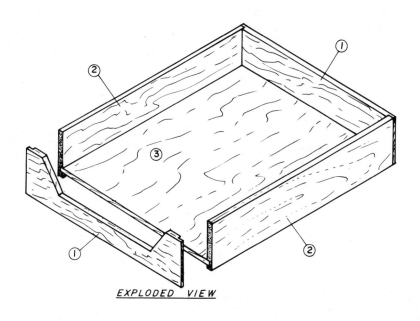

EXPLODED VIEW

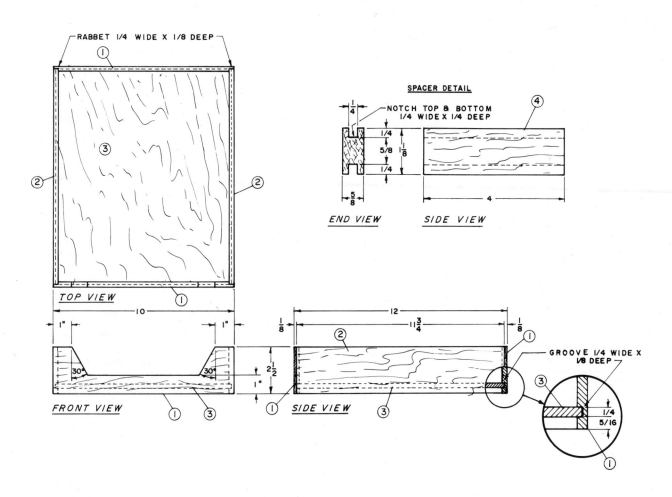

RABBET 1/4 WIDE X 1/8 DEEP

TOP VIEW

SPACER DETAIL

NOTCH TOP & BOTTOM
1/4 WIDE X 1/4 DEEP

END VIEW

SIDE VIEW

FRONT VIEW

SIDE VIEW

GROOVE 1/4 WIDE X
1/8 DEEP

Wall Barometer

This wall-mounted weather station tells the barometric pressure, temperature, and relative humidity. The barometer was invented by an Italian physicist in the mid-1600s, and by the end of the century the British were framing them in elegant cases similar to this one.

The project involves a little inlay work and some very simple carving of the molding.

The inlay, instruments, and brass finial are available from the source given in the Materials List.

1. *Select the stock and cut the parts.* Purchase the instruments before you start building to make sure your instruments will fit the case. Build the case from a hardwood such as cherry, walnut, mahogany, maple, or birch. Cut the parts ½ in. longer and wider than called for and cut them to the dimensions given in the Materials List as you shape them.

2. *Draw a pattern directly on the stock.* The most challenging job in this project is laying out the body (part 1). To avoid errors, it's best to lay out the pattern directly on the wood. Draw a grid with 1-in. squares on the stock for the base. The series of center points and diameters shown in the drawing will help you lay out the circles and arcs that form the base. Transfer the center points to the grid and lay out the curves with a compass. The enlarged detail of the top will help you lay out the curves for the pediment. Lay out the area for the thermometer and barometer by putting them in place on the body. Double-check all dimensions.

3. *Cut the body to shape.* Before I begin cutting the body to shape on the band saw, I head for the drill press. I've found that rather

MATERIALS LIST

Part	Dimensions	Quantity
1. Body	1½″ × 9½″ × 31″	1
2. Barometer flange	¼″ × 9⅛″ dia.	1
3. Front top molding	⅜″ × 2⅛″ × 4¾″	1
4. Side top moldings	⅜″ × 2⅛″ × 2″	2
5. Gooseneck moldings	¼″ × 1¼″ × 4¾″	2
6. Side moldings	Cut from part 5	2
7. Inlay*	2″ dia.	1
8. Pediment cap	⅛″ × 1⅜″ × 1⅝″	1
9. Hygrometer*		1
10. Barometer*		1
11. Thermometer*		1
12. Brass finial*		1
13. Hanger	1½″	1

*Parts are available from Mason and Sullivan Company, 586 Higgins Crowell Road, West Yarmouth, MA 02673. Inlay is #2298-X, finial is #2017-B, thermometer is #4055-X, hygrometer is #4054-X, and barometer is #4056-X.

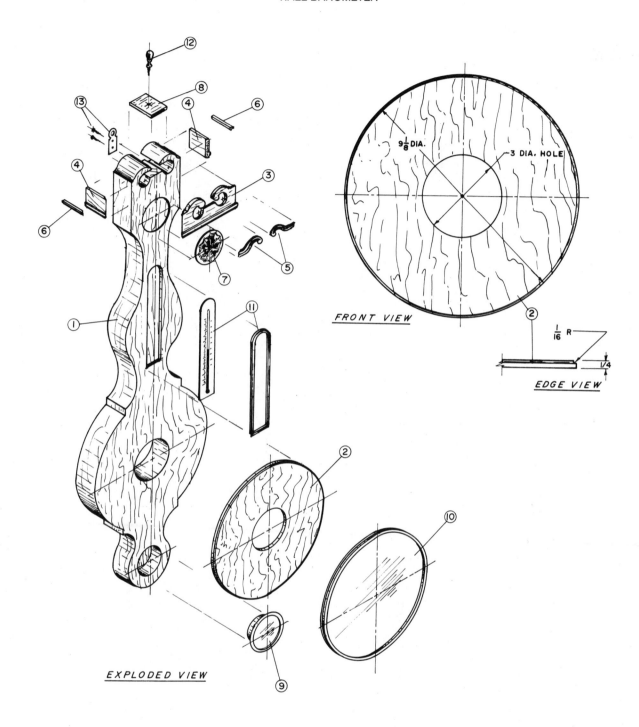

FRONT VIEW

EDGE VIEW

EXPLODED VIEW

than saw curves, it's sometimes easier to drill them out. The results are perfect, symmetrical, and repeatable. With large enough bits, you can even produce the four 1½-in.-radius curves required here. Drill all the holes, except for the two at the pediment. On the band saw, cut out the rest of the body *except for the pediment*. Sand the edges smooth.

4. *Cut out the pediment.* The pediment topping the barometer is built from several pieces: A top molding wraps around the case. Two carved gooseneck moldings are applied over it. A brass finial tops off the piece.

First, cut a piece of stock for the top molding (parts 3 and 4): It should be as wide and thick as the molding and at least 12 in. long. Rout a cove

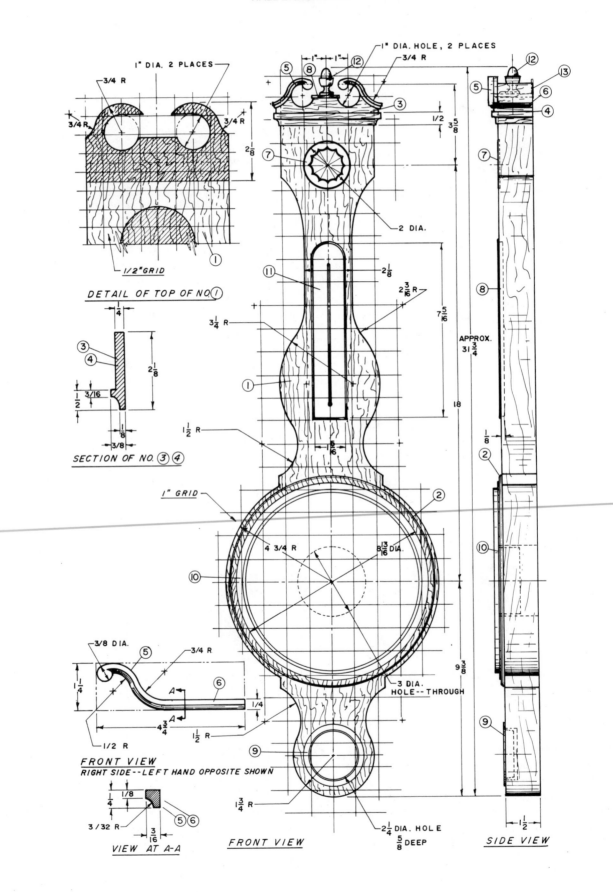

1" DIA. 2 PLACES

3/4 R

3/4 R 3/4 R

2 1/8

1/2" GRID

①

DETAIL OF TOP OF NO ①

SECTION OF NO. ③ ④

③ ④

1/4

2 1/8

1/2 3/16

1/8

3/8

1" DIA. HOLE, 2 PLACES

3/4 R

⑤ ⑧ ⑫

③

1/2 3 5/8

⑦

2 DIA.

⑪

2 1/8

2 3/16 R

3 3/4 R

7 5/16

①

1 1/2 R

5/6

APPROX.
31 3/4

18

1" GRID

⑩

4 3/4 R

8 13/16 DIA.

②

3 DIA.
HOLE — THROUGH

9 3/8

⑫

⑤

⑬

⑥

④

⑦

⑧

1/8

②

⑩

⑨

1 1/2

SIDE VIEW

3/8 DIA.

⑤ 3/4 R

1 1/4

A

A

⑥

1/4

4 3/4

1 1/2 R

1/2 R

FRONT VIEW
RIGHT SIDE — LEFT HAND OPPOSITE SHOWN

1/4 1/8

3/32 R 3/16

⑤ ⑥

VIEW AT A-A

⑨

1 3/4 R

2 1/4 DIA. HOLE
5/8 DEEP

FRONT VIEW

in it, as shown, with a ¼-in.-core box bit. Core box bits are like cove bits, except that they come in smaller sizes and don't have ball-bearing guides. Put the router in a router table and guide the cut against the fence.

Once you've cut the cove, cut the ⅛-in. × 1⅝-in. step above it on the table saw. First, clamp a piece of wood to the saw's fence and move the fence so the wood just touches the blade. Raise the blade to 1⅝ in. Stand the molding on its top edge and put its outside face against the fence to make the cut. Feed the stock against the blade with a push stick.

Cut the stock into three pieces, each about an inch longer than needed to make the molding. Miter the corners, cut the molding to fit, and glue the molding in place.

When the glue dries, drill holes through the top molding and body to define the arches. Band saw the pediment to its final shape and sand smooth.

5. *Make and attach the gooseneck molding.* The front gooseneck moldings (part 5) are not identical; they are mirror images of each other. Two side moldings (part 6) miter into the gooseneck. All four moldings must be carved by hand.

Put the stock for the gooseneck on the bench and trace the shape of the pediment onto it. Use this as a guide to lay out the entire molding, as shown in the drawing. Cut the molding to shape and sand the curves smooth.

The cove around the bottom of the gooseneck is too small to rout, so you will have to carve it. A 9-sweep, 2mm carving gouge is almost perfect for the job, but any small carving gouge will do the trick. Carve both goosenecks and the side moldings that fit into them. Miter and glue all four in place.

Drill a pilot hole in the pediment cap (part 8) to accept the brass finial (part 12). Glue the cap in place but don't mount the finial until after you've applied finish.

6. *Make the recess and holes for the instruments.* To cut the recess for the thermometer (part 11), drill a series of overlapping holes with the appropriate Forstner bit. The width will depend on the thermometer you buy. With Forstner bits, the overlap can be quite large: The center for

one hole need be no more than about ⅛ in. from the next. Clean up the edges of the recess with a sharp chisel.

Drill a hole large enough to accommodate the back of the barometer (part 10). If you don't have a bit large enough, use a circle cutter, coping saw, or jigsaw.

Drill a 2¼-in. hole to accommodate the hygrometer (part 9).

7. *Drill the recess for the inlay.* The inlay (part 7) is made by gluing pieces of veneer to a piece of paper. When purchased ready-made, inlay comes with the paper still attached. Leave it attached.

Drill a hole in the body for the inlay. Put a Forstner bit in your drill press and drill a 2-in.-diameter hole, not quite as deep as the inlay is thick.

Glue the inlay in place with the paper side up. When the glue dries, sand the paper off, and sand the inlay flush. If there are any gaps, fill them with wood filler.

8. *Make the barometer flange.* Cut the circular flange (part 2) on a band saw. The easiest way to cut a circle is to make a simple jig. Screw the center of a square piece of stock to a piece of scrap. Position the jig so that you can cut the circle by rotating the square into the blade. Clamp the jig in place and cut the circle. Cut a cove in the edge with a ⅛-in.-diameter core box bit. (Core box bits this small are also sold as veining bits.) Remember, these bits don't have ball-bearing guides, so you'll have to rout this in a table against a fence. Routing curved surfaces is easier if you band saw a hollow in a wooden fence to match the curve.

Cut or drill a hole in the center of the flange to match the one in the body and glue the flange to the base.

9. *Apply finish.* Sand thoroughly. Temporarily install the three instruments and drill for all screws. The brass screws that come with the instruments may break off, unless pilot holes are drilled for them.

Remove the instruments and varnish the piece. Install the instruments with screws and add the brass hanger (part 13) and brass finial.

Fireboard

What's a fireboard? It is a decorative panel used to block off an unused fireplace. They were a necessity years ago, before fireplaces could be closed with dampers. Early examples usually had handsome primitive paintings on them.

Fireboards can be practical in today's homes as well. At our house, we often go up to bed with warm embers in the fireplace. The damper can't be shut down to keep the fireplace from drawing warm air out of the house, and a fireboard is the answer. A note of caution: The fireboard must be backed with a fireproof heat shield. And even with this shield in place, *never use the fireboard to block a fireplace with a burning fire*. The fireboard conceivably could ignite.

1. *Select the stock and cut the parts.* The choice of wood is yours. Pine would work well. The heat shield and lower shield are made of 16-gauge galvanized steel. The metal runner is made out of steel strapping. All are available from metal suppliers. (Omit parts 11, 12, 13, 14, and 15 if you will not be adding the heat shield.)

Decide if you want the fireboard to fit just inside the fireplace opening or to overlap the outside of the opening. If the fireboard is to be set *inside* the fireplace opening, it should be smaller than the length and width of the opening by ¼ in. The board I've drawn would fit in a 42¼-in. × 33¼-in. opening. Adjust the fireboard to fit your fireplace.

If the fireboard is to be set *outside* the opening, its overall height should be 1 in. more than the width and length of the opening. The board I've drawn would cover a fireplace opening 41 in. × 32 in. Again, adjust the dimensions to fit your fireplace.

Cut the parts to the appropriate dimensions. Adjust the width of the facing boards (part 1), as necessary. Rout ⅛-in. × ½-in.-long slots in each of the battens (part 2), as shown in the exploded view.

MATERIALS LIST

Part	Dimensions	Quantity
1. Facing boards	¾″ × 11″ × 42″	3
2. Battens	¾″ × 3″ × 31″	2
3. Roundhead screws	#8 × 1⅜″	6
4. Washers	#8	6
5. Metal runners	⅛″ × ¾″ × 13″	2
6. Flathead screws	#8 × 1¼″	4
7. Handles	⅞″ dia. × 2¾″	2
8. Lower shield	1/32″ × 4″ × 42″	1
9. Legs	¾″ × 6″ × 12″	2
10. Roundhead screws	#8 × 1½″	4
11. Heat shield	To suit	1
12. Stove bolts	⅜″ dia. × 3″	4
13. Spacer pipes	¾″ outside dia. × 1″	4
14. Washers	#24	4
15. Nuts	⅜″ dia.	4

NOTE: *Alter all dimensions to fit fireplace.*

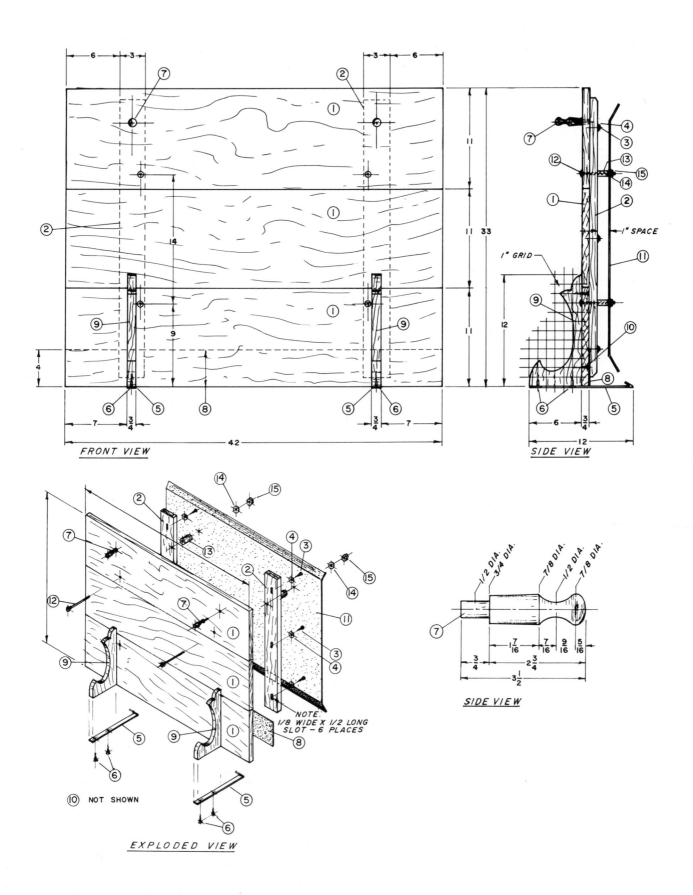

FRONT VIEW

SIDE VIEW

NOTE:
1/8 WIDE X 1/2 LONG
SLOT - 6 PLACES

10 NOT SHOWN

EXPLODED VIEW

1/2 DIA.
3/4 DIA.
7/8 DIA.
1/2 DIA.
7/8 DIA.

SIDE VIEW

2. *Assemble the facing boards.* Glue up facing boards. Tack a 4-in. strip of 16-gauge sheet metal across the bottom to form the lower heat shield (part 8).

Screw the battens to the facing boards with three #8 × 1⅜-in. roundhead screws (part 3). The outer edge of the battens should be 6 in. from either edge of the facing boards. If you will be adding the heat shield (part 11), drill four ⅜-in.-diameter mounting holes through the fireboard and battens. The lower pair of holes is 9 in. up from the bottom of the fireboard, and the upper pair is 14 in. above them.

3. *Make the legs.* Draw a grid with 1-in. squares and enlarge the drawing of the legs (part 9) onto it. Transfer the enlargement to the stock. Cut the parts to shape and sand the edges.

Attach the legs. Screw the legs to the facing board with #8 × 1½-in. roundhead screws (part 10). To avoid splitting the wood, drill a hole slightly larger than the shank of the screw in the facing board; drill a pilot hole slightly smaller than the shank in the leg.

The metal runners (part 5) are made from ⅛-in.-thick steel strapping, ¾ in. wide and 13 in. long. Bend the legs, as shown in the side view. Drill two ⅛-in.-diameter holes in each runner, as shown, and countersink for #8 flathead screws (part 6).

Drill pilot holes in the legs and attach the runners with two flathead screws each.

4. *Add the optional heat shield.* Have a metal worker cut the heat shield (part 11) to the appropriate size and bend it for you. The bends make the shield more rigid and speed the flow of cooling air into the space between the shield and the facing boards. Drill four ⅜-in.-diameter holes in the shield to match those in the facing boards.

Temporarily attach the heat shield with stove bolts, spacers, washers, and nuts (parts 12, 13, 14, and 15). Check to see that the fireboard fits as you had planned.

5. *Add the handles.* Turn the handles (part 7) to the profile shown in the drawing. Drill holes in the facing board for them and glue them in place.

6. *Apply finish.* Disassemble the fireboard. Paint the wooden parts any color that suits your decor; consider using a color that matches the room's trim molding. You can stop there or embellish the fireboard with decorative painting. I had mine painted by a friend who specializes in Early American design.

Reattach the heat shield.

Box for Forstner Bits

I've always wanted a complete set of Forstner bits. When my wife recently gave me a set, my delight was dampened just a bit by the packaging —they were simply wrapped in paper. I hated the thought of their banging around and getting dull.

This box is my solution. You can change the overall dimensions to make a box for other items that need a home. I made a slightly larger box to store router bits. If you pick a handsome wood like walnut, you'll have a box suited for jewelry or important documents.

Like other boxes in this book, I build a sealed box and then cut it open to create the lid. This box has a lipped lid that I create as I cut open the box. I do this by cutting two adjoining grooves: Before assembly, I cut a groove in-

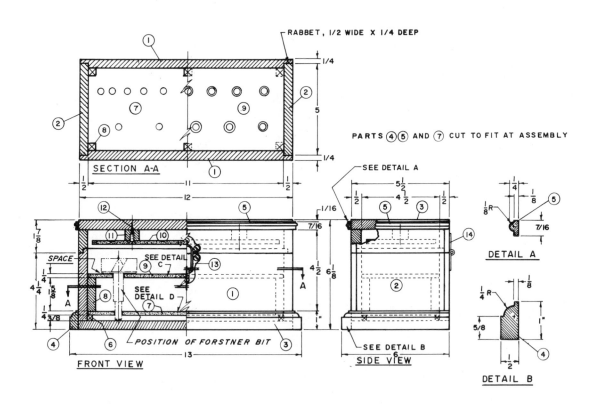

RABBET, 1/2 WIDE X 1/4 DEEP

SECTION A-A

PARTS ④⑤ AND ⑦ CUT TO FIT AT ASSEMBLY

DETAIL A

DETAIL B

FRONT VIEW

POSITION OF FORSTNER BIT

SEE DETAIL B

SIDE VIEW

SEE DETAIL A

SEE DETAIL C

SEE DETAIL D

SPACE

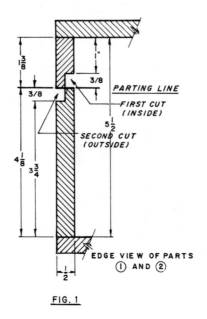

FIG. 1

side the box. After assembly, I cut the second groove on the outside, creating the lip, as shown in Fig. 1.

1. *Select the stock and cut the parts.* Choose any appropriate wood, but I suggest hardwood for the exterior of a box that will see rough use in a workshop. Tempered hardboard works well for the bit supports.

Before you build this box, measure the length of your bits. I've designed the storage box for bits that are no longer than 3¾ in. overall with a shank no longer than 2⅝ in. If your bits are different, adjust the dimensions accordingly.

A piece of wood ½ in. thick and 5½ in. wide × 60 in. long will be enough to make the top, bottom, and all four sides, as shown in Fig. 2. Cut it to form the parts, as described in the next step.

2. *Cut the parts and assemble the box.* Square up the edges of the board and cut off pieces for the top and bottom (part 3) of the box.

Before cutting the remaining piece into four sides, rip a groove ⅜ in. wide and ¼ in. deep, located as shown in Fig. 2. This is the first of two cuts that form the dust lip. Once you've cut the groove, saw the board into the front, back, and ends (parts 1 and 2).

GROOVE 3/8 WIDE — 1/4 DEEP

INSIDE

34⅜

58⅝

BEFORE CUTTING

CUT IN TWO

24⅛

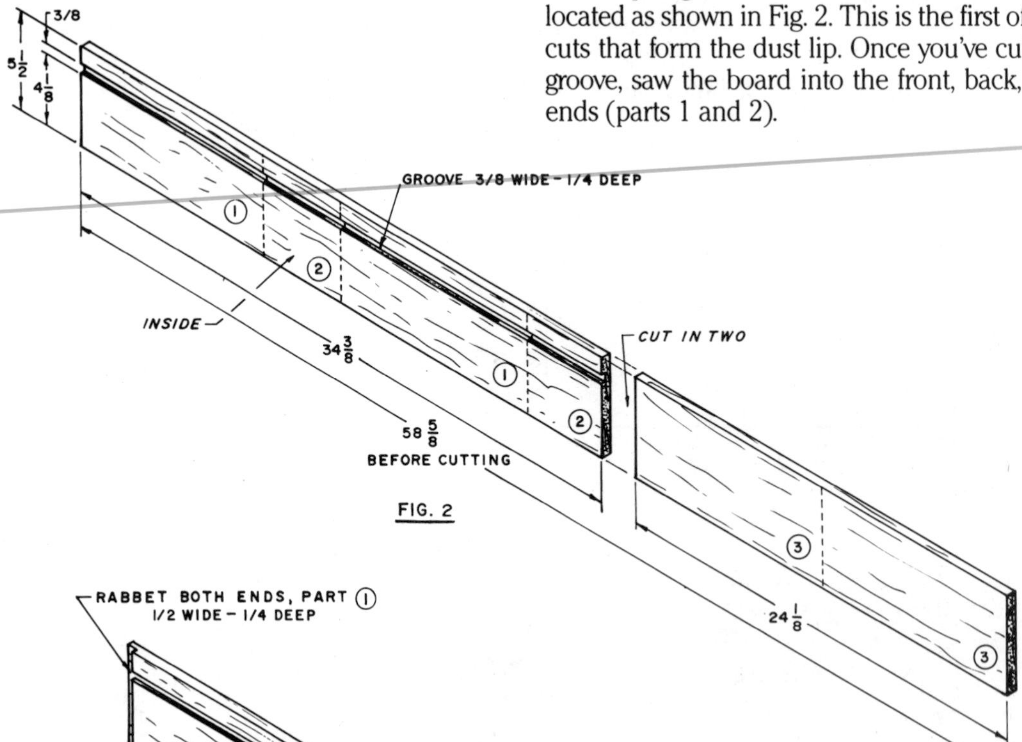

FIG. 2

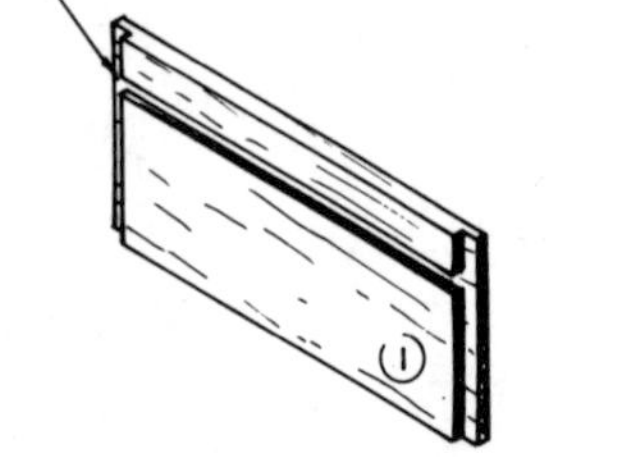

RABBET BOTH ENDS, PART ①
1/2 WIDE — 1/4 DEEP

FIG. 3

Rabbet the front and back pieces to accept the sides, as shown in Fig. 3. Then glue and nail the four sides together, keeping the groove for the dust lip *inside* the box.

3. *Cut off the lid.* Nail the top and bottom in place. After the glue sets, fill the nail holes with wood putty and sand the box smooth, taking care to keep all edges sharp and square.

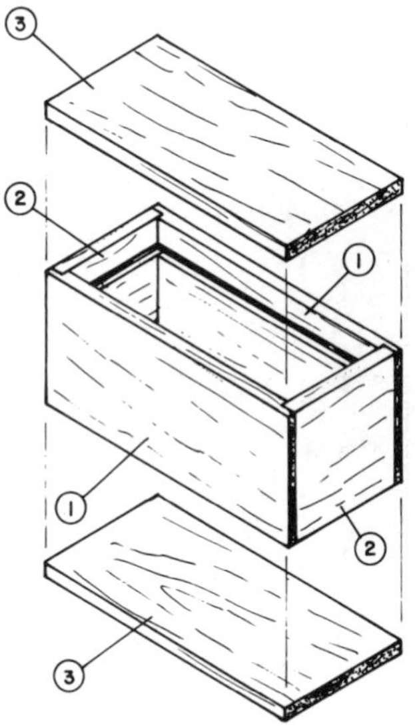
3
2
1
1
2
3

FIG. 4

Cut the second groove that separates the lid from the rest of the box and forms the dust lip. Set the table saw fence to position the cut, as shown in Fig. 1, and cut a groove ¼ in. deep and ⅜ in. wide on the two long sides of the box. To keep the lid from wobbling while cutting the ends of the box, tape ⅜-in.-wide spacers in the kerf before cutting the end grooves, as shown in Fig. 5.

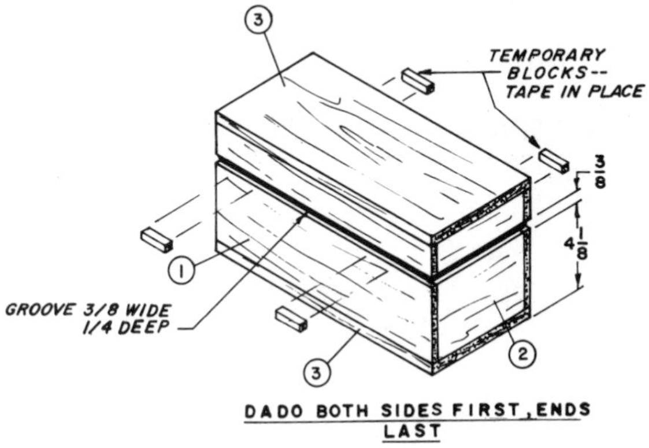
3
TEMPORARY BLOCKS-- TAPE IN PLACE
3/8
4 1/8
1
GROOVE 3/8 WIDE 1/4 DEEP
3
2
DADO BOTH SIDES FIRST, ENDS LAST

FIG. 5

4. *Add the molding.* Cut the molding (parts 4 and 5) with a router or shaper; there is no need to reproduce the moldings illustrated as long as you keep within the overall dimensions. Miter and attach the molding with glue and nails, as shown in Fig. 6.

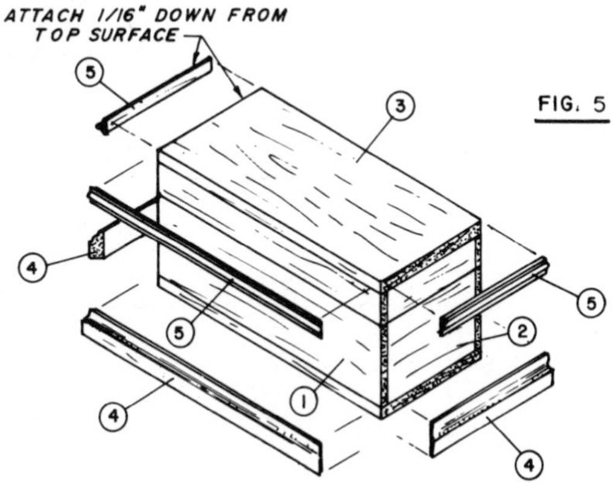
ATTACH 1/16" DOWN FROM TOP SURFACE
5
3
FIG. 5
4
5
5
2
1
4
4

FIG. 6

5. *Make the inside parts.* Cut the inside parts to fit the box. To ensure that the holes will be in the same positions in both the lower base and upper support, tape the two parts together, one on top of the other. Lay out the centers for the 14 holes on either support, as shown in detail C. (Note that these dimensions

MATERIALS LIST

Part	Dimensions	Quantity
1. Front/back	½″ × 5½″ × 12″	1 each
2. Ends	½″ × 5½″ × 5″	2
3. Top/bottom	½″ × 5½″ × 12″	1 each
4. Skirt molding	½″ × 1″ × 36″	1
5. Top molding	¼″ × 7/16″ × 36″	1
6. Base support	⅜″ × ⅜″ × 36″	1
7. Lower base	¼″ × 4½″ × 11″	1
8. Lower spacers	¾″ × ¾″ × 1⅝″	4
9. Upper support	¼″ × 4½″ × 11″	1
10. Upper board	¼″ × 4″ × 10″	1
11. Upper spacers	2″ × 2″ × 1¼″	2
12. Flathead screws	#8 × 2″	2
13. Latch	To suit	1
14. Hinges	¾″ × 2″	2
15. Finishing nails	4d	as needed

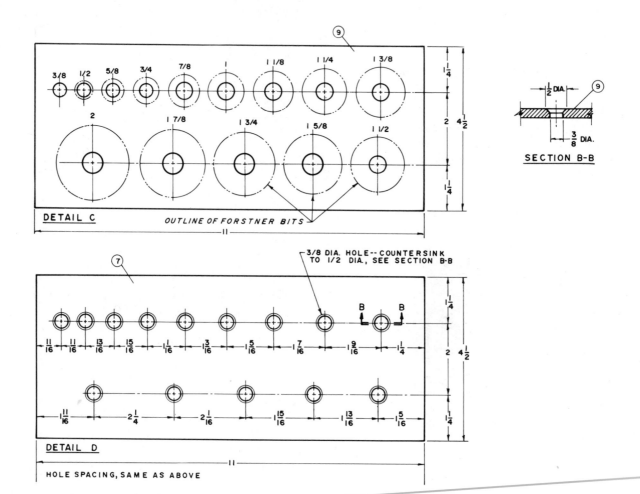

DETAIL C

OUTLINE OF FORSTNER BITS

SECTION B-B

DETAIL D

HOLE SPACING, SAME AS ABOVE

are for a 14-piece set of Forstner bits, ranging in diameter from ⅜ in. to 2 in.; if your set is different, you will have to move the holes to suit.) Using a ¹⁄₁₆-in.-diameter bit, drill the holes through both parts. Separate them.

Use the ¹⁄₁₆-in. holes as layout marks. In the lower base, drill and countersink ⅜-in.-diameter holes centered on the marks, as shown in detail D. In the upper support, drill holes to match your bits.

6. Complete the assembly. Dry-fit the remaining parts and put the bits in their places to make

sure that everything goes together as it should. The bits should fit rather loosely so that moisture doesn't get trapped against them.

Glue the base support (part 6), lower spacers (part 8), lower base (part 7), and upper support (part 9) in place. The upper board (part 10) and upper spacers (part 11) are also in place with screws, as shown. The upper board holds the bits in place in case the box is turned upside down.

7. Apply finish. Finish the box as you choose. Attach the hardware.

Jelly Cupboard

Here is a traditional-looking cover-up for a television set and VCR. Originally, jelly cupboards served as kitchen cabinets. Most were made of pine, an easily worked wood, and many were painted. They came in all shapes and sizes. Some had one or two drawers above the doors, others had drawers below.

Most antique jelly cupboards date between 1830 and 1890. This particular design is a copy of a cupboard from New England. I've widened and deepened it slightly and changed the shelf spacing to accommodate a VCR, cassettes, and a television.

1. *Measure your television.* Before beginning, measure your television and VCR and make sure they will fit. I've designed this to fit my television, which has a 19-in. screen. Measure the overall dimensions of your television: top to bottom; side to side; and from the knobs on the front to the extreme rear of the set. Add at least ½ in. to all the dimensions to be safe. The lines of the cupboard won't be affected much if you have to stretch the dimensions somewhat.

2. *Select the stock.* Except for the top and back, the major parts of the cabinet are all ¾ in. thick. You may need to glue up stock for the wider parts.

3. *Cut the parts for the case.* Cut the sides (part 1), the shelves (part 2), the back (part 3), the front legs (part 4), and the top (part 8) to the sizes given in the Materials List.

Cut rabbets ¼ in. wide and ⅜ in. deep in the backboards, as shown in the exploded view. Note there are rabbets along both edges of the

MATERIALS LIST

Part	Dimensions	Quantity
1. Sides	¾" × 17¼" × 45⅝"	2
2. Shelves	¾" × 17¼" × 25"	5
3. Outer backboards	½" × 9¼" × 45⅝"	2
Center backboard	½" × 8" × 45⅝"	1
4. Front legs	¾" × 2½" × 45⅝"	2
5. Top rail	¾" × 1⅛" × 21"	1
6. Dust stop	¾" × ¾" × 24½"	1
7. Doors	¾" × 10½" × 38"	2
8. Top	⅜" × 20½" × 30"	1
9. Molding	¾" × ¾" × 72"	1
10. Battens	¾" × 2½" × 10"	4
11. Latch	⅜" × ¾" × 2½"	1
12. Brass hinges	1½" × 2"	4
13. Pulls	¾" dia. × 3"	2
14. Square-cut nails	8d	as needed
15. Square-cut nails	4d	2
16. Roundhead screws	#8 × 1¼"	as needed

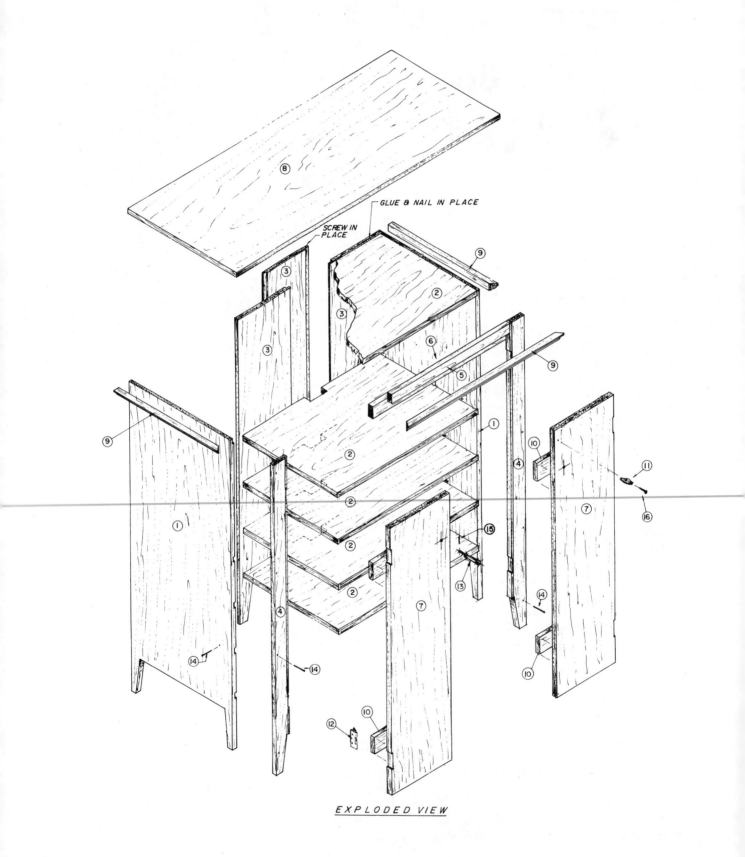

GLUE & NAIL IN PLACE

SCREW IN PLACE

EXPLODED VIEW

JELLY CUPBOARD

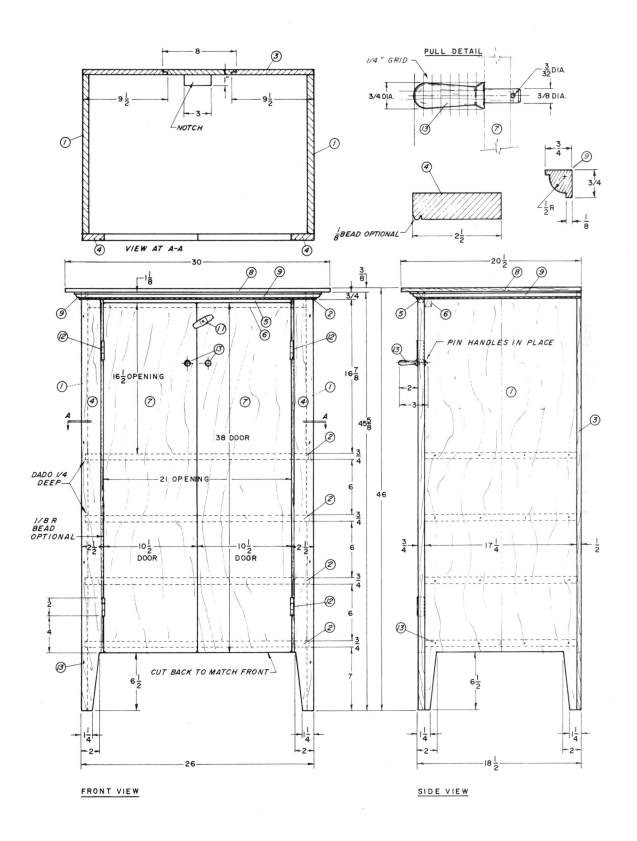

PULL DETAIL

1/4" GRID

3/4 DIA.

3/32 DIA.

3/8 DIA.

⑬

⑦

④

1/8 BEAD OPTIONAL

2 1/2

3/4

⑨

3/4

1/2 R

1/8

8

③

9 1/2

9 1/2

NOTCH

3

1"

①

①

④

④

VIEW AT A-A

30

1 1/8

⑧ ⑨

3/8

3/4

⑨

⑨

⑫

①

④

A

12

①

④

A

16 1/2 OPENING

⑪

⑬

⑦ ⑦

38 DOOR

②

⑫

②

②

⑫

16 7/8

45 5/8

3/4

6

3/4

46

DADO 1/4 DEEP

1/8 R BEAD OPTIONAL

21 OPENING

2 1/2

10 1/2 DOOR

10 1/2 DOOR

2 1/2

②

②

6

3/4

6

1/2

4

②

3/4

⑬

CUT BACK TO MATCH FRONT

6 1/2

7

1 1/4

2

1 1/4

2

26

FRONT VIEW

20 1/2

⑧ ⑨

⑤ ⑥

⑬

PIN HANDLES IN PLACE

⑬

2

3

①

③

3/4

17 1/4

1/2

⑬

6 1/2

1 1/4

2

18 1/2

1 1/4

2

SIDE VIEW

35

center board and along just one edge of the outer boards.

Lay out and cut the rabbet and the dadoes, ¾ in. wide and ¼ in. deep on the sides. Cut a notch in the back of four of the shelves to accommodate wires for the components, as shown in the view at A-A. The fifth shelf that goes at the top of the case is not notched.

4. *Assemble the case.* Put the case face down on the floor and glue and nail the shelves into the sides. Square up the case and begin installing the back. Glue and nail the outer backboards in place; attach the center board with screws only so that you can remove it later to wire the components.

With the case flat on the floor, nail the top in place. Make sure the cabinet is level and square. Let the glue dry overnight.

Make the front legs while the glue dries. Cut a ⅛-in.-radius bead along the inner edges of the front legs, as shown, with a hand plane, router, or shaper. Not all jelly cupboards had this bead, so don't feel that you are sacrificing authenticity if you lack the tools to make it.

Cut the bottom of the leg to the profile shown and sand the edges smooth. When the glue in the case has dried, nail and glue the legs in place.

Cut the top rail (part 5) and the dust stop (part 6) to fit in their openings and nail and glue them in place.

Rout the molding (part 9) to the profile shown with a ½-in.-diameter roundover bit. Miter the molding; cut it to length and nail it in place.

5. *Make and install the doors.* Cut the doors (part 7) to fit the opening. Position the battens (part 10) so that they will not interfere with either shelves or television knobs when the doors are closed. Locate the hinges (part 12) 4 in. from the top and bottom edges of the doors. Mortise the legs to accept the hinges and screw the hinges in place.

Carve or turn the door pulls (part 13) to the shape shown in the detail drawing. While there is no need for the pulls to be identical, you can make a pattern by drawing a ¼-in. grid on a piece of thin plywood. Enlarge the gridded section of the pull onto the plywood and cut out the outline. As you make the pulls, fit the template against them to check their proportions.

When you've made the pulls, drill a hole through each, as shown. Drill ⅜-in.-diameter handle holes in the door 6½ in. down from the top and 1½ in. from the edge. Put the handles through the holes and pin each pull in place with a square-cut nail (part 15) as shown.

Carve the latch (part 11) to the approximate shape shown in the front view. Attach it to the right-hand door with a roundhead screw. The door is held fast with a small hook fastened to an eye inside the cabinet.

6. *Apply finish.* Varnish or paint the cupboard as you see fit. The cupboard in the photograph was decorated by a professional finisher. It has a base coat of paint that was intentionally formulated to check, for the appearance of age. The design was painted over this coat.

Chest of Drawers

This project yields a number of small storage spaces without taking up much floor area. You could make a plain-Jane version to store accessories in the workshop by omitting the dentil molding and using scrap wood and inexpensive pulls.

1. *Select the stock.* I made the chest shown here out of ash simply because I came across a number of old ash table tops that could be had cheaply. Auction houses often sell old furniture at bargain prices, and you can salvage them for their wood. The back can be made of ½-in. plywood. The drawer bottoms can be made of ¼-in. hardboard or plywood.

2. *Cut the parts for the case.* This is one of the more involved projects in the book, so please take the time to go over the plans before cutting any wood.

Build the case first and cut the drawers and molding to fit later. Begin by cutting the sides (part 1) to the dimensions given in the Materials List. Cut dadoes for the drawer runners with a dado blade on a table saw, radial arm saw, or with a router. Cut or rout a rabbet for the back.

Cut the back (part 2) to the shape shown in the drawing. It's easiest if you start with a piece 12½ in. wide and glue two ½-in. wings to it at the bottom. Make the cutout after you've glued the wings in place.

Dry-fit and temporarily clamp the back to the sides. Measure the distance from the bottom

MATERIALS LIST

Part	Dimensions	Quantity
1. Sides	¾" × 9½" × 40"	2
2. Back	½" × 13½" × 42⅞"	1
3. Drawer rails	¾" × 1" × 12½"	11
4. Drawer runners	¾" × ¾" × 8"	22
5. Top	½" × 10¾" × 16"	1
6. Front dentil	½" × 1⅛" × 14½"	1
7. Side dentils	½" × 1⅛" × 10"	2
8. Front molding	¼"-rad. quarter-rd. × 15"	1
9. Side moldings	¼"-rad. quarter-rd. × 10¼"	2
10. Front skirt	¾" × 4" × 15"	1
11. Side skirts	¾" × 4" × 10¼"	2
12. Drawer sides	½" × 3" × 9"	20
13. Drawer backs	½" × 3" × 11½"	10
14. Drawer bottoms	¼" × 8¼" × 11⁷/₁₆"	10
15. Drawer fronts	¾" × 3½" × 12½"	10
16. Pulls*	⅝" dia.	20
17. Finishing nails	4d	as needed

*Pulls can be ordered from Mason & Sullivan Company, 586 Higgins Crowell Road, West Yarmouth, MA 02673; order #2510-B.

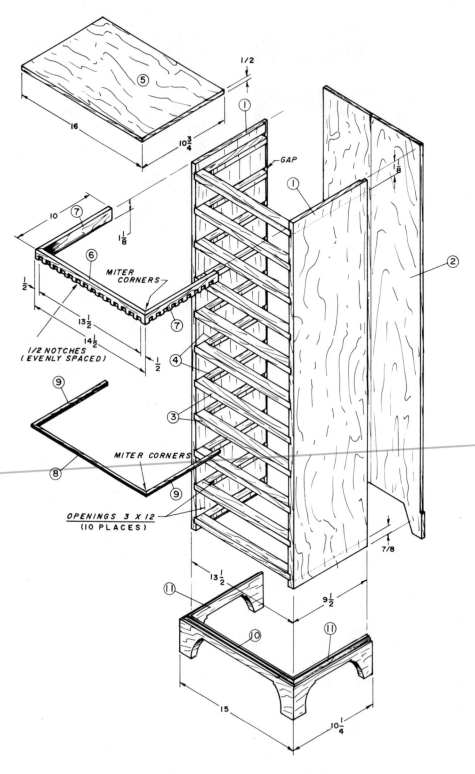

1/2

5

16

10¾

GAP

1⅛

10

7

1⅛

6

MITER
CORNERS

½

7

13½

14½

½

1/2 NOTCHES
(EVENLY SPACED)

9

4

3

8

MITER CORNERS

9

OPENINGS 3 X 12
(10 PLACES)

2

1⅛

7/8

13½

11

9½

10

11

15

10¼

EXPLODED VIEW

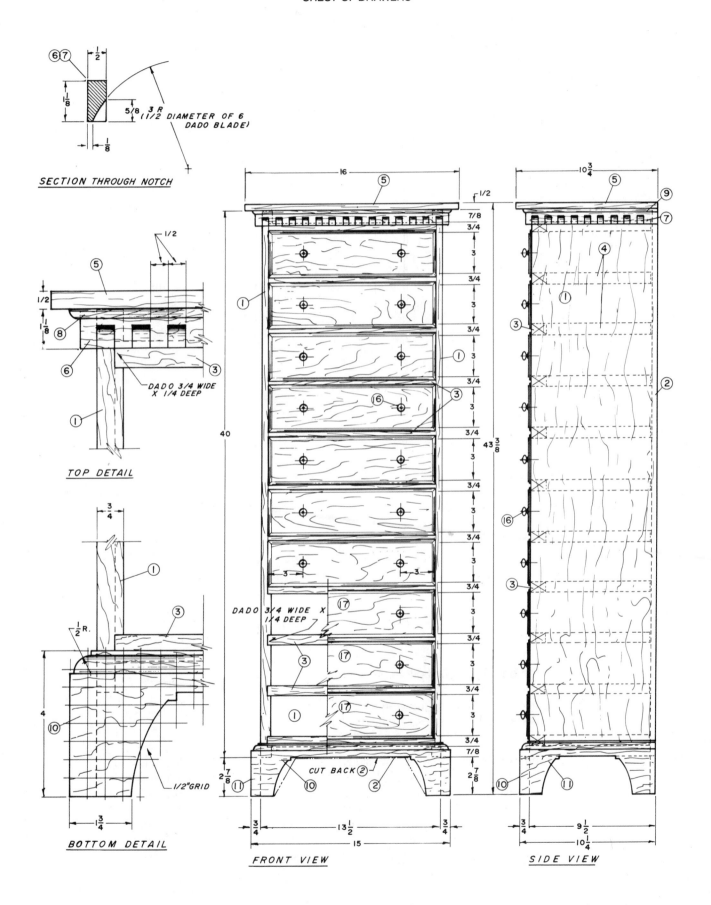

SECTION THROUGH NOTCH

3 R
(1/2 DIAMETER OF 6
DADO BLADE)

TOP DETAIL

DADO 3/4 WIDE
X 1/4 DEEP

BOTTOM DETAIL

1/2"GRID

CUT BACK 2

DADO 3/4 WIDE X
1/4 DEEP

FRONT VIEW

SIDE VIEW

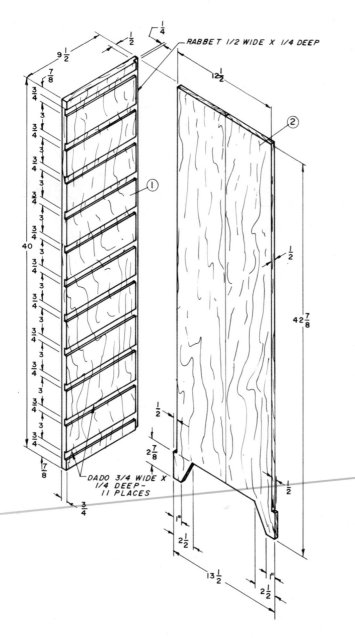

the top (part 5) to the size given in the Materials List and attach it with 4d finishing nails (part 17). Set the nails and putty the holes.

4. Make and install the moldings. Dentil molding usually is made by cutting a series of evenly spaced notches through the wood. This molding (parts 6 and 7) is slightly different: The notches don't go all the way through. Cut the notches with a dado blade on the table saw or radial arm saw but stop ⅛ in. before the cut comes all the way through. The curvature of the blade will leave a sloping wall at the back of the notch, as shown in the notch detail. Make all three dentil moldings an inch longer than necessary to allow for errors. Miter the moldings and cut them to fit the cabinet.

Because the grain of the molding is perpendicular to the sides, it's best to nail the molding in place. Glue would break loose as the wood expanded and contracted with the weather. The front molding can be glued, however, because the grain of the molding and cabinet run in the same direction. Install the moldings.

The ¼-in. quarter-round stock for the front and side molding (parts 8 and 9) is available in pine at most lumber yards. You can also rout or shape it yourself with a ¼-in.-radius roundover bit. Rout the shape on a board wide enough to handle safely and then cut the molding off the edge of the board. Miter the quarter-round molding to fit the cabinet; attach it with glue.

5. Attach the skirts. Rout the top edge of the skirts (parts 10 and 11) to the profile shown with a ½-in.-radius roundover bit. Miter the skirts to fit the case. Then lay out the leg pattern on a ½-in. grid and transfer it to the skirts. Cut out the pattern and sand the edges. Glue the skirts to the case.

6. Make the drawers. Don't let the prospect of making all of those drawers throw you. A drawer is nothing but a box without a top.

Cut the drawer sides, back, bottom, and front (parts 12, 13, 14, and 15) to size. The dimensions in the Materials List will fit the drawer openings *exactly* as drawn. Measure the actual openings. If you need to adjust the size of the drawer, adjust the dimensions accordingly. Once you've cut the parts, dado the sides to house the drawer back. Then cut the grooves in the drawer sides and back to house the drawer bottom.

of a dado on one side to the bottom of a corresponding dado on the other side. Make the measurement across the back of the case to avoid errors caused by wobbling sides. Cut the drawer rails (part 3) to this dimension.

3. Assemble the case. Glue the two sides to the back. Glue the drawer rails in place and clamp the entire assembly together, making sure that everything remains square. When the glue is dry, add the drawer runners (part 4). Glue only the front three in. of the runner so that the sides can expand and contract with the weather. Cut

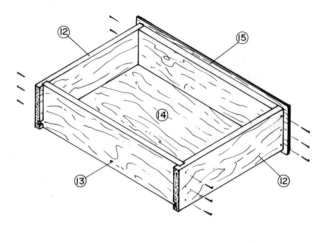

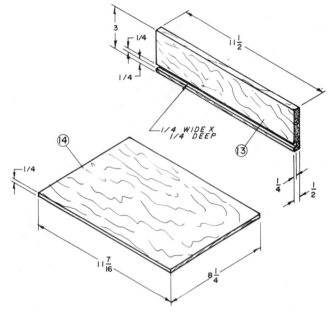

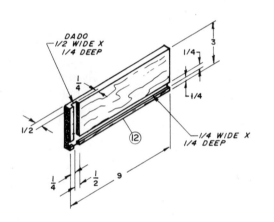

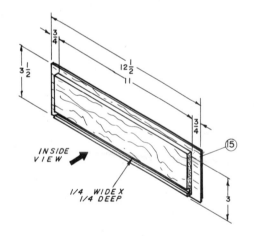

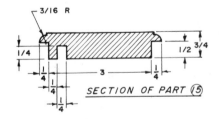

SECTION OF PART ⑮

Now make the drawer fronts. Rout the face of the drawer front to the profile shown with a ³⁄₁₆-in.-radius roundover bit. Then rout or cut the rabbets on the inside. The rabbets are all ½ in. deep, but notice the ones on the sides are wider than those on the top and bottom. Rout the rabbets and cut a groove for the drawer bottom. Locate the groove, as shown in the drawing. If you will be using the pulls (part 16) described in the Materials List, drill two ⅛-in.-diameter holes for them, centered vertically and inset 3 in. from the sides.

Assemble the drawers with glue and 4d finishing nails, except for the bottoms (part 14) that are allowed to float freely in the dadoes cut for them. Check to make sure the drawers are square and allow the glue to dry.

7. Apply finish. Apply a clear finish if you used particularly attractive wood. Otherwise, consider applying a light stain before following with varnish. Add the pulls.

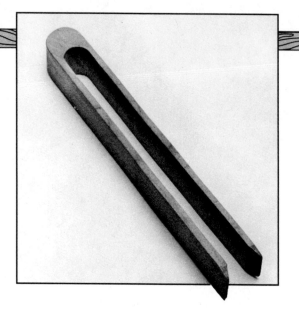

Toaster Tongs

If you are like me, you start off the day in frustration. I can't get the darn toast out of the toaster. Or I couldn't—until I made this simple, handy kitchen implement.

1. Select the wood. There are several ways to make a pair of toaster tongs. My approach was to start with a piece of oversized stock—¾ in. thick × 1⅛ in. wide × 9 in. long—and then work it down to the finished dimensions. Use a hardwood such as maple or cherry.

2. Lay out the tongs. Draw a line down the center of the wide side of the stock. At a point on the line roughly 1½ in. from one end, mark the center of a ⅝-in.-diameter hole and draw the hole. To lay out the insides of the legs, draw two lines: Each one is tangent to the hole and parallel to the sides of the stock, as shown.

To lay out the outside of the tongs, locate a second point on the center line, ⅝ in. above the center of the hole. Swing a ⁷⁄₁₆-in. arc from that point, as shown in the top view. Extend a line from the bottom of the arc to lay out the outside of the legs. If you've measured correctly, the outside lines are ⅛ in. from the inside lines.

3. Cut out the tongs. Drill out the hole and cut along the layout lines with a band saw. Saw just outside the lines and sand down to the final leg thickness of ⅛ in., taking care to make the legs as nearly identical as possible.

4. Finish the tongs. Either leave the wood unfinished or apply a coat of vegetable oil or salad bowl finish. You're now ready to face each morning—at least after a cup of coffee.

7/16 R
5/8
5/8 DIA. HOLE
⅛
5/8 7/8
⅛
TOP VIEW
1 1/16
6 15/16
8
3/4
SIDE VIEW
CHAMFER ENDS AS SHOWN

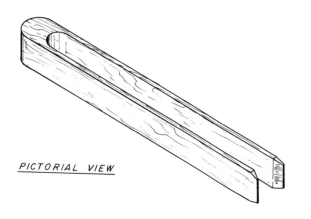

PICTORIAL VIEW

Pasta and Salad Forks

My daughter, Joy, bought an electric pasta maker that makes all shapes and sizes of pasta, but I was more impressed with her new pasta forks. I went right home and made a similar pair. I've found they also make good salad forks.

1. *Select the stock and cut the dowels.* All you need is dowel stock in two diameters. Cut the dowels to the lengths given in the Materials List.

This project will progress more easily if you have a drill press. To keep the dowel from turning as you drill, put it into a long V-shaped groove that you've cut into a block of wood. Clamp the block to the drill press table. Locate and drill the six $3/16$-in.-diameter holes in the support (part 1), making them $5/16$-in. deep. Keep the holes all in a line and drill them at the same angle. Locate and drill the $1/4$-in.-diameter handle hole $3/8$ in. deep. With the support placed so that the six smaller holes are facing downward, this hole will be roughly 30 degrees from vertical, as shown in the side view.

2. *Shape the handle.* Use a sharp knife to chamfer one end of the handle (part 3) and taper the other end down to a diameter of $1/4$ in. The taper should start $1/2$ in. from the end.

3. *Assemble the fork.* Glue the teeth (part 2) in place. When the glue sets, trim the ends to

MATERIALS LIST
(for two forks)

Part	Dimensions	Quantity
1. Supports	$1/2''$ dia. $\times$ $3\,7/8''$	2
2. Teeth	$3/16''$ dia. $\times$ $3\,5/16''$	12
3. Handles	$1/2''$ dia. $\times$ $9''$	2

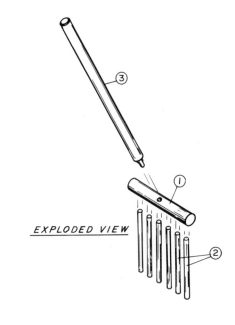

EXPLODED VIEW

the same length with a backsaw. Glue the handle in place.

4. *Finish the fork.* Sand lightly, taking care to remove any sharp edges. Either leave the wood as it is or apply a light coat of salad bowl finish.

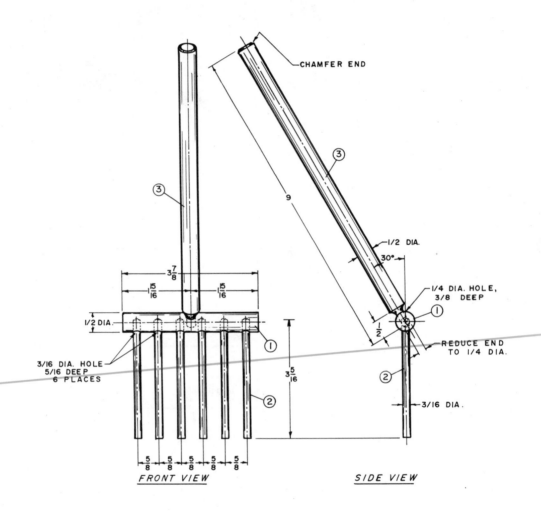

FRONT VIEW

SIDE VIEW

Key Rack

I manage to lose my keys often, and I should have made this project *years* ago.

1. *Select the stock and cut the wood to the overall dimensions.* I suggest using an attractive hardwood and finishing it clear. The key rack in the photo was painted black only so that it would show up clearly in a photograph. You'll need a ¼-in.-thick piece of wood, measuring roughly 4 in. × 11 in. The brass hooks can be picked up at a hardware store.

2. *Make a paper pattern.* Draw a grid with ½-in. squares and enlarge the drawing of the key

onto it. Include the location of the five brass hooks and the centers of all four holes. Transfer the pattern to the wood.

3. *Drill the holes and cut the rack to shape.* Drill the holes. Countersink the ⅛-in.-diameter holes to take flathead screws for mounting the rack. Cut out the key rack. Use an awl to make indentations at the five points where the hooks will be placed. Sand the rack.

4. *Finish the rack.* Stain the rack, if you wish, and apply a clear finish. Screw the hooks in place.

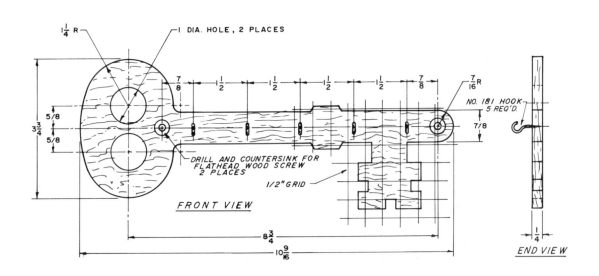

1¼ R

I DIA. HOLE, 2 PLACES

⅞ — 1½ — 1½ — 1½ — 1½ — ⅞

⅞ R

5/8

3¾

5/8

NO. 181 HOOK
5 REQ'D.

7/8

DRILL AND COUNTERSINK FOR
FLATHEAD WOOD SCREW
2 PLACES

1/2" GRID

FRONT VIEW

8¾

10 9/16

END VIEW

¼

Napkin Holder

The pattern for this piece was taken from an antique New England weather vane. Weather vanes are a great design resource for many woodworking projects. If you have a favorite pattern, try using it in place of the crowing rooster shown here.

1. Select the stock and cut out the parts. You'll need ¼- and ⅜-in.-thick stock. I used ash for the piece in the photograph. Cut the parts to the sizes given in the Materials List.

2. Make a paper pattern and cut out the rooster. Draw a grid with ½-in. squares and enlarge the rooster onto it. Transfer the drawing to the front piece (part 1). Note that the holder is slightly taller than it is wide. Orient the grain, as shown. Glue the front and back together with rubber cement so that the pattern faces out.

Drill holes in each of the areas that will be cut out so you can begin the cuts that will remove them. Cut out the design with a jigsaw or a scroll saw and sand the edges.

Cut a 1-in. radius in the top corners of each piece, as shown. Sand what will be the inside of the holder before assembling the pieces.

3. Assemble the holder. Glue the front and back to the base (part 2). Make sure that the front and back are square to the base and parallel to one another.

After the glue sets, lay out and drill the six ⅛-in.-diameter holes that hold the pins (part 3). Place a small amount of glue on each pin and tap them into the holes. Once the glue has dried thoroughly, sand the front and back.

4. Apply finish. Apply a clear finish or paint. Another alternative is to paint only the *outline* of the rooster and then varnish the entire piece.

MATERIALS LIST

Part	Dimensions	Quantity
1. Front/back	¼″ × 6¼″ × 6½″	1 each
2. Base	⅜″ × 2″ × 6¼″	1
3. Pins	⅛″ dia. × ¾″	6

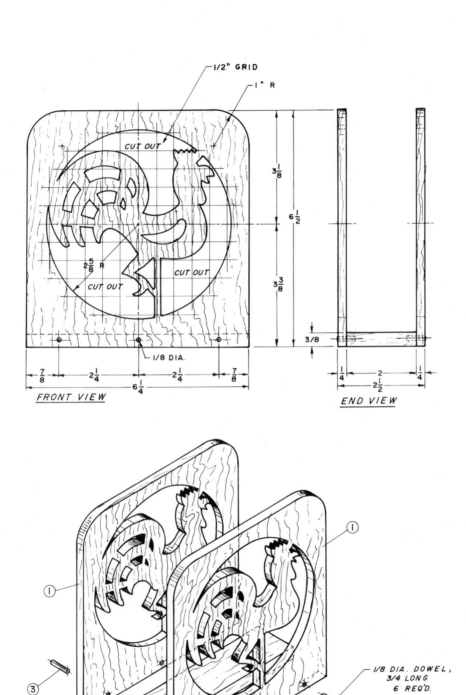

1/2" GRID

1" R

CUT OUT

$3\frac{1}{8}$

$6\frac{1}{2}$

$2\frac{5}{8}$ R

CUT OUT

$3\frac{3}{8}$

CUT OUT

3/8

1/8 DIA.

$\frac{7}{8}$ $2\frac{1}{4}$ $2\frac{1}{4}$ $\frac{7}{8}$

$6\frac{1}{4}$

FRONT VIEW

$\frac{1}{4}$ $\frac{2}{2\frac{1}{2}}$ $\frac{1}{4}$

END VIEW

1/8 DIA. DOWEL,
3/4 LONG
6 REQ'D.

EXPLODED VIEW

47

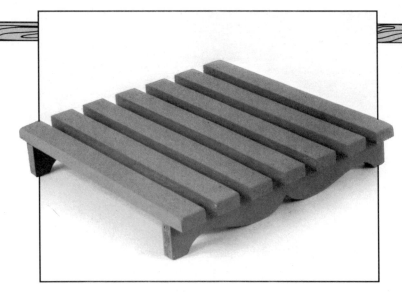

Wooden Trivet

This is a quick project with a practical purpose. These trivets look especially good in traditionally decorated kitchens.

1. *Select the stock and cut the parts.* The entire piece is made out of ½-in.-thick stock. I used pine, but almost any kind of wood will do. Cut the parts to the sizes given in the Materials List. Sand them with a sanding block or an electric palm sander. Make sure you keep the edges sharp.

2. *Make a paper pattern and cut the legs to shape.* Draw a grid with ¼-in. squares and enlarge the outline of the legs (part 1) onto it. Transfer the enlargement to one of the legs. To get identical legs, tape or rubber-cement the legs together with the pattern facing out. Cut out both and sand them together.

3. *Assemble the trivet.* Glue and nail the top boards (part 2) to the legs, taking care that everything is square. Sand thoroughly.

4. *Finish the trivet.* This project can be finished clear or painted if it is to be a display item.

MATERIALS LIST

Part	Dimensions	Quantity
1. Legs	½″ × 1⅛″ × 10″	2
2. Top boards	½″ × 1″ × 10″	7
3. Finishing nails	6d	as needed

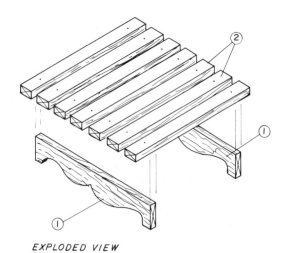

EXPLODED VIEW

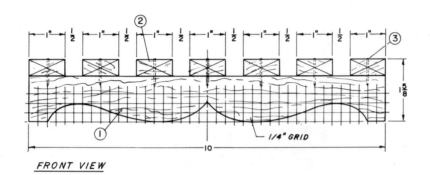

FRONT VIEW

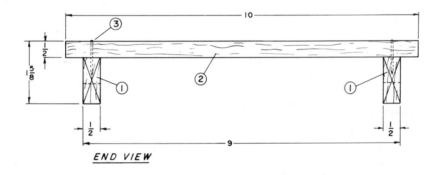

END VIEW

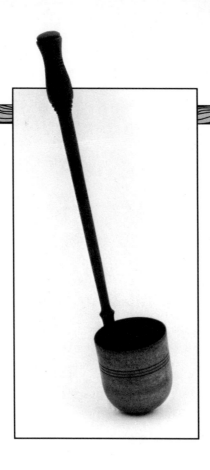

Scoop

Turn the lathe off and apply a coat or two of nonpolyurethane finish. Cut off the piece, sand the ends, and apply finish to them.

3. Turn the cup. Screw the cup blank onto a face plate and mount it on the lathe. Turn the blank to the 2¼-in.-outside diameter along the entire length. Turn off the lathe. Put a drill chuck in the lathe's tailstock and put a 1-in. diameter Forstner bit in the chuck. Bring the bit against the stock and tighten the tailstock. With the lathe running, turn the tailstock wheel to advance the bit into the wood. Drill a hole about 2¼ in. deep. Remember the wood is attached to the face plate with screws. Take care not to drill into them. Back the drill bit out of the way and turn the piece to the profile shown.

Sand the scoop inside and out with the lathe running. Try to sand the top of the cup to the narrow edge, indicated by the hidden lines in the drawing. Cut and darken three grooves, as described, for the handle. Turn off the lathe to apply a coat or two of satin-finish varnish. (If you will be using the scoop for food, finish the inside of the bowl with salad bowl finish instead.)

Cut off the cup, sand the end, and apply finish to match the rest of the cup.

4. Attach the handle. Carefully notch the bottom of the handle with a coping saw so that it fits over the cup, as illustrated. When you have a good, snug joint, attach the handle with epoxy and allow it to dry for 24 hours.

Reinforce the joint with two brass rivets, between ¹⁄₁₆ in. and ³⁄₃₂ in. in diameter and ⅝ in. or ¾ in. long. Hollow rivets are easier to peen over, but you may have trouble finding them at a

I saw a scoop similar to this one at the home of a woodworking friend in Tulsa, Oklahoma. It makes a great woodturning project, whether you use the scoop in the kitchen or simply hang it on a wall. The piece is made of two straight-forward turnings, attached to one another with brass rivets.

1. Select the stock. I suggest using a hard-wood with tight grain, such as maple. The handle is made of a 1-in.-square blank about 12 in. long. The cup is turned from a blank 2½ in. square and about 4 in. long.

2. Turn the handle. Mount the handle on the lathe and turn it down to ¾ in. along its entire length. Then mark off the locations of the different diameters and turn the handle to the profile shown. Sand the entire piece while it is still turning on the lathe. Add the three grooves, as shown, with the heel of a ¾-in.-skew chisel. Make the grooves look darker by holding a length of 20-gauge (about ¹⁄₃₂-in.-diameter) brass or steel wire against them while the piece is turning.

hardware store. If you can't find rivets, use two brass nails with heads. Carefully locate and drill two holes, just wide enough so that the rivets fit snugly. Insert the rivets with the heads inside the cup. (If you are using nails, cut them so that the ends extend 1/16 in. beyond the handle.) To peen over the ends of the rivets (or nails), back the head with a heavy piece of metal. Tap the other end with a nail set and hammer to bend the tip and flare it. Keep flaring until you have formed a second head on the rivet. The rivets should fit snugly but take care to avoid splitting the handle or cup.

Drill a hole in the handle so that you can display the scoop on a wall.

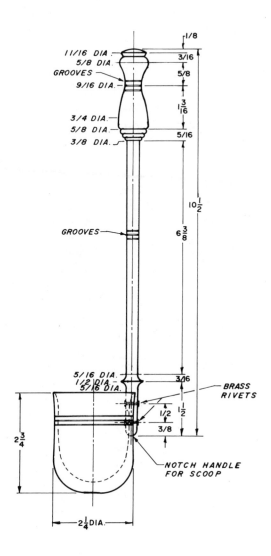

Serving Tray

This project is easy to make. The handle can be cut out quickly, and the rest of the parts go together with little trouble. These trays make great gifts, so consider making two or three of them.

1. *Select the stock.* I suggest using hardwood and applying a clear finish. The tray is made of ½-in.-thick boards. If you can't find a board wide enough for the bottom (part 1), glue it from smaller pieces.

2. *Cut out the parts.* Cut out the ends (part 2), sides (part 3), and bottom rails (part 4) to the dimensions given in the Materials List. Cut the bottom later, so that you can cut it to fit the tray exactly.

3. *Cut out the handles.* Before cutting out the handles, place one end on top of the other. Join them temporarily with tape or rubber cement. On the top piece, draw the outline of the two ¾-in.-diameter holes and the two ⅜-in.-radius arcs. Note the ⅛-in. space between the arcs allows a saw blade to enter and cut the handle in one pass. Draw the 9¼-in.-and 6-in.-radius arcs, as shown. While the ends are still attached to one another, cut the arcs with a band saw, coping saw, or jigsaw. Sand the edges and separate the ends.

4. *Cut the rabbets.* The rabbets all are ½ in. wide and ¼ in. deep. Cut them where shown in the drawing.

5. *Assemble the tray.* Glue and tack the sides together with ¾-in. brads. If the piece is made of hardwood, drill pilot holes for the brads. The best bit for drilling pilot holes is an actual brad. Cut off the head with some wire cutters and tighten the brad in the drill chuck. Drill the hole and drive in a full-length brad. Check that the tray is square.

When the glue has set, measure the opening for the bottom. Cut the bottom to fit and glue and tack it in place as above. Tack the four bottom rails to the bottom with ½-in. brads, spacing the rails, as shown in the end view.

6. *Apply finish.* Sand the entire piece. Stain the tray if you choose and apply two or three coats of varnish. If food is to come in contact with the tray, apply a nontoxic salad bowl finish instead of varnish.

MATERIALS LIST

Part	Dimensions	Quantity
1. Bottom	½″ × 11½″ × 20½″	1
2. Ends	½″ × 3″ × 11½″	2
3. Sides	½″ × 1¾″ × 21″	2
4. Bottom rails	⅛″ × ½″ × 20¾″	4
5. Brads	¾″	as needed
6. Brads	½″	as needed

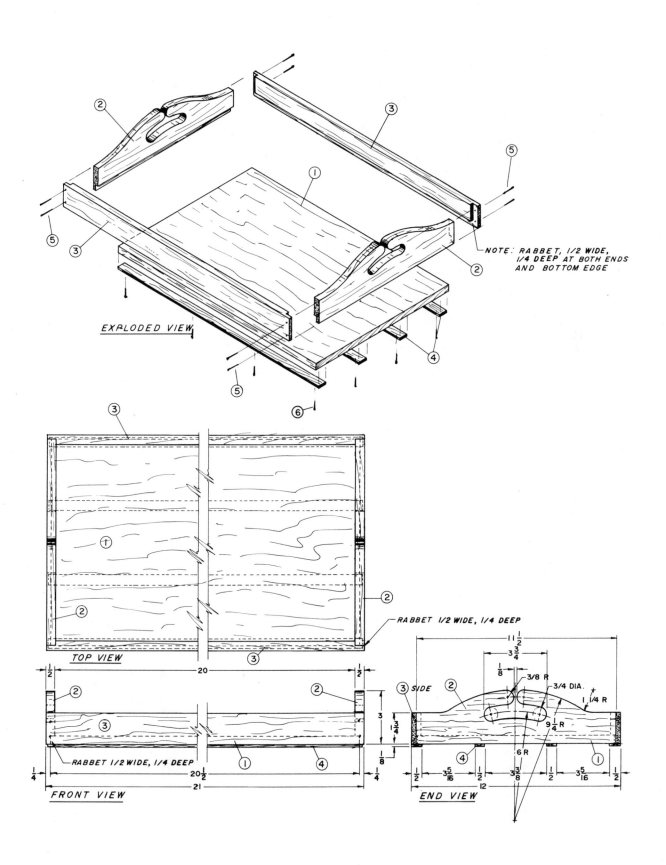

EXPLODED VIEW

NOTE: RABBET, 1/2 WIDE, 1/4 DEEP AT BOTH ENDS AND BOTTOM EDGE

TOP VIEW

RABBET 1/2 WIDE, 1/4 DEEP

FRONT VIEW

RABBET 1/2 WIDE, 1/4 DEEP

END VIEW

SIDE

Candy Dish

For the committed woodworker, a crystal candy dish just won't do. This design is a takeoff of the traditional candy dish, and I prefer it to the glass original. The pedestal and base may look like a turning in the drawing; however, they are square and cut with a band saw.

1. *Select the wood and cut the parts.* Use any wood that appeals to you. Cut all parts to the overall sizes given in the Materials List.

2. *Transfer the pattern and cut the sides to shape.* The four sides (part 4) are exactly the same size and shape. Because the sides slope on the assembled dish, the corner joints are compound angles. The sloped sides also mean that the bottom edge of each side must be beveled.

Cut all these angles before you cut any of the curves. To cut the corner joints, tilt the saw blade to 35 degrees and set the miter gauge to 29 degrees. Make a test-cut on the ends of a couple of pieces of scrap and piece them together to make sure the corner meets at 90 degrees. Adjust your saw settings, if necessary, and cut the ends of your stock.

To bevel the bottom edges, tilt the saw blade to 40 degrees and rip the pieces against your saw's fence. Before you make the cuts, be sure you're cutting the bevel in the correct direction. If your table saw blade tilts to the right, the *inner* face should rest on the table.

Once you've cut the angles, lay out the scalloped edges of the sides. Draw a grid with ¼-in. squares and enlarge the pattern for the sides onto it. Transfer the enlarged pattern to the wood. Band saw the curves with the blade set at a standard 90 degrees.

MATERIALS LIST

Part	Dimensions	Quantity
1. Base	¾" × 5" × 5"	1
2. Pedestal	1¾" × 1¾" × 4¼"	1
3. Tray bottom	¼" × 5⅝" × 5⅝"	1
4. Sides	¼" × 2⅝" × 8¼"	4
5. Flathead screws	#8 × 1¼"	2

3. *Cut the other parts to shape.* To make the pedestal (part 2), lay out the shape on adjacent sides of the 1¾- × 1¾-in. stock. Band saw along the profile you drew on one face but save the scrap. Tape the scrap back around what you've cut out. Then band saw the profile you drew on the second face.

Rout the edges of the base (part 1) with either a single cutter or a ¼-in.-radius cove bit and a ³⁄₁₆-in.-radius roundover bit. Feel free to improvise with any bits that you happen to have.

4. *Assemble the dish.* Dry-fit the four sides. Check that the corners meet tightly. Glue the sides together, "clamping" them with either rubber bands or masking tape. When the glue dries, place the sides on a flat surface to see if their bottom edges are flush; if not, sand as needed. Center the assembled sides on the tray bottom and glue them in place.

To attach the pedestal, drill ⅛-in.-diameter holes through the center of the tray bottom and the base. Countersink the holes to accept flathead screws (part 5). To keep the screws from splitting the pedestal, drill ¹⁄₁₆-in.-diameter pilot holes for them in the top and bottom of the pedestal. Screw the pedestal to the base and to the tray bottom.

5. *Apply finish.* Round-over the top edges of the tray bottom (part 3) with sandpaper. Sand the dish thoroughly. Apply a low-luster varnish.

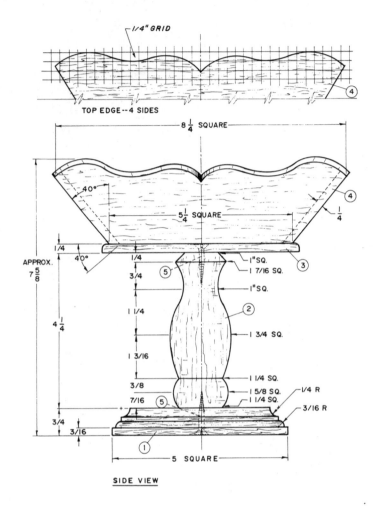

TOP EDGE--4 SIDES

SIDE VIEW

Grocery List Holder

Of the hundreds of projects I've made, my wife appreciates this one the most. The holder is hung on a wall so that it's always handy when someone wants to jot down an item. The printed grocery list pad shown in the photo is available from the source listed in the Materials List, as are the carriage bolts.

1. *Select the stock and cut the parts.* I used ash for this piece but choose any wood you happen to have on hand. Pick out a piece of ¼-in.-thick stock with an eye to the grain, unless you'll be painting the holder to match accessories or trim in the kitchen. Cut the parts to the sizes given in the Materials List.

2. *Lay out the backboard and cut the parts to shape.* Use the given radii to lay out the curves and the handle. Locate the centers of the two ³⁄₁₆-in.-diameter holes for the carriage bolts that hold the locking bar. Cut out the backboard (part 1) and drill the two holes.

Cut the locking bar (part 2) to the dimensions given and drill ³⁄₁₆-in.-diameter holes through it for the carriage bolts (part 3).

3. *Finish the holder.* Sand thoroughly and either varnish or paint the piece. Use the locking bar and carriage bolts to clamp a pad of paper in place.

MATERIALS LIST

Part	Dimensions	Quantity
1. Backboard	¼" × 4¾" × 15½"	1
2. Locking bar	¼" × ¾" × 4⅝"	1
3. Carriage bolts, with washers, butterfly nuts*	1½"	2
4. Grocery list pad*		1

*Hardware is available from Meisel Hardware Specialties, P.O. Box 70, Mound MN 55364. Pair of bolts with washers and nuts is #C.B., and printed grocery list pad is #14-P.

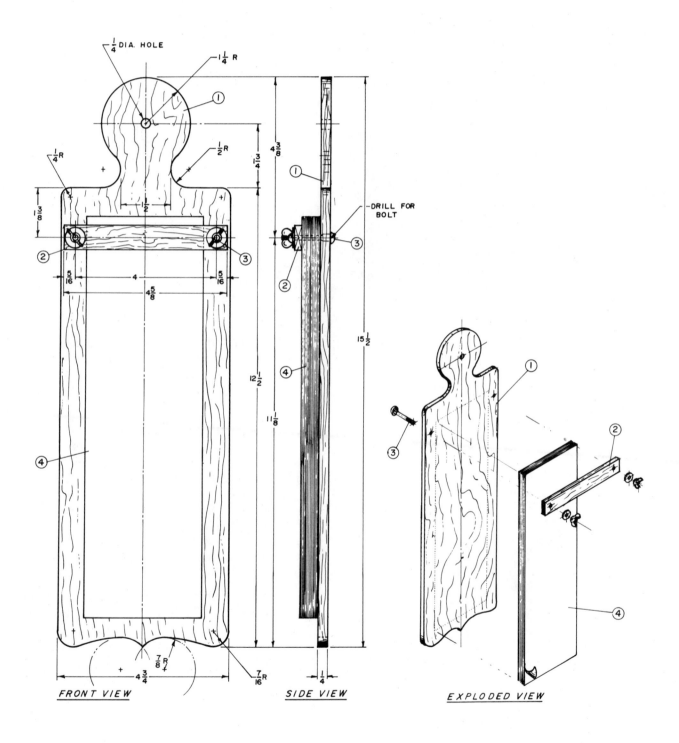

FRONT VIEW   SIDE VIEW   EXPLODED VIEW

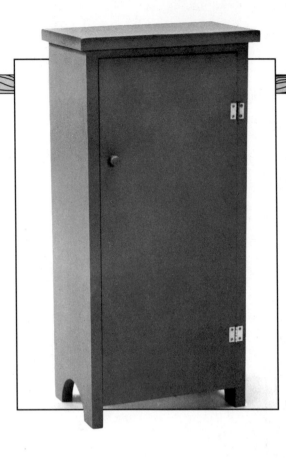

Small Jelly Cupboard

The size of this project sets it apart. Because butt joints are used throughout, the cupboard is easy to make.

1. *Select the stock and cut the parts.* Use softwood for this project. Cut all the parts except the door to the sizes given in the Materials List. Lay out and cut the curves for the feet on the two sides (part 1).

2. *Assemble the cupboard.* The parts are assembled with glue and finishing nails (part 10). Attach the back (part 2) to the sides. Add the rail (part 6) and dust stop (part 7). Nail the three shelves (part 3) to the case. Add the top (part 4), centering it as shown, and nail it in place. Measure the opening and cut the door, allowing for a 1/32-in. gap between the edges of the door and the cabinet. Temporarily attach the door (part 5) and the hinges (part 8) to check the fit.

3. *Apply finish.* Remove the hinges from the door and case. Fill the nail holes with putty and sand thoroughly. Add the wooden pull (part 9). Paint with the color of your choice. Reinstall the hinges and hang the door.

MATERIALS LIST

Part	Dimensions	Quantity
1. Sides	¾" × 7" × 23¼"	2
2. Back	½" × 9⅜" × 21¼"	1
3. Shelves	½" × 5¾" × 9⅜"	3
4. Top	¾" × 7½" × 11⅞"	1
5. Door	¾" × 9⅜" × 21¼"	1
6. Rail	½" × ¾" × 9⅜"	1
7. Dust stop	¾" × ¾" × 9⅜"	1
8. Brass hinges	½" × 1"	2
9. Wooden pull	½" dia.	1
10. Finishing nails	4d	as needed

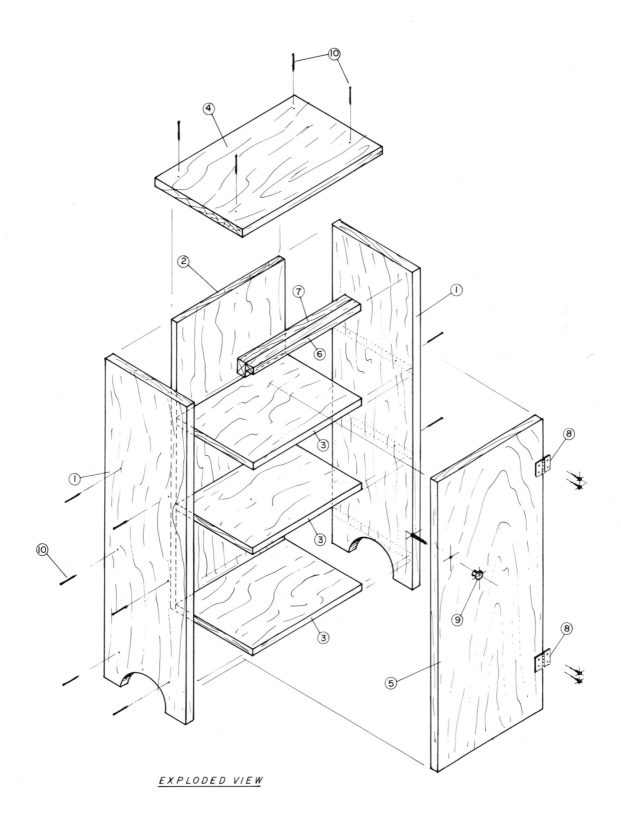

EXPLODED VIEW

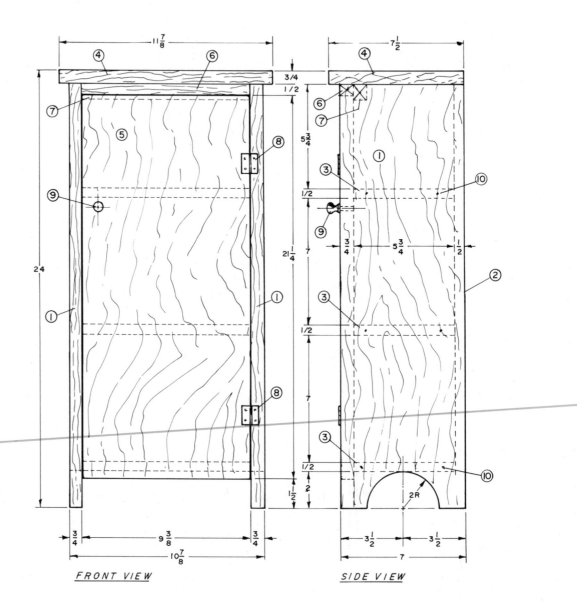

FRONT VIEW

SIDE VIEW

Bathroom Shelf

Use this shelf in the bathroom or anywhere else in the house. You can make it longer by adding spindles on 2½-in. centers; a 41-in.-long shelf would have eight more spindles than the project illustrated here. If you won't be turning spindles and can't find them in local stores, you can buy them from the source given in the Materials List.

1. Select the stock and cut the parts. The shelf in the photo was made from ash; I bought the oak spindles through the mail. Cut the parts to the sizes given in the Materials List.

MATERIALS LIST

Part	Dimensions	Quantity
1. Shelf	½" × 6" × 21"	1
2. Front rail	½" × 1" × 21"	1
3. Side rails	½" × 1" × 6"	2
4. Splines	⅛" × 1" × 1"	2
5. Spindles*		13
6. Wall braces	½" × 4" × 5"	2
7. Metal hangers*	As available	2
8. Nails	6d	as needed

*Parts are available from Meisel Hardware Specialties, P.O. Box 70, Mound, MN 55364. Spindles are #S-4, and brass hangers are #7269.

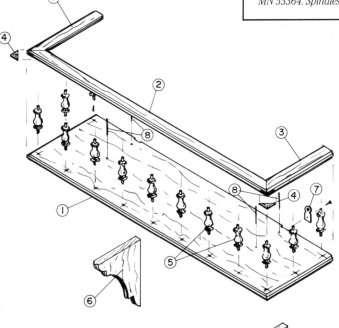

EXPLODED VIEW

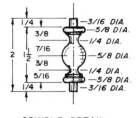

SPINDLE DETAIL

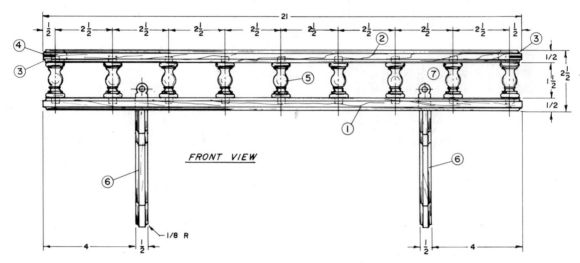

FRONT VIEW

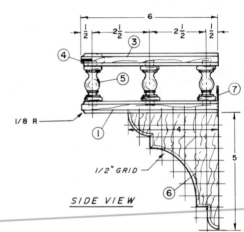

1/8 R

1/2" GRID

SIDE VIEW

2. *Cut the parts to shape.* Notch the rear edge of the shelf (part 1) to accept whichever metal hangers (part 7) you will use. Brass hangers are available from the source given in the Materials List.

Miter the ends of the front rail (part 2) and side rails (part 3) where they will meet. Glue the rails together, making sure that the corners they form are square. After the glue sets, strengthen the joints with splines (part 4). Let the glue dry and then sand the entire rail.

The spindles I bought fit nicely in $3/16$-in.-diameter holes that were $3/8$ in. deep. Mark the center of each hole on the rail and on the shelf with an awl. Make sure that the points on the shelf line up *exactly* with those on the rail and then drill to fit your spindles (part 5).

Draw a grid with $1/2$-in. squares and enlarge the drawing of the wall brace (part 6) onto it. Transfer the enlarged drawing to the wood. Cut the two braces to shape.

3. *Cut the molded edges.* Rout coves into edges of the shelf, the wall braces, and the rail with a $1/8$-in.-radius cove bit that has a ball-bearing guide. Clean up the routing on the inside corners of the brace with a gauge. The router may tend to tip when routing the narrow rail. You can steady

it by placing a scrap $1/2$ in. thick $\times$ 6 in. wide $\times$ 18 in. long between the rails while routing.

4. *Assemble the shelf.* Sand the entire shelf. Dry-assemble the spindles in the holes in the shelf and then fit the glued-up rail in place. Make any necessary adjustments. Disassemble the parts, apply a little glue to the top and bottom of the spindles, and put the parts back together.

When the glue dries, position the wall braces 4 in. from the outer edges of the shelf and nail them in place with 6d finishing nails (part 8).

5. *Apply finish.* Sand the entire shelf and paint or varnish it.

Cookbook Holder and Trivet

This piece helps conserve counter space in the kitchen by holding cookbooks and hot pans at the same time.

1. *Select the stock and cut the parts.* Use hardwood for this project. Cut the parts to the sizes given in the Materials List and make sure that all of the dowels (part 3) are exactly the same length.

MATERIALS LIST

Part	Dimensions	Quantity
1. Supports	½″ × 6½″ × 6½″	2
2. End	½″ × 1½″ × 6½″	1
3. Dowels	½″ dia. × 18″	5

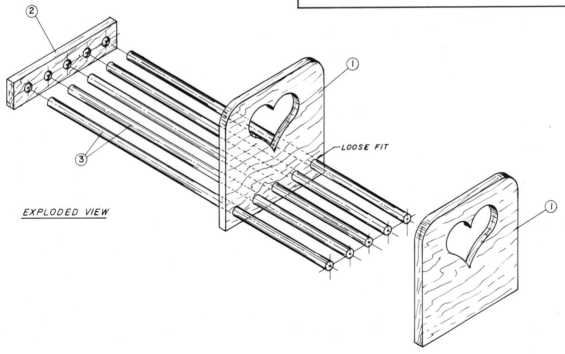

LOOSE FIT

EXPLODED VIEW

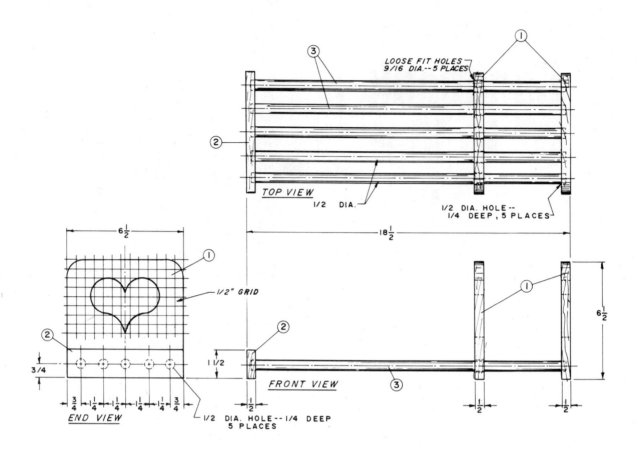

TOP VIEW

LOOSE FIT HOLES
9/16 DIA.--5 PLACES

1/2 DIA.

1/2 DIA. HOLE --
1/4 DEEP, 5 PLACES

18½

6½

1/2" GRID

6½

END VIEW

3/4

3/4 ¼ ¼ ¼ ¼ 3/4

1 1/2

½

FRONT VIEW

1/2 DIA. HOLE -- 1/4 DEEP
5 PLACES

½ ½

2. *Make a paper pattern and cut the supports to shape.* Draw a grid with ½-in. squares and enlarge the drawing of the supports (part 1) onto the grid. Transfer the enlargement to one of the supports. Tape the supports together and then cut the outline and the heart shape. While the supports are still taped together, lay out five ½-in.-diameter holes in the top support. Set a drill press or use a stop on a hand drill to make the holes exactly ¾ in. deep; the holes should penetrate the top support but go just ¼ in. into the lower support. This lower support will be the stationary one, as shown in the exploded view.

Separate the two supports and redrill the five through-holes in what was the top support with a ⁹⁄₁₆-in. bit; this will allow the support to slide freely over the dowels.

Locate and drill the five ½-in.-diameter holes in the end (part 2) to a depth of ¼ in.

Sand the parts thoroughly. Give particular attention to smoothing the entire length of the dowels so that the center support will slide easily.

3. *Assemble the holder and trivet.* Glue the five dowels to the support with the stopped holes. Slide the center support over the dowels. Glue the end in place.

4. *Apply finish.* Because the center support should slide easily over the dowels, it's best to varnish the piece rather than apply a thicker coat of paint.

Wall Spice Box

This box can be mounted on an empty bit of wall area to give you a place to tuck all sorts of odds and ends. The drawers are all small and simple: It's a good piece for practicing your drawer making.

1. Select the stock and cut the parts. I used ash for the box shown here simply because that's what I had on hand at the time. Use whatever wood you'd like. The pulls are white glass with brass centers. You can order them from the source given in the Materials List.

Cut the back (part 1), the side (part 2), and the dividers (part 3) to the dimensions given in the Materials List.

2. Cut the back and sides to shape. Lay out and cut the back, as shown. Drill the ¼-in.-diameter hole for hanging the box.

Draw a grid with ½-in. squares and enlarge the drawing of the sides (part 2) onto the grid. Transfer the enlargement to the actual side. Tape the sides together and cut the sides to shape. Sand the edges while the pieces are still joined.

Separate the sides and lay out the dadoes for the dividers. The sides are not identical: They

are mirror images of each other. Rout the dadoes with a ½-in. straight bit. Clamp a straight edge to the side and guide the router against it. Stop all the dadoes ½ in. from the back edge.

3. Dry-assemble the case. Without using glue, test-fit the back, sides, and dividers (part 3) to make sure that everything comes together properly. Make any necessary adjustments and glue up the parts. Make sure the case is square before the glue sets. Sand the case and dividers when the glue dries.

4. Make the drawers. In drawer making, the Materials List is only a guide. Always fit a drawer to its opening.

Cut eight drawer fronts (part 4) to fit snugly in the drawer openings and rabbet them to accept the drawer sides (part 5). Measure the distance between the rabbets and cut the drawer back (part 6) to that length.

Cut the sides to fit next. In this case, measure the depth of the opening and subtract ½ in. Rabbet the front to accept the drawer bottom (part 7). Temporarily assemble the drawers and cut bottoms to match.

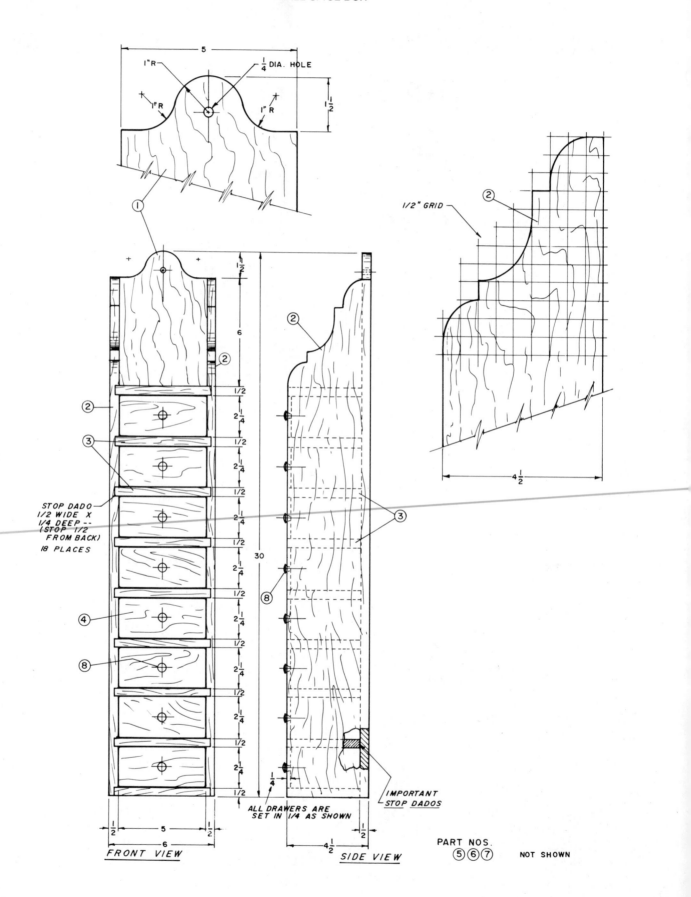

5

1"R

¼ DIA. HOLE

1"R

1"R   1"R

1½

①

②

1/2" GRID

4½

+   +

1½

6

②

STOP DADO
1/2 WIDE X
1/4 DEEP --
(STOP 1/2
FROM BACK)
18 PLACES

②

1/2

2¼

③

1/2

2¼

1/2

2¼

30

④

1/2

2¼

⑧

1/2

2¼

②

③

⑧

1/2

2¼

1/2

2¼

1/2

¼

ALL DRAWERS ARE
SET IN 1/4 AS SHOWN

IMPORTANT
STOP DADOS

½   5   ½

6

FRONT VIEW

4½

1/2

SIDE VIEW

PART NOS.
⑤⑥⑦   NOT SHOWN

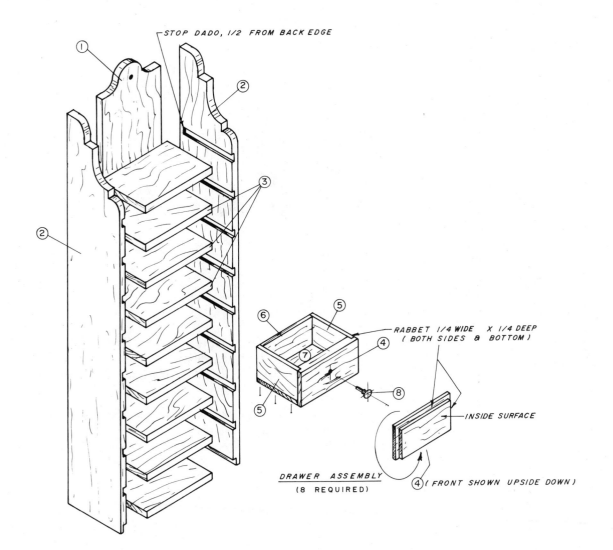

STOP DADO, 1/2 FROM BACK EDGE

RABBET 1/4 WIDE × 1/4 DEEP
(BOTH SIDES & BOTTOM)

INSIDE SURFACE

DRAWER ASSEMBLY
(8 REQUIRED)

④ (FRONT SHOWN UPSIDE DOWN)

EXPLODED VIEW

Glue the drawers together, leaving the bottoms off for now. Use rubber bands as clamps and make sure that all sides are square. After the glue has set, tack the drawer bottom in place with 1-in. wire brads. Sand all surfaces until the drawer slides smoothly in the opening.

Drill a hole for the pull (part 8) in the center of each drawer front.

5. Apply finish. Varnish or paint the case and drawers.

MATERIALS LIST

Part	Dimensions	Quantity
1. Back	½″ × 5″ × 30″	1
2. Sides	½″ × 4½″ × 28½″	2
3. Dividers	½″ × 4″ × 5½″	9
4. Drawer fronts	½″ × 2¼″ × 5″	8
5. Drawer sides	¼″ × 2″ × 3⅝″	16
6. Drawer backs	¼″ × 2″ × 4½″	8
7. Drawer bottoms	¼″ × 3⅝″ × 5″	8
8. Drawer pulls*	⅝″ dia.	8
9. Brads	1″	as needed

*Pulls are available from Mason & Sullivan Company, 586 Higgins Crowell Road, West Yarmouth, MA 02673; order #2510 B.

Adjustable Corner Shelves

I find that fixed shelves usually are either too close together or too far apart. The corner shelves shown here solve that problem. Each shelf rests on ⅝-in. dowels so the shelf can be raised or lowered as needed. The supports are like two ladders kept erect by shelves that hook over the rungs.

1. Select the stock and cut the parts. The shelves in the photograph are maple; you can substitute any hardwood or softwood. You'll probably have to get out the pipe clamps and glue up two or more pieces of wood to make the individual shelves (part 3). To make a taller or shorter set of shelves, just lengthen the rails (part 1) and add a few more dowels (part 2).

MATERIALS LIST

Part	Dimensions	Quantity
1. Rails	¾" × 2" × 53"	4
2. Dowels	⅝" dia. × 2⅛"	26
3. Shelves	¾" × 14" × 34"	4

Cut all parts to the sizes given in the Materials List; be exact in measuring and cutting the dowels. Sand thoroughly. Lay out and drill the holes in each rail.

2. Lay out the shelves and cut them to shape. On a piece of wood that you've cut for shelving, lay out the shape of a shelf. First, lay out a 90-degree angle. Swing the arcs shown in the bottom view to lay out the curved front.

Cut the straight edges of the shelves with a portable circular saw guided by a straight edge. If you don't have a circular saw, you can band saw along the waste side of the line and then trim the cut with a router guided by a straight edge.

Cut or rout the dadoes, as shown in the view at A-A, along the straight edge of each shelf.

In sawing the curved front edge, you can save some time and get consistent results by stacking the shelves and cutting them together. Attach the boards temporarily with rubber cement or double-sided tape. Cut the shelves and sand the edges before separating them.

3. Assemble the sides. Put glue on the ends of the dowels and insert them in the holes in the rails. Try to confine glue to the holes and clean any drips with a damp cloth. It's vital to keep everything square. When the glue dries, have a helper hold the supports in position as you put each shelf where you'd like it.

4. Apply finish. Take the shelves off the supports and finish each with either varnish or paint.

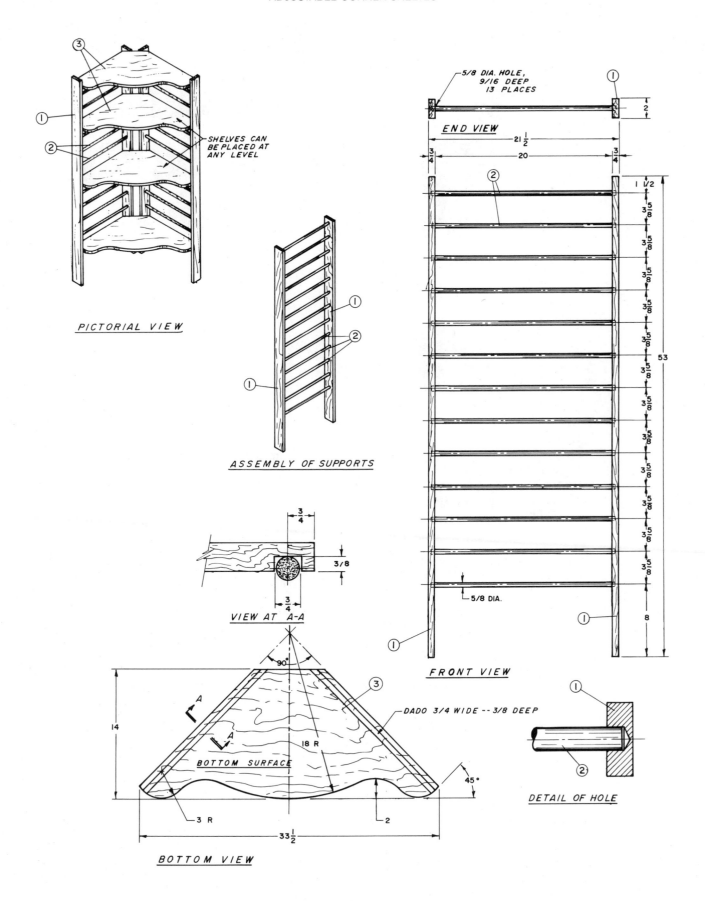

PICTORIAL VIEW

SHELVES CAN BE PLACED AT ANY LEVEL

ASSEMBLY OF SUPPORTS

5/8 DIA. HOLE, 9/16 DEEP 13 PLACES

END VIEW

21 1/2

20

3/4

3/4

2

1 1/2

3 5/8

53

5/8 DIA.

8

FRONT VIEW

3/4

3/8

3/4

VIEW AT A-A

90°

A
A

14

18 R

BOTTOM SURFACE

3 R

2

45°

DADO 3/4 WIDE -- 3/8 DEEP

33 1/2

BOTTOM VIEW

DETAIL OF HOLE

69

Rooster and Turkey on Sticks

These birds aren't very impressive at first glance, I'll admit. But I have found they sell very well to people who are fond of folk art. Both shapes are taken directly from old weather vanes.

1. Select the stock and cut the parts. Use any wood you have on hand for both the bird and its base. Cut the parts to the sizes given in the Materials List.

2. Make a paper pattern. Draw a grid with ½-in. squares and enlarge the bird's body (part 1) onto it. Transfer the pattern to the wood and cut out the bird with a saber saw or band saw. To make several at a time, make a stack of the wood pieces and hold them together with double-sided tape or rubber cement.

Round the edges of the beak with sandpaper to make it look more realistic. Drill a ¾-in.-deep hole in the bird and a 1-in.-deep hole in the base (part 2) to take the welding rod stand (part 3); size the drill bit according to the diameter of the rod. Take care to angle the bore into the bird, as shown, so that the bird will stand upright. Welding rods are available at larger hardware stores, but if you have trouble finding them, you can make a thicker bird and substitute ³/₁₆-in.-diameter dowels.

3. Assemble the bird. Insert one end of the welding rod in the bird and insert the other end in the base. Add a few drops of epoxy if the fit is loose.

4. Apply finish. Paint the body a flat off-white shade. When the paint has dried, add a brick red beak and comb and any other details that strike your fancy. Let your imagination run a bit.

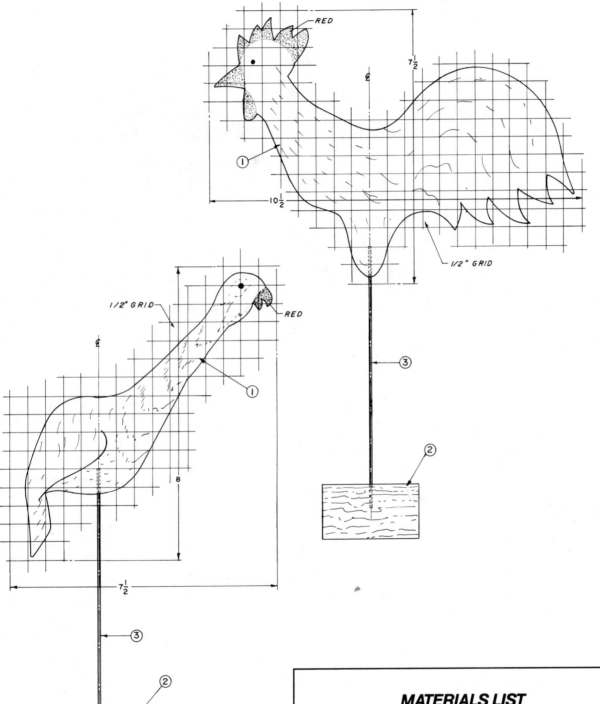

MATERIALS LIST

Part	Dimensions	Quantity
1. Rooster or turkey body	⅜″ × 7½″ × 10½″ ⅜″ × 7½″ × 8″	1
2. Base	1½″ × 2¾″ × 2¾″	1
3. Welding rod	Dia. as available × 7½″	1

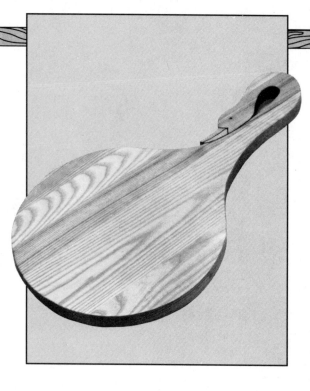

Swan Cutting Board

I've found that the most popular animal shape for cutting boards is that of the pig, but this board takes the shape of a resting swan. I saw one like it at a flea market, and the dealer claimed to know it was old and came from South Carolina. The original was about one-third larger than this pattern, a size that might be too large for today's kitchens.

1. Select the stock. Use knot-free, straight-grained hardwood, ¾ or 1 in. thick. If possible, find a 12-in.-wide board and make the project out of one piece of wood. Otherwise, you'll have to glue up the blank from two or more pieces. You can make good use of scrap pieces in this way.

2. Transfer the pattern. Draw the swan's body directly on the wood with a large compass, following the dimensions shown on the drawing.

Make a paper pattern for the swan's head. Draw a grid with ½-in. squares and enlarge the swan's head and neck onto it. Line up the enlarged drawing so that the dots marked "end of arcs" run into the 5¾-in.-radius curves on the swan's body. The centerline of the head pattern, indicated by long and short dashes, should align with the centerline of the body. Transfer the drawing to the wood.

3. Cut out the cutting board. Cut just outside the layout line with a band saw, saber saw, or jigsaw. Drill a hole in the cutout within the bend of the neck, slip a coping or jigsaw blade through it, and saw out the teardrop shape. Sand the entire piece and round the ends slightly to remove any rough edges.

Use a sharp carving knife or wood-burning tool to define the beak and neck, as shown in the photograph.

4. Apply finish. Sand the piece and buff it with 0000 steel wool. Protect it with salad bowl finish.

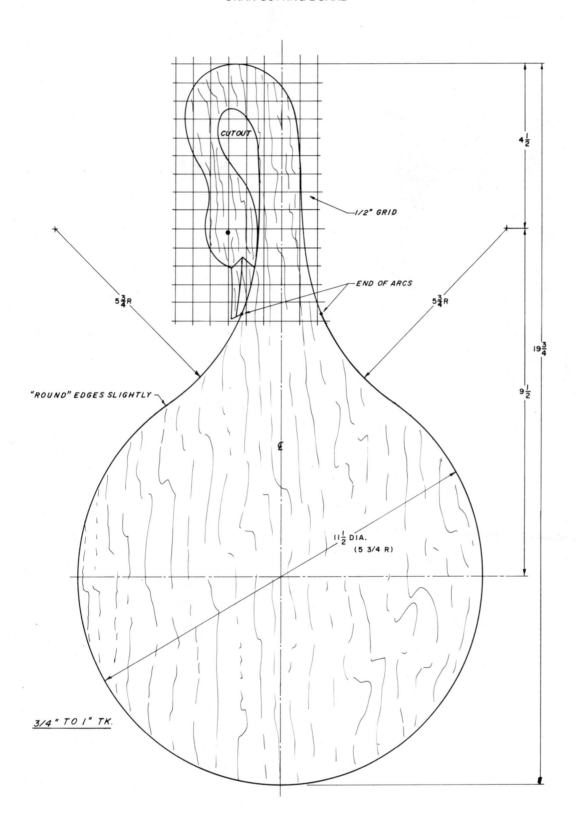

CUTOUT

1/2" GRID

5¾R

5¾R

END OF ARCS

19¾

9½

4½

"ROUND" EDGES SLIGHTLY

11½ DIA.
(5 3/4 R)

3/4" TO 1" TK.

Cat on a Stand

Here is my idea of a pet. You don't have to feed it, pet it, or let it out of the house day and night. It's housebroken, and it won't climb on the furniture. This cat just sits quietly and asks nothing of you at all.

1. Select the stock and cut out the parts. Both the body and the base are made from ¾-in.-thick hardwood. Cut the two parts to the sizes given in the Materials List. Pay particular attention to the grain direction shown in the drawing of the cat.

2. Make a paper pattern. Draw a grid with ½-in. squares and enlarge the drawing of the cat onto the grid. You don't have to be exact—after all, no two *real* cats are alike. Transfer the enlargement to the body (part 1) and cut it out. On the

base (part 2), lay out and cut the 1½-in. radii at either end.

3. Attach the cat to the base. Center the body on the base and trace lightly around the paws with a pencil. Remove the body and locate the centers of the four paw outlines. Countersink and drill a clearance hole in the base, slightly larger than the shank of a #8 flathead wood screw.

Glue the body to the base, making sure that the paws fit within the outlines. When the glue has set, drill pilot holes slightly smaller than the screw shank through the base and about ¾ in. into the cat's legs. Screw the cat to the base.

4. Finish the cat. Paint the cat any color you wish; the drawing suggests a black cat on a brown base.

MATERIALS LIST

Part	Dimensions	Quantity
1. Body	¾″ × 13″ × 22″	1
2. Base	¾″ × 3″ × 15½″	1
3. Flathead screws	#8 × 1½″	4

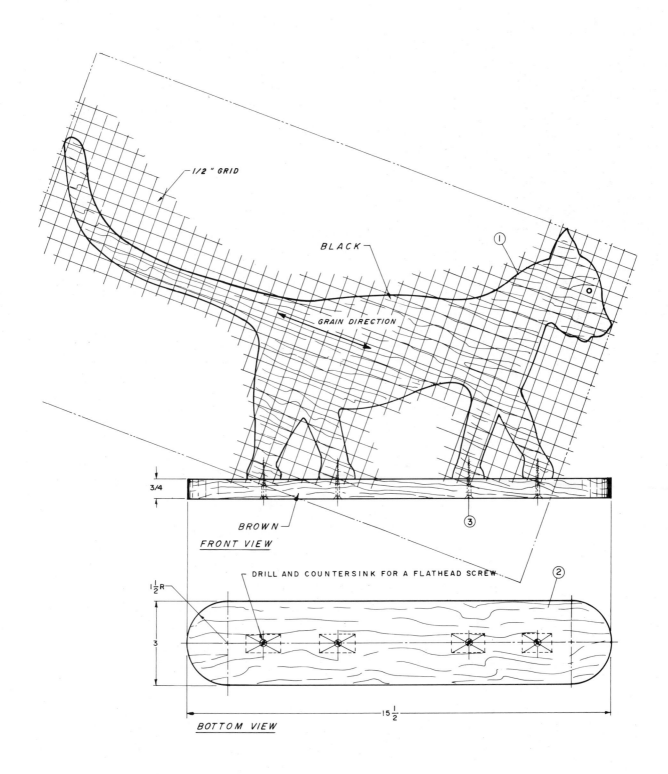

1/2 " GRID

BLACK

GRAIN DIRECTION

3/4

BROWN

FRONT VIEW

DRILL AND COUNTERSINK FOR A FLATHEAD SCREW

1 1/2 R

3

BOTTOM VIEW

15 1/2

Tulips on a Stand

Here in New Hampshire we have very short summers—I believe summer fell on July 7th last year—and these bright wooden flowers can help make winter bearable. By the way, pieces like this seem to sell readily at craft fairs.

1. *Select the stock and cut the parts.* Except for the ¼-in. dowel used for the stems, all you need are ¾-in.-thick scraps of any wood.

2. *Make a paper pattern.* Draw a grid with ¼-in. squares and enlarge the drawing of the leaves (part 2) and flowers (part 3) onto the grid. Transfer the enlargements to the wood and cut them to shape. You can save time by drawing the patterns on just one flower and one leaf and cutting out several of the same pieces at once. Stack similar pieces and attach them to each other with either double-sided tape or rubber cement.

Draw curves at both ends of the base (part 1) and cut them out. Locate and drill the ¼-in.-diameter holes in the flowers, leaves, and base, as directed on the drawings. Sand each part entirely.

3. *Assemble the tulips.* Apply glue to each stem at the location of the leaf. Slide the leaves over the dowel stems (part 4). Spread glue on the tops of the stems and insert them into the flower blossoms. Spread glue on the bottoms of the stems and insert them into the base. Wipe off any excess glue.

4. *Finish the tulips.* Paint as you choose. The front view suggests colors for the various parts, along with stain for the base to represent soil. To make the piece more interesting, try varying the shade of green you use on the leaves and stems.

MATERIALS LIST

Part	Dimensions	Quantity
1. Base	¾″ × 4″ × 16″	1
2. Leaves	¾″ × 4½″ × 3½″	5
3. Flowers	¾″ × 2½″ × 2½″	5
4. Stems	¼″ dia. × 7¾″	5

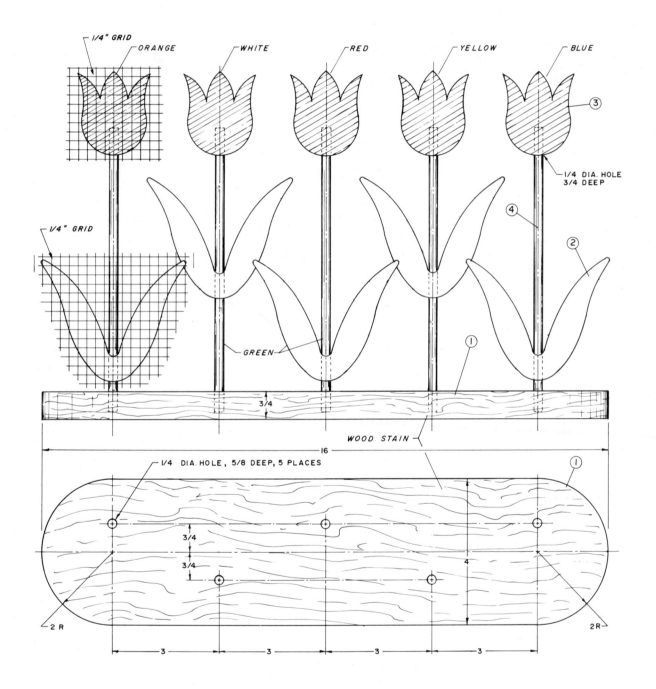

Duck Basket

MATERIALS LIST

Part	Dimensions	Quantity
1. Front/back	¾″ × 6″ × 4¾″	1 each
2. Head	¾″ × 4″ × 10⅝″	1
3. Bottoms	⅜″ × 1⁵⁄₁₆″ × 9⅝″	4
4. Side boards	⅜″ × 1¼″ × 14¼″	8
5. Tail feathers	⅜″ × 1½″ × 6″	3
6. Flathead screws	#6 × 1½″	2
7. Tacks	¾″	as needed

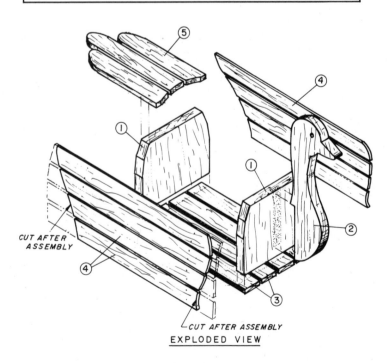

CUT AFTER
ASSEMBLY

CUT AFTER ASSEMBLY
EXPLODED VIEW

Baskets come in all shapes and sizes, but this is the first one I've seen posing as a duck. A lot of people must love these baskets because I have a friend who has built and sold 2,000 of them. When his baskets were featured on a regional television show, they were referred to as "New Hampshire baskets." Whatever you want to call them, my wife tells me that they make great planters for holding potted plants.

1. *Select the stock and cut the parts.* The front, back, and head are made of ¾-in.-thick stock; the rest of the pieces are ⅜-in.-thick slats. Use any wood you have on hand. Cut the parts to the dimensions given in the Materials List.

2. *Lay out the parts.* Lay out the front and back (part 1), as shown in the front view.

Make a paper pattern to lay out the head. Draw a grid with ½-in. squares and enlarge the drawing of the duck's head (part 2) onto the grid. Transfer the enlarged drawing to ¾-in.-thick wood.

3. *Cut the parts to shape, except for the side boards.* Stack and tape the front and back together. Cut them at the same time to make certain they are identical. Cut out the head. Don't overlook the ⅜-in. notch in the head where it is attached to the front board; the notch is labeled on the side view. To drill the ¼-in.-diameter eye hole cleanly, bore through the head until the point of the bit just pokes through. Turn the head over and finish drilling from the other side. Do not attach the head to the body yet.

Cut the tail feathers to shape. A grid is provided for them, as shown in the top view, but there is no need to bother with a pattern unless you will be turning out dozens of these baskets. Simply sketch the shape directly on the wood.

4. *Assemble the basket.* Assemble the parts with ¾-in. tacks (part 7), preferably brass. Begin

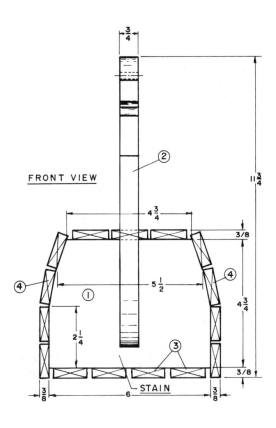

FRONT VIEW

by tacking the bottom slats (part 3) to the front and back. Make sure that the front and back are perpendicular to the bottom.

Attach the side boards (part 4); they should extend 1⅝ in. beyond the front and 2⅞ in. beyond the back, as shown in the side view. Sketching directly on the side boards, lay out the duck's front and back profile, which are labeled *CUT AFTER ASSEMBLY* in the side view. As with the tail feathers (part 5) a ½-in. grid is given for guidance, but you don't have to take the trouble to make a pattern. Cut along the sketched line. The cut can be made most easily on the band saw by laying the duck on its side.

5. *Apply finish and add the head and tail.* Stain the duck's body and paint the head and tail feathers a matte black. When the parts are dry, attach the head with two flathead screws (part 6). To prevent splitting, predrill a clearance hole through the front that is slightly *larger* than the diameter of the screw shank. Drill a pilot hole slightly *smaller* than the shank diameter into the head. Tack the three tail feathers to the back. Apply a coat or two of stain over the entire assembled duck.

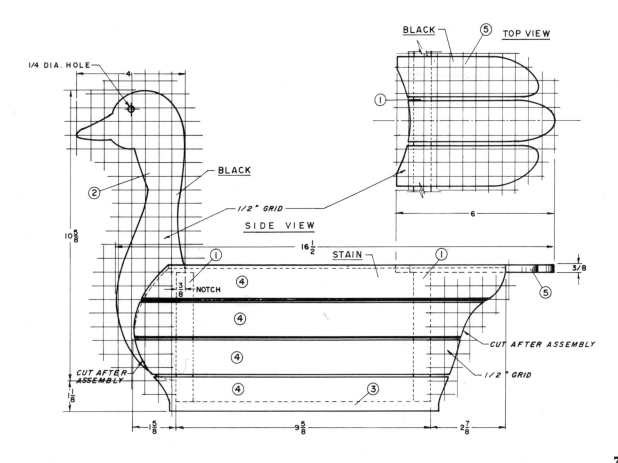

Pull Toys

These old-time pull toys can be painted however you wish. Don't feel that you have to reproduce faithfully either of the designs shown here.

1. Select the stock. All stock is ¾ in. thick. Any wood will do. Poplar accepts paint particularly well.

2. Make a paper pattern and cut the horse to shape. Draw a grid with ½-in. squares and enlarge the horses onto it. (If you want to make smaller horses, use a smaller grid. A ¼-in. grid, for example, will give you horses half the size of those illustrated.) If you expect to make a lot of horses, make durable cardboard or plywood patterns.

Transfer the pattern to the wood and cut out the body (part 1). Locate and drill the ¼-in.-diameter holes for the axles (part 3). Drill the ⅛-in.-diameter hole for the pull string.

Cut the wheels (part 2) from scrap left from the horse. When making the wheels, either an adjustable circle cutter or a hole saw, available at most hardware stores, will cut a perfect circle when put in a drill. If necessary, enlarge the center holes these tools leave to ¼-in. holes. (If you choose, you can buy ready-made wheels appropriate to the design.) Cut the axles to size.

3. Apply finish. Life will be a lot easier if you paint the horse *before* assembling it. Sand the piece well before painting. The drawings offer painting suggestions, but you're on your own. Don't paint the axles or get paint into the axle holes. If you are turning out a number of horses, challenge yourself by making each one unique.

4. Assemble the horse. Insert the axles and use glue sparingly to attach the wheels. Tie on a pull string.

MATERIALS LIST

Part	Dimensions	Quantity
1. Body	¾″ × 7″ × 10″	1
2. Wheels	1½″ or 1¾″ dia. × ¾″	4
3. Axles	¼″ dia. × 2½″	2

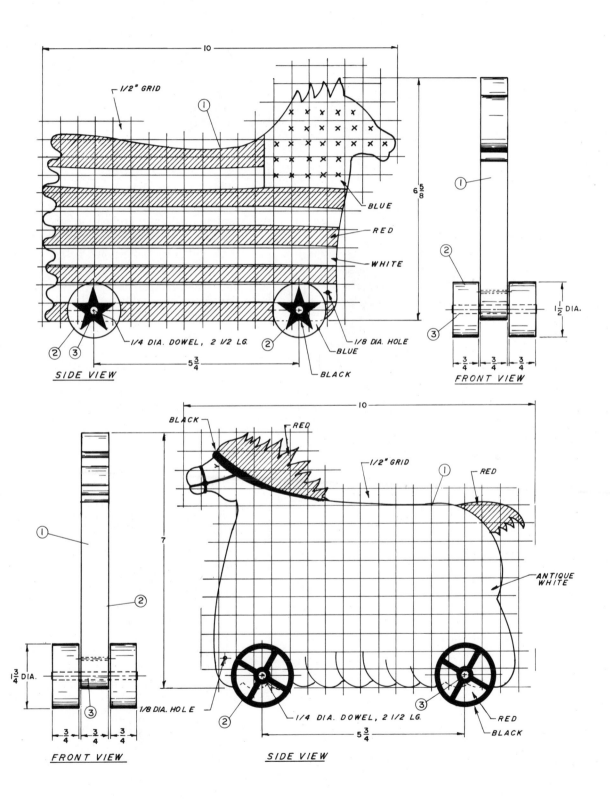

Office Bird

Here is a project that is tacky and tasteless beyond question, and for that reason you might find it fun to make and give to others. Most of us woodworkers take our hobby very seriously, and it should come as a relief to build a piece for which measurements are anything but crucial.

I presented an office bird to my son-in-law, a bank manager, to display in his office, and now I keep one on my own desk as a reminder to take myself less seriously.

1. *Select the stock and cut the parts.* Any wood will do. Cut the parts to the sizes given in the Materials List, noting the grain direction for the neck, as indicated in the side view. Cut the platform (part 4) from a 2-in.-diameter dowel.

2. *Make a paper pattern and cut the parts to shape.* Draw a grid with ½-in. squares and enlarge the bird onto it. Lay out the leg (part 2) and the two wings (part 3) separately. Transfer the enlargements to the wood and cut the parts to shape. If copied as illustrated, the bird should balance nicely. Cut a notch at the top of the leg by hand to fit the body (part 1). Cut a saw kerf, as shown in the front view, to create two distinct legs. Sand the parts and round the corners slightly.

3. *Assemble the bird and apply finish.* Assemble the parts with glue. Offset the two wings as shown.

Paint the bird as you wish. A few color suggestions are given in the side view. The tackier the better. You have the option of either using drafting ink to draw in the eyes or gluing on the jiggle eyes (part 6), available from the source given in the Materials List. If you would like to affix a corny message to the bird for presentation to a friend, type it on a piece of paper that will fit on the platform. Protect this label with a spray of clear plastic fixative then attach it to the wood with rubber cement.

MATERIALS LIST

Part	Dimensions	Quantity
1. Body	½″ × 4½″ × 13″	1
2. Leg	¾″ × 2″ × 9″	1
3. Wings	3/16″ × 2″ × 4¼″	2
4. Platform	2″ dia. × 3¾″	1
5. Base	¼″ × 3¼″ × 3¼″	1
6. Jiggle eyes*		1 pair

*Part is available from Meisel Hardware Specialties, P.O. Box 70, Mound MN 55364; order #7647.

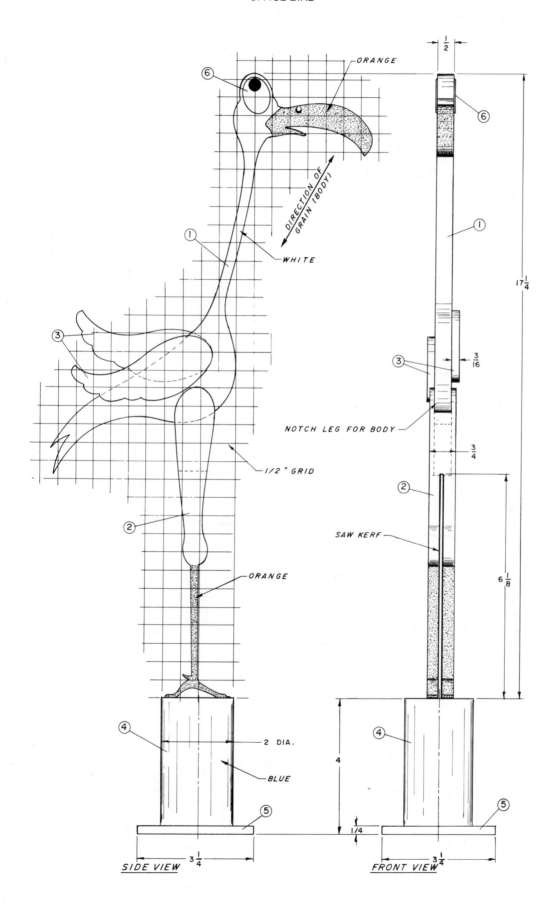

ORANGE

⑥

DIRECTION OF
GRAIN (BODY)

WHITE

①

③

NOTCH LEG FOR BODY

②

SAW KERF

ORANGE

2 DIA.

BLUE

④

⑤

SIDE VIEW

1/2 " GRID

½

⑥

17¼

①

3/16

③

¾

②

6⅛

④

⑤

FRONT VIEW

4

¼

3¼

3¼

Knickknack Shelf

The intricate decorative cuts shown here were especially popular with woodworkers back in the 1930s and 1940s. The designs are cut out of ¼-in.-thick stock with a jigsaw.

1. *Select the stock.* Use a knot-free wood such as mahogany. If you can't plane your own wood, you can buy ¼-in.-thick wood from suppliers listed in the appendix.

2. *Make a paper pattern.* Draw a grid with ½-in. squares and enlarge the parts onto it. Transfer the enlargement to the wood.

3. *Cut the parts to size.* To make the cutouts, first drill ¼-in.-diameter holes in each so that you can start cutting with the jigsaw. After making the cutouts, saw along the outside of the design. Sand thoroughly but don't round the corners.

4. *Assemble the shelf.* This project is put together with glue and finishing nails (part 4). If you think the wood might split, then drill pilot holes before nailing. Attach the shelf (part 3) to the brace (part 2) then add the backboard (part 1).

5. *Apply finish.* If you wish, apply stain and varnish. Hang the shelf through the teardrop-shaped hole at the top of the backboard.

MATERIALS LIST

Part	Dimensions	Quantity
1. Backboard	¼″ × 7½″ × 12″	1
2. Brace	¼″ × 3⅞″ × 4⅝″	1
3. Shelf	¼″ × 4⅛″ × 6¾″	1
4. Finishing nails	4d	as needed

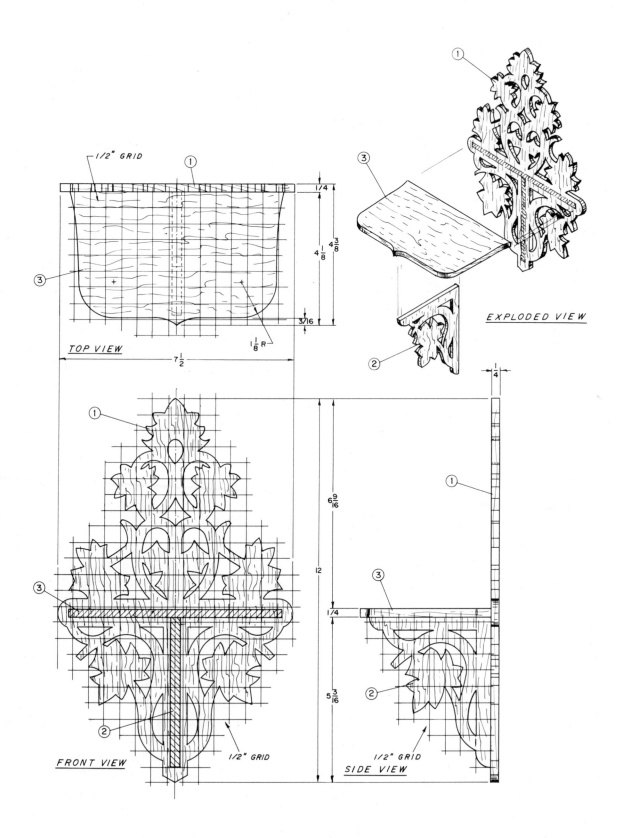

—1/2" GRID

①

1/4

4 3/8

4 1/8

③

3/16

TOP VIEW

1 1/8 R

7 1/2

③

EXPLODED VIEW

②

1/4

①

①

6 9/16

③

12

1/4

②

5 3/16

①

②

③

1/2" GRID

FRONT VIEW

1/2" GRID

SIDE VIEW

Miniature Rocking Horse

My daughter, Joy, collects folk art horses, and this one fits right into her collection. You can glue up scraps to make them. I've found they sell quickly at craft fairs.

1. *Select the stock.* Make the pins from dowels. Note the flat pieces are made from several different thicknesses of wood. For the greatest strength, orient the wood grain, as shown in the drawing.

2. *Transfer the pattern and cut the parts to shape.* Draw a grid with ½-in. squares. Enlarge the individual parts of the drawing onto it to make five different patterns. Transfer the enlargements to the wood and cut out all the parts. Drill the holes for the dowel pins and the two decorative holes in each rocker. Sand thoroughly.

3. *Assemble the base.* Stack the rocker, spacer, links, and pins (parts 1, 2, 3, 4, and 5); align the holes. Brush glue on the dowel pins and drive the pins through the holes. Clamp the pieces together. When the glue dries, drill a hole in the top of the spacer for the support pin (part 10).

4. *Assemble the horse.* Stack the body, front and rear legs, and pins (parts 6, 7, 8, and 9) and assemble as above. Then spread glue on the ends of the support pin and mount the horse.

5. *Apply finish.* I suggest pastel colors for this project; you can consult the cover of the book for ideas on a paint scheme.

MATERIALS LIST

Part	Dimensions	Quantity
1. Rocker	⅜″ × 3½″ × 11″	2
2. Spacer	¾″ × 1″ × 2½″	1
3. Links	⅛″ × 1″ × 2½″	2
4. Pins	¼″ dia. × 1¾″	2
5. Pins	¼″ dia. × 1½″	2
6. Body	½″ × 4½″ × 9½″	1
7. Front legs	¼″ × 1¼″ × 4″	2
8. Rear legs	¼″ × 1½″ × 4″	2
9. Pins	¼″ dia. × 1″	2
10. Support pin	¼″ dia. × 4″	1

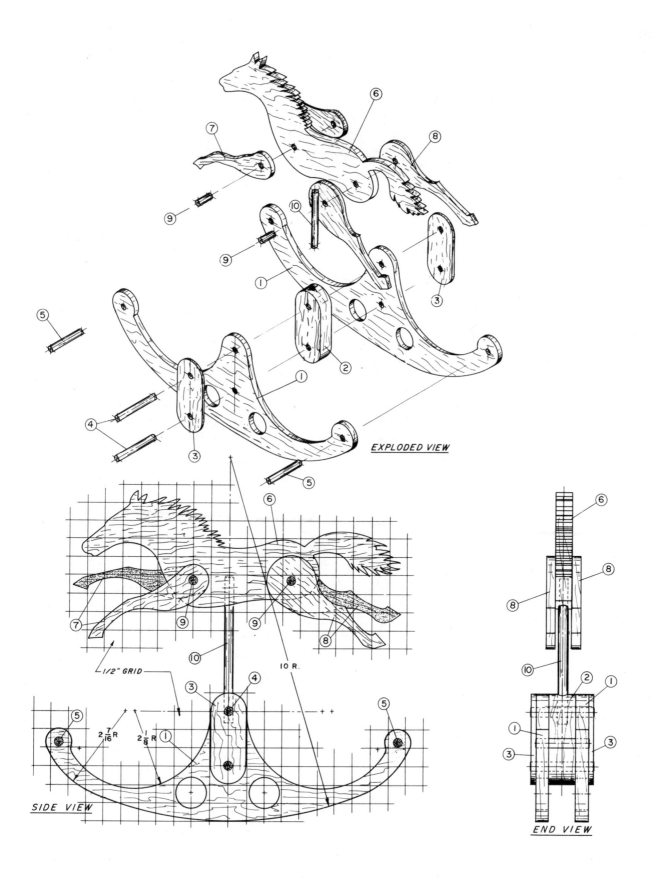

EXPLODED VIEW

1/2" GRID

10 R.

$2\frac{7}{16}$ R. $2\frac{1}{8}$ R.

SIDE VIEW

END VIEW

Chip-Carved Jewelry Box

The chip-carved border of this box is easy to make. You simply cut out small chips of wood to make a design. The tools are inexpensive, and the wood can be quite ordinary.

1. *Select the stock and cut the parts.* I suggest using poplar for this project because it carves so readily. Otherwise, find a good grade of straight-grained, knot-free pine. You'll need stock ¼ in. thick.

Instead of building the lid and box separately, I build a sealed box and then cut it open to create the lid. The dimensions in the Materials List compensate for the wood lost in cutting open the box. Cut the parts to the sizes given in the Materials List.

MATERIALS LIST

Part	Dimensions	Quantity
1. Front/back	¼" × 4⅛" × 10"	1 each
2. Ends	¼" × 4⅛" × 5¾"	2
3. Top/bottom	¼" × 6" × 10"	1 each
4. Hinges*	13/16" × 13/16"	2
5. Hasp*		1
6. Feet*		4

**Hardware is available from Meisel Hardware Specialties, P.O. Box 70, Mound, MN 55364. Hinges with screws are #1632, hasp with pin is #1604, and feet are #421/SMS612.*

2. *Make the box.* Cut rabbets in the ends of the front and back (part 1), as shown in the view at A-A. Glue the ends (part 2) to the front and back, keeping everything square.

Glue the top and bottom (part 3) in place. Hold the piece together with clamps or rubber bands until the glue sets. This creates a sealed cube. You'll be cutting off a lid in the next step.

Round-over the top edges of the box with a ⅛-in.-radius roundover bit with a ball-bearing guide in your router.

3. *Cut off the lid.* Place the fence of the table saw to make a 3¼-in.-wide cut and set the blade just over ¼ in. high. Stand the box on its end. Hold the bottom against the fence and push the box across the blade. Repeat on the other end. To keep the end kerfs open for the next two cuts, tape scraps of wood into both of them. Then make the cuts along the front and back to separate the lid from the box.

4. *Chip-carve the box.* You can do the carving with two knives. Woodcraft Supply Corporation, listed in the appendix, sells chip-carving tools, as well as a good introductory text, *Chip Carving: Techniques and Patterns,* by Wayne Barton.

Lay out the pattern on the lid of the box.

Each "chip" is made with three strokes of the chip-carving knife and is actually pyramid shaped. Note how the cut progresses, as shown in the illustration. The first and second cuts begin at the point that looks darker in the drawings; they start out about ⅛ in. deep. Raise the knife

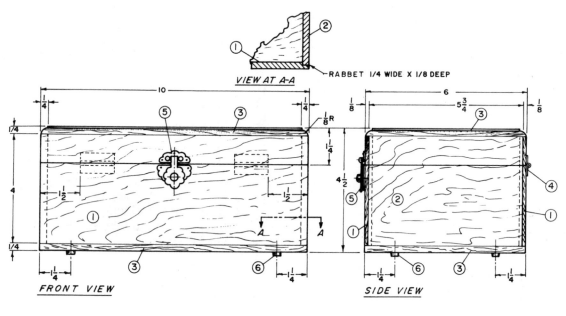

VIEW AT A-A

RABBET 1/4 WIDE X 1/8 DEEP

FRONT VIEW

SIDE VIEW

CENTER 4 1/2 X 8 1/2 CHIP-CARVING PATTERN
ON TOP ③ APPROX. 3/4 IN FROM SIDES.

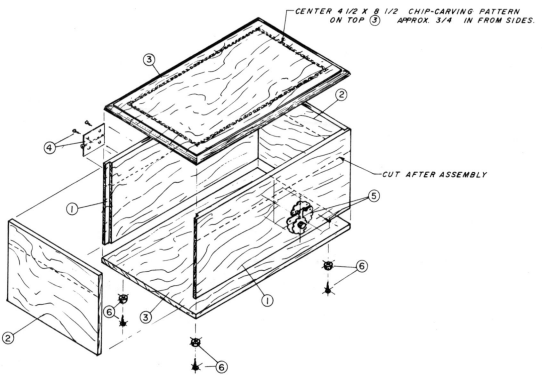

CUT AFTER ASSEMBLY

EXPLODED VIEW

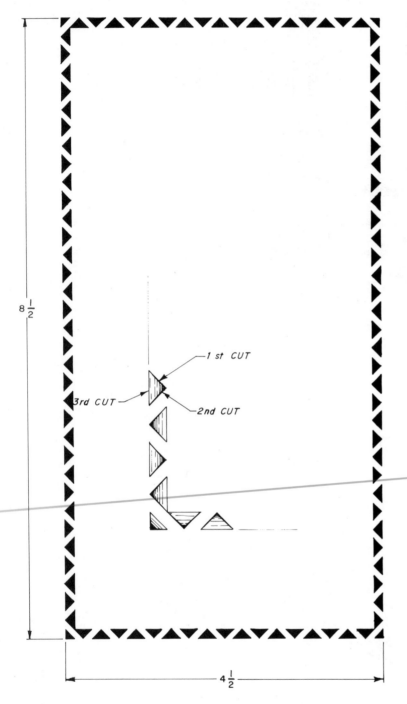

out of the wood as you cut, so the cut finishes nearly flush with the surface. The chip is released with the third cut, which starts at the surface and goes to a depth of ⅛ in. The work goes more quickly if you make the first cut on all of the triangles then proceed to make all the second cuts and finally, to make all the third cuts.

In sanding the surfaces of the box, don't try to work the paper down into the chipped-out areas. Leave the edges crisp by using a palm sander or sandpaper wrapped around a block of wood.

5. *Apply finish.* A light stain will emphasize the chip-carving. Protect the box with two or three coats of a clear varnish. Add the hinges (part 4), placing them 1½ in. from the ends, the hasp (part 5), and the four ½-in.-diameter rubber feet (part 6).

Folk-Art Birdhouse

It seems that every woodworker eventually gets around to making a birdhouse. So, if you *have* to build one, you might as well build one with some style. This design is distinctive. It's also a fine project to work on with a child.

1. *Select the stock and cut the parts.* Most of the birdhouse is made out of ½-in. stock. If you can't find wood that thickness, either resaw thicker stock or plane down ¾-in. boards.

Cut the parts to the dimensions in the Materials List. Rip the top edge of the sides (part 2) at a 34-degree angle. Two of the shingles (part 6) have an edge beveled to 75 degrees so they can meet at the ridge, as shown. The rest of the shingles have 90-degree edges.

2. *Make a paper pattern and cut the front and back to shape.* Draw a grid with ½-in. squares and enlarge the front pattern (part 1) onto it. Transfer the enlargement to the wood. Cut both pieces at once by tacking them together and sand the edges before separating them. Locate and drill the ¼- and 1-in.-diameter holes in the front piece only. (You may want to change the size of the larger hole to suit the species of bird you hope to attract.)

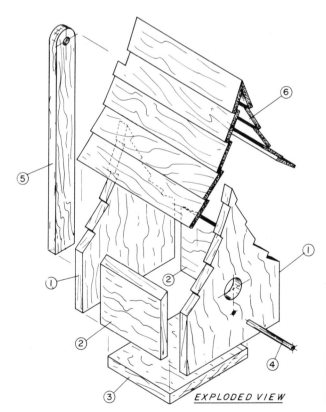

EXPLODED VIEW

MATERIALS LIST

Part	Dimensions	Quantity
1. Front/back	½″ × 6″ × 9½″	1 each
2. Sides	½″ × 3⅝″ × 4¼″	2
3. Bottom	½″ × 4¼″ × 5″	1
4. Perch	¼″ dia. × 3″	1
5. Hanger	½″ × 1¼″ × 12″	1
6. Shingles	³/₁₆″ × 1¾″ × 6¼″	10
7. Finishing nails	4d	as needed

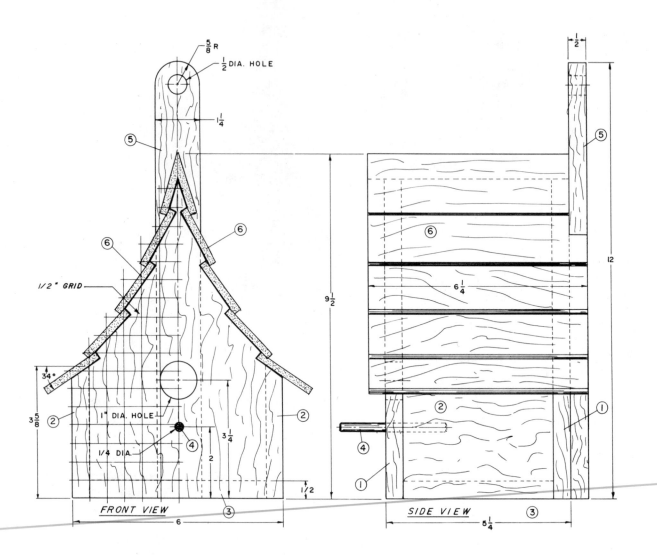

FRONT VIEW

SIDE VIEW

3. Assemble the birdhouse. Sand the parts thoroughly then dry-fit them, making adjustments if necessary. Glue and nail (part 7) the front and back to the sides. Check for squareness and glue and nail the bottom (part 3) in place. If you want to remove the bottom for cleaning, substitute screws for the glue and nails.

Glue and nail the shingles to the eaves, starting from the bottom. To prevent the shingles from splitting, predrill the holes. The best drill bit for this is a 4d nail with the head cut off. Glue the shingles that form the ridge together and nail them in place.

Notch the shingles at the back of the birdhouse with a backsaw to accommodate the hanger

(part 5). Shape the hanger and drill a hanger hole in it. Attach the hanger to the back of the birdhouse with glue and nails.

Glue the perch (part 4) in the hole provided for it. The perch should extend about 1¼ in. in front of the house.

4. Apply finish. Because this is a folk-art birdhouse, you can let your imagination run free. Use bright paint that is intended for exterior use. I painted mine white with a red roof and a green hanger.

Hang the birdhouse on the side of the house or an outbuilding or nail it to a tree.

Weather Vane

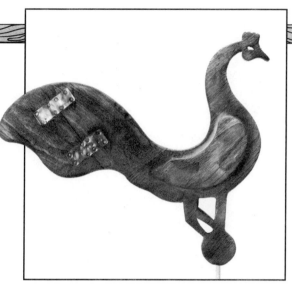

As a boy living in rural New England, I was in awe of the weather vanes that topped most barns. Today, most of these bold examples of folk art have disappeared, either because of the elements or because of collectors.

My fascination with weather vanes led me to write a book on them several years ago, featuring 68 full-size patterns. Just after it went off to the publisher, I came upon the beautiful design shown here. The original weather vane was made of wood around 1755 and stood 34 in. high and 45 in. wide. It perched atop a barn at the old Fitch Tavern in Bedford, Massachusetts, where the Minute Men assembled for battle in 1775. The rooster came down in 1930 when the barn was dismantled.

1. *Select the stock and cut the parts.* Use pine for this project, aligning the grain as shown in the illustration. Note that the grain of the body (part 1) and tail (part 3) are at right angles to each other—an unusual practice, but the original weather vane held up well enough over the years.

Cut the parts to the dimensions given in the Materials List. Note that you can scale down the rooster for indoor display. For a bird of half the given size, use a ½-in. grid in the following step.

2. *Make a paper pattern and cut the parts to shape.* Draw a grid with 1-in. squares and enlarge the wooden parts of the weather vane onto it. Transfer the enlargements to the wood, keeping the grain direction in mind. Mark the location of the eyes, wings, and optional hole at the bottom of the body. Before cutting the final shape of the parts, carefully drill a hole for the shaft into the lower edge of the body. Note that if you want an operable weather vane, the shaft should fit loosely in this hole. Cut out the parts with a jigsaw, band saw, or coping saw and sand thoroughly.

3. *Assemble the weather vane.* Attach the tail to the body with a waterproof resorcinol glue. To make sure that the tail would stay put on my rooster, I reinforced this joint with two ¼-in.-diameter dowels, 1 in. long. I want this project to last as long as the Bedford rooster!

Locate the wings (part 2) and attach them with waterproof glue. Sand thoroughly.

4. *Apply finish.* If you wish, you can artificially weather the weather vane to make it look as though it has spent 200 years atop a barn. Scorch the edges and sides with a torch, varying how deeply you burn from place to place. Do this outdoors and have a bucket of water handy

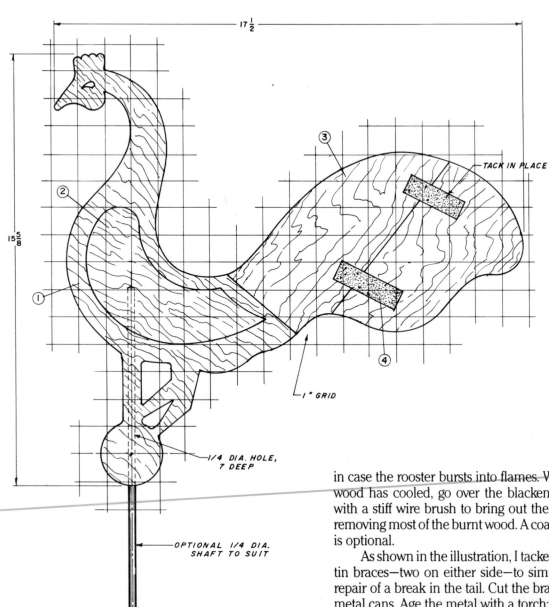

17 ½

15 ⅝

③ ← TACK IN PLACE

②

①

④

—1" GRID

1/4 DIA. HOLE, 7 DEEP

← OPTIONAL 1/4 DIA. SHAFT TO SUIT

in case the rooster bursts into flames. When the wood has cooled, go over the blackened areas with a stiff wire brush to bring out the grain by removing most of the burnt wood. A coat of paint is optional.

As shown in the illustration, I tacked on four tin braces—two on either side—to simulate the repair of a break in the tail. Cut the braces from metal cans. Age the metal with a torch: Grip the metal with a pair of pliers and heat it until it turns blue. You can even go so far as to suggest a break by cutting a shallow groove across either side of the tail, as shown running under the braces.

The rooster can be mounted on a ¼-in.-diameter steel rod for display, or it can be used atop a building.

MATERIALS LIST

Part	Dimensions	Quantity
1. Body	¾″ × 15″ × 15″	1
2. Wings	½″ × 6″ × 8″	2
3. Tail	¾″ × 9″ × 10″	1
4. Braces	¾″ × 2½″	4

Sailboat Half Model

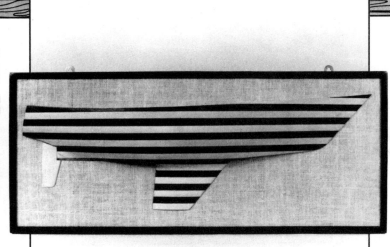

Traditionally, wooden half models were a step in designing the hulls of ships. The models look so handsome that woodworkers now make them just for display.

I made the half model, as shown, out of two contrasting woods, maple and walnut, to demonstrate how the project is glued up. I prefer the way they look; however, most hulls that I have seen are made of a single wood.

1. *Select the stock and cut the parts.* The model requires $11/32$-in.-thick stock—not a standard item at your local home center. If you don't have access to a planer, have the boards planed at a mill that does custom work.

Cut all the parts slightly larger than given in the Materials List. Label each layer so you can keep them straight.

2. *Lay out the pattern.* Draw a series of grids with ½-in. squares and enlarge each of the eighteen sections onto them. Parts 1-18 form the hull of the ship. Scraps from parts 9-18 form the rudder. Include the exact location of the lines *E, H,* or *J* on the appropriate patterns; these points help align the sections during assembly. Label the patterns by number so you can keep them straight and then cut them out.

Stack the patterns in their proper order, top to bottom, with reference lines *E, H,* and *J* aligned. Check that the boat's lines all flow from one pattern to the next and adjust as necessary.

3. *Cut the layers to shape.* Transfer each pattern to the corresponding piece of wood, including the reference lines. Cut each layer out, cutting on the waste side of the layout line.

4. *Assemble the half model and rudder.* Glue all the layers together. Align the reference lines. Make sure the back of the hull that mounts on the wall is flat. Hold the pieces together with a single clamp until the glue has dried.

Shape the general form of the hull with a spokeshave. In the flatter areas, you can do some of the work with a small hand plane. Bring the model to its final shape with either an electric sander or a sanding block, using coarse paper. Be sure that the hull flows smoothly from one layer to the next. Sand again with medium-grit paper and a final time with an extra-fine grit paper. Sand the rudder to shape and glue it in place, leaving a gap at the top, as shown.

5. *Display the half model.* I mounted the hull in the photo on a sheet of ½-in. plywood. I covered the plywood with good quality burlap I

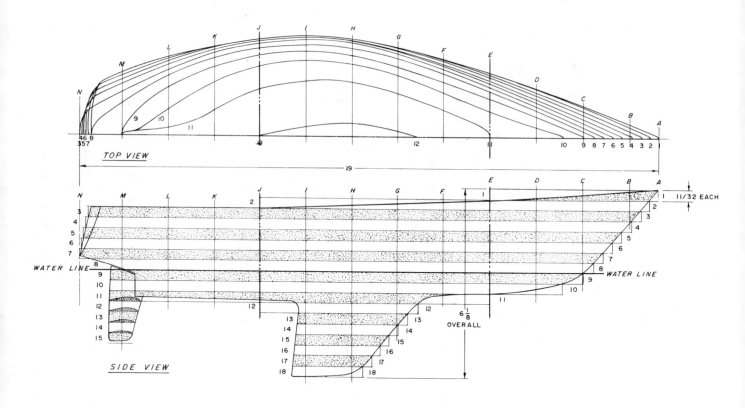

TOP VIEW

19

WATER LINE

SIDE VIEW

11/32 EACH

WATER LINE

6 1/8 OVERALL

bought at a fabric store. I wrapped the burlap around the front of the board and stapled it to the edges of the plywood. Two flathead screws, driven through the back of the plywood, hold the hull in place. A simple picture frame around the plywood really sets off the piece. To display the model on a wall, screw flat brass wall hangers to the plywood rather than to the frame.

MATERIALS LIST

Part	Dimensions	Quantity
1.	2″ × 5½″	1
2.	3¼″ × 13″	1
3.	3¼″ × 18″	1
4.	3¼″ × 18″	1
5.	3¼″ × 18″	1
6.	3¼″ × 17½″	1
7.	3¼″ × 17″	1
8.	3″ × 16½″	1
9.	2¾″ × 15″	1
10.	2½″ × 15″	1
11.	2″ × 12″	1
12.	½″ × 5½″	1
13.	⅜″ × 4″	1
14.	⅜″ × 3½″	1
15.	¼″ × 3½″	1
16.	¼″ × 3″	1
17.	¼″ × 2½″	1
18.	¼″ × 2″	1

NOTE: *All stock is* $^{11}/_{32}$″ *thick.*

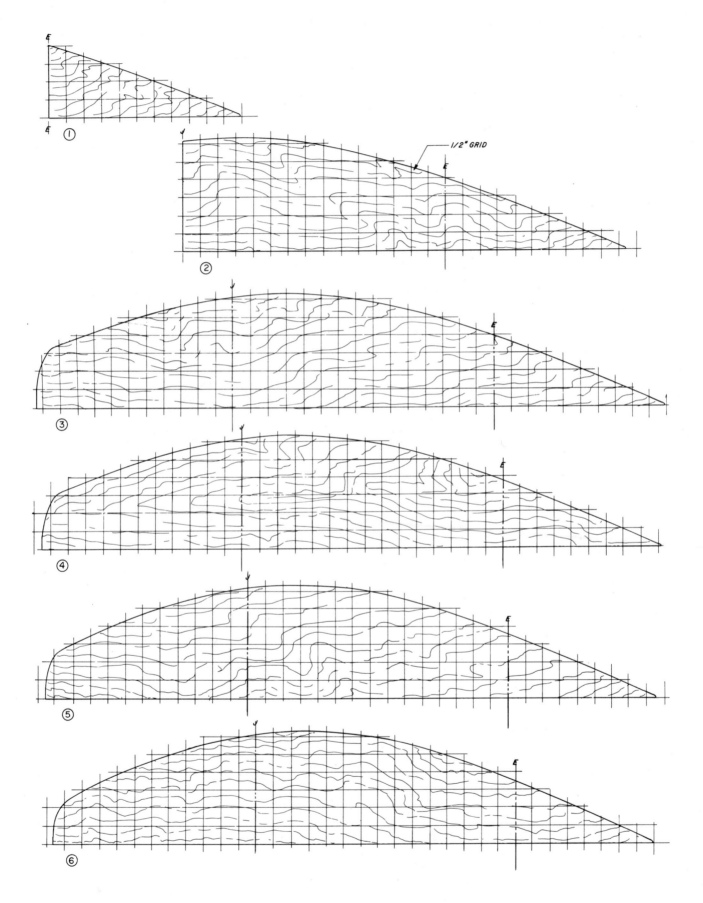

1/2" GRID

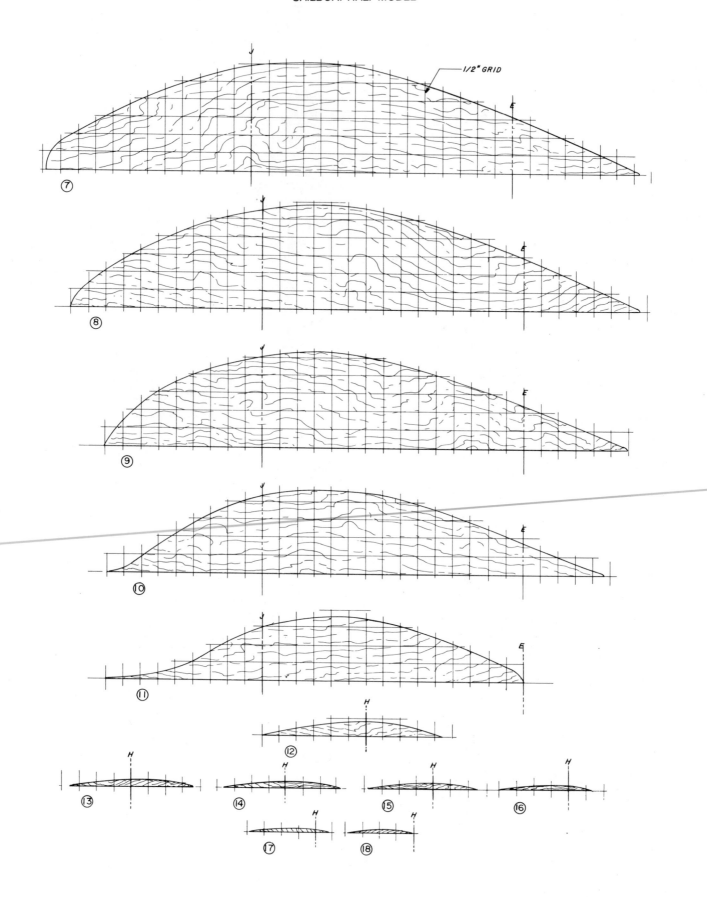

1/2" GRID

⑦

⑧

⑨

⑩

⑪

⑫

⑬   ⑭   ⑮   ⑯

⑰   ⑱

Candle Box

This candle box can be used to hold potted plants and any number of things other than candles. Hang the box on the wall or place it on a shelf. The example shown here has been painted with a stylized floral design, but that's optional. I patterned the box after one I saw in a Maine antique shop.

1. *Select the stock and cut the parts.* The box is made out of ½-in.-thick stock. Cut the parts to the sizes given in the Materials List.

MATERIALS LIST

Part	Dimensions	Quantity
1. Back	½″ × 12″ × 8½″	1
2. Sides	½″ × 3¾″ × 4¾″	2
3. Front	½″ × 3¾″ × 12″	1
4. Bottom	½″ × 4″ × 11″	1
5. Brads	1″	as needed

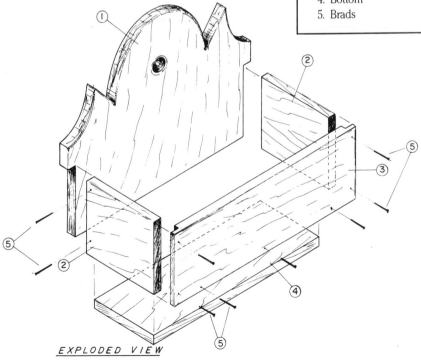

EXPLODED VIEW

CANDLE BOX

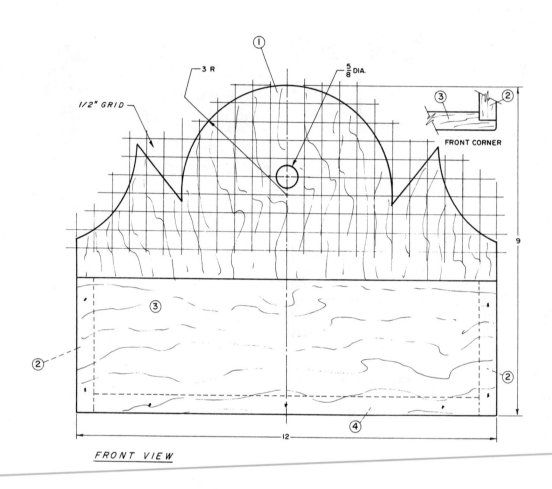

3 R

5/8 DIA.

1/2" GRID

③ FRONT CORNER ②

②

③

②

②

④

9

12

FRONT VIEW

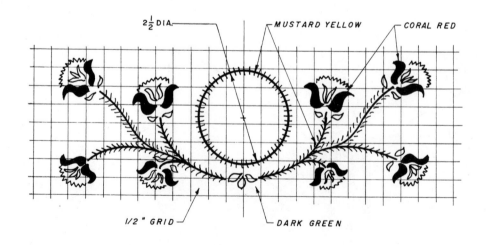

2 1/2 DIA.

MUSTARD YELLOW

CORAL RED

1/2" GRID

DARK GREEN

2. *Make a paper pattern for the back.* Draw a grid with ½-in. squares and enlarge the pattern for the back (part 1) onto it. Transfer the enlargement to the wood and cut it out. Notch the back to receive the sides (part 2), as shown in the exploded view. Locate and drill a ⅝-in.-diameter hanger hole in the back.

Rout a rabbet ½ in. wide and ¼ in. deep along the inside edges of the front (part 3), as shown in the front corner detail.

3. *Assemble the box.* Dry-fit the parts of the box and make any necessary adjustments. Glue and tack the corners together with 1-in. brads (part 5), keeping everything square. Glue the bottom (part 4) in place.

4. *Apply finish.* The original box was painted a light gray-green that you can approximate by using a subtle shade from an early American line of paint.

The floral pattern shown here is optional. To copy this design, reproduce it on a ½-in. grid and transfer it to the box; paint with the colors noted on the drawing.

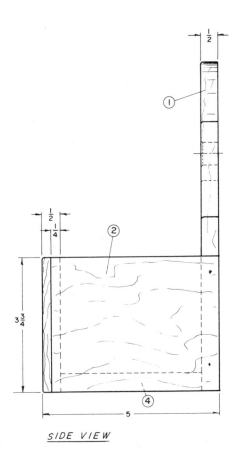

SIDE VIEW

Toy Blocks

If you tend to make an incorrect cut now and then and waste a little wood—as I do—you can recycle these leftovers by turning them into children's blocks. You don't have to reproduce the exact shapes shown here, of course. I offer these as examples.

To make it a little easier for kids to fit the blocks together, restrict yourself to a few overall widths and heights. The shapes in the drawings are in increments of a full inch. As illustrated, they're all ¾ in. thick, but again that's up to you.

Sand the blocks lightly, rounding the corners somewhat and removing splinters. You can finish them with a coat of salad bowl finish or a nontoxic paint. For the safety of younger children who might gnaw on blocks, don't use leftover paints that may contain toxic chemicals.

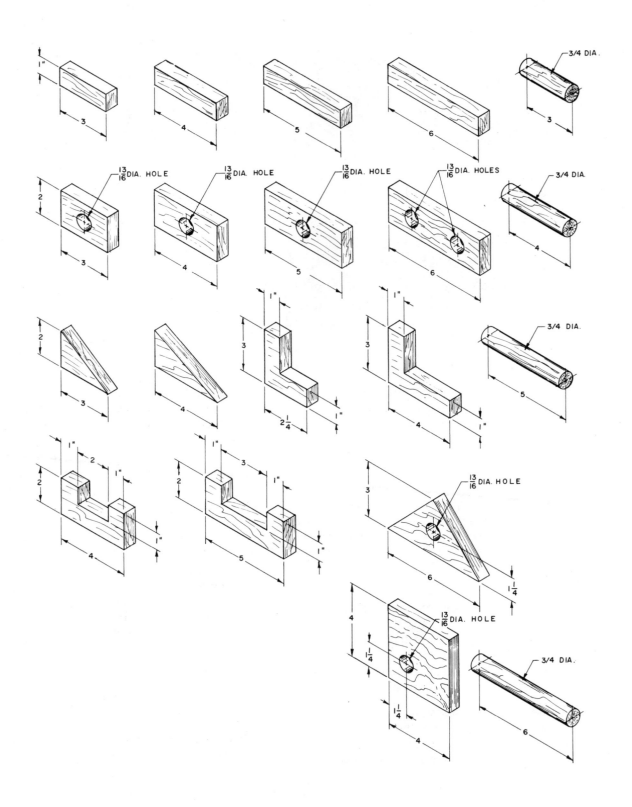

Jigsaw Puzzle

Here is a simple eight-piece puzzle for younger children. You can make it with a frame, as shown in the photograph, or without one, as shown in the drawing.

1. *Select the stock.* Use ¾-in. plywood or knot-free, straight-grained solid wood.

To make a framed puzzle, start with a piece measuring roughly 12 in. square. You'll also need a piece of ¼-in.-thick plywood to make the backing. If you don't want a frame, the wood needs to be only as large as the overall dimensions of the elephant.

2. *Make a paper pattern.* Draw a grid with ½-in. squares and enlarge the elephant onto it. Include the outline of each piece, as well as that of the eye and hat. Transfer the enlargement to the wood. For a framed puzzle, center the elephant in the square of wood.

3. *Cut out the puzzle.* The first step in making a framed puzzle is to cut out the elephant and make the frame. Once you've made the frame, the steps for making a framed and unframed puzzle are identical.

Start the frame by cutting the elephant out of the stock. Begin the saw cut by drilling a very small hole at the inner corner of the mouth, as shown in the drawing. Take the blade out of your scroll saw, insert it in the hole, and reattach it to the saw. Cut along the outline of the elephant.

Remove the elephant's body from the square of wood. Glue a plywood backing to the square to make the frame. If you'd like to cover the edges of the frame and plywood, glue on a simple 1-in.-deep frame with mitered corners.

Cut out the elephant, working from left to right. First, cut out the hat. Then cut two horizontal lines: One begins above the eye and goes across the top; The other begins at the mouth and goes across the middle.

Piece the three strips back together. Cut along the line that begins behind the hat and runs just in front of the rear leg. Disassemble the pieces to make the short last cut along the vertical line behind the eye.

4. *Apply finish.* Paint with nontoxic colors of your choice.

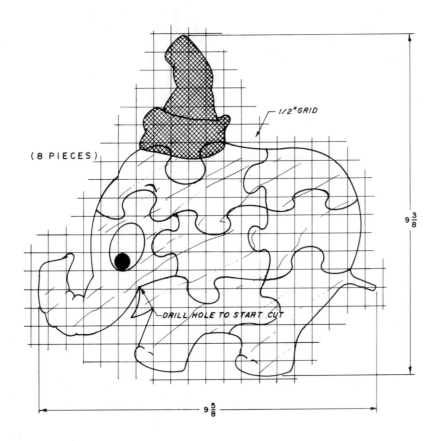

(8 PIECES)

1/2" GRID

9 3/8

9 5/8

DRILL HOLE TO START CUT

Elephant Pull Toy

The elephant in the previous project reappears here as a pull toy. Once you've drawn up a full-size elephant pattern, you may want to hold on to it for use on other pieces.

1. Select the stock and cut the parts. The body (part 1) is made from 1-in.-thick stock. If you can't find wood that thick, glue up two ½-in. pieces. Cut the parts to the sizes given in the Materials List.

2. Make a paper pattern and cut the parts to shape. Draw a grid with ½-in. squares and enlarge the elephant and his ears onto it. Transfer the pattern to wood. Note that the ears (part 2) are a single piece of wood and that they slide into a notch cut in the bottom of the body. Cut the body and the ears to shape. Cut the notch with a band saw or jigsaw.

Cut the saddles (part 5) to shape and glue them to the body. Drill a 3/16-in.-diameter hole for the tail (part 3) and a 1-in.-diameter hole for the rider (part 6). The rider can be lathe-turned or carved from a 1-in.-diameter dowel.

You can order the 2-in.-diameter wheels (part 8) from the source given in the Materials List or cut them yourself with a hole saw from ¾-in.-thick stock.

Drill ¼-in. holes in the base for the axle pegs (part 9).

3. Assemble the elephant. Glue the ears and tail to the body. Glue the body to the base (part 7). When the glue has set, drill and countersink for two flathead screws (part 10) and screw the elephant to the base. Slide the wheels over the axle pegs and glue the pegs in place, making sure that the wheels have enough room to turn freely. Add the eye screw (part 11).

4. Apply finish. Paint with nontoxic colors of your choice and add the jiggle eyes (part 4), if you wish.

MATERIALS LIST

Part	Dimensions	Quantity
1. Body	1″ × 7½″ × 7½″	1
2. Ear	½″ × 4″ × 5½″	1
3. Tail	3/16″ dia. × 1¼″	1
4. Jiggle eyes*		1 pair
5. Saddles	¼″ × 2″ × 2″	2
6. Rider	1″ dia. × 2″	1
7. Base	¾″ × 4″ × 7¾″	1
8. Wheels*	2″ dia. × ¾″	4
9. Axle pegs*		4
10. Flathead screws	#8 × 1½″	2
11. Eye screw		1

*Parts are available from Meisel Hardware Specialties, P.O. Box 70, Mound, MN 55364. Pair of jiggle eyes is #7647, wheels are #W20320, and axle pegs are #AP-4.

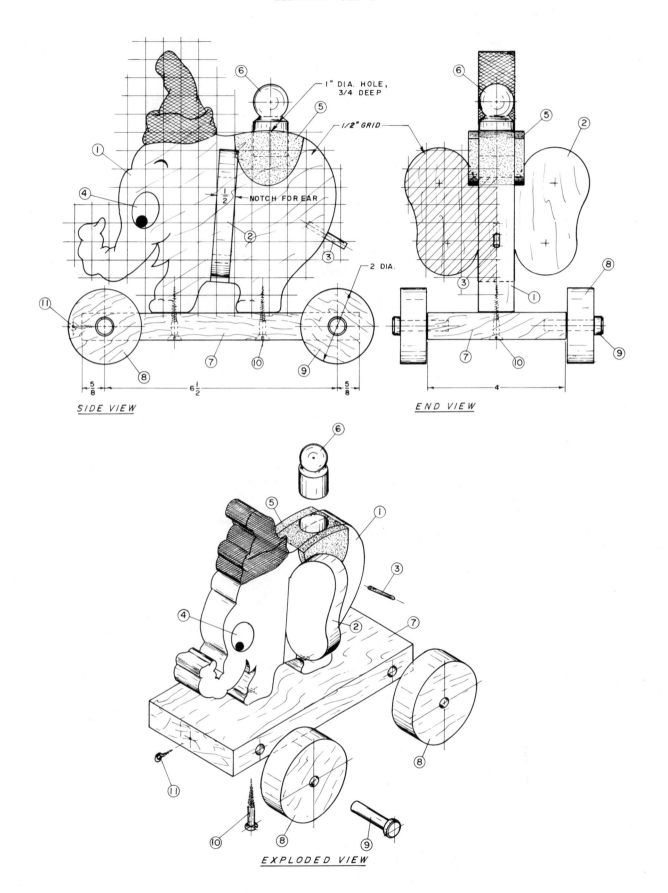

1" DIA. HOLE, 3/4 DEEP

1/2" GRID

1/2 NOTCH FOR EAR

2 DIA.

5/8   6 1/2   5/8

SIDE VIEW

END VIEW

4

EXPLODED VIEW

Toy Top

The top is one of the oldest toys. Eskimos made them of ice, native Americans made them of bone, and South Sea islanders used volcanic ash. This project is an improved design with a string that rewinds automatically. To work it, just pull the string and let go—the string rewinds itself, ready for another pull.

1. *Select the stock.* For durability and weight, turn the top from hardwood. If you can't find a piece thick enough for the body, glue up stock. Use the same kind of wood throughout so that the weight will be distributed evenly.

2. *Turn the parts.* Turn the handle (part 1) to the profile shown in the front view. Sand the handle and other wooden parts while they are turning on the lathe. Sand the section of the handle that goes through the rewind loop a bit more than the rest. The smaller diameter that results will ensure that the handle spins freely in the rewind loop. With the lathe turned off but with the handle still mounted on it, drill the 1/16-in.-diameter hole in the handle for the string.

The 1/4-in hole through the rewind loop (part 2) is easiest to drill *before* you turn the loop because the wood is still square at this point. Drill the hole through what will be the axis of the loop; center it in the block as well.

Band saw the outer diameter of the loop roughly to shape. Mount the stock on the lathe between centers and turn the outer diameter to the profile shown. Drill out the inner hole with a 1 1/4-in. drill bit. While not absolutely necessary, you'll find that Forstner bits make a smoother cut than regular spade bits.

If you've glued up stock to turn the body (part 3), let it dry thoroughly before turning it. To make drilling the 1/4-in.-diameter hole for the handle easier, mount the top so its wide end is nearest the tailstock. After you've turned the body to the profile shown, mount a brad-point or Forstner bit in a chuck in the lathe tailstock. Center the drill spur on the top's axis and lock the tailstock in place. With the lathe turned on, gradually feed the bit into the body. While this works well when drilling the 1/4-in. hole, your best bet for drilling the 1/8-in.-diameter hole is to clamp the top in a vice and drill with an electric hand drill.

3. *Assemble the parts.* Check that the rewind loop turns freely on the handle. With the loop on the handle, glue the handle into the body. Be sure to leave 1 3/8 in., as shown, so the rewind loop won't bind on the handle.

Make the tip (part 4) by rounding the point of a 10d common nail with a file or grinding wheel. Cut a 7/8-in. length off the end. Place it into the hole in the bottom of the top body. Epoxy it in place, if necessary.

4. *Apply finish.* Old tops often were decorated with bright pin stripes, so you may want to add them. Finish with varnish or paint. When finishing the handle, only finish the top end to avoid binding the return loop.

Attach a 20-in. length of string through the hole in the handle, and you're ready to revolve.

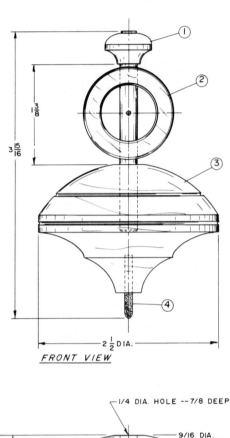

① ② ③ ④

3 15/16

3 1/8

2 1/2 DIA.

FRONT VIEW

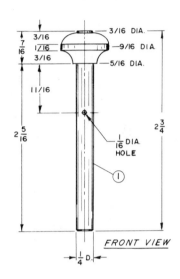

3/16 DIA.

7/16

3/16

1/16

3/16

9/16 DIA.

5/16 DIA.

11/16

2 5/16

1/16 DIA. HOLE

2 3/4

①

1/4 D.

FRONT VIEW

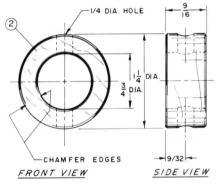

②

1/4 DIA. HOLE

9/16

1 1/4 DIA.

3/4 DIA.

CHAMFER EDGES

9/32

FRONT VIEW   SIDE VIEW

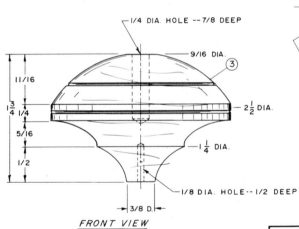

1/4 DIA. HOLE -- 7/8 DEEP

9/16 DIA.

③

11/16

1 3/4   1/4

5/16

1/2

2 1/2 DIA.

1 1/4 DIA.

1/8 DIA. HOLE -- 1/2 DEEP

3/8 D.

FRONT VIEW

MATERIALS LIST

Part	Dimensions	Quantity
1. Handle	5⁄8″ × 5⁄8″ × 5″	1
2. Rewind loop	9⁄16″ × 1½″ × 1½″	1
3. Top body	2¾″ × 2¾″ × 4″	1
4. Common nail	10d	1
5. String	Cut to fit	as needed

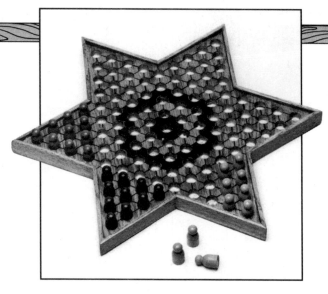

Chinese Checkers

This old game does not have its origins in China, but in Sweden, where it was highly popular in the 1800s. The star-shaped game board has 121 holes in it. The trickiest part of this project is laying them all out. You'll also get a chance to practice your wood burning skills when you mark all the lines on the board.

In case you didn't know, the object of the game is to be the first to move all of your pawns to the opposite point of the star. You can jump over other pawns, either yours or those of opponents. If there are two players, each gets 15 pawns; if there are three players, each gets 10.

1. *Select the stock.* The game board (part 1) is cut from a sheet of ¾-in. plywood. The game will look better if you use plywood with a hardwood veneer. I chose oak-veneer plywood with its interesting grain, but if you decide to paint the board, birch offers a smoother surface.

MATERIALS LIST

Part	Dimensions	Quantity
1. Base	¾″ × 14″ × 16″	1
2. Frames	¼″ × 1″ × 5½″	12
3. Pawns*	⅝″ dia. × 1¼″	45

Pawns are available from Meisel Hardware Specialties, P.O. Box 70, Mound, MN 55364; order #GP2.

2. *Lay out the game board.* Your measurements and drawing must be *exact* throughout this step. If possible, lay out the game board with a drawing board and T-square to ensure accuracy.

Draw the pattern on a piece of paper, measuring at least 15 in. × 18 in. Draw two perpendicular lines that cross in the center of the paper, as shown in Fig. 1. Set a compass for a radius of exactly 6¹⁵⁄₁₆ in. and scribe a circle from this center point.

Using a 30/60-degree triangle, construct an equilateral triangle with three 12-in. sides and three 60-degree angles, as shown in Fig. 2. Check to see each side is exactly 12 in. long and redraw, if necessary.

Rotate the drawing 180 degrees and construct a second triangle on top of the first and identical to it, as shown in Fig. 3.

Measure along each leg of both triangles and make sharp, precise marks at 1-in. intervals, as shown in Fig. 4. At the end of each leg, you should end up with a 1-in. space; if not, check your drawing.

With a sharp 4H pencil and a straightedge, construct the lines, as shown in Fig. 5. If your layout is correct, all lines should cross exactly as shown. You can be off by ¹⁄₃₂ in. but not much more. Correct your lines, if necessary—you will be drawing them with a woodburning set later, and mistakes at that point cannot be erased.

Measure ½ in. beyond the outline of the star to draw the outer line, as shown in Fig. 6.

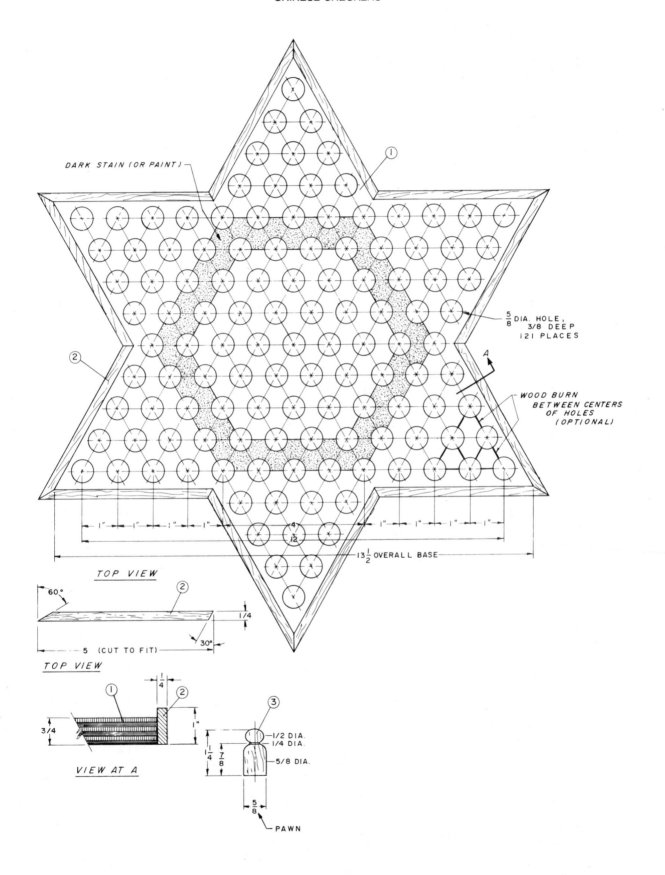

DARK STAIN (OR PAINT)

①

②

$\frac{5}{8}$ DIA. HOLE,
3/8 DEEP
121 PLACES

WOOD BURN
BETWEEN CENTERS
OF HOLES
(OPTIONAL)

A

1" 1" 1" 1"

$\frac{4}{12}$

1" 1" 1" 1"

$13\frac{1}{2}$ OVERALL BASE

TOP VIEW

60°

②

1/4

30°

5 (CUT TO FIT)

TOP VIEW

$\frac{1}{4}$

①

②

1"

3/4

VIEW AT A

③

1/2 DIA.
1/4 DIA.

$1\frac{1}{4}$

$\frac{7}{8}$

5/8 DIA.

$\frac{5}{8}$

PAWN

111

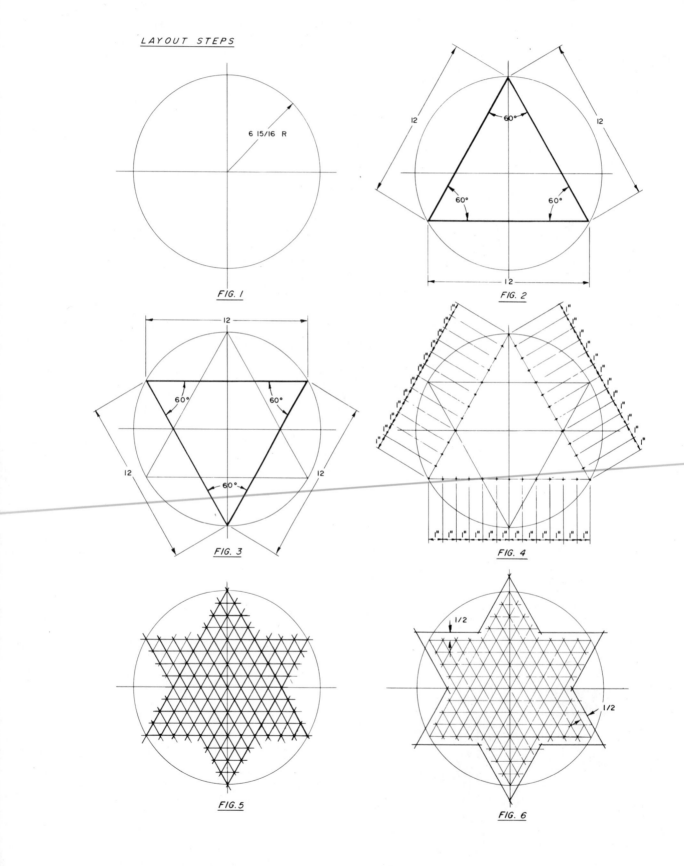

LAYOUT STEPS

FIG. I

FIG. 2

FIG. 3

FIG. 4

FIG.5

FIG. 6

3. *Transfer the pattern and burn it in.* To transfer the pattern, tape it to the wood and prick the intersections of all lines with an awl. Mark the corners of the star in the same way. Remove the paper and connect the awl pricks with a sharp pencil. Then burn in the lines with a woodburning set guided by a steel straightedge. To keep the straightedge from shifting, tape it to the wood with double-sided tape. Try to burn the lines so the width is consistent.

4. *Bore the holes.* Bore holes for the pawns at each mark made by the awl, even if the burned lines strayed slightly from these marks. Bore holes with a ⅝-in.-diameter bit in a drill press, if you have one. Set the drill press to make ⅜-in.-deep holes. If you use a hand drill, place a commercially available drill stop on the bit. Sand the board.

5. *Cut out and assemble the game board.* Cut out the star with a band saw or jigsaw. Keep the edges as straight as possible. Cut the twelve frames (part 2) to fit; note that the ends of each are mitered at 30 and 60 degrees, as shown in the detail. Glue and nail the frames in place. Set and fill the nail holes.

6. *Turn the pawns.* You can turn the 45 pawns (part 3), as shown in the detail drawing, if you choose. You can also buy pawns but make sure the diameter is no more than ⅝ in. Purchase at least three sets of pawns, each set a different color.

7. *Apply finish.* There are all sorts of ways to finish the board, with stain or paint or both. The game board shown in the photograph has a dark stain in the center, followed by a light golden oak stain over the entire board. Two coats of varnish or shellac should be added to protect the board. Sand between coats. Complete the job with a coat of paste wax. If you turned your own pawns, paint them as you choose.

Elephant Bank

Here is still another elephant project. It must be obvious by now that I am fond of elephants.

This particular animal is hollow, to store a child's coins. The bottom is attached with two screws, which can be removed without too much trouble when it is time to withdraw the funds.

1. Select the stock. This elephant is something of a sandwich, with a hollowed-out body (part 1) capped by two sides (part 2). Cut the parts to the sizes given in the Materials List but don't glue them together yet.

2. Make a paper pattern. Draw a grid with ½-in. squares and enlarge the elephant, his ears (part 7), and his legs (parts 5 and 6) onto it. Be

sure to locate the mortise for the ears, as shown in the side view. Transfer the patterns to the wood. Cut out the ears and legs but not the body or sides.

3. Hollow out the body. Cut the body along the dashed lines shown in the side view. Then cut the mortises for the ears in the side pieces: Draw a line down the center of the mortise and center a series of adjoining ⁷/₁₆-in. holes along this line. Cut out the edges of the mortise with a sharp chisel. Check the fit of the ears as you chisel.

4. Glue the sides to the body and cut to shape. Glue the sides to the body.

Screw the bottom to the elephant. Drill clearance holes slightly larger than the shank of the screw (part 4) in the bottom and pilot holes slightly smaller than the screw shank in the body. Screw the bottom in place.

Cut the outline of the body.

5. Add the ears, legs, and tail. Locate and cut out the slot for coins in the top of the body; you can first drill ⅛-in.-diameter holes at either end of the slot and then saw out the portion in between.

The legs are notched and then attached to the body, as shown in the exploded view. To lay out the notch, place a ¾-in. piece of wood between the bottom of the elephant and the workbench. This puts the elephant at the height it will be when the legs are attached. Hold a leg in place with the foot flat on the bench and trace the outline of the bottom and sides on the leg. Use a fine-tooth saw or chisel to cut the notches. Repeat

MATERIALS LIST

Part	Dimensions	Quantity
1. Body	1″ × 6½″ × 7¼″	1
2. Sides	¼″ × 6½″ × 7¼″	2
3. Bottom	¼″ × 1″ × 3″	1
4. Roundhead screws	#6 × ⅝″	2
5. Front legs	½″ × 1½″ × 1¾″	2
6. Rear legs	½″ × 1½″ × 2″	2
7. Ears	½″ × 2½″ × 3¾″	2
8. Tail	⅛″ dia. × ¾″	1
9. Jiggle eyes*		1 pair

*Part is available from Meisel Hardware Specialties, P.O. Box 70, Mound MN 55364; order #7647.

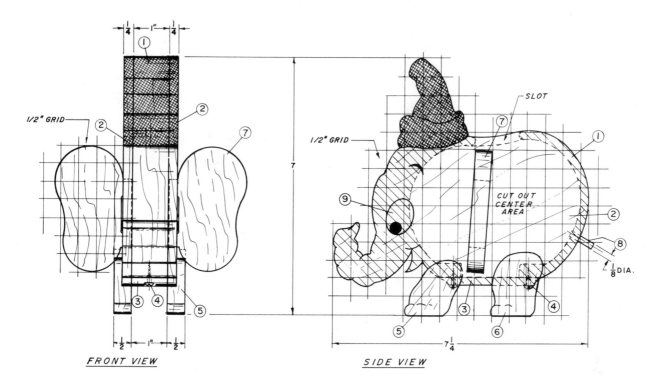

1/2" GRID

7

FRONT VIEW

SLOT

1/2" GRID

CUT OUT CENTER AREA

1/8 DIA.

7 1/4

SIDE VIEW

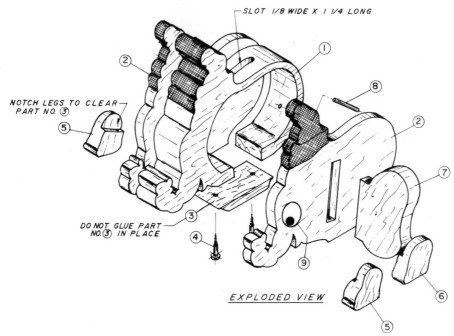

SLOT 1/8 WIDE X 1 1/4 LONG

NOTCH LEGS TO CLEAR PART NO. ③

DO NOT GLUE PART NO.③ IN PLACE

EXPLODED VIEW

for the remaining legs. Glue the legs in place.

Drill a ⅛-in.-diameter hole at an angle for the tail (part 8), as shown in the side view, and glue the tail in place. Glue the ears in place, making sure they are in line with each other.

Sand thoroughly.

6. *Apply finish.* Remove the bottom. Decorate the elephant with nontoxic paints. You might want to use the same color pattern for several of the book's elephant projects, if the pieces will be in the same room. Reattach the bottom. Attach the jiggle eyes (part 9).

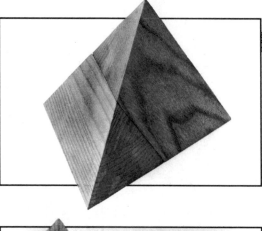

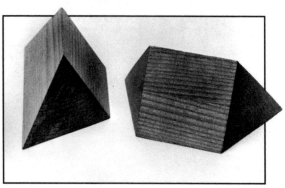

Pyramid Puzzle

Are you intrigued by three-dimensional puzzles? If so, you should like this one. It involves just two identical pieces, each made with four saw cuts. The trick is to assemble the pieces to form a three-sided pyramid.

How difficult is this puzzle? You'll have to make it before you can find out.

1. Select the stock. I suggest straight-grained hardwood. You'll need a block 2¼ × 2⅝ × 16 in. You'll be able to get both puzzle pieces out of this block. If you can't come up with 2¼-in. stock, glue up three pieces of ¾-in. hardwood.

2. Cut the pieces. Cut the block into two 7½-in. lengths. The drawings give step-by-step illustrations for the remaining cuts. I made cuts on a band saw. Remember: You are making two identical puzzle pieces.

To make the first cut, set the saw blade to exactly 30 degrees and cut, as shown. Turn the block 180 degrees and make the second cut with the same blade setting. Be sure to keep the base a full 2⅝ in. wide.

For the third and fourth cuts, use the miter gauge to saw off the ends with the blade still set at 30 degrees. These cuts *must* leave a base that is exactly 2⅝ in. square if the puzzle is to work.

3. Apply finish. Use rubber cement to temporarily attach the two pieces, labeled parts 1 and 2 in the drawings. Sand the pieces, keeping surfaces flat and the corners very sharp. Take the pieces apart and sand the square surfaces that were joined.

I've found that it's best to either leave the puzzle unfinished or to apply varnish so that the grain is visible. When assembled, the grain in one part is perpendicular to the grain in the other. This is the only clue I give people, and it's great fun to watch them at work.

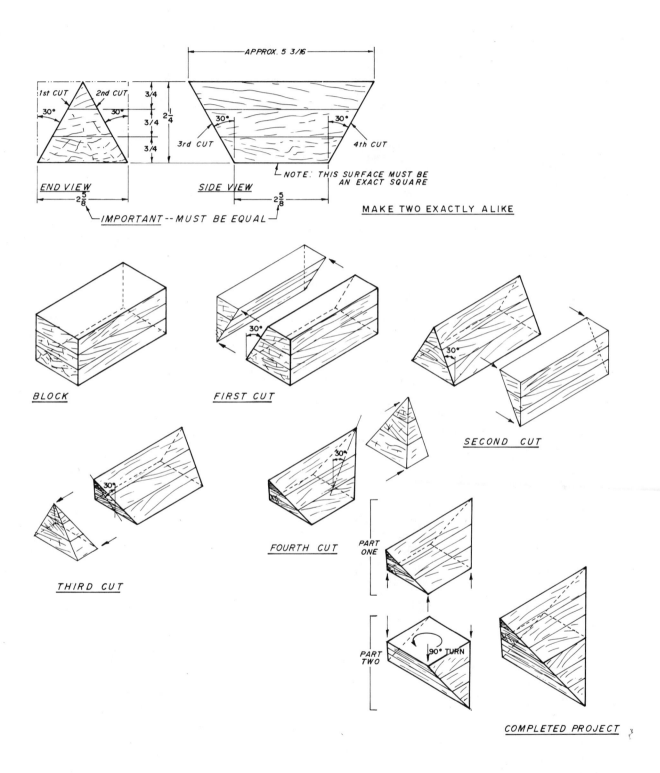

END VIEW

SIDE VIEW

IMPORTANT -- MUST BE EQUAL

MAKE TWO EXACTLY ALIKE

NOTE: THIS SURFACE MUST BE AN EXACT SQUARE

APPROX. 5 3/16

BLOCK

FIRST CUT

SECOND CUT

THIRD CUT

FOURTH CUT

PART ONE

PART TWO

90° TURN

COMPLETED PROJECT

Dog Pull Toy

A good friend of mine bought a miniature dachshund and spent hours teaching the dog to do tricks. I was impressed with the dog and based this toy on it.

1. *Select the stock and cut the body segments.* I suggest using straight-grained maple or birch. First, make paper patterns of both the dog and his ears (parts 1 and 2). Draw a grid with ½-in. squares and enlarge the parts onto it. Transfer the enlargements to the stock, leaving at least ½ in. between the segments.

Cut the parts to shape.

2. *Drill the hinge pin holes.* Temporarily assemble the three body segments and tape them together. Make sure that they are in proper alignment and that the hinge joints are snug. Locate

and drill the holes for the two hinge pins (part 3), as shown in the top view, taking care to drill straight down.

Temporarily put the hinge pins—made from ⅛-in.-diameter hardwood dowels—in place and remove the tape. Sand the profile of the dog so that one segment seems to flow into the other along the length of the body. This work goes quickly on a drum sander mounted on a drill press.

Remove the hinge pins and round the hinge joints with a rasp so that the segments can each swivel approximately 90 degrees in either direction. Refer to the exploded view to see the finished shape of the hinges. As you work, check your progress by reassembling the dog. The fit should be loose but not sloppy.

3. *Make the wheels and axles.* You can either cut the wheels (part 5) out of ⅝-in.-thick stock with a circle cutter in a drill press or order them from the source given in the Materials List.

Cut out the axles (part 4). Notch them to take the feet of the dog. Drill ⁷⁄₃₂-in.-diameter holes, roughly 1¼ in. deep, in the center of the axle ends to take the axle pegs (part 6).

4. *Assemble the dog.* You can glue up axle pegs or turn them if you have a lathe, but I've found it's easier to purchase them from the source given in the Materials List. Slip the pegs through the wheel holes and glue them in the axles, making sure the cap on the end of the axle doesn't bind against the wheel. Glue the dog's feet to the axles and glue on the ears.

5. *Apply finish.* You can leave the dog unfinished or apply a varnish or fanciful paint job. When the finish has dried, glue the hinge pins in place; place the glue in the top and bottom holes only, or the joints won't turn.

Install the eye screw (part 7), tie on a length of string (part 8), and take your dog for a walk.

MATERIALS LIST

Part	Dimensions	Quantity
1. Body	½″ × 6½″ × 14″	1
2. Ears	⅛″ × 2″ × 2¾″	2
3. Hinge pins	⅛″ dia. × 2½″	2
4. Axles	¾″ × ¾″ × 4″	2
5. Wheels*	⅝″ × 2″ dia.	4
6. Axle pegs*	⁷⁄₃₂″ dia. × 1½″	4
7. Eye screw		1
8. String	Cut to fit	as needed

Parts are available from Meisel Hardware Specialties, P.O. Box 70, Mound, MN 55364. Wheels are #20020, and axle pegs are #AP1.

DOG PULL TOY

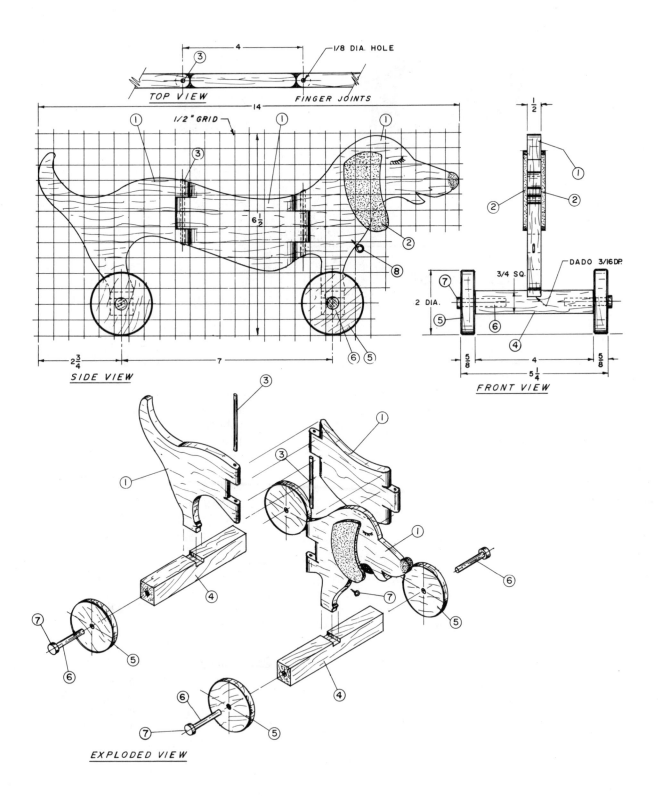

TOP VIEW FINGER JOINTS

1/8 DIA. HOLE

4

14

1/2" GRID

6 1/2

SIDE VIEW

2 3/4

7

1/2

2 DIA.

3/4 SQ.

DADO 3/16 DP.

5/8   4   5/8

5 1/4

FRONT VIEW

EXPLODED VIEW

Toy Train

| | MATERIALS LIST | |

Part	Dimensions	Quantity
Engine		
1. Base	$7/16'' \times 2\frac{1}{4}'' \times 7\frac{1}{4}''$	1
2. Sides	$7/16'' \times 2^{5}/16'' \times 2\frac{3}{4}''$	2
3. Front	$7/16'' \times 2^{5}/16'' \times 7/8''$	1
4. Top	$7/16'' \times 2\frac{1}{8}'' \times 3\frac{1}{2}''$	1
5. Boiler	$1\frac{5}{8}''$ dia. $\times 3^{9}/16''$	1
6. Stack	$1\frac{1}{8}''$ dia. $\times 1^{11}/16''$	1
7. Horn	$5/8''$ dia. $\times 1\frac{1}{8}''$	1
8. Wheels*	$1\frac{3}{4}''$ dia.	16
9. Axle pegs*		16
Tender		
10. Base	$7/16'' \times 2\frac{1}{4}'' \times 5''$	1
11. Sides	$7/16'' \times 1\frac{5}{8}'' \times 3\frac{1}{4}''$	2
12. Front	$7/16'' \times 1\frac{5}{8}'' \times 7/8''$	1
Cars		
13. Bases	$7/16'' \times 2\frac{1}{4}'' \times 6\frac{1}{2}''$	2
14. Sides	$7/16'' \times 1^{9}/16'' \times 5\frac{1}{4}''$	4
15. Tops	$7/16'' \times 1\frac{7}{8}'' \times 6''$	2
Hardware		
16. Hooks**		3
17. Eye screws**		3

*Wheels and axle pegs are available from two sources:
1. Woodworker's Supply of New Mexico, 5604 Alameda Place NE, Albuquerque, NM 87113. Wheel is #110-163, and axle is #110-164.
2. The Woodworkers' Store, 21801 Industrial Boulevard, Rogers, MN 55374. Wheel is #B1463, and axle is #B1471.

**Instead of hooks and eyes, you can use 1/2-in.-dia. ceramic magnets, available from Cherry Tree Toys Inc., P.O. Box 369, Belmont, OH 43718. Magnets are #430, and roundhead annular nails to attach them are #410.

I based the design for this train on a toy made in the 1930s. The toy appeared to have been homemade, but I suppose it might have been mass-produced.

A few simple turnings are needed to make the engine, but otherwise the project is straightforward, using only butt joints. The original train was coupled with large hooks and eye screws between the cars, but I suggest substituting the ceramic magnets available from the source given in the Materials List. The magnets are a bit safer and are easier to use for little fingers. The wheels and axles pegs also can be purchased through sources given in the Materials List.

1. Select the stock and cut the parts. Any wood will do for this project. Cut the parts to the sizes given in the Materials List.

2. Turn the engine parts. Turn the boiler, (part 5), stack (part 6), and horn (part 7). Lay out and drill the holes in the boiler, as shown in the top view of the boiler. Make the flat spot on the bottom of the boiler by sliding it over sandpaper; take off 1/8 in. or so, as shown.

3. Drill the axle holes. The trickiest task is to accurately locate and drill the holes for the axle pegs (part 9). The holes must be drilled exactly the same distance from the bottom surface of the bases (parts 1, 10, and 13), or the cars will not all sit on the same level. Use a self-centering doweling jig, if possible. (I didn't, and my string of cars is not level.)

4. Assemble the cars. Assemble the cars, as shown in the exploded view. Round the corners,

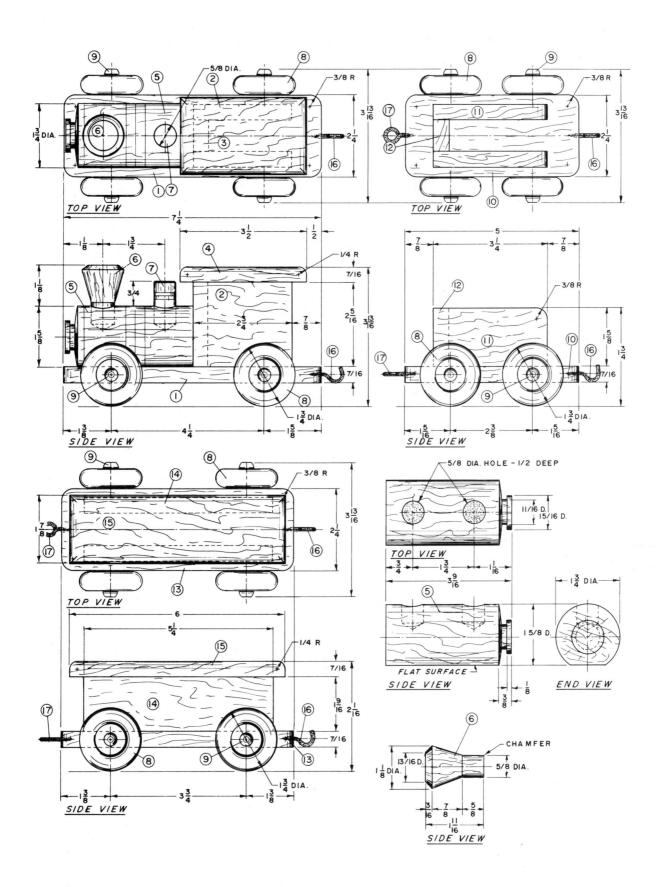

as shown. Glue the axle pegs in place, leaving enough space for the wheels to turn freely. If you will be painting the train, do so before adding the axles and wheels.

5. *Apply finish.* Use bright, cheerful colors of nontoxic paint. Add the hooks and eye screws or the magnets. When attaching the magnets, make sure to have all of the magnets of one pole at the same end of the cars, or the cars won't couple.

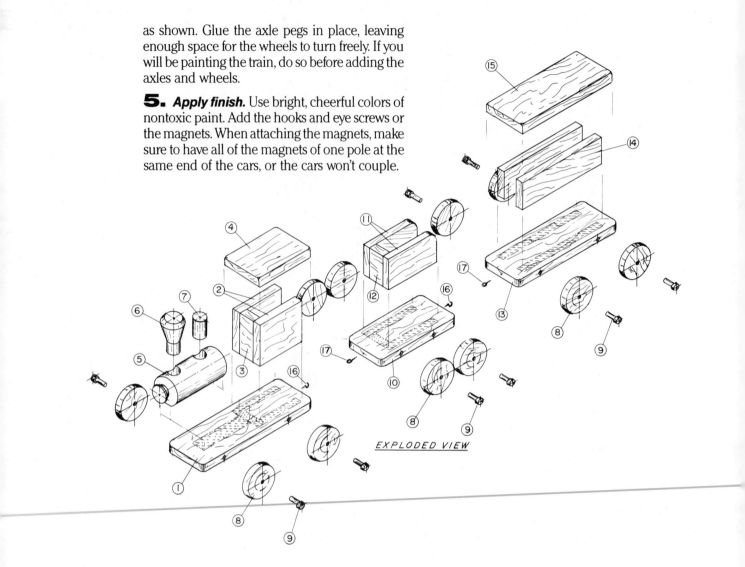

EXPLODED VIEW

Model T Runabout

The Model T Ford was the car that put America on wheels. The first one was made in 1908, and by the time the last one came off the line in 1927, more than 15 million had been produced. Aside from providing transportation, they were adapted to plow fields, saw wood, pump water, store grain, and run machinery.

This toy is patterned after a 1914 Model T, a car with a crank starter, carbide headlights, kerosene cowl lights, and a rubber bulb horn. As the by-now famous saying goes, "It came in any color you wanted, as long as you wanted black." I owned one of them a few years ago, and it was a lot of fun to drive.

Since even a slight deviation may affect the assembly, dry-fit each part before gluing it. You'll find that cutting the parts is far easier if you have a parallel-arm scroll saw, but you can make-do with a coping saw.

1. *Select the stock.* Because of the intricate cutting that you'll have to do, use a wood with tight, straight grain. Maple and birch are good choices. I used ash because I have a plentiful supply, but it was hard work.

Cut the parts to the sizes given in the Materials List. Make the engine compartment (part 4) 12 in. long for now so that it will be easier to chamfer when the time comes. Cut the base (part 1) to the profile shown.

2. *Make paper patterns.* Draw grids with the appropriately sized squares and enlarge the outer body and fenders onto it. Transfer the patterns to the stock.

3. *Make the body.* The body is a sandwich made of two outer bodies and one inner body. The two outer bodies (part 2) are particularly complex. Cut them at the same time, temporarily gluing two $3/16$-in.-thick pieces of stock to each other with rubber cement. Cut out the parts with a jigsaw or coping saw. Begin the two cutouts, as marked in the side view, by drilling a small hole. Slip the saw blade into the hole before attaching the blade to the saw.

Use one of the outer bodies as a pattern to draw the inner body (part 3) on a piece of stock. Leave out the roof supports but add a seat, as shown in the detail of the inner body. Cut out the inner body.

Lay out and drill a $1/8$-in.-diameter steering wheel hole through the front of the inner body; it is $3/8$ in. from the left side, roughly $5/8$ in. up from the bottom and at a 45-degree angle to the floor.

Make a saw kerf, $1/16$ in. wide and $1/4$ in. deep, to accept the windshield in the inner body. Locate and cut out the rear window, as shown.

Glue the outer bodies to either side of the inner body. When the glue has dried, sand the edges between the parts. This completes the body subassembly.

4. *Make the engine compartment.* Cut the 45-degree chamfers, as shown in the front view

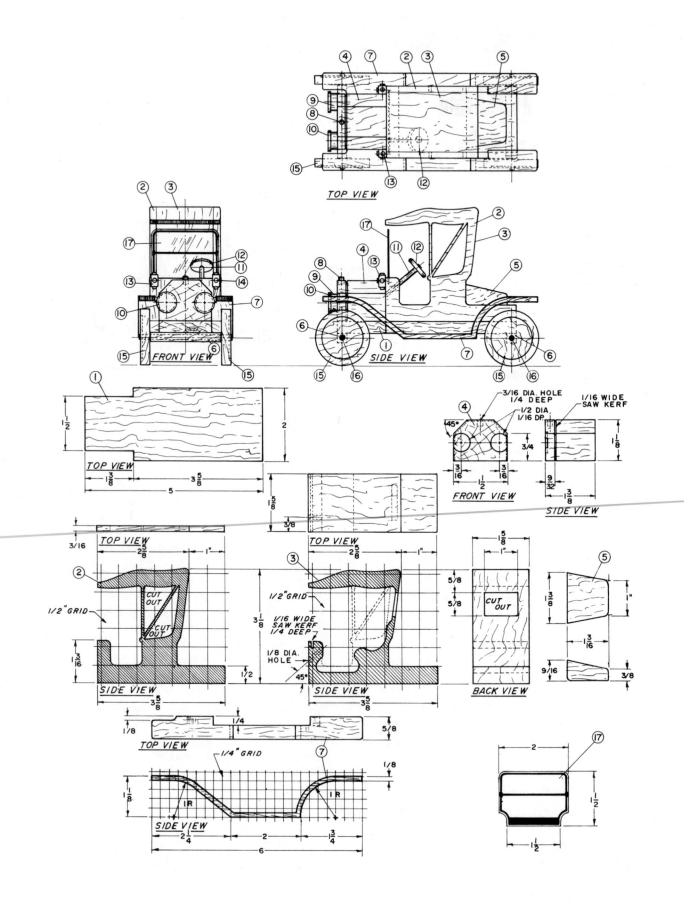

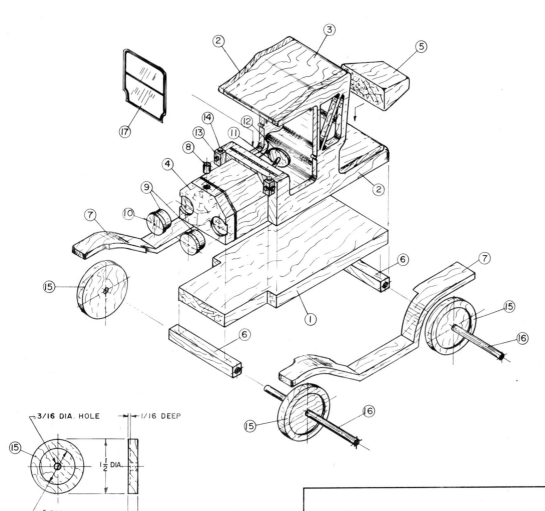

3/16 DIA. HOLE — 1/16 DEEP

1½ DIA.

1" DIA. --
1/16 DEEP

¼

FRONT VIEW   **SIDE VIEW**

of the engine compartment (part 4). You can rip these on the table saw, if you begin with a piece at least 12 in. long. Chamfer it and then cut it to the proper length.

Lay out and drill the two holes for the head-lights, as shown in the front view of the engine compartment. Position the holes exactly as shown. The drill bit overhangs the edge of the compartment when drilling, leaving a hole with one flat side.

Cut a slot around the engine compartment with a thin-bladed saw, as shown in the side view of the engine compartment. Lay out and drill the hole for the radiator cap.

5. *Assemble the body, base, engine compartment, and trunk.* Glue the base and engine

MATERIALS LIST

Part	Dimensions	Quantity
1. Base	$\frac{3}{8}'' \times 2'' \times 5''$	1
2. Outer body	$\frac{3}{16}'' \times 3\frac{1}{8}'' \times 3\frac{5}{8}''$	2
3. Inner body	$1\frac{5}{8}'' \times 3\frac{1}{8}'' \times 3\frac{5}{8}''$	1
4. Engine compartment	$1\frac{1}{8}'' \times 1\frac{1}{2}'' \times 1\frac{3}{8}''$	1
5. Trunk	$\frac{9}{16}'' \times 1\frac{3}{8}'' \times 1\frac{3}{16}''$	1
6. Axle supports	$\frac{1}{4}'' \times \frac{1}{4}'' \times 2''$	2
7. Fenders	$\frac{5}{8}'' \times 1\frac{1}{8}'' \times 6''$	2
8. Cap	$\frac{3}{16}''$ dia. $\times \frac{3}{8}''$	1
9. Headlight bodies	$\frac{1}{2}''$ dia. $\times \frac{1}{4}''$	2
10. Headlight lenses	$\frac{5}{8}''$ dia. $\times \frac{1}{16}''$	2
11. Steering post	$\frac{1}{8}''$ dia. $\times 1\frac{1}{4}''$	1
12. Steering wheel	$\frac{5}{8}''$ dia. $\times \frac{1}{8}''$	1
13. Lamps	$\frac{3}{16}'' \times \frac{3}{16}'' \times \frac{5}{16}''$	2
14. Lamp details	$\frac{1}{8}''$ dia. $\times \frac{1}{8}''$	8
15. Wheels	$1\frac{1}{2}''$ dia. $\times \frac{1}{4}''$	4
16. Axle pins	$\frac{3}{16}''$ dia. $\times 2\frac{3}{4}''$	2
17. Windshield	$1\frac{1}{2}'' \times 2''$ (thickness variable)	1

compartment to the body subassembly. When the glue has dried, fill any gaps with a matching wood putty and sand thoroughly, smoothing the edges between the parts. Glue the trunk (part 5) in place.

6. *Make the fenders.* Use the pattern you made earlier to lay out the fenders (part 7). Sand or file as necessary to fit the fender to the car body. Only the top of the left-hand fender is shown. You need to make a set of right-hand and left-hand fenders. Glue the fenders to the body and fill and sand as necessary to eliminate any gaps.

7. *Complete the assembly.* Drill $3/16$-in.-diameter holes through the length of the axle supports (part 6). To position the axle supports, temporarily mount the wheels in them. Put the supports underneath the car so that the wheels are centered inside the fender wells. Glue the supports in place.

When the glue dries, check the fit of the axle pins (part 16) in the axle supports. Slide the axle pins into the supports and make sure the wheels can turn freely. You might have to sand the pins slightly. Adjust as necessary, slip an axle

pin through the supports, and glue the wheels in place.

Glue the steering post (part 11) and steering wheel (part 12) in place.

Glue the lamp details (part 14) onto the lamps (part 13). Note that on each lamp, one detail is aimed away from the car—the right-hand and left-hand lamps will not be identical. Mount the lamps on the body, as illustrated.

Slice the headlight bodies and lenses (parts 9 and 10) from sections of $1/2$-in. and $5/8$-in.-diameter dowel. Glue them together and then glue the assembly to the body.

Glue the cap (part 8) on top of the radiator.

Cut out the windshield (part 17) from a piece of clear plastic measuring up to $1/16$ in. thick. I used plastic from an overhead projector transparency. Outline the border in black, as shown, with a pen that will write on plastic. Attach the plastic in the kerf with a general-purpose household cement designed for plastics.

8. *Apply finish.* You can leave the car as it is or add a couple coats of clear varnish. Of course, you also can paint it black like the original Model T.

Jeep

The Jeep was literally the workhorse of the Army in World War II, replacing the horses used in World War I. This toy borrows the more graceful lines of today's Jeep.

When making small-scale projects such as this vehicle, even a slight deviation from the given sizes may affect the assembly. So, as you proceed, dry-fit each part before gluing it, and make adjustments as necessary.

1. *Select the wood and cut the parts.* Use a hardwood for the Jeep and cut the parts to the dimensions given in the Materials List. You may have to glue up the hood (part 3) and seat (part 16) because they require thicker pieces.

2. *Transfer the patterns and cut the parts to shape.* Draw full-size patterns on the individual pieces of wood. Cut the shapes. Note the two fenders (part 5) are not identical: They are mirror images of each other. Drill holes, as indicated on the drawing, except for the holes on the grill, which you will drill later.

3. *Make the wheels.* Buy the wheels (part 18) from the source given in the Materials List. You can also cut them with a circle cutter or turn them on a lathe. I made my wheels with a circle cutter that had a $5/16$-in.-diameter drill in the center, so I had to adjust the diameter of the axles (part 17) to fit. You will also have to adjust the axle size if you mail-order the wheels.

4. *Assemble the body.* Glue the hood (part 3) and the rear panel (part 4) between the sides (part 2). When the glue dries, sand thoroughly.

Cut a $1/8$-in.-thick slice from the front of the assembled body to make the grill (part 7), as shown in the exploded view. Lay out and drill the holes for the headlights and parking lamps. You can leave the larger holes, as shown in the plans, or make headlights with $3/16$-in. lengths of $3/4$-in.-diameter dowel, as in the photograph.

Create the grill effect by cutting grooves about $1/16$ in. deep in the grill with a hand saw. Space the slots evenly, as shown. Cut seven fillers from a piece of scrap that is the width and depth of the kerfs and about 7 in. long. Each filler is about $5/16$ in. long. Glue them into the lower ends of the kerfs.

Glue the grill back onto the front of the body. When the glue has dried, sand the joint smooth.

5. *Assemble the Jeep.* Glue the body sub-assembly to the base (part 1), and when the glue dries, sand the joint between the two to make it inconspicuous.

Taper the top of the hood about 2 degrees, as shown in the side view of part 3. Start the taper just ahead of the door openings and sand or plane the hood to create the slope. Round the edges of the hood, as shown in the side view of the completed vehicle, with a rasp and sandpaper. This shaping gives the Jeep an up-to-date look.

The fenders, which you cut to shape in Step 1, may need some final shaping to fit the body. Shape as needed and glue the fenders in place.

Add the post and steering wheel (parts 14 and 15). Make the windshield (part 13) from four

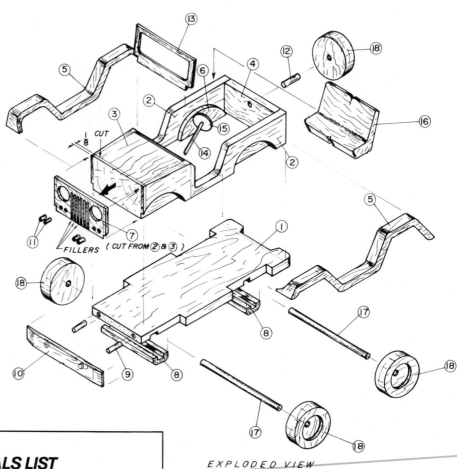

MATERIALS LIST

Part	Dimensions	Quantity
1. Base	⅜″ × 4″ × 9⅜″	1
2. Sides	⅜″ × 1⅞″ × 8⅞″	2
3. Hood	1⅞″ × 3¼″ × 3″	1
4. Rear panel	⅜″ × 1⅝″ × 3¼″	1
5. Fenders	1″ × 1¾″ × 9⅛″	2
6. Wheel wells	⅛″ × 1⅛″ × 3″	2
7. Grill	Cut from parts 2 and 3	1
8. Axle supports	⅜″ × ¾″ × 3¼″	2
9. Bumper supports	¼″ dia. × ⅝″	2
10. Bumper	³/₁₆″ × ¾″ × 5″	1
11. Parking lights	³/₁₆″ dia. × ³/₁₆″	4
12. Tire support	¼″ dia. × 1″	1
13. Windshield	⅛″ × ½″ × 12″	1
14. Post	³/₁₆″ dia. × 1¼″	1
15. Steering wheel	⅞″ dia. × ³/₁₆″	1
16. Seat	1¾″ × 2⅛″ × 3⅛″	1
17. Axles	¼″ dia. × 4¾″	2
18. Wheels*	2¼″ dia. × ¾″	5

Wheels are available from Cherry Tree Toys, Inc., P.O. Box 369, Belmont, OH 43718; order wheel #15.

⅛-in.-thick scraps, as shown in the detail for it. Sand and glue it in place. Attach the wheel wells (part 6), seat (part 16), bumper supports, (part 9) bumper (part 10), and parking lights (part 11).

6. *Add the wheels.* Glue the spare tire (part 18) to the tire support (part 12) and glue the support in the hole provided for it in the body. Glue the wheels to the axles. The wheels and axles are held in place by the axle supports (part 8). Make the supports by cutting a groove ¼ in. wide and ⅛ in. deep, down the center of a piece ¾ in. wide, as shown. Chamfer the edges to approximate the illustrated shape. To simplify adding a finish, you might want to add the wheels after completing Step 7.

7. *Apply finish.* Either paint the Jeep with brilliant nontoxic colors or apply a clear varnish, as shown in the photograph.

JEEP

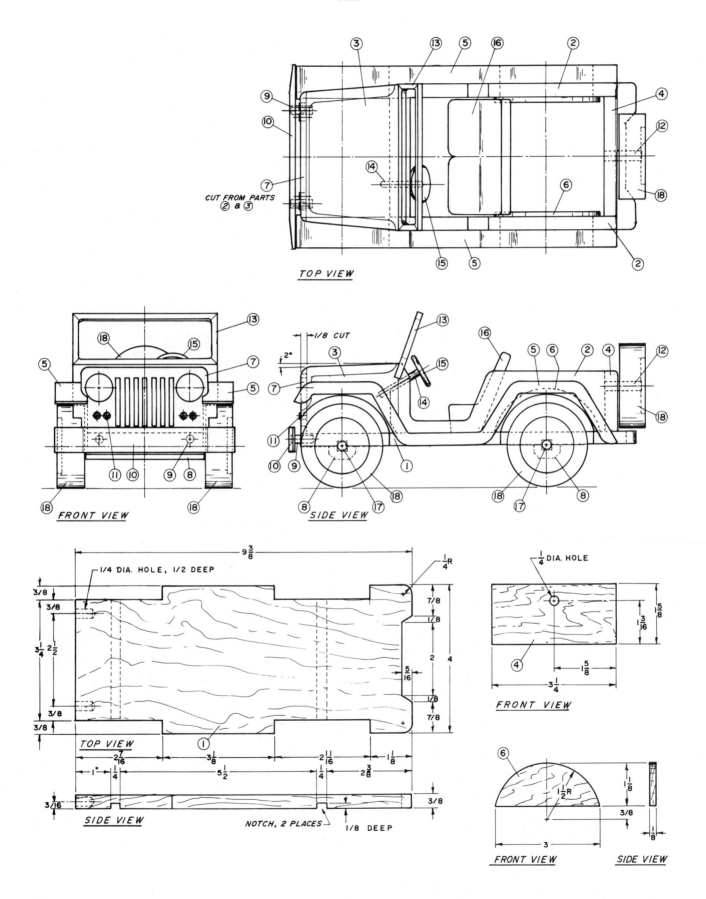

TOP VIEW

FRONT VIEW

SIDE VIEW

1/8 CUT

CUT FROM PARTS
② & ③

9 3/8

1/4 DIA. HOLE, 1/2 DEEP

1/4 R

TOP VIEW

SIDE VIEW

NOTCH, 2 PLACES   1/8 DEEP

1/4 DIA. HOLE

FRONT VIEW

FRONT VIEW   SIDE VIEW

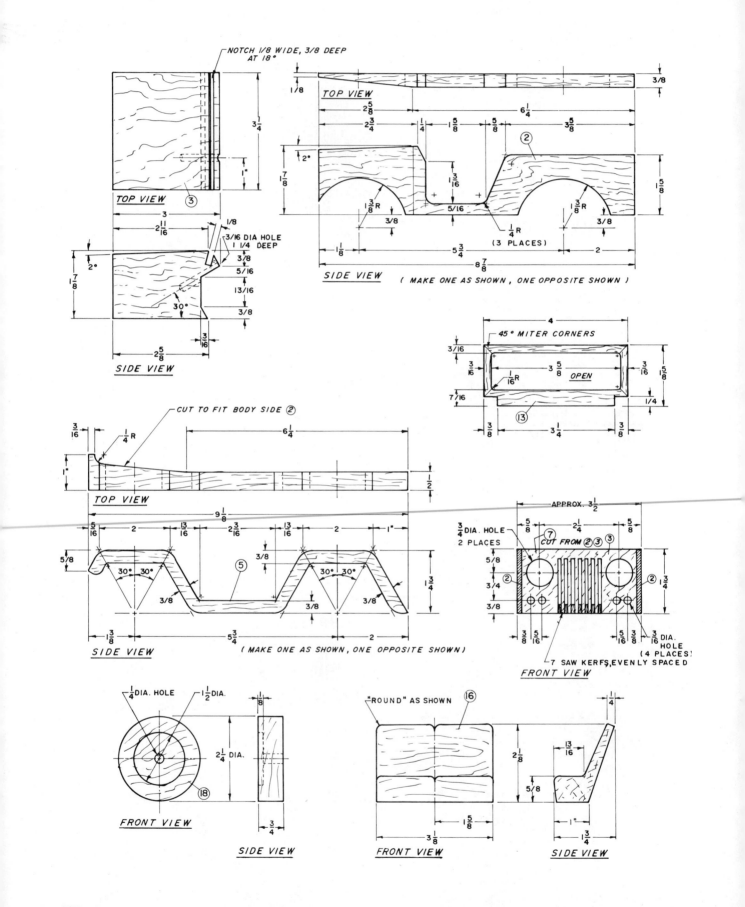

NOTCH 1/8 WIDE, 3/8 DEEP AT 18°

TOP VIEW ③

3¼

1"

3

2 11/16

1/8

3/16 DIA HOLE 1 1/4 DEEP

3/8

5/16

13/16

3/8

2°

1 7/8

30°

3/16

2 5/8

SIDE VIEW

1/8

TOP VIEW

3/8

2 5/8

2 3/4

¼

1 5/8

5/8

3 5/8

6¼

②

2°

1 7/8

1 3/16

3/8 R

3/8

5/16

¼ R (3 PLACES)

1 3/8 R

3/8

1 5/8

1⅛

5¾

2

8⅞

SIDE VIEW   (MAKE ONE AS SHOWN , ONE OPPOSITE SHOWN)

4

45° MITER CORNERS

3/16

3/16

3 5/8   OPEN

3/16

1/16 R

7/16

1/4

3/8

3 ¼

3/8

1 5/8

⑬

CUT TO FIT BODY SIDE ②

3/16

¼ R

1"

6¼

1½

TOP VIEW

9⅛

5/16

2

13/16

2 13/16

13/16

2

1"

5/8

30° 30°

3/8

30° 30°

⑤

3/8

3/8

3/8

1 3/4

1 3/8

5¾

2

SIDE VIEW   (MAKE ONE AS SHOWN, ONE OPPOSITE SHOWN)

APPROX. 3½

3/4 DIA. HOLE 2 PLACES

5/8

2¼

5/8

⑦ CUT FROM ② ③ ③

5/8

②

3/4

②

3/8

②

1 3/4

3/8 5/16

5/16 3/8

3/16 DIA. HOLE (4 PLACES)

7 SAW KERFS, EVENLY SPACED

FRONT VIEW

¼ DIA. HOLE

1½ DIA.

1/8

2¼ DIA.

⑱

3/4

FRONT VIEW

SIDE VIEW

"ROUND" AS SHOWN ⑯

¼

2⅛

5/8

13/16

1"

1 3/4

3⅛

1 5/8

FRONT VIEW

SIDE VIEW

130

Dump Truck

This toy truck is built for rugged play. I based the design on a couple of actual dump trucks, but if you want, you can omit the dump subassembly (parts 27, 28, 29, 30, 31, 32 and 33) to make a simpler utility truck.

You can buy treaded wheels, and I think their realism adds a lot to the project. You can order them from the source given in the Materials List.

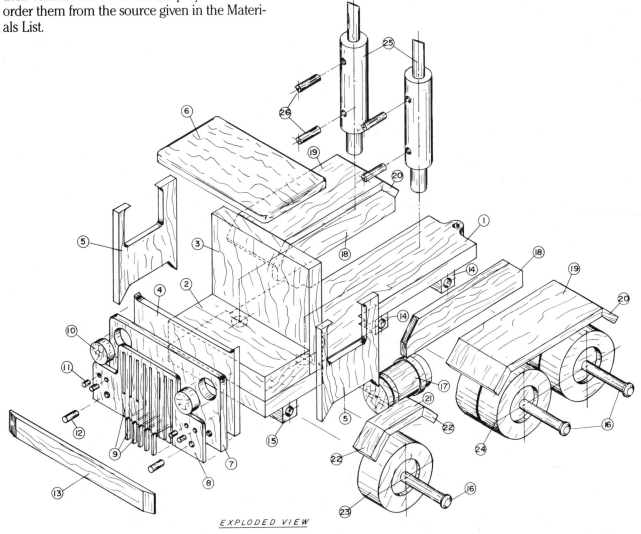

EXPLODED VIEW

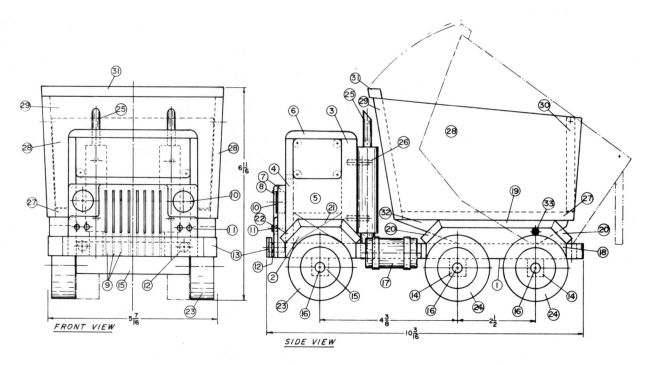

FRONT VIEW $5\frac{7}{16}$ $3\frac{7}{16}$

SIDE VIEW $4\frac{3}{8}$ $2\frac{1}{2}$ $10\frac{3}{16}$

This project looks difficult at first glance, but it fits together as nicely as a puzzle. Note that four parts are turned on a lathe.

1. Select the stock and cut the parts.
Use any hardwood for this one. I made the truck shown here out of ash.

Cut the parts to the sizes given in the Materials List. To save yourself the trouble of cutting tight radii in the corners of the cab front (part 4) and sides (part 5), lay out and drill the ¼-in.-diameter holes *before* cutting out the parts.

2. Lay out the parts and cut them to shape.
Use the measurements in the drawing to lay out the various parts. Drill all holes before cutting the parts to their final shapes so that the parts will be easier to hold.

If you're building the dump subassembly, drill the ¼-in.-diameter hole in the dump support (part 32) and use this hole as a guide for drilling the ¼-in.-diameter holes in the wheel housing (part 18).

As you cut out the parts, dry-fit them so that you can catch any errors at the earliest possible stage.

3. Turn the gas tanks and mufflers.
Turn the gas tanks (part 17) and mufflers (part 25) on a lathe. If you don't have a lathe, substitute dowels: Make the gas tanks from two 1⅝-in. lengths

of 1-in.-diameter dowel; make the mufflers from three dowels with diameters of ⅞ in., ¹¹⁄₁₆ in., and ¼ in.

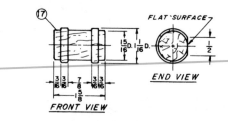

FRONT VIEW   END VIEW   FLAT SURFACE

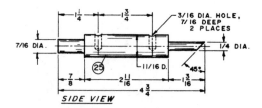

SIDE VIEW

4. Make subassemblies.
Assemble the truck in a series of smaller subassemblies.

First, make two rear wheel wells from parts 18, 19, and 20. Make front fender assemblies from parts 21 and 22. Make the grill subassembly from parts 7, 8, 9, 10, and 11. Make the cab from parts 2, 3, 4, 5, and 6 and dry-fit the cab to the base (part 1). Trim the base if necessary. Glue the cab to the base and then glue the grill subassembly to it.

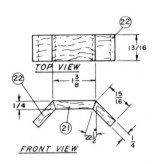

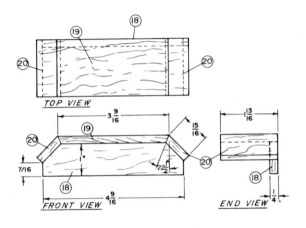

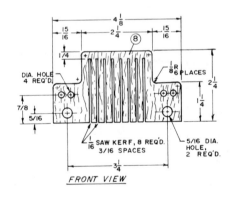

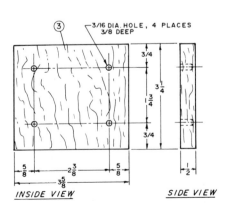

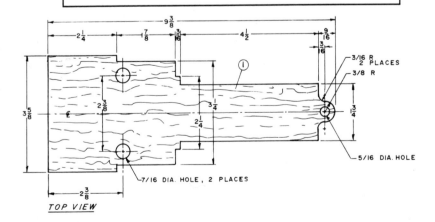

MATERIALS LIST

Part	Dimensions	Quantity
1. Base	$\frac{1}{2}" \times 3\frac{5}{8}" \times 9\frac{3}{8}"$	1
2. Seat	$1" \times 1\frac{1}{2}" \times 3\frac{5}{8}"$	1
3. Back	$\frac{1}{2}" \times 3\frac{5}{8}" \times 3\frac{1}{4}"$	1
4. Front	$\frac{1}{4}" \times 3\frac{5}{8}" \times 2\frac{5}{8}"$	1
5. Sides	$\frac{1}{4}" \times 2\frac{1}{4}" \times 3"$	2
6. Top	$\frac{1}{4}" \times 2\frac{1}{4}" \times 4\frac{1}{8}"$	1
7. Hood	$\frac{1}{4}" \times 4\frac{1}{8}" \times 2\frac{1}{4}"$	1
8. Grill	$\frac{1}{8}" \times 4\frac{1}{8}" \times 2\frac{1}{4}"$	1
9. Lower grills	$\frac{1}{16}" \times \frac{1}{8}" \times \frac{3}{4}"$	8
10. Headlights	$\frac{5}{8}"$ dia. $\times \frac{5}{16}"$	2
11. Parking lights	$\frac{3}{16}"$ dia. $\times \frac{3}{16}"$	4
12. Bumper supports	$\frac{5}{16}"$ dia. $\times \frac{9}{16}"$	2
13. Bumper	$\frac{3}{16}" \times \frac{5}{8}" \times 5\frac{5}{8}"$	1
14. Axle supports	$\frac{1}{2}" \times \frac{1}{2}" \times 2\frac{1}{4}"$	2
15. Axle support	$\frac{1}{2}" \times \frac{1}{2}" \times 3\frac{5}{8}"$	1
16. Axle pegs*	$\frac{5}{16}"$ dia. (length to suit)	6
17. Gas tanks	$\frac{1}{16}"$ dia. $\times 1\frac{5}{8}"$	2
18. Housings	$\frac{1}{4}" \times 1" \times 4\frac{9}{16}"$	2
19. Wheel tops	$\frac{1}{4}" \times 1\frac{13}{16}" \times 3\frac{9}{16}"$	2
20. Wheel ends	$\frac{1}{4}" \times 1\frac{13}{16}" \times \frac{15}{16}"$	4
21. Wheel tops	$\frac{1}{4}" \times \frac{13}{16}" \times 1\frac{3}{8}"$	2
22. Wheel ends	$\frac{1}{4}" \times \frac{13}{16}" \times \frac{15}{16}"$	4
23. Front wheels*	$\frac{3}{4}" \times 2"$ dia.	2
24. Rear wheels*	$\frac{3}{4}" \times 2"$ dia.	8
25. Mufflers	$\frac{11}{16}"$ dia. $\times 4\frac{3}{4}"$	2
26. Muffler supports	$\frac{3}{16}"$ dia. $\times \frac{3}{4}"$	4
27. Dump base	$\frac{1}{4}" \times 5" \times 5\frac{9}{16}"$	1
28. Dump sides	$\frac{1}{4}" \times 3\frac{3}{4}" \times 6\frac{3}{4}"$	2
29. Dump front	$\frac{1}{4}" \times 3\frac{7}{8}" \times 5\frac{7}{8}"$	1
30. Dump board	$\frac{1}{4}" \times 3" \times 5\frac{1}{4}"$	1
31. Top board	$\frac{5}{16}" \times \frac{1}{2}" \times 5\frac{7}{8}"$	1
32. Dump support	$\frac{3}{4}" \times 1\frac{3}{4}" \times 5\frac{9}{16}"$	1
33. Pin	$\frac{1}{4}"$ dia. $\times 2\frac{1}{4}"$	1

*Parts are available from Meisel Hardware Specialties, P.O. Box 70, Mound, MN 55364. Axle peg is #AP5, and wheels are #705020.

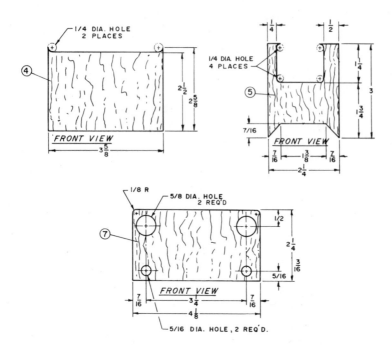

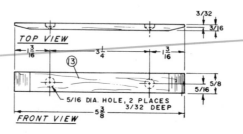

Cut the bumper (part 13). Drill holes in it for the bumper support (part 12). Glue one end of the bumper support in the bumper and the other end in the grill. Glue it in place.

Glue the rear wheel wells to the base. Fit the front fenders to the cab. You may have to notch the front fender slightly to fit over the hood. Glue the fenders in place.

Glue the muffler to the base and cab. Glue the gas tank in place.

Make the dump subassembly from parts 27, 28, 29, and 31 but don't attach the dump support (part 32) to it yet. Attach the dump board (part 30) with 4d finishing nails or ¾-in. lengths of ¹⁄₁₆-in.-diameter dowel. Be sure to drill before nailing to avoid splitting the wood. Check that the dump board moves freely.

5. *Dry-fit the wheels.* Order the axle pegs and wheels (parts 16 and 23). Drill holes in the supports to suit the peg length and diameter. Make sure the wheels turn freely but do not glue them in place.

Glue the six axle supports (parts 14 and 15) in place, as shown in the side view of the assembled truck. The given distances between the axle centers are only an approximate guide: Center the wheels within the wheel wells, as shown in this view.

6. *Add the dump subassembly.* If you don't care to have an operable dumping bed, simply glue the bed to the base. Otherwise, proceed as follows:

Enlarge the ¼-in.-diameter hole in the dump support with a ⁹⁄₃₂-in. drill bit. Attach the dump support to the truck by putting the pin (part 33) through the hole in one of the wheel wells, into the hole in the dump support, and out through the second wheel well.

Glue the dump to the dump support, positioning it so it will not hit any parts as it moves. Make sure that the dump subassembly looks centered when seen from the top, both sides, and the rear. Use large rubber bands to hold everything together until the glue sets.

7. *Apply finish.* The truck can be left unfinished, protected with clear varnish (as is the toy in the photo on page 131), or painted. Glue the axle pegs in place.

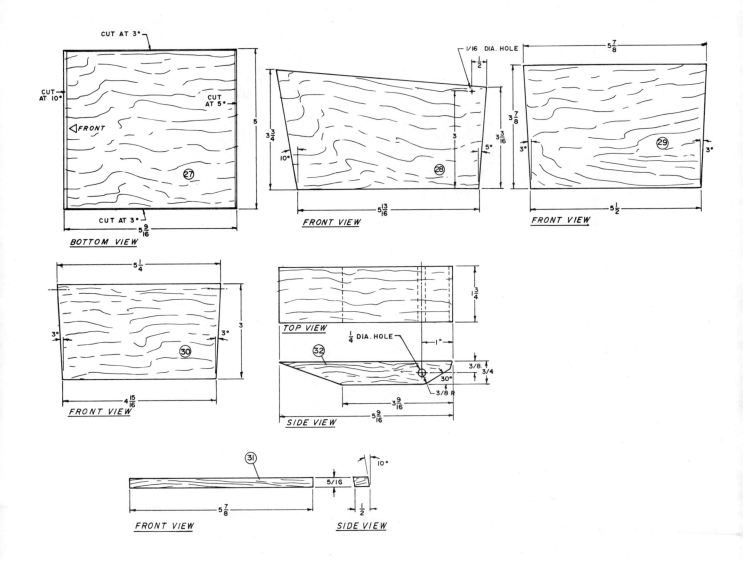

CUT AT 3°

CUT AT 10°

CUT AT 5°

◁FRONT

27

5

CUT AT 3°

5 9/16

BOTTOM VIEW

1/16 DIA. HOLE

1/2

3 3/4

3

10°

3 3/16

5°

28

5 13/16

FRONT VIEW

5 7/8

3 7/8

3°

29

3°

3°

5 1/2

FRONT VIEW

5 1/4

3°

3°

30

3

4 15/16

FRONT VIEW

1 3/4

TOP VIEW

1/4 DIA. HOLE

32

1"

3/8

3/4

30°

3/8 R

3 9/16

5 9/16

SIDE VIEW

31

5/16

10°

5 7/8

1/2

FRONT VIEW

SIDE VIEW

Tractor Trailer

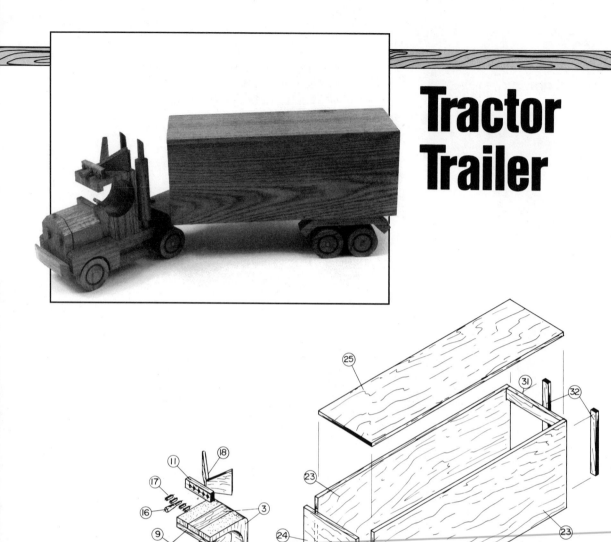

EXPLODED VIEW

I never really enjoyed making wooden toys until I tackled this project. Now I face the job of making a fleet of them for my nieces, nephews, and granddaughter.

1. Select the stock and cut the parts. For durability I suggest making all toys from a hardwood. This tractor trailer was made out of oak.

You'll find the parts that require shaping (parts 2, 3, 5, 12, 18, 22, 27, and 29) will be easier to shape if you leave them slightly longer and wider than given in the Materials List. Cut the balance of the parts to the dimensions given in the Materials List.

Note that the three ¾-in.-thick blocks glued up to make the cab (part 3) are not identical. The grain in the center piece is perpendicular to the grain of the outside pieces. This cross-grain structure strengthens the roof of the cab. Glue the cab together before you shape it.

2. Transfer the patterns and cut the parts to shape. Draw full-size patterns and transfer them to the wood. If you anticipate mass-producing a fleet of trucks, make sturdy patterns out of cardboard or thin plywood.

Before cutting the final shapes, drill all the holes, as shown in the drawings. Note that both front fenders are made by drilling a hole into a single oversized piece and then cutting the piece to form two fenders. To prevent tear-out, you can use Forstner bits to drill this hole and the 2-in.-hole in the cab. Drill a ¼-in.-diameter hole through the axle supports (parts 7, 8, and 28).

Cut the parts to their final shapes. Saw the kerfs in the hood (part 2) and cab, as shown in the details for those parts. Sand the parts all over.

3. Make the stacks and wheels. You can turn the stacks (part 6) on a lathe, or you can glue them up from dowels. If you make them from dowels, drill holes ¾ in. deep in the ends of the center dowel to accept the other two dowels.

The wheels (part 20) can be made with an adjustable circle cutter in a drill press. First, set the cutter to score a shallow 1⅛-in.-diameter groove that defines the edge between the tire and wheel. Then set the cutter to a diameter of 1¾ in. and cut out the wheel. If necessary, redrill the center hole to fit the axle.

4. Assemble the tractor. Assemble the tractor, as shown in the exploded view. For durability, you can epoxy the stacks in the holes in the base. Wait until after you've applied a finish to attach the wheels.

5. Assemble the trailer. Assemble parts 22, 23, 24, 25, 27, 31, and 32, being sure that everything is square. Wait until after you've applied a finish to attach the wheels.

6. Finish the tractor trailer. The toy can be left unfinished (as in the photo on page 136), or you can varnish or paint it. Glue the flaps (part 30) to the back of the rear fenders. They can be made of canvas or a similar heavy, flexible material. Complete the project by attaching the wheels. I placed a flat washer between each pair of rear wheels to space them more realistically.

MATERIALS LIST

Part	Dimensions	Quantity
1. Base	⅝″ × 2¼″ × 7¼″	1
2. Hood	2″ × 2¼″ × 2¼″	1
3. Cab parts	¾″ × 2½″ × 3¾″	3
4. Step	⅝″ × 1¹⁵/₁₆″ × 3¼″	1
5. Spacer	⅜″ × 1³/₁₆″ × 1¹¹/₁₆″	1
6. Stacks	⅝″ dia. × 5½″	2
7. Front axle support	⅝″ × ⅝″ × 2¼″	1
8. Rear axle support	⅝″ × ⅝″ × 1³/₁₆″	1
9. Brace	¼″ × ¼″ × 2¼″	1
10. Bumper	³/₁₆″ × ⅝″ × 3¼″	1
11. Light support	⁵/₁₆″ × ⁷/₁₆″ × 2″	1
12. Front fender	½″ × 2⅞″ × 3¼″	1
13. Bumper spacers	¼″ dia. × ½″	2
14. Headlights	⅝″ dia. × ³/₁₆″	2
15. Cap	¼″ dia. × ⅜″	1
16. Horn	⅜″ dia. × 1″	1
17. Clearance lights	¼″ dia. × ⁷/₁₆″	4
18. Wind deflectors	³/₁₆″ × 1⅜″ × 1½″	2
19. Steering wheel	¾″ dia. × 1⅛″	1
20. Wheels	½″ × 1¾″ dia.	14
21. Front axles	¼″ dia. × 3⁵/₁₆″	2
22. Trailer base	½″ × 3½″ × 14⅛″	1
23. Trailer sides	¼″ × 4½″ × 12½″	2
24. Trailer front	¼″ × 4″ × 3½″	1
25. Trailer top	¼″ × 4″ × 12½″	1
26. Pin	⁵/₁₆″ dia. × 1⁹/₁₆″	1
27. Axle spacers	½″ × 1″ × 3⅝″	2
28. Axle supports	⅝″ × ⅝″ × 1¹⁵/₁₆″	2
29. Rear fenders	1¹/₁₆″ × 1″ × 5″	2
30. Flaps	¹/₃₂″ × ¾″ × 1¹/₁₆″	2
31. Top rail	¼″ × ½″ × 3½″	1
32. Side stiles	¼″ × ⅜″ × 3½″	2
33. Rear axles	¼″ dia. × 4¹/₁₆″	2

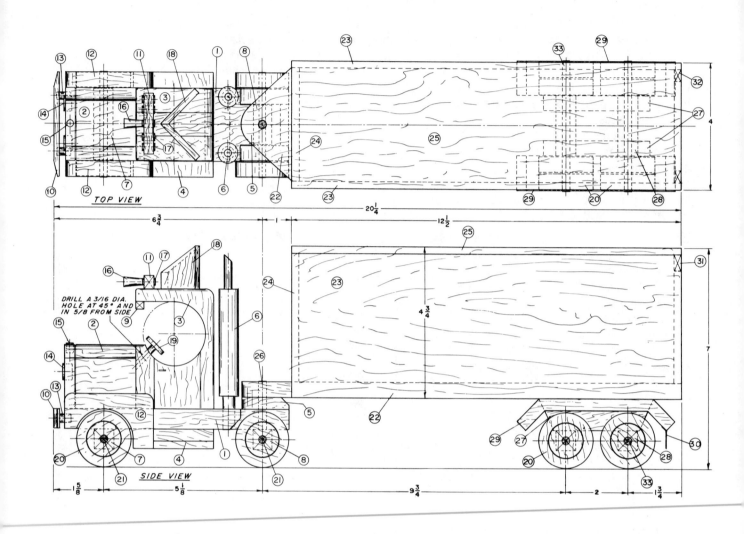

TOP VIEW

SIDE VIEW

DRILL A 3/16 DIA.
HOLE AT 45° AND
IN 5/8 FROM SIDE

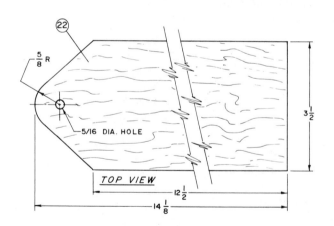

5/8 R

5/16 DIA. HOLE

TOP VIEW

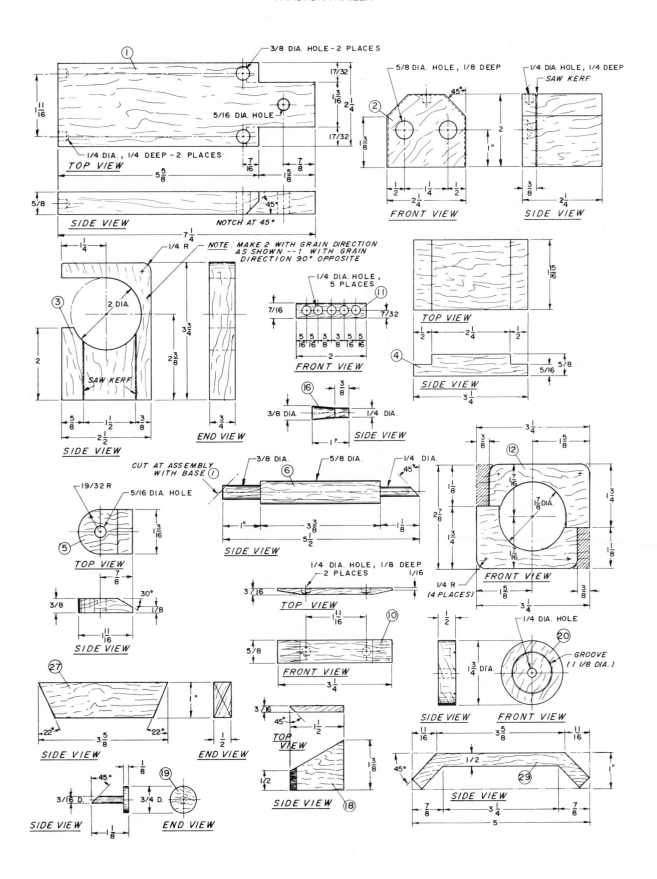

Merry-Go-Round

This is a copy of an antique toy merry-go-round I saw for sale at a shop in northern New Hampshire. You simply turn the platform to wind the strings around the pole and then let it go. The animals will spin back and forth several times—a simple effect, but one that seems to fascinate children forever. I've substituted wild circus animals for the four horses on the original in order to add more color.

As you look at the drawings, note that the platform supporting the animals rotates independently from the pole and base.

1. Select the stock and cut the parts. The platform and animals are made from ½-in. stock; the base is ¾ in. thick. Make the animals from straight-grained stock.

Cut the parts to the sizes given in the Materials List. The base (part 1) and platform (part 2) are circles. Locate and drill a ⁵⁄₁₆-in.-diameter hole in the center of the base and a ⅜-in.-diameter hole in the center of the platform. The pole (part 3) should fit snugly in the hole in the base while allowing the platform to rotate freely.

2. Make a pattern for the animals and cut them out. On paper, draw a grid with ¼-in. squares and enlarge the animals (part 5, 6, 7, and 8) onto it. Include the painted details in the enlargement and be sure to lay out the hole for the mounting stick (parts 9, 10, 11, and 12). Transfer the patterns to the wood. Before cutting the animals to shape, drill the holes for the mounting sticks. Cut out the animals with a jigsaw, coping saw, or band saw.

MATERIALS LIST

Part	Dimensions	Quantity
1. Base	¾″ × 6″ dia.	1
2. Platform	½″ × 7½″ dia.	1
3. Pole	⁵⁄₁₆″ dia. × 12⅛″	1
4. Tip ball	¾″ dia.	1
5. Camel	½″ × 3″ × 3¼″	1
6. Lion	½″ × 2″ × 3¼″	1
7. Bear	½″ × 2¼″ × 4″	1
8. Elephant	½″ × 3½″ × 7″	1
9. Camel mounting stick	³⁄₁₆″ dia. × 4″	1
10. Lion mounting stick	³⁄₁₆″ dia. × 2¾″	1
11. Bear mounting stick	³⁄₁₆″ dia. × 2⅞″	1
12. Elephant mounting stick	³⁄₁₆″ dia. × 4½″	1
13. Balls	½″ dia.	8
14. Feet	½″ dia.	4
15. Colored twine	24″	2
16. Roundhead screws		4

3. *Drill holes in the balls.* I purchased the balls (part 13) for the merry-go-round through the mail. Several good mail-order sources are listed in the appendix. Drill ³/₁₆-in. diameter holes, ¼ in. deep in four of the ½ in. balls. These balls will go atop the sticks supporting the animals. In the other four balls, drill ¹/₁₆-in.-diameter holes all the way through. The twine that runs from the platform to the top of the pole will be threaded through these balls. Drill a ⁵/₁₆-in.-diameter hole in the ¾-in.-diameter tip ball (part 4), ³/₈ in. deep Make two cuts with a backsaw at the top of the pole to take the twine; they should be ½ in. deep and at right angles to each other.

4. *Assemble the merry-go-round.* Glue the mane on the lion and the ears on the elephant. Drill a ¹/₁₆-in.-diameter hole for a tail in each of the animals. Glue a thick string tail in the hole in the lion and ¹/₁₆-in.-diameter dowel tails in the other three animals.

Glue the animals on the sticks, as shown in the patterns for each. Glue the balls on top of the four sticks. Drill ³/₁₆-in.-diameter holes through the platform for each stick; the holes are placed at equal intervals around a 6½-in.-diameter circle centered on the platform. Drill ¹/₁₆-in.-diameter holes in the platform for the string: These holes are on a 6¼-in.-diameter circle and are located midway between the animals.

Place the platform over the center post and see if it rotates freely. If not, sand either the post or the hole in the platform.

Cut two 24-in. lengths of colored twine (part 15). As shown in the side view, tie a knot at one end of each length; thread it up through a hole in the platform and add a ½-in. diameter ball. Pass the thread through a notch at the top of the post and reverse the entire process on the other side. Tie the final knot so that the platform is suspended about ⅛ in. above the base. Press the tip ball over the top of the post to hold the twine in place.

5. *Apply finish.* Remove the tip ball and twine and paint the toy with the colors of your choice. Follow the lines transferred onto the animals. I painted the rest of the merry-go-round white, except for the red paint on the balls and on the triangle decoration around the platform edge. Unless you paint the animals before assembly, you might want to mask the platform to protect it from paint splatters.

To make the triangle pattern on the edge of the platform, first paint the platform its base color and allow the paint to dry completely. Attach a strip of masking tape around it and make a mark every 10 degrees (approximately ¹¹/₁₆ in.), as shown in the side view. Use these marks to lay out the triangles. Cut out the lower row of triangles with an X-ACTO knife and paint the spaces with a contrasting color. When this second coat of paint has dried, peel off the rest of the tape.

Reassemble the toy, and attach the four plastic or rubber feet (part 14) with screws.

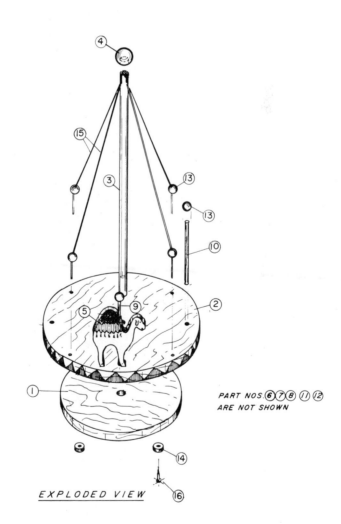

PART NOS. ⑥⑦⑧ ⑪ ⑫ ARE NOT SHOWN

EXPLODED VIEW

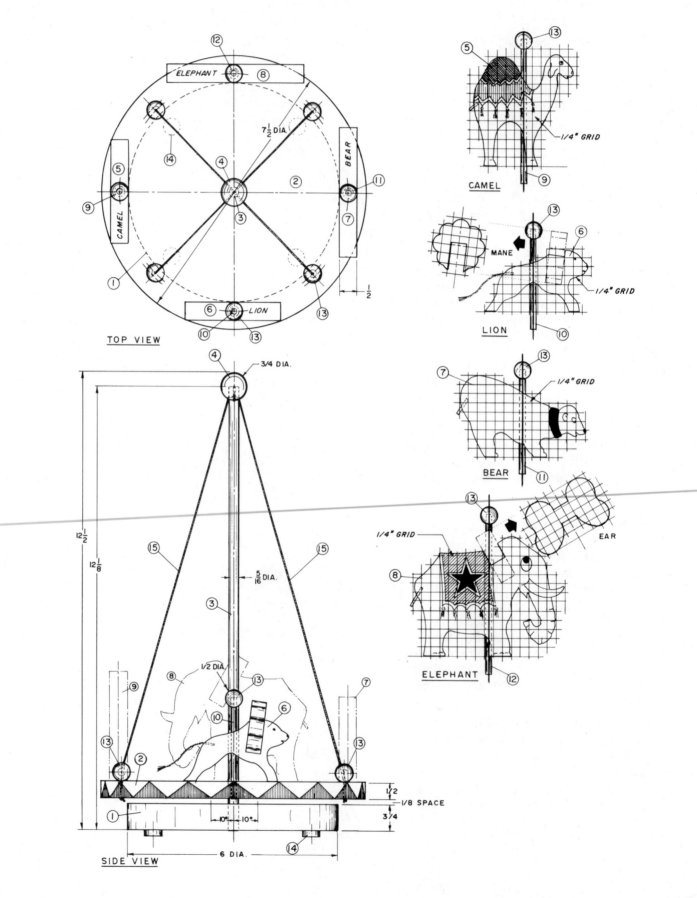

TOP VIEW

7½ DIA.

½

ELEPHANT

BEAR

CAMEL

LION

CAMEL

1/4" GRID

LION

1/4" GRID

MANE

BEAR

1/4" GRID

1/4" GRID

ELEPHANT

EAR

SIDE VIEW

3/4 DIA.

12½

12⅛

5/16 DIA.

1/2 DIA.

1/2

1/8 SPACE

3/4

10°   10°

6 DIA.

142

Circus Toy

There are a lot of details in this one, but none of them are particularly difficult. Because the toy will appeal to small children, take great care to glue the parts securely. Annular (or ring) nails are used to help keep the wheels and magnets in place.

1. *Select the stock and cut the parts.* Use any wood for the wagon; the animals should be hardwood for durability. In selecting wood for the animals, arrange the shapes so that thin areas will run with the grain, such as along the neck of the giraffe. Note that the clown is cut from two stock thicknesses. The more unusual hardware items can be ordered from the source given in the Materials List.

Leave parts that require shaping slightly longer and wider than listed in the Materials List and cut them to size as you shape. Cut the rest of the parts to the sizes given in the Materials List.

2. *Cut the wagon parts to shape.* Cut a notch in the base (part 1) to take the ramp, as shown in the section view at A-A.

Cut the ends of the long and short top rails (parts 2 and 3) to make tight-fitting lap joints, as shown in the side and end views. Glue the four rails together to make a frame, checking to see that it is square; the overall dimensions of this frame should be exactly the same as those of the base.

Drill the holes for the bars (part 4) next: Lay out the holes on the bottom of the base. Clamp the top support on top of the base, lining up the sides exactly. Using a stop on a drill bit or drill press, drill each of the holes for the bars through the base and 5⁄8 in. into the supports. This ensures that the holes will be aligned for the bars.

Rout coves in the base and top rails with a 1⁄8-in.-radius cove bit and a ball-bearing guide. The profile of the cove is shown in the view at C-C. The section view at A-A shows the location of the coves.

Cut the bars and chamfer the edges slightly so that they will fit into place more easily. Glue the bars into the base and allow the glue to dry before adding the top support frame to the bars. Make sure the support and base are parallel and 7¼-in. apart, as shown in the side view.

Next, cut the four axle supports (part 5) to the shape shown in the side view. It's easiest if you chamfer a long block and cut it to form the four axle supports. Drill a 3⁄8-in.-diameter axle hole through the center of each support.

Cut the two axles (part 6) and chamfer the ends slightly. Temporarily slide the axles through the axle supports to align the supports. Position the supports, as shown in the side and end views. After the glue sets, reinforce the joint with finishing nails (part 32).

3. *Make the ramp.* Cut the ramp (part 8) to shape and saw the 1⁄16-in.-deep kerfs, as shown in the side view, with a hand saw. Drill the 3⁄16-in.-diameter holes in the base for the ramp hinge pins (part 9).

CIRCUS TOY

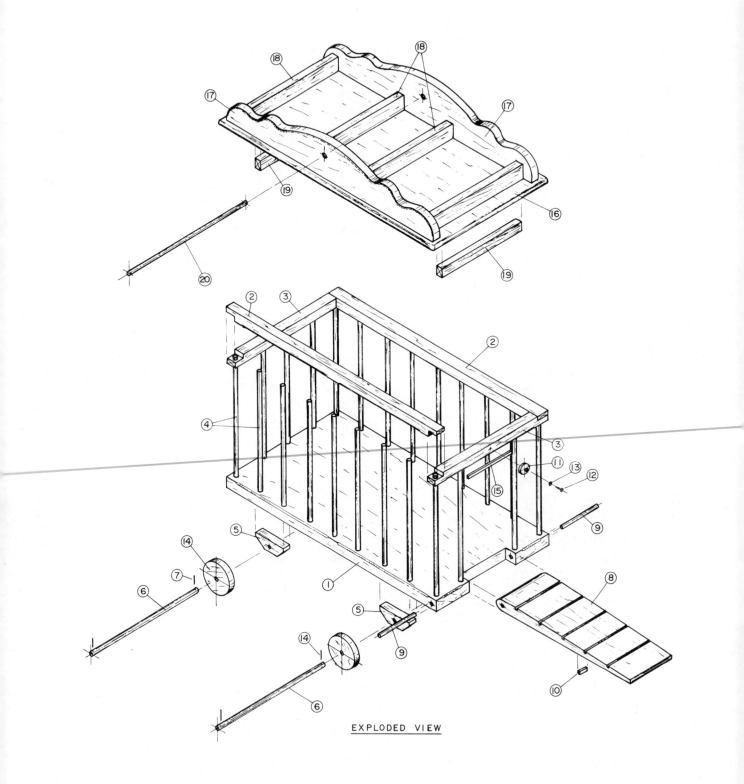

EXPLODED VIEW

144

To hang the ramp, drill through the holes you just made from the base into the ramp. Drill about 1 in. from each side into the ramp. Put the ramp temporarily in place. Before gluing the hinge pins in place, make sure that the ramp works as it should. Make necessary adjustments so that the ramp closes just below the short top support. Then glue the ramp hinges in place, taking care to glue them to the base only. Add the ramp stop (part 15) to the short top support.

Glue the ramp handle (part 10) to the ramp, as shown.

The ramp lock (part 11) is simply a ¼-in.-thick slice of a ¾-in.-diameter dowel mounted through an off-center hole. Drill a clearance hole for the screw ³/₁₆ in. from the center of the dowel. Counterbore it to take a #4 × 1-in. roundhead screw and #4 washer (parts 12 and 13); Screw the ramp lock to the top support.

4. Make the wagon wheels. The wheels (part 20) can be made with an adjustable circle cutter in a drill press.

Cut the wheels (part 14) from ⅝-in.-thick stock with an adjustable circle cutter. First, set the cutter to score a shallow 2¼-in.-diameter groove that defines the edge between the tire and wheel, as shown in the detail of the wagon wheel. Then set the cutter to a diameter of 2⅞ in. and cut out the wheel. If necessary, redrill the center hole to fit the axle.

Put the axles temporarily in the axle supports, slide on the wheels, and mark the proper location of the wheel pins on the axles. Allow about ¹/₃₂-in. clearance between the wheels and the base, then drill the ⅛-in.-diameter holes for the pins. Cut the four wheel pins (part 7), but do not drill holes for them yet.

5. Make the top board and trim. Rout the edges of the top board (part 16) with a ⅛-in.-radius router bit and sand to the profile shown.

On paper, draw a grid with ½-in. squares and enlarge the top trim (part 17) onto it. Transfer the pattern to the stock and cut the trim to shape. To make certain the two trim pieces will match, attach them to one another with rubber cement or double-sided tape and then cut them out. Drill the ⁵/₁₆-in.-diameter hole and sand the edges before taking them apart. Rout a ⅛-in.-radius cove in the edge, as shown in the view at B-B. Don't cut all the way to the edges, as indicated by the side view.

MATERIALS LIST

Part	Dimensions	Quantity
1. Base	¾" × 7¼" × 13¾"	1
2. Long top supports	¾" × ¾" × 13¾"	2
3. Short top supports	¾" × ¾" × 7¼"	2
4. Bars	⁵/₁₆" dia. × 7⅛"	23
5. Axle supports	¾" × ¾" × 2¼"	4
6. Axles	⅜" dia. × 9"	2
7. Wheel pins	⅛" dia. × ¾"	4
8. Ramp	¾" × 3¹/₁₆" × 5¾"	1
9. Ramp hinges	³/₁₆" dia. × 3"	2
10. Ramp handle	¼" × ¼" × 1"	1
11. Ramp lock	¾" dia. × ¼"	1
12. Roundhead screw	#4 × 1"	1
13. Flat washer	#4	1
14. Wagon wheels	2⅞" dia. × ⅝"	4
15. Ramp stop	¼" × ¼" × 3¼"	1
16. Top board	⁵/₁₆" × 7½" × 14"	1
17. Top trim	⁹/₁₆" × 2⅛" × 13¾"	2
18. Braces	⅝" × ¾" × 6"	4
19. Cleats	⅝" × ¾" × 5¾"	2
20. Ladder support	⁵/₁₆" dia. × 8"	1
21. Ladder rails	⅜" × ¾" × 14½"	4
22. Ladder rungs	¼" dia. × 2½"	18
23. Animals	¾" × 8" × 54" (makes 7)	1
24. Animal wheels	1¼" dia. × ⁵/₁₆"	32
25. Ball	1⅝" dia. × ¾"	1
26. Magnets*	½" dia.	17
27. Roundhead annular nails*	¾"	18
28. Flathead annular nails*	¾"	32
29. Clown body	½" × 2" × 5"	1
30. Clown arms/legs	¼" × 2" × 6"	2 each
31. Post and screw*	2" × 1⅛"	1 each
32. Finishing nails	4d	as needed

Hardware is available from Cherry Tree Toys, Inc., P.O. Box 369, Belmont, OH 43718. Magnets are #430, roundhead annular nails are #410, flathead annular nails are #420, and post and screw is #908.

Glue the top trim to the top board. For now, glue only the front and back braces (part 18) to the trim and top board, placing them about 1 in. from the front and back of the top. You will add the two inner braces later.

Glue the two cleats (part 19) to the underside of the top, allowing approximately ¹/₁₆-in. clearance with the top support frame. The cleats serve to keep the top, which is removable, centered on the wagon.

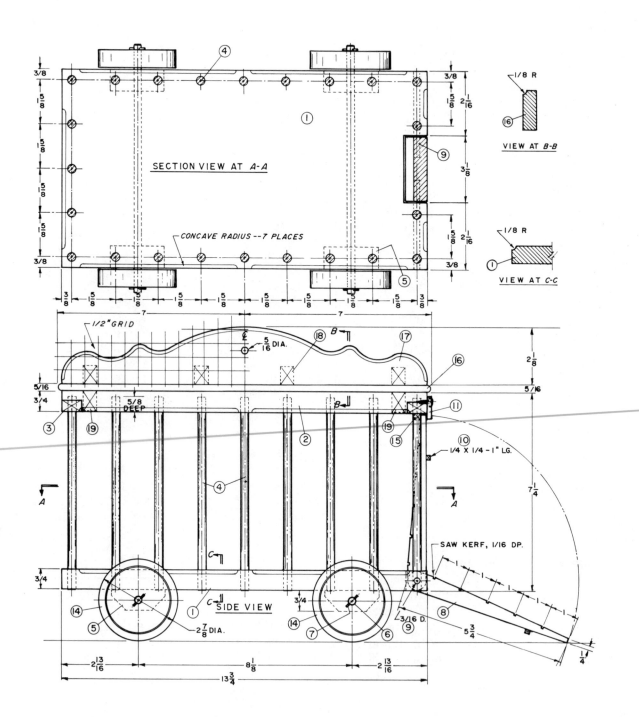

SECTION VIEW AT *A-A*

CONCAVE RADIUS -- 7 PLACES

VIEW AT *B-B*

1/8 R

VIEW AT *C-C*

1/8 R

1/2" GRID

5/16 DIA.

5/8 DEEP

2 7/8 DIA.

SIDE VIEW

SAW KERF, 1/16 DP.

1/4 X 1/4 – 1" LG.

3/16 D.

6. ***Make the ladders.*** There are two ladders. One is attached to the roof by the ladder support (part 20). The other ladder simply leans against the wagon.

Drill rung holes in the ladder rails and drill the hole for the ladder support, as shown in the detail of the ladder. Make sure that the holes on the pairs of rails are aligned. Glue up the rails and rungs (parts 21 and 22), keeping everything square.

Round the ends of the ladder support. Attach the ladder to the wagon by running the ladder support through the holes both in the top trim and in the ladder rails; glue the support in the holes in the trim. Position the two remaining braces so that they keep the ladder at roughly a 60-degree angle. Glue the braces in place and tack them in place when the glue has dried.

7. ***Cut the animal and clown parts to shape.*** The wagon is done; now it's time to build a clown and some animals for it. Sand the face of the boards from which you'll cut the animals before making any cuts. It will make the job of sanding easier later. Draw the patterns on a ½-in. grid; transfer the patterns to the wood and cut out the parts.

The animal wheels (part 24) are ⁵⁄₁₆-in.-thick slices of 1¼-in. dowel. Counterbore the wheels so the heads of the nails that attach them will be recessed. If you have a drill press, a simple jig makes this easy.

To make the jig, clamp a piece of scrap to the drill press. Drill a 1¼-in.-diameter hole ¼ in. deep in the scrap. Without moving the scrap, put a ⅜-in.-diameter bit in the chuck. Set the depth stops for a hole ⅛ in. deep. Put each wheel in turn into the jig and drill the counterbore. Then put a drill bit, slightly wider than the annual nails that will hold the wheels in place, into the drill press. Drill holes through all the wheels.

Glue the ears on the elephant, the mane on the lion, and the assorted tails on the animals.

8. ***Apply finish.*** Paint the circus wagon and animals with bright, nontoxic colors. For inspiration, you might go to the library for a book with color photos of circuses.

9. ***Add the magnets and wheels and assemble the clown.*** After the paint has dried, attach the ceramic magnets (part 26) with roundhead

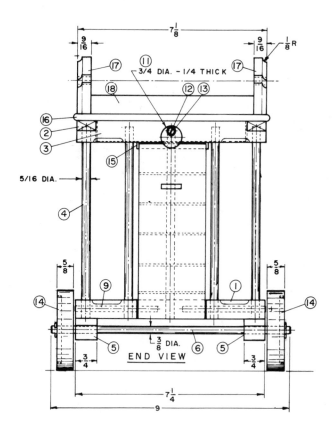

annular nails (part 27). The polarity of the magnets is marked with plus and minus symbols; make sure that all of the pluses are at the front and the minuses at the back, or the animals won't parade around obediently. The seal gets a roundhead nail in its nose (part 23) to attract the magnet in the ball (part 25).

When attaching the animal wheels, put a bit of candle wax into the counterbored holes for lubrication. Attach the wheels to the bodies with flathead annular nails (part 28).

Attach the wagon wheels to the wagon. Glue the wheel pins in place.

Assemble the clown (parts 29 and 30) with a self-locking post and screw (part 31). If necessary for a snug fit, place thin flat washers between the body and the arms and legs. Make sure that the posts and screws are very tight so that they won't come apart in a child's hands. Check them for tightness from time to time. You might ask at a hardware store for a special adhesive that locks threaded parts and use it on the screw.

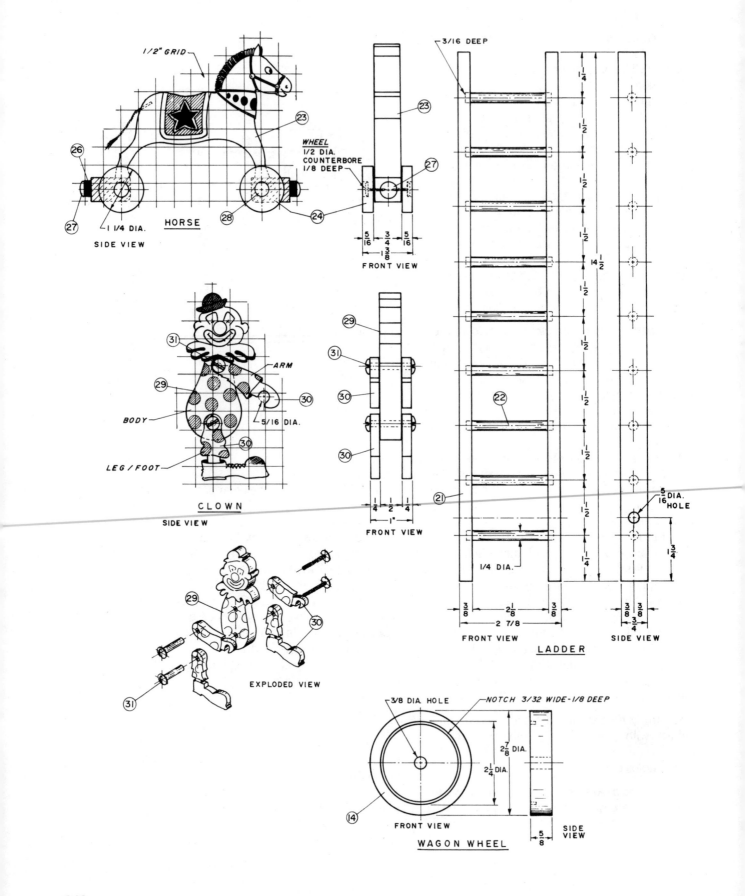

1/2" GRID

WHEEL
1/2 DIA.
COUNTERBORE
1/8 DEEP

HORSE

SIDE VIEW

1 1/4 DIA.

FRONT VIEW

3/16 DEEP

ARM

BODY

5/16 DIA.

LEG/FOOT

CLOWN

SIDE VIEW

FRONT VIEW

1/4 DIA.

LADDER

FRONT VIEW

SIDE VIEW

5/16 DIA. HOLE

14 1/2

1 1/4
1 1/2
1 1/2
1 1/2
1 1/2
1 1/2
1 1/2
1 1/2
1 1/2
1 1/4

3/8   2 1/8   3/8
2 7/8

3/8 3/8
3/4

1 3/4

EXPLODED VIEW

3/8 DIA HOLE

NOTCH 3/32 WIDE-1/8 DEEP

2 7/8 DIA.

2 1/4 DIA.

FRONT VIEW

SIDE VIEW

5/8

WAGON WHEEL

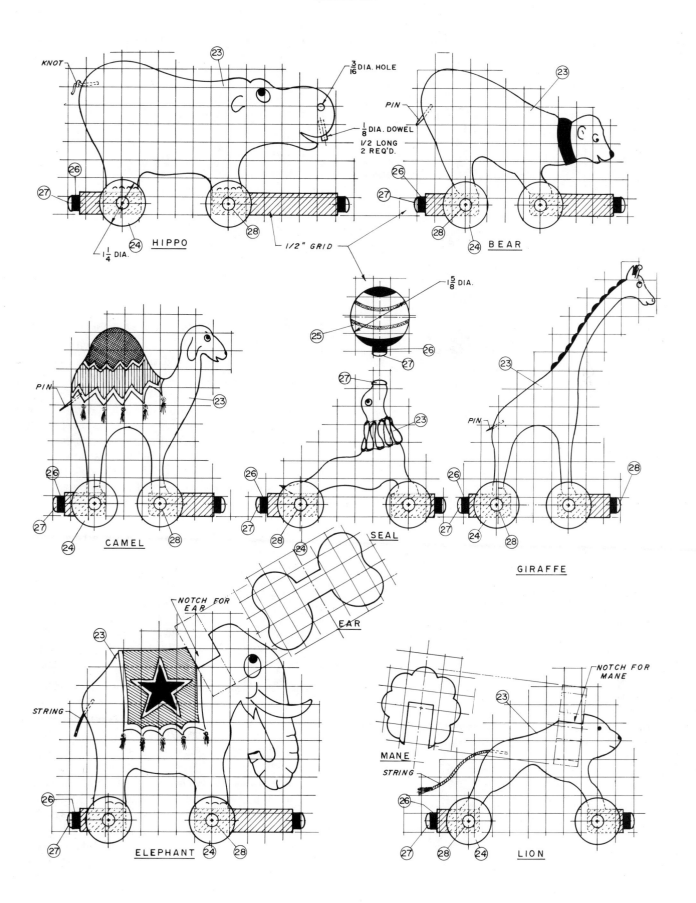

Flying Elephant Toy

Who says that elephants can't fly? When you spin the top of this toy, the animals swing out on their dowels. Kids seem to be quite enchanted by the simple mechanics of the flying elephants.

The project will go more quickly if you have an electric scroll saw, but you can make do with a jigsaw. Be forewarned that you're apt to spend a lot more time painting than cutting, especially if you follow an intricate decoration scheme.

1. *Select the stock and cut the parts.* This project requires several thicknesses of wood, so consult the Materials List before getting underway. Cut the parts to their overall sizes as given in the Materials List. Note that the base (part 1) is circular.

Cut the five dowels (part 8) to length and drill a 1/16-in.-diameter hole through the center of each, 7/8 in. from one end, as shown in the front view. Drill a 5/16-in.-diameter hole into an end of the center post (part 4), 1/2 in. deep. Slightly chamfer that end.

2. *Make the stars.* Use a compass to lay out the three star patterns on the wood. The technique is fairly straightforward. Follow the same procedure I described for making the elephant table lamp on page 14. Alter the dimensions as needed.

Cut a total of five stars: one large star (part 5) and two each of the medium and small stars (parts 2 and 3). Cut slots in the large star for the dowels that hold the elephant: Drill three 3/16-in.-diameter holes in a row and file the surfaces until flat and smooth. Drill the rest of the

MATERIALS LIST

Part	Dimensions	Quantity
1. Base	3/4" × 9½" dia.	1
2. Medium stars	3/8" × 4" dia.	2
3. Small stars	1/4" × 2" dia.	2
4. Center post	5/8" dia. × 8¾"	1
5. Large star	1/2" × 9" dia.	1
6. Wooden pin	5/16" dia. × 1⅛"	1
7. Finial ball	5/8" dia.	1
8. Dowels	3/16" dia. × 6⅜"	5
9. Steel pins	1/32" dia. × 3/4"	5
10. Bodies	5/8" × 5" × 5"	5
11. Ears	5/16" × 2½" × 4"	5
12. Saddles	1/8" × 1" × 1⅜"	10
13. Riders	5/8" dia. × 1"	5
14. Tails	1/8" dia. × 1"	5
15. Top balls	1/2" dia.	5
16. Feet	1/2" dia.	4

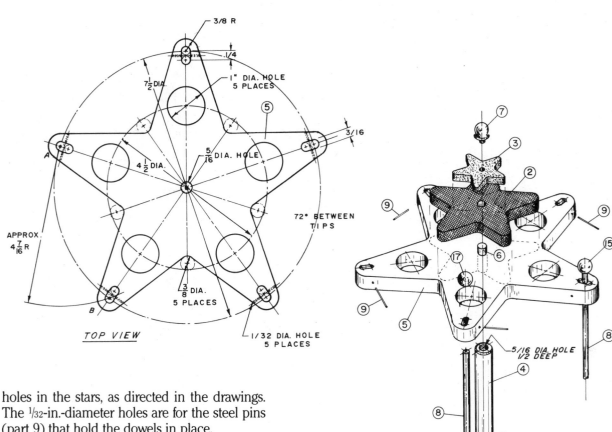

TOP VIEW

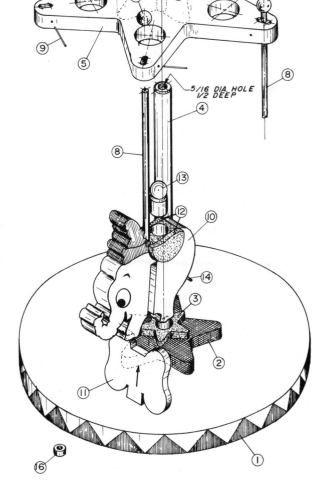

EXPLODED VIEW

holes in the stars, as directed in the drawings. The 1/32-in.-diameter holes are for the steel pins (part 9) that hold the dowels in place.

3. *Make a paper pattern for the elephant.* Draw a grid with 1/2-in. squares and enlarge the body (part 10) and the ears (part 11) and the saddle (part 12) onto it. Note on the body pattern the location and angle of the holes to be drilled for the dowel, rider, and tail. Transfer the pattern to pieces of wood and cut them out. To save time and ensure consistency, you can stack all five pieces for each part and tape them together with doubled-sided tape. Cut the entire stack at once. Sand the edges and separate the parts.

Glue the ears and saddles (two for each elephant) to the body. Cut the tail (part 14) from a 1/8-in.-diameter dowel or whittle it from a dry twig.

Lay out and drill holes for the rider, the tail, and the dowel in each body.

4. *Assemble the merry-go-round.* Glue a small star on top of a medium star and glue the medium star on top of the large star, aligning them as shown in the top view. When the glue has dried, drill a 5/16-in.-diameter hole from the bottom of the center of the large star, halfway through the medium star. Drill a smaller hole for the finial ball (part 7) down through the center of the small star.

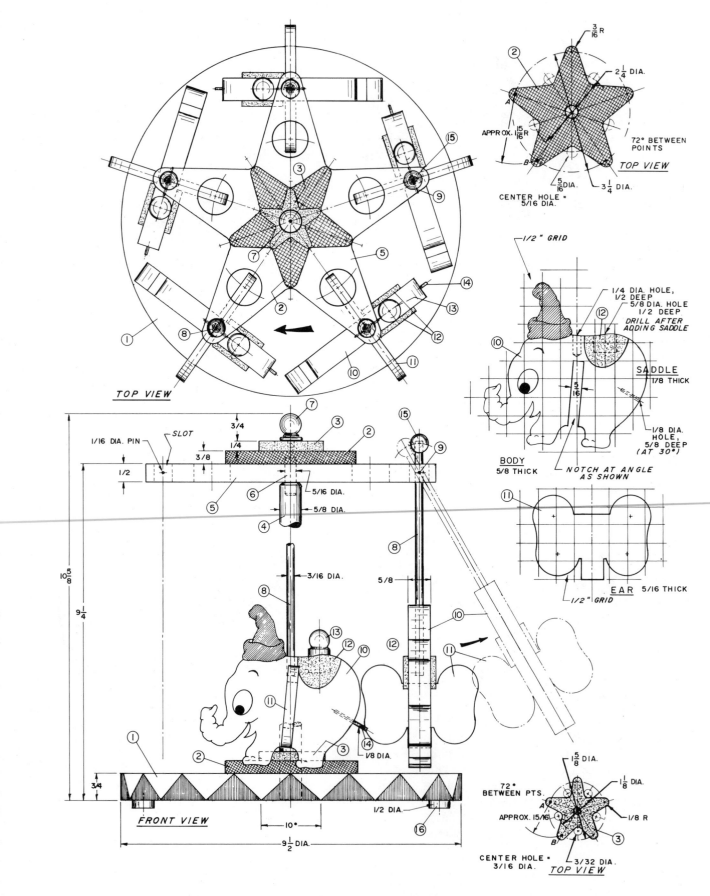

TOP VIEW

③④R

2¼ DIA.

APPROX. 1⁵⁄₁₆ R

72° BETWEEN POINTS

⁵⁄₁₆ DIA.

3¼ DIA.

TOP VIEW

CENTER HOLE = 5/16 DIA.

1/2" GRID

1/4 DIA. HOLE, 1/2 DEEP

5/8 DIA. HOLE 1/2 DEEP

DRILL AFTER ADDING SADDLE

SADDLE 1/8 THICK

5/16

1/8 DIA. HOLE, 5/8 DEEP (AT 30°)

BODY 5/8 THICK

NOTCH AT ANGLE AS SHOWN

EAR 5/16 THICK

1/2" GRID

TOP VIEW

3/4

1/4

3/8

1/2

SLOT

1/16 DIA. PIN

5/16 DIA.

5/8 DIA.

3/16 DIA.

5/8

1/8 DIA.

10⁵⁄₈

9¼

3/4

FRONT VIEW

10°

1/2 DIA.

9½ DIA.

1⁵⁄₈ DIA.

1⅛ DIA.

1/8 R

72° BETWEEN PTS.

APPROX. 15/16

CENTER HOLE = 3/16 DIA.

3/32 DIA.

TOP VIEW

152

Place the wooden pin (part 6) into the hole in the top of the center post, and make sure that it rotates freely; if not, sand the pin a bit. Glue the wooden pin into the hole in the bottom of the stars.

Now mount the remaining stars on the base. Glue the remaining small star to the remaining medium star and glue the medium star to the base. When the glue has dried, drill a ⅝-in.-diameter hole for the center post through the center of the small star, medium star, and base; a Forstner bit will help prevent the small star from splitting. Glue the center post into this hole, making the bottom of the post flush with the bottom surface of the base.

5. *Attach the elephants.* Glue a ³⁄₁₆-in.-diameter dowel into each body. Put the top ends of the dowels through the slots in the large star and hold them in place with the steel pins. (The pins can be cut from a steel coat hanger.) The dowels should fit loosely enough on the pins to swing in and out freely. Temporarily add the ½-in.-diameter top balls (part 15). Glue the finial ball in place.

Place this top subassembly on the center post. The elephants should swing out freely 4 or 5 in. when you spin the top. If not, enlarge the slots in the large star to remedy the problem.

6. *Apply finish.* Remove the elephants from the toy. Lightly sand all over. From here, it's up to you. Pick the colors you like best. Use nontoxic paint only. To paint the triangles around the edge of the base, see the directions given for the merry-go-round on page 140.

Once the paint has dried, add the four rubber feet (part 16). Reinstall the elephants and glue the ½-in.-diameter top balls to the ends of the dowels. Put the riders in the holes provided for them.

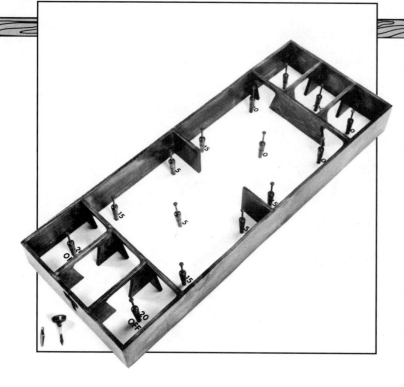

Skittles

For many centuries the British have gathered in pubs to play a game called skittles. The object of the game is to spin a top across the board and knock down as many of the 15 pins (called skittles) as you can.

The moving parts of the game are turned on a lathe. If you do not have a lathe, have them turned by a local woodworking shop, or by the mail-order source named in the Materials List. If you go to a woodworking shop, give the turner a copy of the detail drawings of the top, pin, and handle.

To play the game, wind twine around the top and put it in a cutout at one end of the playing board. Slip the string through the ⅛-in. slot in the cutout. Pull the string to send the top on its journey, knocking down skittles as it travels from room to room. You can play until a player reaches a predetermined number of points, or you can give each player a certain number of turns and total the scores.

1. *Select the stock.* Make the bottom (part 7) from ¼-in. tempered hardboard. Make the sides (part 1) and dividers (parts 3, 4, 5, and 6) from ½-in. stock, either solid wood or a good grade of plywood that is smooth and defect-free on *both* sides.

2. *Cut the parts.* Cut the parts to the sizes given in the Materials List.

Lay out and cut the rabbets and dadoes in the sides, ends (part 2), and dividers. All are ½ in. wide and ¼ in. deep. Sand thoroughly.

3. *Make cutouts in the dividers and in one end.* On a piece of paper, draw full-size patterns for the door openings in the dividers. Also make a pattern for the starter hole, as shown in the detail drawings. Indicate the centerlines and the drill centers on these patterns.

MATERIALS LIST

Part	Dimensions	Quantity
1. Sides	½" × 5" × 48½"	2
2. Ends	½" × 5" × 18"	2
3. Two-door divider	½" × 4½" × 18"	1
4. Three-door divider	½" × 4½" × 18"	1
5. Small dividers	½" × 4½" × 8½"	4
6. Center dividers	½" × 4½" × 5"	2
7. Bottom	¼" × 18" × 48"	1
8. Battens	¼" × ¼" (cut to fit)	4
9. Top*	1¾" dia. × 3⅜"	1
10. Pins*	⅞" × 5"	15
11. Handle*	½" dia. × 2½"	1
12. Finishing nails	4d	as needed
13. Finishing nails	6d	as needed
14. Flathead screws	#6 × ¾"	7
15. Twine	15"	as needed

Parts can be custom-turned by River Bend Turnings, R.D. 1, P.O. Box 364, Wellsville, NY 14895.

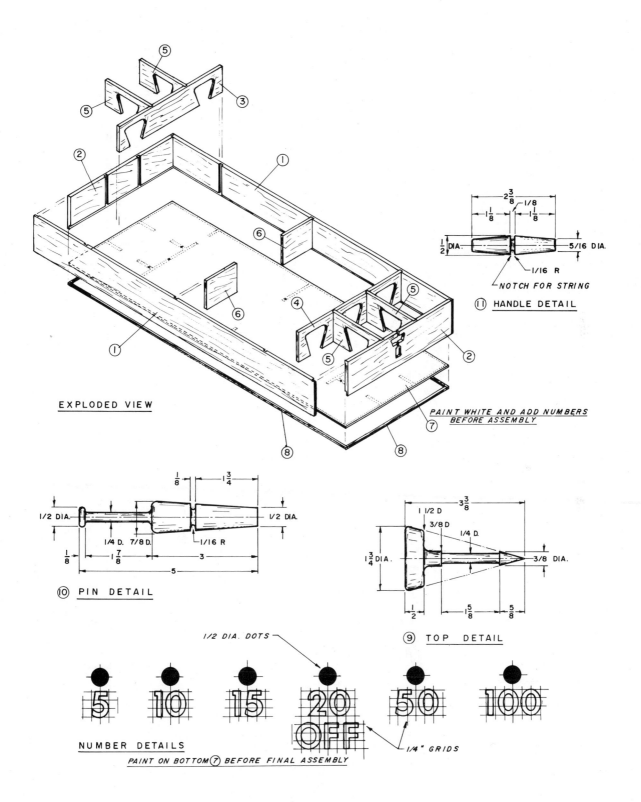

EXPLODED VIEW

⑪ HANDLE DETAIL

NOTCH FOR STRING

2 3/8   1/8
1 1/8   1 1/8
1/2 DIA.   5/16 DIA.
1/16 R

PAINT WHITE AND ADD NUMBERS
BEFORE ASSEMBLY

⑩ PIN DETAIL

1/2 DIA.   1/2 DIA.
1/8   1 3/4
1/4 D.   7/8 D.   1/16 R
1/8
1 7/8
3
5

⑨ TOP DETAIL

3 3/8
1 1/2 D
3/8 D
1/4 D.
1 3/4 DIA.   3/8 DIA.
1/2   1 5/8   5/8

1/2 DIA. DOTS

NUMBER DETAILS

5   10   15   20   50   100

OFF

1/4" GRIDS

PAINT ON BOTTOM ⑦ BEFORE FINAL ASSEMBLY

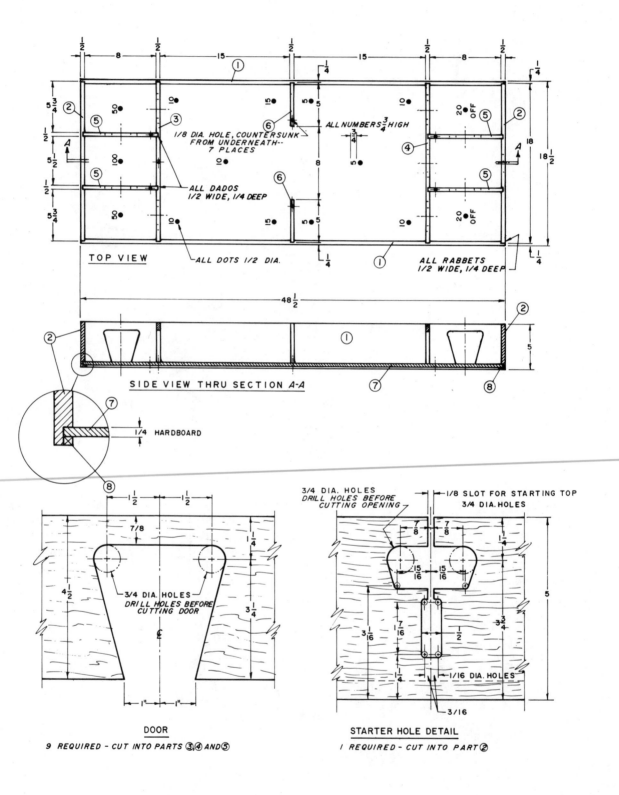

TOP VIEW

1/8 DIA. HOLE, COUNTERSUNK FROM UNDERNEATH-- 7 PLACES

ALL NUMBERS 3/4 HIGH

ALL DADOS 1/2 WIDE, 1/4 DEEP

ALL DOTS 1/2 DIA.

ALL RABBETS 1/2 WIDE, 1/4 DEEP

SIDE VIEW THRU SECTION A-A

1/4 HARDBOARD

DOOR

9 REQUIRED - CUT INTO PARTS ③,④ AND⑤

3/4 DIA. HOLES DRILL HOLES BEFORE CUTTING DOOR

3/4 DIA. HOLES DRILL HOLES BEFORE CUTTING OPENING

1/8 SLOT FOR STARTING TOP 3/4 DIA.HOLES

1/16 DIA. HOLES

3/16

STARTER HOLE DETAIL

1 REQUIRED - CUT INTO PART②

On the wood pieces, lay out the centerlines in pencil, using a square for guidance. Cut out the paper pattern, line up the center lines, and trace around it. Transfer the drill centers by pricking the pattern with an awl.

The four small dividers will be more consistent if you stack, drill, and cut them as a unit. Temporarily glue the parts together with rubber cement. Drill the holes and make straight cuts between them. Sand the edges before taking them apart.

4. *Assemble the game board.* With the exception of the bottom and the battens (part 8), assemble all the parts with glue and 6d finishing nails (part 13). Keep everything flat and square. Set the nails, fill the holes with putty, and sand as needed.

When the glue has set, place the bottom into the rabbet in the base of the game board. Trace the location of the dividers on the bottom's upper face. Remove the bottom and locate and drill screw holes exactly in the middle of the divider outlines you have drawn. Countersink each hole from the underside to take a flathead wood screw (part 14). Do not assemble the bottom or battens until after the game board is painted.

5. *Turn the top, pin, and handle.* Turn the top (part 9), pin (part 10), and handle (part 11) to the dimensions shown. Tie a 15-in. length of twine to the handle.

6. *Apply finish.* Paint or stain the walls. Prime the bottom and then paint it white with a semi-gloss enamel, sanding lightly between coats. Rub lightly with 0000 steel wool.

Lay out and draw in the fifteen pin locations and outline the ¾-in. high letters, as shown. Use a steel-nib drawing pen and black waterproof ink, such as India ink. Note that the numbers and letters are positioned to be read from the playing end of the game board.

Apply a thin coat of varnish over the top of the bottom board and lightly rub again with 0000 steel wool. Add a coat of paste wax, and you're ready to attach the bottom to the game board. Put it in place, drive the seven screws up into the dividers, and install the battens with 4d finishing nails (part 12).

Sand the point of the top slightly to make it travel a more eccentric path.

English Rocking Horse

American antiques are becoming harder to find, and when you *can* find them, their prices are steep. In response to this scarcity, dealers are bringing in antiques from England and other European countries. This rocking horse is a copy of one made in England around 1860. It is ruggedly built, as testified to by at least five generations of use.

The original had a padded seat with large-headed tacks holding a leather cover in place. Note that this design is different from most rocking horses made in the United States because it has footrests on each side but doesn't have the hand-hold dowels found on most of our horses. You may find this horse a bit tippy, and it may be a good idea to add hand-hold dowels. This copy has relatively simple joinery and is easy to cut out and assemble.

1. *Select the stock and cut the parts.* I recommend using a hardwood such as maple, oak, or ash for this project. Softwood may not hold up over the decades as well as the ash used to make the original.

Cut the parts to the sizes given in the Materials List.

2. *Make paper patterns of all parts.* Draw the separate grids with the size squares noted on the drawings and enlarge each individual piece onto the grids. Take special care to draw a *smooth* 28½-in. radius for the rocker (part 5). Note that the top of the rocker has a step that accepts the notched footrest. Measure accurately so that these pieces will come together properly. Transfer the patterns to the wood.

MATERIALS LIST

Part	Dimensions	Quantity
1. Body	¾″ × 11″ × 21″	1
2. Front legs	¾″ × 3″ × 14″	3
3. Rear legs	¾″ × 6″ × 16″	2
4. Mane	½″ × 4″ × 9″	2
5. Rocker	¾″ × 6½″ × 31″	2
6. Footrests	¾″ × 2¼″ × 22″	2
7. Runners	½″ × 2¼″ × 8½″	2
8. Spacers	¾″ × 3″ × 8″	3
9. Seat	¾″ × 2¾″ × 4¾″	1
10. Seat supports	½″ × 2½″ × 4¾″	2
11. Seat supports	½″ × 2¼″ × 2″	2
12. Flathead screws	#8 × 2″	12
13. Flathead screws	#8 × 1½″	4
14. Finishing nails	4d	as needed
15. Finishing nails	6d	as needed
16. Dowels	⅜″ dia. × 1⅛″	12

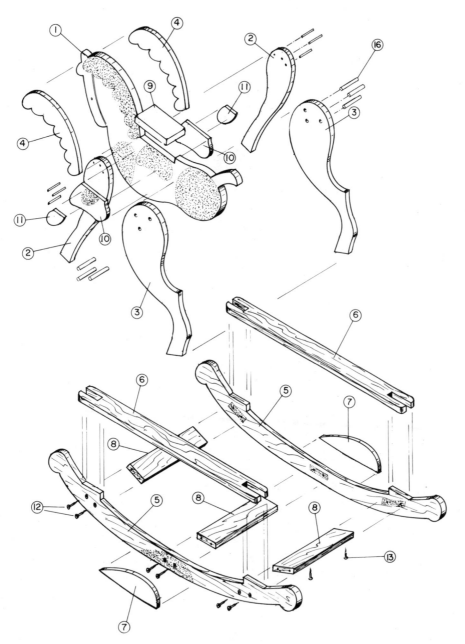

EXPLODED VIEW

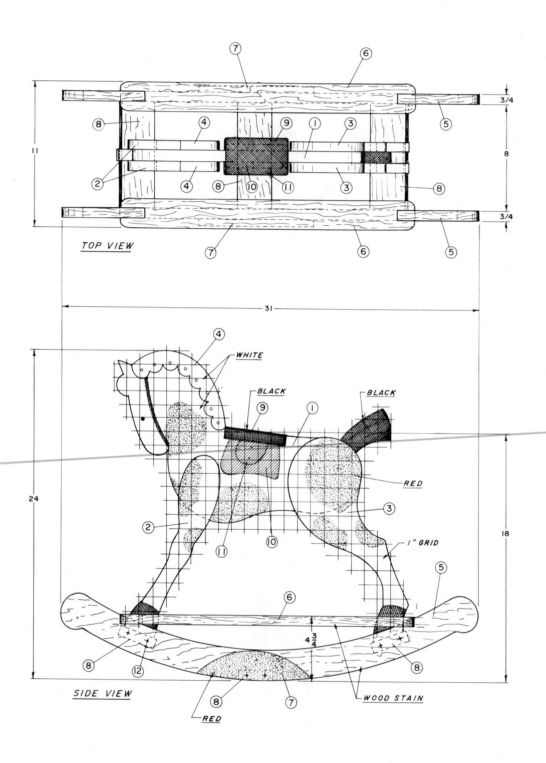

TOP VIEW

SIDE VIEW

WHITE

BLACK

BLACK

RED

1" GRID

WOOD STAIN

RED

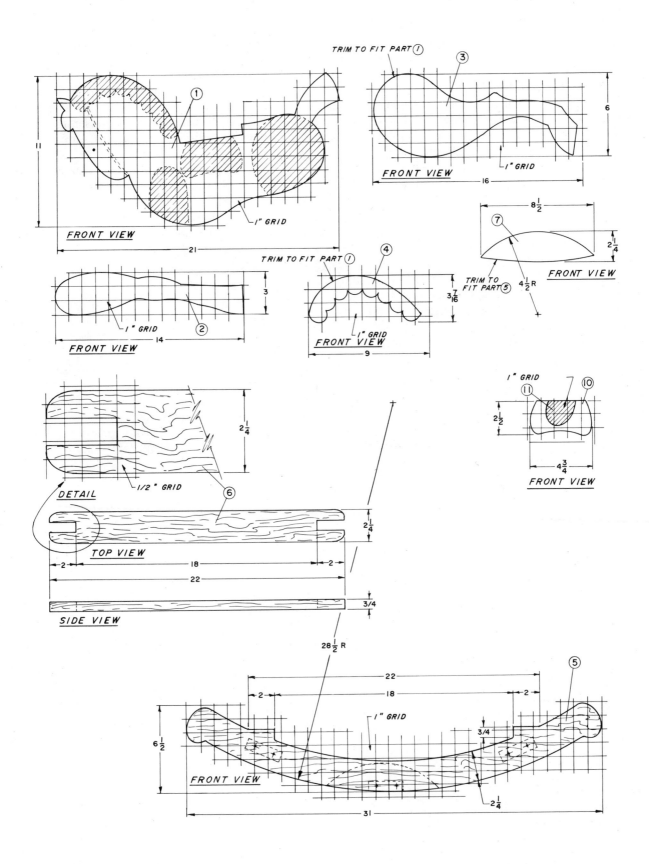

TRIM TO FIT PART ①

③

FRONT VIEW

6

1" GRID

16

①

11

FRONT VIEW

1" GRID

21

8½

⑦

2¼

TRIM TO
FIT PART⑤

FRONT VIEW

4½ R

TRIM TO FIT PART ①

④

FRONT VIEW

3

1" GRID

②

14

3 7/16

1" GRID

FRONT VIEW

9

1" GRID

⑪ ⑩

2½

4¾

FRONT VIEW

2¼

DETAIL

1/2" GRID

⑥

TOP VIEW

2¼

2

18

2

22

SIDE VIEW

3/4

28½ R

22

18

2

2

3/4

1" GRID

⑤

6½

2¼

FRONT VIEW

31

3. *Cut the parts to shape.* To save time, double up when cutting identical parts. Tape the pairs together with double-sided tape, or temporarily tack them together with small finishing nails (the holes can be filled in later). After cutting all the parts to shape, sand their edges while the pairs are still together. This saves time and ensures that the matching parts really match. Take particular care when cutting the bottom edge of the rockers so that the horse will rock evenly.

Two cross pieces run between the rockers and are attached with screws. Before taking the two rockers apart, drill and countersink six screw holes slightly larger than the screw shank, as shown in the front view. Then separate the rockers.

You'll need to drill holes in the spacers (part 8), too, to keep the screws from splitting them. The easiest way to locate these holes is to temporarily clamp the spacers in place and drill through the rocker holes into the spacers. Drill holes slightly smaller than the screw shank.

4. *Assemble the horse.* Dry-fit all parts, making any necessary adjustments. Glue the footrests (part 6) to the rockers. Screw the spacers between the rockers with #8 2-in flathead screws. Make sure everything is square. Glue the runners (part 7) in place. Sand the entire rocker, rounding the edges slightly.

Glue the mane (part 4) and the seat supports (parts 10 and 11) to the body, as shown. Attach the seat (part 9) with glue. To ensure that

these parts don't move, drive 4d finishing nails (part 14) through the mane and supports, and 6d finishing nails (part 15) through the seat.

Clamp the legs (parts 2 and 3) onto the body (part 1) and adjust them until all four rest squarely on the spacers. Trace the outline of the legs on the body. Remove the clamps and add glue. Guided by the outlines, clamp the legs to the body again. After the glue has set, reinforce this joint by running a ⅜-in. diameter dowel (part 16) through each pair of legs and halfway into the body. Glue the dowels in place and sand the ends flush with the legs.

Finally, glue the legs to the spacers and screw them in place with #8 1½-in.-flathead wood screws (part 13).

5. *Apply finish.* The original horse was painted and had a stained rocker assembly, as shown in the side view. My wife wanted to make the horse brighter, so she painted the rockers solid blue. The spots labeled "red" were actually an orangy brick red on the original. Be sure to use nontoxic paint.

To make the horse look older, paint it as noted in the plans and, when thoroughly dry, sand all the edges slightly to give them a worn look. Then apply a light coat of cherry stain over all the painted surfaces.

A simpler alternative is to stain the entire horse rather than paint it.

Bootjack

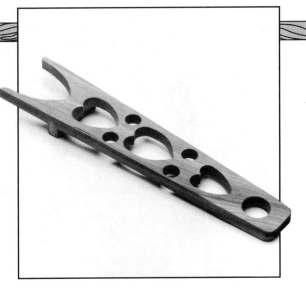

Here is an item that isn't quite as useful today as it was in the days when tall boots were standard footwear. Still, a bootjack is an interesting novelty, and I don't believe I've ever seen a more ornate one than the one in this design.

1. *Select the stock and cut the parts.* Both the bootjack and the leg it sits on are cut out of ¾-in.-thick stock. For a functional bootjack, pine will serve well, but consider a more attractive hardwood if the piece will be largely ornamental.

2. *Make a paper pattern.* Draw a grid with ½-in. squares and enlarge the bootjack (part 1) onto it. The pattern should include the location of all the holes and of the dado for the leg. Transfer the pattern to the wood, cut the dado, and drill the holes. Cut out the remaining area of the hearts with a coping saw or jigsaw.

Nail the leg (part 2) in the dado with 6d finishing nails (part 3). Cut out the outline of the bootjack and sand all surfaces and edges.

3. *Apply finish.* Apply varnish. The bootjack can be hung on the wall when not in use to show off its unusual shape.

MATERIALS LIST

Part	Dimensions	Quantity
1. Bootjack	¾" × 4" × 15"	1
2. Leg	½" × 1" × 4"	1
3. Finishing nails	6d	as needed

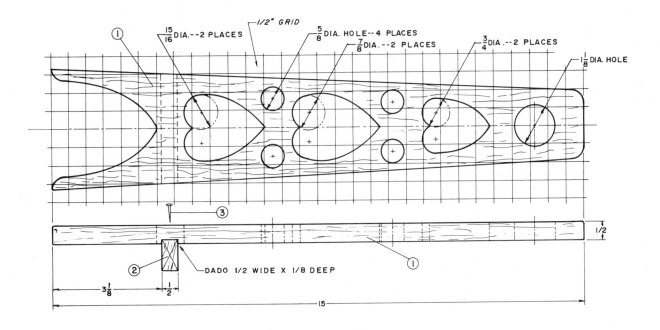

Footstool

In colonial times, footstools were known as crickets and often could be found before a chair in front of the fireplace. Designs for them vary greatly, I suppose, because we all have our own ideas about what a footstool should look like. The original model for this footstool comes from eighteenth century New England. It is easy to make and very sturdy.

1. *Select the stock and cut the parts.* Your choice of wood will be influenced by whether or not you plan on painting the footstool. Poplar or pine take paint well; a clear finish calls for an attractive hardwood.

Cut the parts to the sizes given in the Materials List.

2. *Lay out the legs and skirts.* To save a bit of time, tape the legs (part 1) together with double-sided tape before you lay out the curves with a compass. Make your layout lines on the top piece only and cut out both pieces at once. Lay out the notch that houses the skirt and cut it with a backsaw.

Draw a grid with ½-in. squares to make a pattern for the skirt (part 2). Enlarge the drawing of the skirt onto the grid. Tape the skirts together and transfer the enlargement to the wood. Lay the hearts out directly on the wood.

Sand the edges while the pieces are still together. Separate the parts and sand the surfaces.

3. *Assemble the footstool.* Attach the legs to the skirts with glue and finishing nails (part 4). Be sure to keep everything square. Once the glue has set, line up the top (part 3), and attach it with glue and 6d nails.

4. *Apply finish.* Sand thoroughly, rounding the top edges. The footstool can be either varnished or painted.

MATERIALS LIST

Part	Dimensions	Quantity
1. Legs	⅝″ × 6″ × 5⅜″	2
2. Skirts	½″ × 1⅞″ × 12″	2
3. Top	⅝″ × 6″ × 12″	1
4. Finishing nails	6d	as needed

FOOTSTOOL

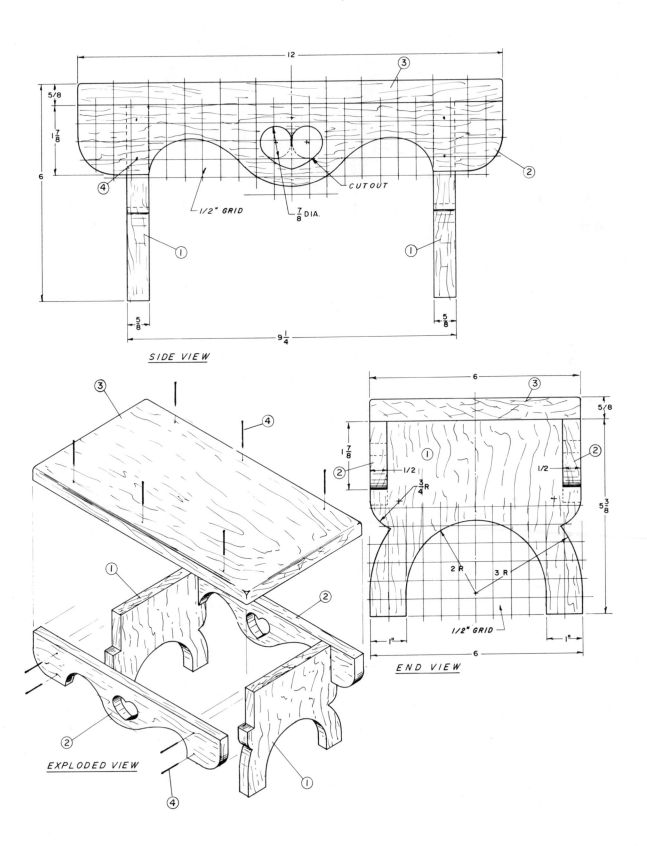

SIDE VIEW

12

5/8

1 7/8

6

④

1/2" GRID

CUTOUT

7/8 DIA.

③

②

①

①

5/8

5/8

9 1/4

EXPLODED VIEW

③

④

①

②

②

①

④

END VIEW

6

③

5/8

1 7/8

②

1/2

②

3/4 R

①

②

1/2

5 3/8

2 R

3 R

1"

1/2" GRID

1"

6

165

Silver Tray

This is an exact copy of an antique tray for holding silver. I can't understand why silver trays aren't as popular today as they were 150 years ago. They are still very handy and show off silverware to good advantage.

1. Select the stock and cut the parts. I suggest cutting all the parts ½ in. longer and wider than the dimensions given in the Materials List and then cutting them to size as assembly progresses.

2. Cut the joints. Because the sides of this tray slope, the corners are compound miters, and the bottom and top of each must be bevelled. Cut the compound miters first.

Tilt the blade on your table saw to 80¼ degrees, and set the miter gauge at 44¼ degrees. Cut a sample joint and check to make sure it meets at 90 degrees without gaps. Adjust as necessary and cut the joints on the long and short sides (parts 1 and 2). Cut each side to length when you cut the *second* miter on it. Dry-fit all four sides to make sure that they meet tightly and at 90 degrees.

Rip a 10-degree bevel along the top and bottom of the sides, as shown in the side section. Cut the sides to width when cutting the second bevel.

Rout a dado in the center of the short sides to house the handle. The dado is ⅜ in. wide and ³/₁₆ in. deep and stops ⅜ in. from the bottom edge.

3. Assemble the tray. Clamping a piece with sloping sides can be difficult. Try this: Put a long strip of masking tape on the bench, sticky side up. Lay a side on part of the tape, outside face down. Tape the adjoining side to it so that the corners of the miters are in contact along their entire length. Repeat this process for the neighboring corners. When you are done, all four sides should be taped together in one long strip. Put glue in the joints, and fold the corners to form the box. "Clamp" with heavy-duty rubber bands and check for squareness.

4. Cut the bottom to fit. When the glue dries, set the table saw blade to cut a 10-degree bevel and cut the bottom (part 3) to fit snugly between the sides and ends. Glue it in place. Reinforce all of the joints with square-cut nails (part 5).

5. Make a paper pattern and cut the handle. Before you cut the scroll work on the handle (part 4), cut it to fit in the dadoes. Measure the distance between the dadoes at the bottom of the box. Set the miter gauge to 80 degrees and

MATERIALS LIST

Part	Dimensions	Quantity
1. Long sides	⅜" × 2¼" × 11¾"	2
2. Short sides	⅜" × 2¼" × 6½"	2
3. Bottom	⅜" × 5¾" × 11"	1
4. Handle	⅜" × 6⅞" × 12"	1
5. Square-cut nails	1"	24

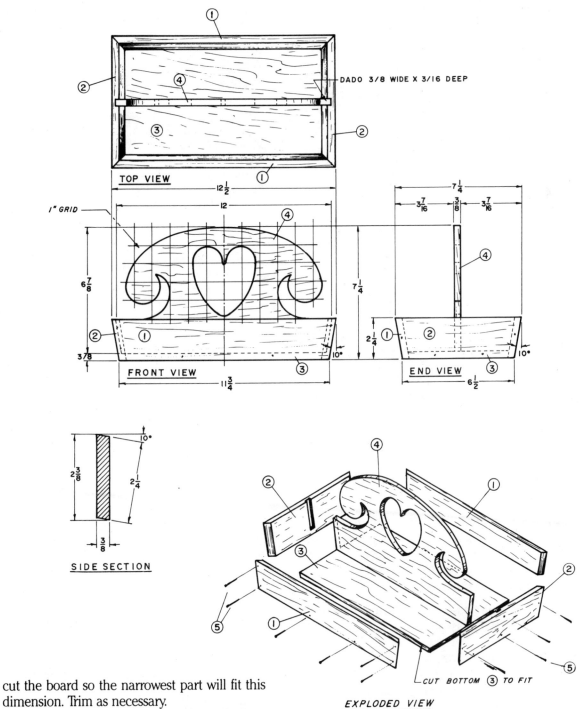

DADO 3/8 WIDE X 3/16 DEEP

TOP VIEW

1" GRID

FRONT VIEW

END VIEW

SIDE SECTION

EXPLODED VIEW

CUT BOTTOM ③ TO FIT

cut the board so the narrowest part will fit this dimension. Trim as necessary.

When the handle fits correctly in the box, cut the scroll work. Make a paper pattern by drawing a grid with 1-in. squares and enlarge the drawing of the handle onto it. Transfer the enlargement to the wood. Cut the scroll work with a jigsaw or coping saw.

6. *Apply finish.* Sand the tray and paint it. The original was painted blue-gray.

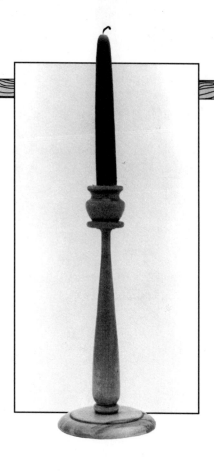

Early American Candlestick

This project is an exact copy of an antique candlestick I found in Maine. The original was maple, but you might also try turning one from cherry or walnut.

1. *Select the stock.* This candlestick is a two-piece construction. The base is turned from a blank, 9/16 in. thick and 4¼ in. square. The stem is turned from a blank, 1¾ in. square and 10 in. long.

2. *Turn the base.* Scribe a 4¼-in. circle on the base with a compass, and cut out this circle with a bandsaw or saber saw.

The 1/16-in. recess, shown in the dashed lines at the bottom of the base, is designed to keep the candlestick from rocking on an uneven surface.

Turn the recess first. Mount the base between centers on the lathe. Center the drive spur on the center of the circle you drew and center the tailstock against the other side of the wood. Scrape the recess, using standard turning techniques. There will be a small plug you cannot reach because of the tailstock. Remove the base from

the lathe and pare off the plug with a chisel. Center a faceplate in the recess and screw the faceplate to the base. Make sure the screws are as long as possible, but not long enough to come through the top of the base.

Turn the base to the profile shown. Looking at the drawing, note the hidden line on the *top* surface of the base: it indicates a shallow groove turned into the top of the base.

After you've turned the groove, drill a hole in the top of the base to hold the stem. You can do this while the piece is still on the lathe: First, put a chuck in the tailstock and then put a drill bit in the chuck. Lock the tailstock in place and, with the lathe running slowly, advance the bit to drill the hole. Sand the piece while it is turning on the lathe. Remove it from the lathe but not from the faceplate.

3. *Turn the stem.* Mount the stem blank on the lathe and turn it to the profile shown. The stub tenon that fits into the base should be the closest to the headstock. Turn it carefully—it must fit snugly into the ½-in.-diameter hole in the base. Turn the section immediately above the cup that holds the candle to a diameter of ¾ in. Sand the entire profile. Drill a hole for the candle. Remove the stem from the lathe.

The lathe makes a perfect clamp for holding the pieces together during the glue-up. Put the faceplate and base back on the lathe. Put glue both on the stub tenon and in the hole for it. Insert the tenon in the hole, center the tailstock against the stem, and tighten it gently. Allow the glue to set for at least 24 hours and remove the candle stand from the lathe and from the faceplate.

4. Apply finish. Apply two coats of a satin-luster finish of your choice.

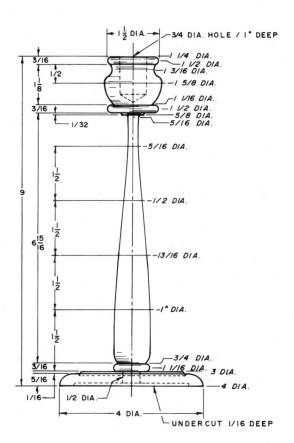

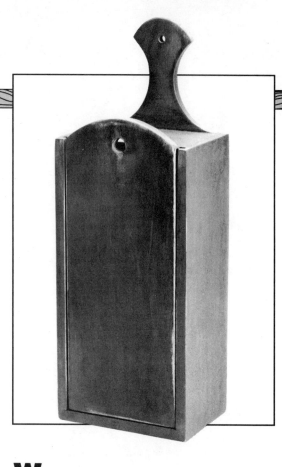

Wall Candle Box

When the electricity went off in a storm, I used to hunt all over the house for candles. Not anymore. This box, a copy of an antique, keeps candles in plain sight, ready for use.

1. *Select the stock.* I suggest maple, cherry, oak, ash, or poplar for this project.

2. *Cut the parts to size.* Because the sides, (part 1) and the bottom (part 2) have identical rabbets and identical grooves, cut the rabbets and grooves in one long board and then cut the board to form the separate parts, as shown in Fig. 1 and 2.

3. *Cut the joinery.* Once you've cut the boards to length, cut a ⅜-in. × ³⁄₁₆-in.-deep rabbet along the bottom of each side. Cut a similar rabbet along the top of each side *but stop it as soon as it hits the groove for the front.* See the exploded view to get an idea of what the finished side should look like.

Rip the top (part 3) to width, as shown in Fig. 3.

4. *Assemble the box.* Dry-fit the sides, bottom, and top, and make any necessary adjustments. Glue the parts and assemble them with large rubber bands to keep everything together. Check for squareness.

5. *Make a paper pattern for the back.* Draw a grid with ½-in. squares, and enlarge the drawing of the back (part 5) onto it. Adjust the overall width of the back to fit your box, if necessary. Transfer the enlargement to the wood and cut it out. Lay out and drill a ¼-in.-diameter hole, as shown.

Put the back in place, and if it fits correctly, glue it in place. As an option, you may want to reinforce the joints of the box with ¾-in. square-cut nails.

6. *Make the lid.* Cut the lid (part 4) to fit the box: Measure from the bottom of one of the grooves it travels in to the bottom of the other groove. Cut the lid ¹⁄₃₂ in. smaller than this dimension.

Cut a rabbet to make a lip that fits in the groove. The lid must be able to slide freely in its track without being too loose. As a rule of thumb,

MATERIALS LIST

Part	Dimensions	Quantity
1. Sides	⅜″ × 3½″ × 10″	2
2. Bottom	⅜″ × 3½″ × 8″	1
3. Top	⅜″ × 2¾″ × 4⅝″	1
4. Lid	⅜″ × 4⅝″ × 11³⁄₁₆″	1
5. Back	⅜″ × 4⅝″ × 13¹³⁄₁₆″	1

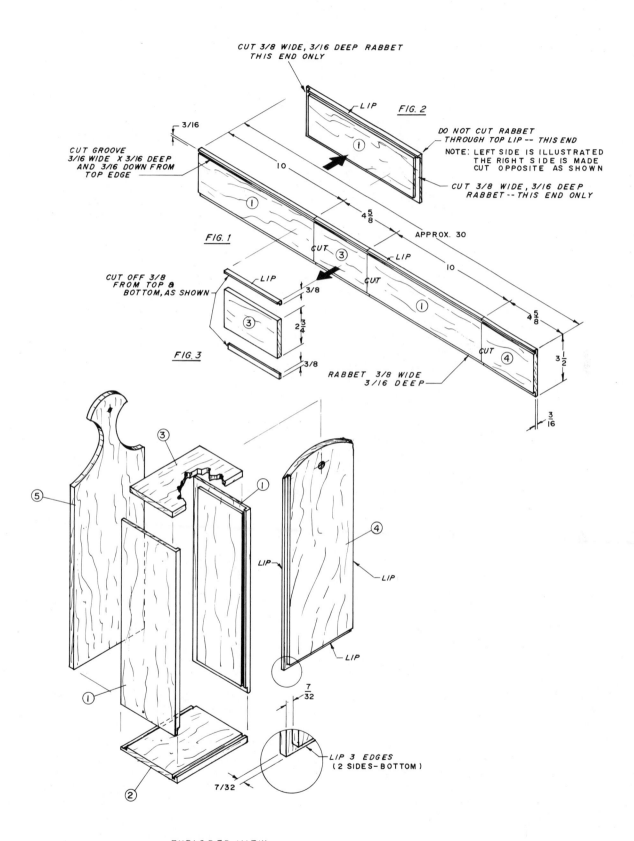

CUT 3/8 WIDE, 3/16 DEEP RABBET
THIS END ONLY

LIP

FIG. 2

DO NOT CUT RABBET
THROUGH TOP LIP -- THIS END

NOTE: LEFT SIDE IS ILLUSTRATED
THE RIGHT SIDE IS MADE
CUT OPPOSITE AS SHOWN

CUT 3/8 WIDE, 3/16 DEEP
RABBET -- THIS END ONLY

3/16

CUT GROOVE
3/16 WIDE X 3/16 DEEP
AND 3/16 DOWN FROM
TOP EDGE

10

$4\frac{5}{8}$

APPROX. 30

FIG. 1

CUT ③ LIP

CUT OFF 3/8
FROM TOP &
BOTTOM, AS SHOWN

LIP

3/8

CUT

10

$2\frac{3}{4}$

③

$4\frac{5}{8}$

FIG. 3

3/8

RABBET 3/8 WIDE
3/16 DEEP

CUT ④

$3\frac{1}{2}$

$\frac{3}{16}$

③

⑤

①

②

①

LIP

LIP

④

LIP

$\frac{7}{32}$

LIP 3 EDGES
(2 SIDES-BOTTOM)

7/32

EXPLODED VIEW

171

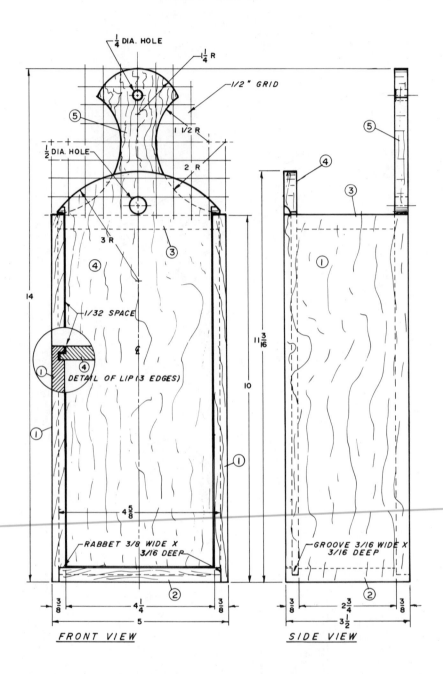

FRONT VIEW SIDE VIEW

there should be a 1/32-in. gap, as shown in the front view.

When the lid fits correctly, lay out and cut a 3-in.-radius arc to form the rounded end of the lid. Lay out and drill a finger hole in the lid, as shown in the front view. The hole is 15/16 in. from top of the arc and centered from left to right on the lid.

7. Apply finish. Some candle boxes were varnished. Others were painted. I prefer them painted on the outside only. Take care to avoid applying finish where it may bind the lid.

Hang the box in a handy spot so that you won't have much trouble finding it in the dark. And don't forget to tuck a book of matches in the box along with the candles.

Colonial Shelf

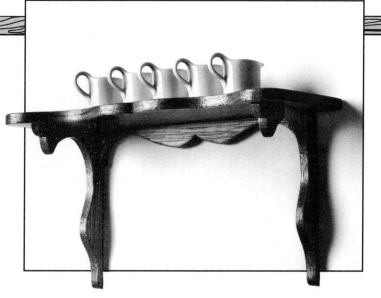

Our forefathers had a great sense of proportion when it came to designing wall shelves. Their shelves were graceful and beautiful, with lines that computer-assisted design can't improve.

I found the model for this project in Maine, where it was made sometime during the eighteenth century. I was attracted to its smooth lines. It is rather small, but it may be just right for holding a clock or a favorite object.

1. Select the stock. This shelf can be made of any kind of wood, but I think that hardwood suits it best. There are only four parts: two sides, a brace, and a shelf, all made from ⅜-in. stock. Cut them to the sizes given in the Materials List.

2. Make a paper pattern and cut the parts to shape. Draw a grid with ½-in. squares and enlarge the drawing of the parts onto it. Transfer the patterns to the stock and cut the parts to shape. To ensure that the sides (part 1) are identical, attach one on top of the other with double-sided tape and cut them as a unit. While the pieces are still together, sand the edges, and cut a notch for the brace.

Drill two ⅛-in.-diameter mounting holes in the brace (part 2) and countersink them from the front.

3. Assemble the shelf. Glue up the parts. Before the glue sets, make sure the sides are square with the brace. To make the shelf look like the original, attach the shelf (part 3) with ⅞-in. square-cut brads (part 4).

4. Apply finish. Sand thoroughly, rounding the edges slightly. Finish with a low-luster varnish.

MATERIALS LIST

Part	Dimensions	Quantity
1. Sides	⅜″ × 4¾″ × 7⅛″	2
2. Brace	1½″ × 2″ × 12″	1
3. Shelf	⅜″ × 5½″ × 14½″	1
4. Square-cut brads	⅞″	as needed

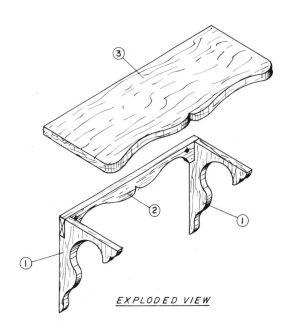

EXPLODED VIEW

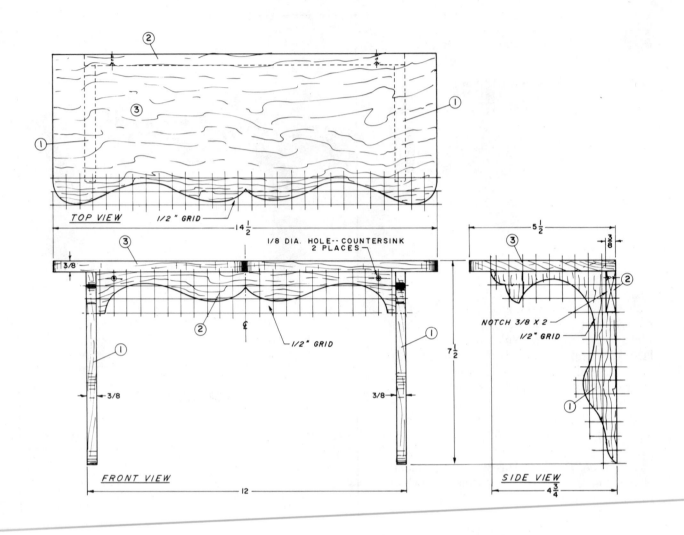

TOP VIEW   1/2" GRID

14 1/2

3/8

FRONT VIEW

1/8 DIA. HOLE -- COUNTERSINK
2 PLACES

1/2" GRID

3/8   3/8

12

5 1/2

3/8

7 1/2

NOTCH 3/8 X 2

1/2" GRID

SIDE VIEW
4 3/4

Pipe Box with Two Drawers

This type of box was used to store long-stem clay pipes. It is unusual because it has two drawers, one slightly larger than the other.

1. *Select the stock and cut the sides and dividers.* Use any hardwood. A secondary wood can be used for all of the drawer parts except the front. Cut the sides (part 2) and the dividers (part 4) to the dimensions given in the Materials List. Rout two stopped dadoes and a stopped rabbet, ⅜ in. wide and ⅛ in. deep, in each of the sides, as shown. All stop ⅜ in. short of the back edge. Guide the router against a fence clamped to the side.

2. *Assemble the sides and dividers.* Dry-fit the dividers in the sides. If everything comes together as it should, glue the sides and dividers together. Make sure the assembly is square before the glue dries.

3. *Cut the front and back to fit.* This project uses simple butt joints to attach the front and back, as did the box from which I took this design. Cut the front and back (parts 3 and 1) to fit.

Make a paper pattern for the curves on the front and back. Draw a grid with ½-in. squares

and enlarge the curved sections of the back and the front onto it. Transfer the patterns to the stock and cut the parts to shape. Sand the edges.

Glue the front and back in place.

4. *Make the drawers.* Always make drawers to fit the opening, no matter how simple the project. Cut the drawer parts, (parts 5, 6, 7, 8, 9, 10, and 11) to the width and thickness given in the Materials List but leave each part about ½ in. long.

Cut the drawer fronts to fit snugly in the openings. Cut the rabbets ³⁄₁₆ in. wide × ¼ in. deep in the drawer fronts to accept the drawer sides.

Cut the sides so that the drawer front will be flush when the drawer is pushed all the way back. Take the depth of the rabbet into account when calculating the proper length.

Dado the sides for the back. Test-fit the three parts. Make sure they are square in relation to one another and then measure the distance between the dadoes. Cut the back to this dimension.

Cut a ⅛-in.-wide, ¹⁄₁₆-in.-deep groove in all the drawer parts to accept the bottom. Cut the bottom to fit. Test-fit all the parts and adjust as

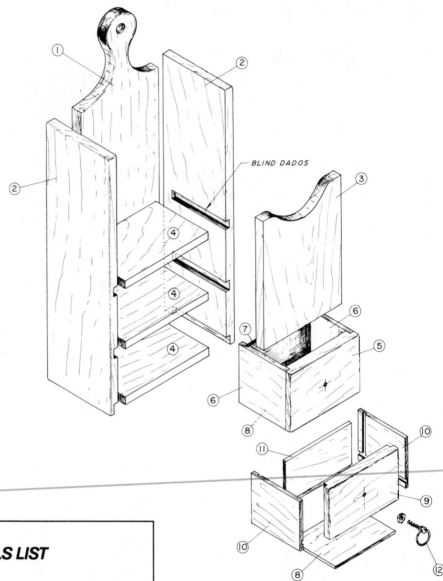

BLIND DADOS

EXPLODED VIEW

MATERIALS LIST

Part	Dimensions	Quantity
1. Back	$\frac{3}{8}'' \times 4\frac{1}{4}'' \times 18''$	1
2. Sides	$\frac{3}{8}'' \times 4'' \times 14''$	2
3. Front	$\frac{3}{8}'' \times 4\frac{1}{4}'' \times 7\frac{1}{8}''$	1
4. Dividers	$\frac{3}{8}'' \times 3\frac{5}{8}'' \times 4\frac{1}{2}''$	3
5. Upper drawer front	$\frac{1}{2}'' \times 3\frac{1}{8}'' \times 4\frac{1}{4}''$	1
6. Upper drawer sides	$\frac{3}{16}'' \times 3\frac{1}{8}'' \times 3\frac{3}{8}''$	2
7. Upper drawer back	$\frac{3}{16}'' \times 3\frac{1}{8}'' \times 4\frac{1}{16}''$	1
8. Drawer bottoms	$\frac{1}{8}'' \times 2\frac{7}{8}'' \times 4''$	2
9. Lower drawer front	$\frac{1}{2}'' \times 2\frac{5}{8}'' \times 4\frac{1}{4}''$	1
10. Lower drawer sides	$\frac{3}{16}'' \times 2\frac{5}{8}'' \times 3\frac{3}{8}''$	2
11. Lower drawer back	$\frac{3}{16}'' \times 2\frac{5}{8}'' \times 4''$	1
12. Pulls*		2

Pulls with 1-in.-dia. rings are available from Ball and Ball, 463 West Lincoln Highway, Exton, PA 19341; order #G22-158.

necessary. When the parts fit, glue all the parts together except the bottoms, which are allowed to float in the grooves cut for them. Sand the sides until the drawers travel smoothly.

Drill the drawer fronts for the pulls (part 12).

5. *Apply finish.* Sand thoroughly. Paint, stain and varnish, or simply varnish this project.

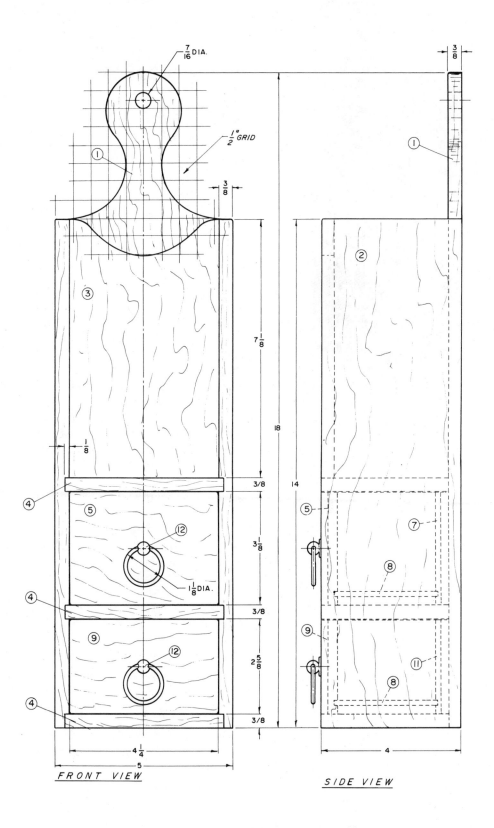

FRONT VIEW   SIDE VIEW

Colonial Pipe Box

In the early days of this country, long before the Surgeon General's warnings about tobacco, pipe smoking was a popular custom. The pipe box served as a place to store both tobacco and the fragile, long-stemmed clay pipes that were the fashion. Pipe boxes flourished from 1745 until late in the century, but few remain today. Chances are you'll have to go to a museum to see one.

It seems that no two pipe boxes were made from the same pattern. They ranged from stocky, crude designs to delicately built containers. Most have an open top compartment for the pipes and a small tobacco drawer below. Cherry, maple, mahogany, and walnut were the most commonly used woods, with an occasional box made out of pine.

This project is modeled after a green-painted pine pipe box made in eastern Massachusetts around 1750. The original can be seen at the Strawberry Banke Museum in Portsmouth, New Hampshire.

Today, a pipe box can be used to store envelopes and stamps or candles and matches.

1. *Select the stock and cut the parts.* The pipe box is made from five different stock thicknesses. If you can't plane or resaw the boards yourself, find a mill that can do the work for you. To simplify matters, you can substitute ⅜-in. stock for the ¹¹/₃₂-in. pieces called for here.

Cut the parts to the sizes given in the Materials List.

2. *Make a paper pattern and lay out the curves.* Draw a grid with ½-in. squares and enlarge the curves in the drawing onto it. Transfer

MATERIALS LIST

Part	Dimensions	Quantity
1. Back*	¹¹/₃₂″ × 6½″ × 16⅝″	1
2. Sides*	¹¹/₃₂″ × 4¹/₃₂″ × 11⅛″	2
3. Front*	¹¹/₃₂″ × 6½″ × 6¼″	1
4. Divider*	¹¹/₃₂″ × 3¹¹/₁₆″ × 5¹³/₁₆″	1
5. Bottom	⅜″ × 4⅝″ × 6⅞″	1
6. Drawer front	⁹/₁₆″ × 2¾″ × 6⅛″	1
7. Drawer sides	¼″ × 2¾″ × 3¾″	2
8. Drawer back	¼″ × 2⅜″ × 5¹¹/₁₆″	1
9. Drawer bottom	³/₁₆″ × 3¾″ × 5⁷/₁₆″	1
10. Drawer pull	½″ dia. × 1½″	1
11. Pin	(Square-cut nail, to fit)	1
12. Square-cut brads	⅞″	21
13. Eye screws		2

*You can substitute ⅜″ stock for these parts.

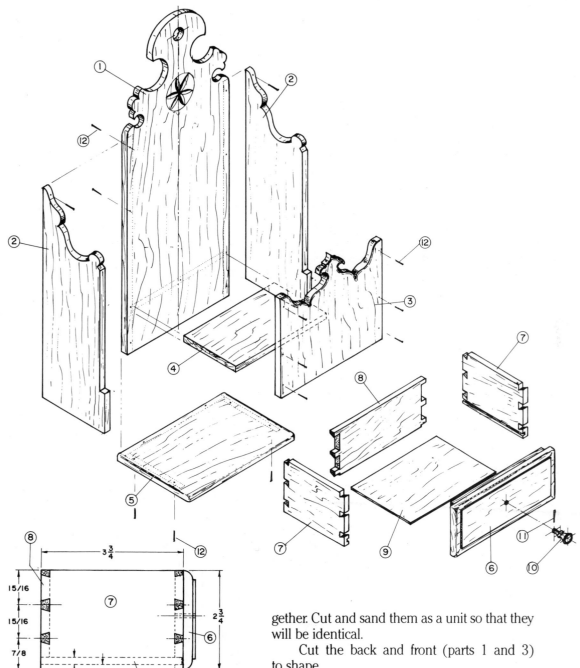

SIDE VIEW DETAIL OF DRAWER DOVETAIL

3 3/4

15/16

15/16

7/8

2 3/4

3/16   3/16

the enlarged curves to the wood. Some of the tighter curves will be drilled out rather than cut, so mark the drill centers on the stock, too.

3. Cut the parts to shape. Place one side (part 2) on top of the other and tape them to-

gether. Cut and sand them as a unit so that they will be identical.

Cut the back and front (parts 1 and 3) to shape.

4. Chip-carve the back. The original pipe box has a flower chip-carved into the back. If you have never tried chip-carving, this is a good beginner's project. The necessary tools are available from Woodcraft, a company whose address is listed in the appendix. Woodcraft also sells an excellent book on the subject, *Chip Carving: Techniques and Patterns*, by Wayne Barton. If you don't feel like carving the flower, you could simply paint it or leave it out altogether.

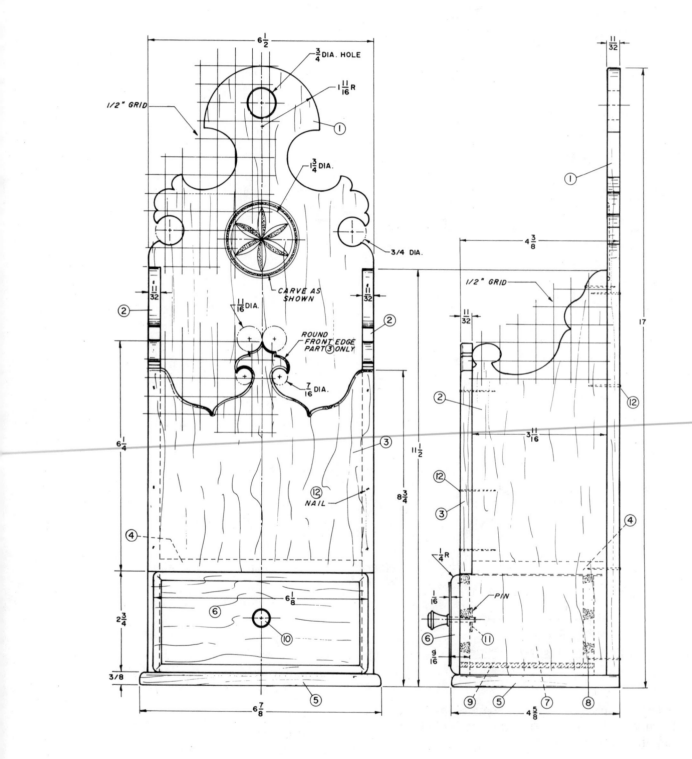

$6\frac{1}{2}$

$\frac{3}{4}$ DIA. HOLE

$1\frac{11}{16}$ R

1/2" GRID

①

$1\frac{3}{4}$ DIA.

3/4 DIA.

CARVE AS SHOWN

$\frac{11}{16}$ DIA.

$\frac{11}{32}$

②

$\frac{11}{32}$

②

ROUND FRONT EDGE PART ③ ONLY

$\frac{7}{16}$ DIA.

$6\frac{1}{4}$

③

$11\frac{1}{2}$

⑫ NAIL

$8\frac{3}{4}$

④

⑥

$6\frac{1}{8}$

$2\frac{3}{4}$

⑩

3/8

⑤

$6\frac{7}{8}$

$\frac{11}{32}$

①

$4\frac{3}{8}$

17

1/2" GRID

$\frac{11}{32}$

②

⑫

$3\frac{11}{16}$

③

⑫

④

$\frac{1}{4}$ R

$\frac{1}{16}$

PIN

⑥

⑪

$\frac{9}{16}$

⑨ ⑤ ⑦ ⑧

$4\frac{5}{8}$

5. *Assemble the box.* Dry-assemble the parts to check that everything will go together correctly. If necessary, make any adjustments. Glue and nail the sides to the back with 7/8-in. square-cut brads. Glue and nail the front in place, and make sure the box is square. Insert the divider (part 4) and glue it to the front and back. Sand the box, leaving the edges square. Position the bottom (part 5) and nail it to the box. Note that the scroll work on the front has a slightly rounded front edge. Use a rasp or sandpaper to get this effect.

6. *Make the drawer.* The original drawer is dovetailed together. If the prospect of making dovetails intimidates you, build the drawer with rabbet joints instead. Rabbeted drawers weren't at all uncommon on early pipe boxes, so you won't be compromising the authenticity of the project.

Cut the drawer parts to fit the opening.

The heights specified for the drawer sides (part 7) are the same as the height of the drawer opening. Since this won't allow for expansion of the drawer in humid weather, make the drawer height 1/32 in. to 1/16 in. less than the *actual* drawer opening. The drawer back (part 8) is even narrower so that you can slide the bottom into the completed drawer.

Rout the drawer front to the profile shown, with a 1/4-in.-radius roundover bit and bearing.

The drawer front (part 6) overlaps the pipe box on either side and has rabbets cut in it to make this possible. Rout a 3/16 × 1/4-in. deep rabbet along the inside left and right drawer front edges.

Cut dovetails in the drawer, as shown.

Cut 3/16 × 1/8-deep grooves in the drawer front and sides to house the drawer bottom.

Dry-assemble the drawer, starting with the front. Make adjustments as necessary, then glue it up. Slide the bottom in place after assembly. The grain of the bottom runs parallel to the drawer front so that the bottom can expand and contract without pushing against the drawer sides. You can buy a drawer pull (part 10) or turn one, complete with a tenon. Drill a hole for the tenon in the drawer front, and pin it with a square-cut nail (part 11), as shown in the side view of the pipe box.

7. *Apply finish.* Sand the entire pipe box with very fine sandpaper. In an attempt to match the green of the original box, I painted mine with Wild Bayberry green, number 1214, available from Stulb Paint and Chemical Company, whose address is listed in the appendix. Apply a single coat of paint and allow it to dry. To suggest the effects of aging, rub the piece all over with 0000 steel wool, wearing away at the edges in particular. Apply a coat of paste wax.

Courting Mirror

In colonial America, glass was so expensive that some very early mirrors were made with broken pieces of other mirrors, held in a crude makeshift frame.

The design shown here is more refined. It is a courting mirror, presented by a man when proposing to a prospective bride. It was said that if the woman smiled into the mirror, she surely would accept.

This early mirror is decorated with dentils and three hearts, one of them right side up and the others upside down. It is made of walnut, but you can use almost any hardwood.

You might hang a courting mirror on a wall where a larger mirror or picture can't be squeezed in.

1. *Select the stock and cut the parts.* The entire mirror is made of ¼-in. hardwood. Cut the parts to the sizes given in the Materials List. Study the exploded drawing: To prevent warping, the grain runs across the bottom batten (part 4) in the same direction as that in the bottom section (part 1).

2. *Make a paper pattern.* Draw a grid with ½-in. squares and enlarge the entire mirror onto it. The three hearts in the top section are laid out with a compass. Transfer the patterns to the stock.

3. *Cut the parts to shape.* Lay out and drill the holes for each heart in the top section. Cut out the remaining area of the hearts with a jigsaw or coping saw. Cut the outline of the top section.

In the bottom section, carefully locate the centers of the holes that form the corners of the cutout for the mirror. Drill the holes, then saw the rest of the cutout. With a router and a ¼-in. roundover bit, round the edges of the cutout to the profile shown in the cross section.

Locate and drill the two ⅜-in.-diameter holes that help to define the top corners of the bottom section. Then cut out the remainder of the section's outline.

Lay out the dentils along the top edge. You can cut them on a table saw with a dado blade. Hold the bottom section with its top edge down and guide it through repeated passes with the miter gauge.

The pinwheel can be scratched into the stock at any time in the construction process. Scratch the outline into the wood. You can either follow the pattern, or scratch a series of arcs with a drafting compass that has a steel point instead of pencil lead.

Taper the back board (part 6) on all four sides, as shown in the cross section with a hand plane.

4. *Assemble the mirror frame.* Dry-assemble the wood parts of the frame. As shown in the cross section, the top, the sides, and the bottom battens combine to form a rabbet that holds the mirror glazing and backboard in place. For the mirror to fit properly, the rabbet should be ¼-in.

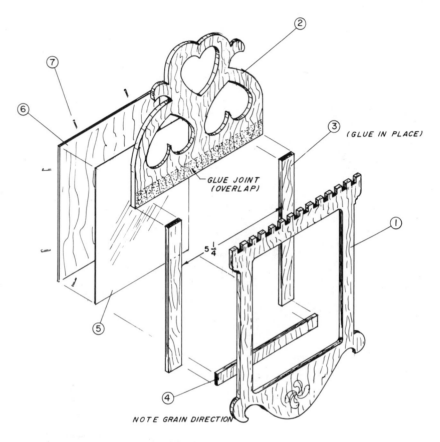

GLUE IN PLACE

GLUE JOINT
(OVERLAP)

$5\frac{1}{4}$

NOTE GRAIN DIRECTION

EXPLODED VIEW

wide all around the mirror cutout, as shown. Trim the battens, if necessary. Glue up the frame. Glue the two side battens (part 3) flush with the sides of the bottom section. Glue the top (part 2) in place so the overall height of the mirror frame is 17½ in. Glue the bottom batten ¼ in. below the lower edge of the cutout.

Attach two small eye screws to the back and string a length of picture wire between them.

5. Apply finish. Before installing the mirror glazing (part 5) and backboard, varnish the frame.

6. Cut the mirror glazing. Cut the mirror glazing to size and check the fit—it should not be snug, or the expansion of the surrounding wood might crack the glass. Add the backboard and hold it in place securely by driving eight square-cut headless brads (part 7) into the lip.

MATERIALS LIST

Part	Dimensions	Quantity
1. Bottom section	¼" × 9¾" × 11⁵/₁₆"	1
2. Top section	¼" × 8¾" × 7½"	1
3. Side battens	¼" × 7⅞" × 1¹/₁₆"	2
4. Bottom batten*	¼" × 5¼" × ¾"	1
5. Mirror glazing	³/₃₂" × 5³/₁₆" × 7¹/₁₆"	1
6. Backboard	¼" × 5³/₁₆" × 7⅛"	1
7. Square-cut headless brads	⅞" long	8
8. Eye screws	⅞"	2

Note that grain direction runs width of part.

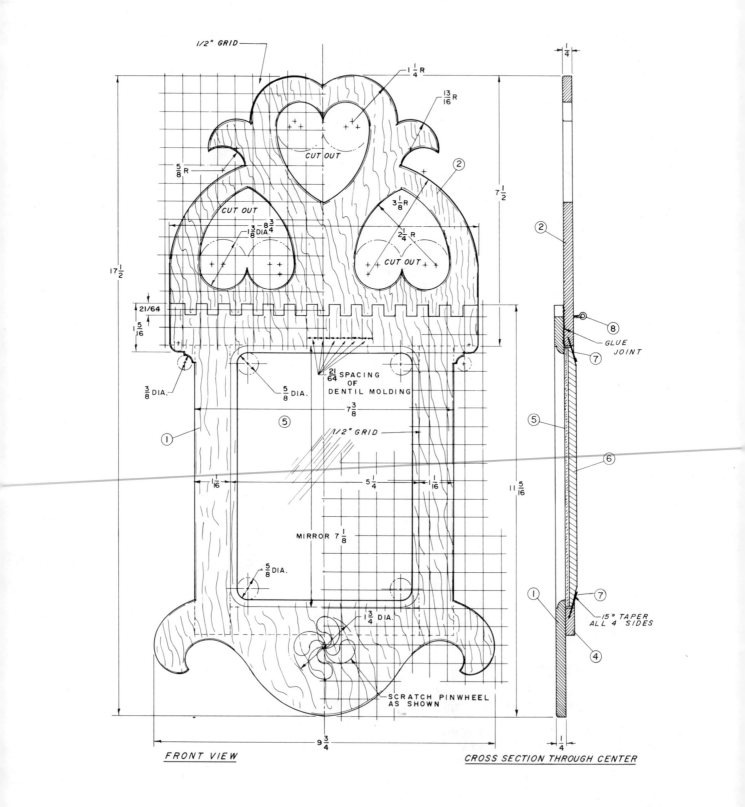

1/2" GRID

1 1/4 R

13/16 R

5/8 R

CUT OUT

CUT OUT

CUT OUT

3 1/8 R

2 1/4 R

7 1/2

1 3/8 DIA — 8 3/4

2

21/64

1 5/16

21/64 SPACING OF DENTIL MOLDING

3/8 DIA.

5/8 DIA.

7 3/8

5

1/2" GRID

1

1 1/16

5 1/4

1 1/16

11 5/16

MIRROR 7 1/8

5/8 DIA.

1 3/4 DIA.

SCRATCH PINWHEEL AS SHOWN

9 3/4

17 1/2

FRONT VIEW

1/4

2

8

GLUE JOINT

7

5

6

1

7

15° TAPER ALL 4 SIDES

4

1/4

CROSS SECTION THROUGH CENTER

Miniature Blanket Chest

This project is based on a chest made in Pennsylvania around 1820. The original was made of pine and poplar, and it is unusual for its small size—just 16 in. wide, 10¼ in. deep, and 12 in. high. You might use such a box to store jewelry, important papers, or any number of other things.

You still can buy hardware very similar to that used on the original, as noted in the Materials List.

1. Select the stock. I used mahogany to make the miniature chest shown in the photograph because that happened to be the only wood I had around at the time. I painted the piece powder blue, although the original was painted green. Note that most of the parts must be planed down to a thickness of ⅜ in. The drawer is made of still thinner stock. It would be a good idea to make the drawer bottoms out of plywood or hardboard so that they won't push the drawers apart as they expand and contract. Glue up the wider pieces specified in the Materials List, if necessary.

2. Cut the parts. Cut the sides (part 1), the front (part 2), back (part 3), and bottoms (part 4) to the sizes given in the Materials List. Everything else will be cut to fit later. The chest has two bottoms: a "false" bottom above the drawers and a second bottom below the drawers. Cut stopped dadoes for each in the sides. These dadoes end ⅜ in. from the back surface.

3. Assemble the case. The case is put together with simple butt joints. Dry-assemble the sides, the back, and both bottoms, as shown in the exploded view. Cut the four drawer guides (part 5) to fit. Note the grain direction. Glue and nail the pieces together.

Make a cutout in the front piece to line up with the openings in the chest. Glue and nail the front panel in place. Sand all surfaces.

4. Attach the lid. The lid (part 6) should be 1/32 in. longer and wider than the case. Cut it to size based on the actual chest. Notch the back for the hinges (part 14) and temporarily attach them to the lid and case. Check to see that the lid fits well. Check for proper fit again and then remove all the hardware until after you have applied a finish.

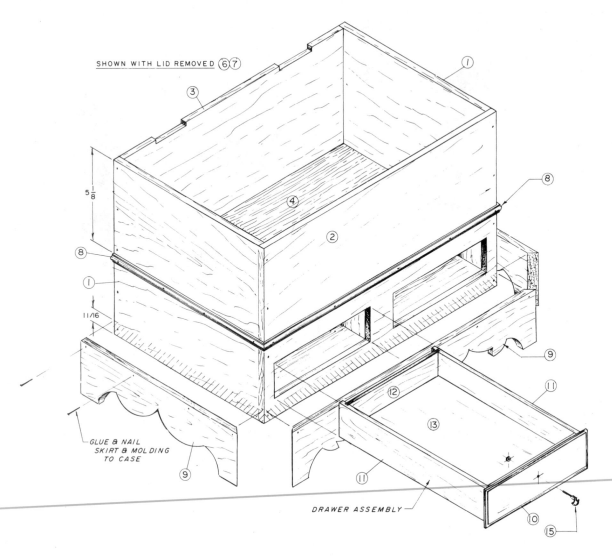

SHOWN WITH LID REMOVED ⑥⑦

5 1/8

11/16

GLUE & NAIL
SKIRT & MOLDING
TO CASE

DRAWER ASSEMBLY

EXPLODED VIEW

5. *Build the drawers.* Measure the drawer openings. Actual sizes often vary: Make sure the drawer components (parts 10, 11, 12, and 13) in the Materials List will work. Adjust the sizes as necessary.

Rout or shape a 3/16-in. radius on all four sides of each drawer front, as shown in detail D. Rabbet the drawer front, as shown. Look at both the top and side view of the drawers. The rabbets on the top and bottom are different.

Cut dadoes in the sides to accept the back.

Cut grooves in all the parts to receive the drawer bottoms. Dry-assemble the drawer, keeping everything square, and glue and nail it together if you're satisfied with the fit.

Drill for the drawer pulls (part 15) and add them.

6. *Attach the skirt and moldings.* Shape or rout the moldings and the skirts (parts 7, 8, and 9) to the profile shown in details A, B, and C. Make each an inch or so longer than necessary, and then miter and trim them to fit the chest. Glue and nail each to the chest. To locate the center molding, measure 5⅛ in. down from the top of the case.

7. *Finish the chest.* You can try your hand at grain painting, if you want to be true to the original chest. Or, simply stain and varnish or paint the piece. Finally, add the hinges.

186

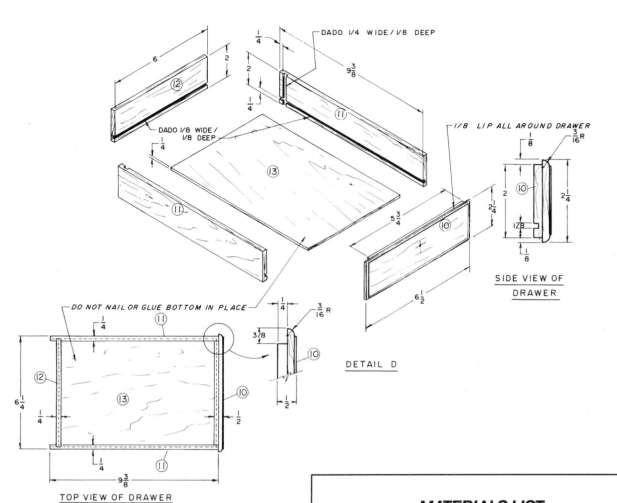

DADO 1/4 WIDE/1/8 DEEP

DADO 1/8 WIDE/1/8 DEEP

1/8 LIP ALL AROUND DRAWER

SIDE VIEW OF DRAWER

DO NOT NAIL OR GLUE BOTTOM IN PLACE

DETAIL D

TOP VIEW OF DRAWER

MATERIALS LIST

Part	Dimensions	Quantity
1. Sides	$\frac{3}{8}'' \times 9\frac{1}{2}'' \times 9\frac{7}{8}''$	2
2. Front	$\frac{3}{8}'' \times 9\frac{1}{2}'' \times 15\frac{1}{4}''$	1
3. Back	$\frac{3}{8}'' \times 9\frac{1}{2}'' \times 14\frac{1}{2}''$	1
4. Bottoms	$\frac{3}{8}'' \times 9\frac{1}{8}'' \times 14\frac{7}{8}''$	2
5. Drawer guides	$\frac{3}{8}'' \times 2'' \times 9\frac{1}{8}''$	4
6. Lid	$\frac{3}{8}'' \times 9\frac{29}{32}'' \times 15\frac{5}{16}''$	1
7. Lid molding	$\frac{3}{8}'' \times \frac{3}{4}'' \times 40''$	1
8. Center molding	$\frac{1}{4}'' \times \frac{3}{8}'' \times 40''$	1
9. Skirt	$\frac{3}{8}'' \times 2\frac{7}{8}'' \times 40''$	1
10. Drawer fronts	$\frac{1}{2}'' \times 2\frac{1}{4}'' \times 6\frac{1}{2}''$	2
11. Drawer sides	$\frac{1}{4}'' \times 2'' \times 9\frac{3}{8}''$	4
12. Drawer backs	$\frac{1}{4}'' \times 2'' \times 6''$	2
13. Drawer bottoms	$\frac{1}{8}'' \times 6'' \times 8\frac{7}{8}''$	2
14. Hinges*	$\frac{1}{2}'' \times 2''$	2
15. Drawer pulls*	$\frac{3}{4}''$ wide	2
16. Square-cut nails	$\frac{3}{4}''$	60

*Brass hardware is available from Anglo-American Brass Company, P.O. Box 9487, San Jose, CA 95157.

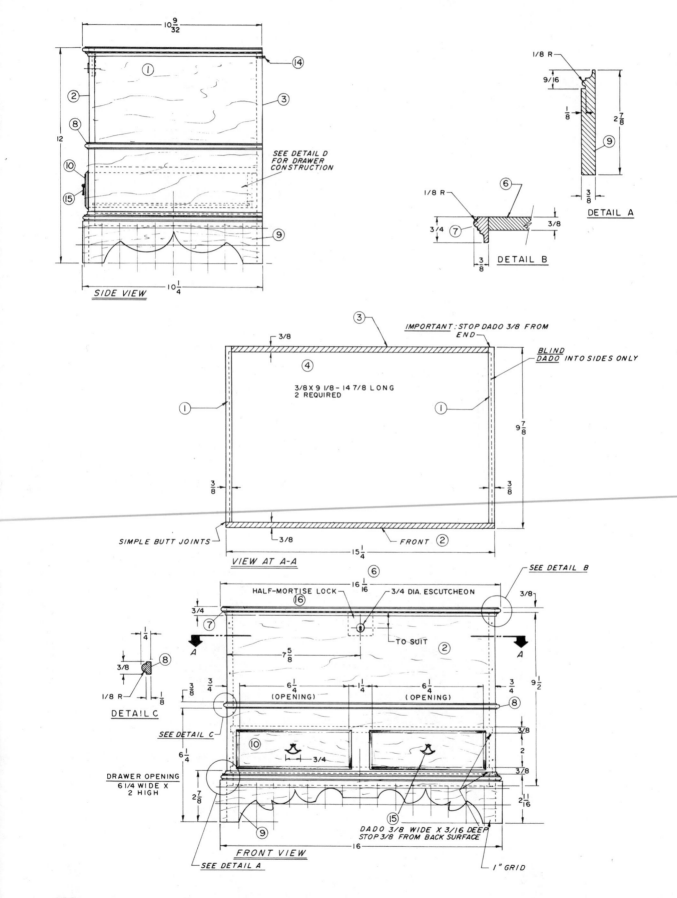

$10\frac{9}{32}$

⑭

①

②

⑧

⑩

⑮

12

SEE DETAIL D
FOR DRAWER
CONSTRUCTION

③

⑨

$10\frac{1}{4}$

SIDE VIEW

1/8 R

9/16

1/8

$2\frac{7}{8}$

⑨

3/8

DETAIL A

1/8 R

⑥

3/4

⑦

3/8

3/8

DETAIL B

③

IMPORTANT: STOP DADO 3/8 FROM
END

3/8

④

BLIND
DADO INTO SIDES ONLY

3/8 X 9 1/8 - 14 7/8 LONG
2 REQUIRED

①

①

$9\frac{7}{8}$

3/8

3/8

SIMPLE BUTT JOINTS

3/8

FRONT ②

$15\frac{1}{4}$

VIEW AT A-A

⑥

SEE DETAIL B

$16\frac{1}{16}$

HALF-MORTISE LOCK

⑯

3/4 DIA. ESCUTCHEON

3/8

3/4

⑦

⑧

TO SUIT

②

$9\frac{1}{2}$

$7\frac{5}{8}$

1/4

3/8

1/4

3/8

3/4

$6\frac{1}{4}$
(OPENING)

$1\frac{1}{4}$

$6\frac{1}{4}$
(OPENING)

3/4

3/8

1/8

⑧

1/8 R

DETAIL C

SEE DETAIL C

⑩

3/8

3/4

2

3/8

$6\frac{1}{4}$

DRAWER OPENING
6 1/4 WIDE X
2 HIGH

$2\frac{7}{8}$

⑮

$2\frac{11}{16}$

⑨

DADO 3/8 WIDE X 3/16 DEEP
STOP 3/8 FROM BACK SURFACE

FRONT VIEW

16

SEE DETAIL A

1" GRID

188

MINIATURE BLANKET CHEST

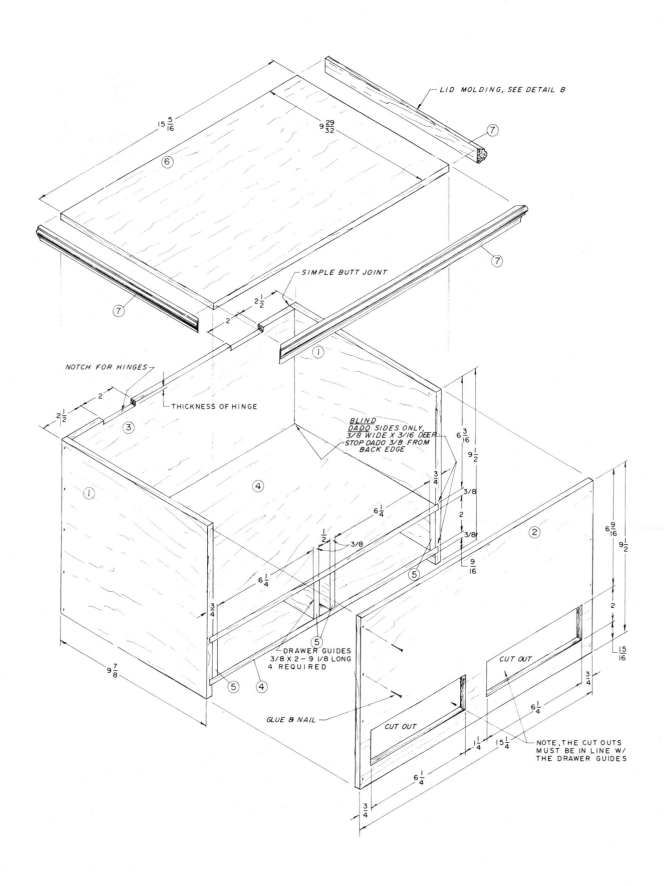

189

Victorian Nightstand

This is a copy of an original made in the late 1800s. It was a mass-produced piece made of solid oak. I happened to find the original in a curious way.

My wife and I had just moved into our first home, an old cottage in northern Vermont. In the process of shoveling through 2 feet of snow, I kept finding odd pieces of oak and tossed them into a pile to get them out of the way. In time I realized that these were the pieces of a table of some kind. In fact, the whole thing was there, and I glued the parts back together.

The table is still with us after 32 years and has survived moves to California, Rhode Island,

and now New Hampshire. Someday it will be passed down to the kids.

1. *Select the stock and cut the parts.* Any hardwood will do, although oak and walnut were particular Victorian favorites. Glue up the stock for the top.

Cut the parts as specified in the Materials List but leave the skirts (parts 4 and 5) and the post (part 1) 2 in. longer than called for. Note the direction of the grain on the legs (part 2); this is done for the sake of strength.

2. *Make a paper pattern for the leg.* Draw a grid with ½-in. squares and enlarge the drawing of the leg onto it. Be careful to maintain an *exact* angle of 90 degrees between the bottom of the leg and the surface which joins it to the post. This angle is called out on the leg detail. Use a large carpenter's square to double-check this angle. If it is off, the legs won't sit squarely on the floor.

3. *Make the legs.* Transfer the outline of the leg to the wood, making sure that the grain runs down the length of the shape. If you have a saw that can handle the job, cut out all four legs at once by taping them together with double-sided tape. Sand the edges before separating them. If your saw won't handle a stack of legs, cut one leg and use it as a pattern to cut the other three.

Locate and drill holes for the dowel pins (part 7) in each leg.

MATERIALS LIST

Part	Dimensions	Quantity
1. Post	1½″ × 1½″ × 23¾″	1
2. Legs	¾″ × 3½″ × 14½″	4
3. Top	¾″ × 14″ × 16¾″	1
4. Front/back skirts	5/16″ × 1⅝″ × 13¾″	1 each
5. Side skirts	5/16″ × 1⅝″ × 11″	2
6. Top support	¾″ × 2¼″ × 9½″	1
7. Dowel pins	¼″ dia. × 1¼″	8
8. Flathead screws	#8 × 1¼″	2

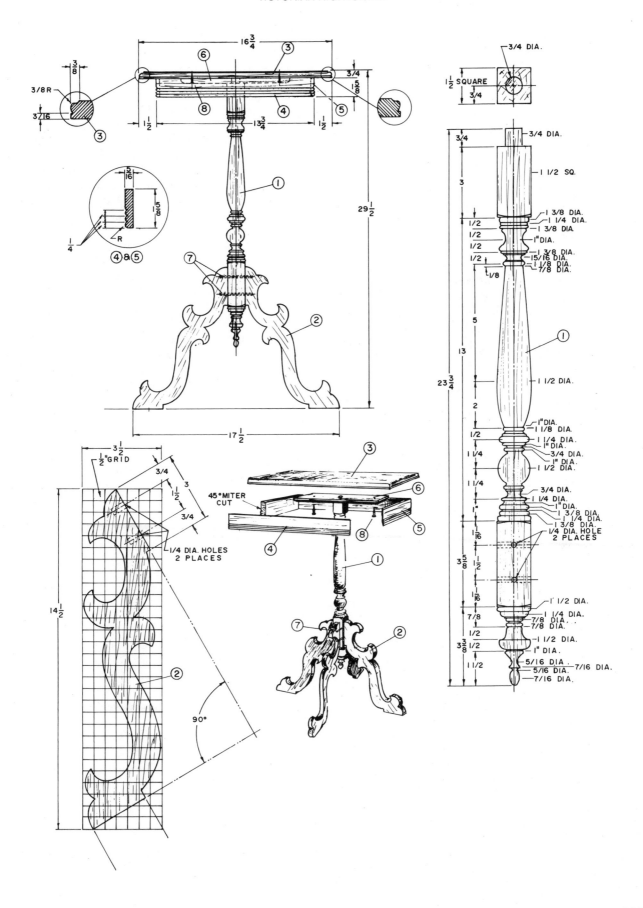

4. *Turn the post.* Turn the post to the profile shown. To help prevent chipping, try wrapping masking tape around the post at the three places where it goes from a square to a round shape.

Make sure you maintain the ¾-in.-diameter at the top end, so that will fit snugly in the top support (part 6).

When you're done turning, lay out the holes in the post by putting dowel centers, available at most hardware stores, into the holes already drilled in the legs. Position the legs on the post and push the points of the dowel center into the post. Drill ¼-in. diameter × ¾-in. holes at the marks in the post.

5. *Make the skirts.* Cut beads on the skirts with a router or shaper to the profile shown. After you've cut the beads, miter the corners, cutting the skirts to length in the process.

6. *Make the top and top supports.* Cut the top (part 3) to size. Rout the four edges as closely as possible to the profile shown, using the bits available to you.

Cut the top support to size and drill a hole in it to accept the post. Drill and countersink holes for the flathead screws (part 8).

7. *Assemble the table.* Glue the four legs to the post, using the eight dowel pins. Glue the skirts to the underside of the top. Glue the top support to the post, aligning it with one of the pair of legs. When the glue dries, attach the top support to the top with two flathead screws. The top support is centered on the underside and runs parallel with the longer sides of the top.

8. *Apply finish.* Sand thoroughly. If you used oak or another porous wood, go over the night stand with a wood filler to fill the grain. Wipe the filler *across* the grain and allow it to dry for a few minutes. Wipe off the excess in the same direction, using a rough rag. Take care not to pull the filler out of the wood pores in the process. Sand thoroughly. The original had a light oak stain and a high-gloss varnish; I used a similar stain and a satin finish on the reproduction pictured here.

Large Blanket Chest

Blanket chests were among the first pieces of furniture to arrive with settlers to colonial America. In fact, the Pilgrims brought six-board blanket chests with them on the Mayflower.

I copied this design from a chest in an antique dealer's showroom in Peterborough, New Hampshire. I would guess the original was made around 1840. It is perhaps the biggest blanket chest I have seen, so before getting started you should measure the room in which it is to go and make sure it will fit.

1. *Select the stock and cut the parts.* The original chest was made of pine, as is the chest shown here. Six-board blanket chests were named because each side was made from a single wide board. I was able to use 2-foot-wide boards for my reproduction, but you may have to glue up the wider parts. Even if you machine plane your boards, consider a final pass with the hand plane to give them the gently wavy surface that distinguishes traditional woodworking.

Cut the sides (part 1) and shelf dividers (2) to the dimensions given in the Materials List. Cut the rest to fit later.

2. *Make a paper pattern and cut the parts to shape.* Draw a grid with 1-in. squares and enlarge the front and side legs onto it. Transfer each enlargement to the appropriate part. Cut along the lines with a jigsaw or band saw.

Cut two dadoes in each side to house the shelf dividers.

3. *Assemble the chest.* Nail and glue the shelf dividers to the sides. Check to make sure the assembly is square. Cut the front and back (parts 3 and 4) to fit. Glue and nail them to the sides.

Glue the spacers (part 8), the front legs (part 5), and the skirt (part 7) in place. Check again to make sure the cabinet is square. When the glue dries, glue and nail the back legs (part 6) in place.

4. *Make the lid.* The lid of the original chest was a 1¼-in.-thick board. Because it is hard to come by such a massive piece, I glued up a sandwich of two boards (parts 9 and 10). When the glue has dried, use a hand plane or rasp to round the top, front, and sides, as shown; do not round the back edge.

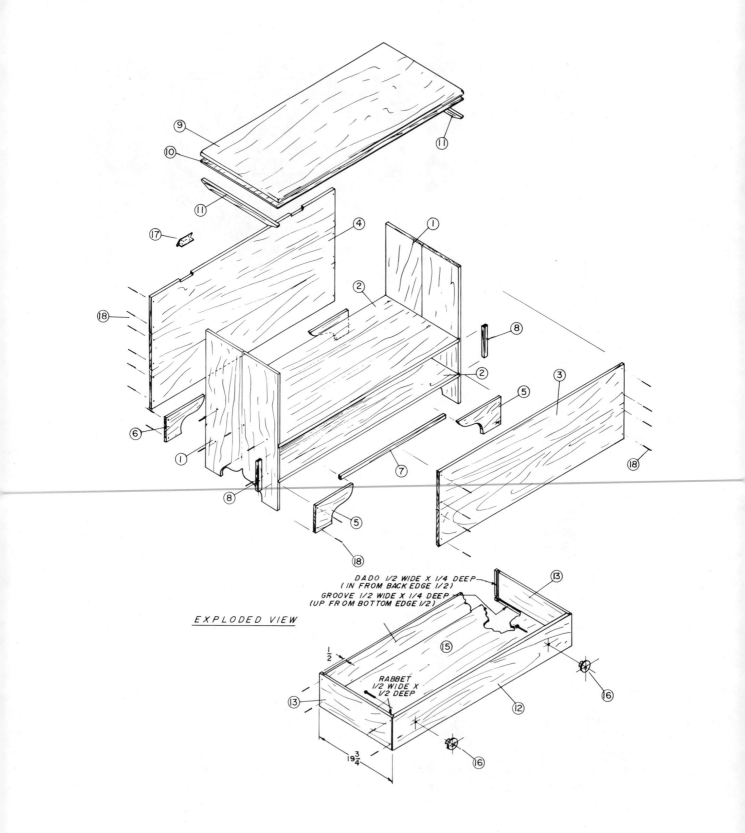

EXPLODED VIEW

DADO 1/2 WIDE X 1/4 DEEP
(IN FROM BACK EDGE 1/2)
GROOVE 1/2 WIDE X 1/4 DEEP
(UP FROM BOTTOM EDGE 1/2)

RABBET
1/2 WIDE X
1/2 DEEP

$1\frac{1}{2}$

$19\frac{3}{4}$

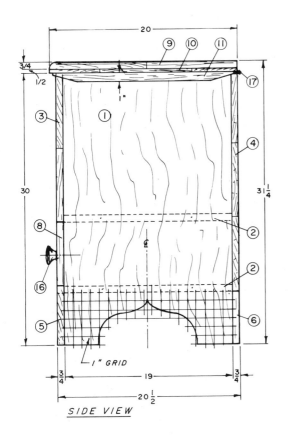

SIDE VIEW

I" GRID

MATERIALS LIST

Part	Dimensions	Quantity
1. Sides	$\frac{3}{4}'' \times 19'' \times 30''$	2
2. Shelf dividers	$\frac{3}{4}'' \times 19'' \times 47''$	2
3. Front	$\frac{3}{4}'' \times 16\frac{1}{2}'' \times 48''$	1
4. Back	$\frac{3}{4}'' \times 23\frac{1}{2}'' \times 48''$	1
5. Front legs	$\frac{3}{4}'' \times 6\frac{1}{2}'' \times 10''$	2
6. Back legs	$\frac{3}{4}'' \times 5\frac{3}{4}'' \times 10''$	2
7. Skirt	$\frac{3}{4}'' \times \frac{13}{16}'' \times 28''$	1
8. Spacers	$\frac{3}{4}'' \times \frac{13}{16}'' \times 7''$	2
9. Outside lid	$\frac{3}{4}'' \times 20'' \times 49\frac{3}{4}''$	1
10. Inside lid	$\frac{1}{2}'' \times 20'' \times 49\frac{3}{4}''$	1
11. Battens	$\frac{3}{4}'' \times 1'' \times 19\frac{1}{2}''$	2
12. Drawer front	$\frac{3}{4}'' \times 7'' \times 46\frac{1}{2}''$	1
13. Drawer sides	$\frac{1}{2}'' \times 7'' \times 19\frac{1}{2}''$	2
14. Drawer back	$\frac{1}{2}'' \times 6'' \times 46''$	1
15. Drawer bottom	$\frac{1}{2}'' \times 18\frac{3}{8}'' \times 46''$	1
16. Pulls	$2''$ dia.	2
17. Hinges	$1\frac{1}{2}'' \times 3''$	2
18. Finishing nails	6d and 8d	as needed

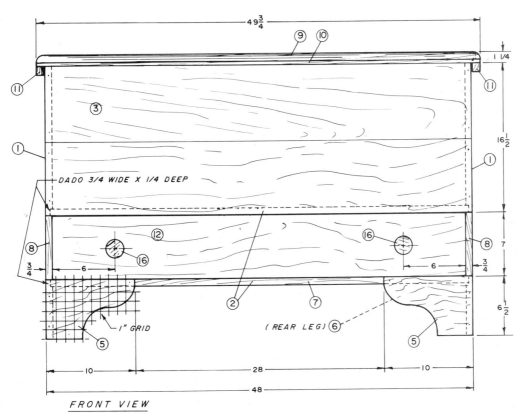

DADO 3/4 WIDE X 1/4 DEEP

I" GRID

(REAR LEG)

FRONT VIEW

Attach the battens (part 11), making sure that they will clear the sides of the case. Mortise the back for the hinges (part 17) 8 in. from each end and attach the lid. You can add a chain stop to the lid (not shown here) to prevent it from falling back too far.

5. *Make the drawer.* The original drawer was not dovetailed together, which is surprising given its age.

There is a knack to fitting a drawer. The dimensions given are simply guidelines. Cut the drawer front (part 12) so that it fits snugly in its opening and then rabbet it for the sides.

Cut the drawer sides (part 13) to a length that will make the drawer front flush with the chest front when the drawer is closed. Rabbet the sides for the back.

Dry-assemble the pieces so that they are square in relation to each other. Measure the distance between the dadoes and cut the back to this dimension.

Cut grooves in the drawer front and sides to house the drawer bottom (part 15). There is no groove in the drawer back (part 14). The drawer back sits *on top* of the drawer bottom so that the drawer can expand and contract underneath it after the drawer is built.

Dry-fit the parts of the drawer, and make any necessary adjustments. Slip the bottom in the sides, and build the drawer around them. Glue and nail the drawer together. Check to make sure it is square and let the glue dry. Put the drawer in place to check the clearance. Sand or plane the sides for a good fit.

Drill two holes in the drawer front for the pulls (part 16), inset 6 in. from the ends. Add the pulls. Standard 2-in.-diameter wooden pulls will look good on the piece.

6. *Apply finish.* Sand the chest thoroughly and paint it. The original was painted a traditional blue-green shade.

Wall Shelf

This is a copy of an antique shelf, to which I've added an optional dish rail. The design features cyma curves with a step between each.

1. Select the stock and cut the parts. The original shelf was made of pine. The entire piece is made from ¾-in.-thick stock.

Cut the parts to the sizes given in the Materials List.

2. Make a paper pattern and cut the sides to shape. Draw a grid with 1-in. squares and enlarge the drawing of the sides onto it. Include the dadoes for the shelves in the pattern.

Temporarily tack the two sides (part 1) together; try placing the tacks in the center of the top and bottom dadoes. Transfer the pattern to the top piece of wood and cut the sides to shape.

Sand the edges while they are still together, and then separate them.

Cut the dadoes for the shelves in each side. If you choose, cut a dish rail groove in each shelf, 1⅝ in. from the back edge.

Drill ½-in. holes, ¼ in. deep for the wooden plugs that cover the four hanging holes. Drill the ³/₁₆-in.-diameter hanging holes on the same centers as the ½-in. holes.

3. Assemble the shelf. Glue and nail the shelves (part 2) to the sides with square-cut nails (part 3). Check that everything is square and will lay evenly on a flat surface.

4. Apply finish. Sand thoroughly. Stain and varnish or simply varnish. Drive screws through the hanging holes to hang the shelf. Cover them with the four plugs (part 4).

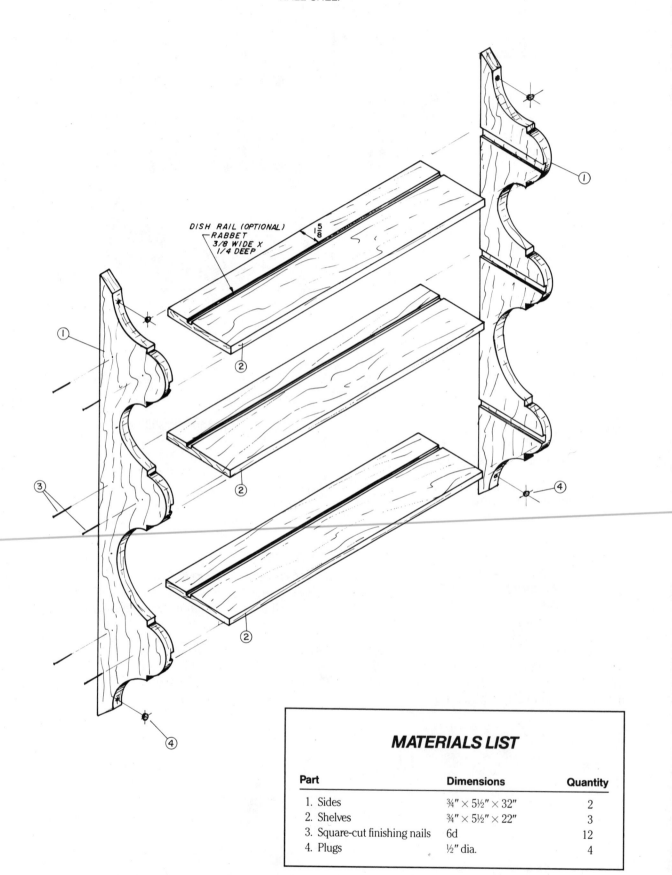

DISH RAIL (OPTIONAL)
RABBET
3/8 WIDE X
1/4 DEEP

MATERIALS LIST

Part	Dimensions	Quantity
1. Sides	¾" × 5½" × 32"	2
2. Shelves	¾" × 5½" × 22"	3
3. Square-cut finishing nails	6d	12
4. Plugs	½" dia.	4

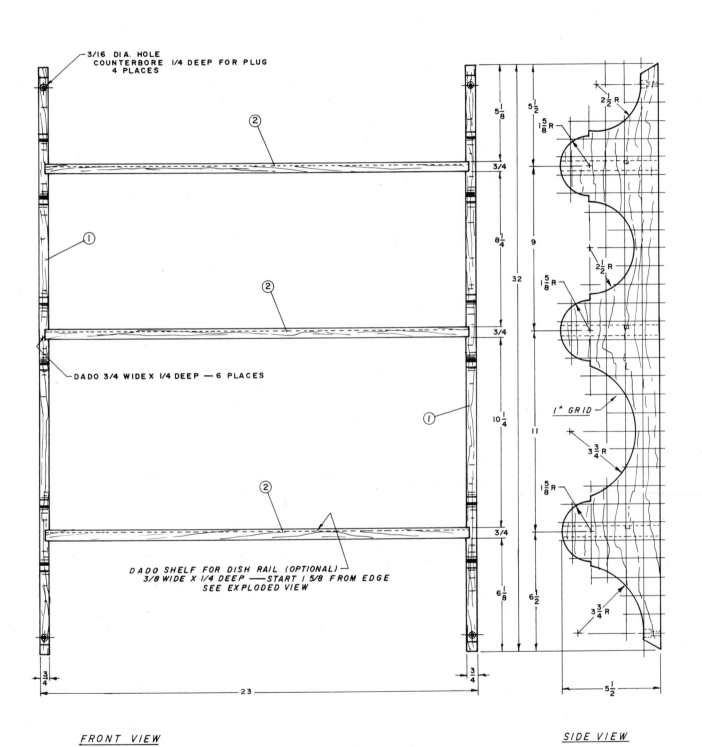

3/16 DIA. HOLE
COUNTERBORE 1/4 DEEP FOR PLUG
4 PLACES

DADO 3/4 WIDE x 1/4 DEEP — 6 PLACES

DADO SHELF FOR DISH RAIL (OPTIONAL)
3/8 WIDE X 1/4 DEEP — START 1 5/8 FROM EDGE
SEE EXPLODED VIEW

FRONT VIEW

SIDE VIEW

Wall Cupboard

Here is one of the earliest designs in this book. The original is said to have been made around 1725 and was found in Lancaster, Pennsylvania. The large iron butterfly hinges and escutcheon plate shown here are true to the antique version. Exact copies of this hardware can be ordered through the source given in the Materials List.

1. Select the stock and cut the parts of the case. The original cupboard was made from butternut and painted. Cut parts 1 through 10 to the sizes given in the Materials List.

2. Make a paper pattern and cut the parts to shape. Draw a grid with 1-in. squares and enlarge the profile of the side panel onto it. Transfer the enlargement to the stock. To ensure that both sides (part 2) are identical, tack them together with finishing nails and cut them out at the same time. Separate them and cut the dadoes and rabbets in the sides, as shown.

Make a pattern for the bottom skirt (part 10) and cut out the skirt. Cut the notch for the drawer opening in the two front boards (part 5), taking care to made both parts identical and all cuts exactly 90 degrees.

3. Assemble the case. Glue and nail the shelves (parts 3 and 4) to the side panels. Nail the back (part 1) and the back support (part 6) in place, keeping everything square.

When the glue dries, nail the bottom skirt and top board (part 9) in place.

4. Make and install the trim. Rout or shape the top moldings (parts 12 and 14) to the profile shown in the drawing. Miter and cut the molding to fit the cabinet. Glue the molding to the front support (part 7) but simply nail the molding to the sides.

MATERIALS LIST

Part	Dimensions	Quantity
1. Backboard	½" × 14¾" × 25¼"	1
2. Side panels	¾" × 7¼" × 25¼"	2
3. Shelves	½" × 7¼" × 14¾"	2
4. Bottom shelf	½" × 3½" × 14¾"	1
5. Front board	¾" × 3" × 20½"	1
6. Back support	¾" × 1½" × 14"	1
7. Front support	¾" × 2¼" × 14"	1
8. Trim	¾" × 2" × 9½"	1
9. Top board	¾" × 9¾" × 19"	1
10. Bottom skirt	¾" × 2¼" × 14¾"	1
11. Door	¾" × 9½" × 11½"	1
12. Top molding	¾" × 1½" × 40"	1
13. Door pull	½" × ¾" × 11½"	1
14. Bottom molding	½" × 15½"	1
15. Drawer face	¾" × 4¾" × 14¾"	1
16. Drawer front/back	½" × 4¼" × 13½"	1 each
17. Drawer sides	½" × 4¼" × 6¾"	2
18. Drawer bottom	⅜" × 6¼" × 13½"	1
19. Drawer pull	1" dia. × 2⁷⁄₁₆"	1
20. Escutcheon*		1
21. Butterfly hinges*		2
22. Half-mortise lock		1
23. Square-cut nails	1½"	30
24. Brad	⅞"	1

Hardware is available from Ball and Ball, 463 West Lincoln Highway, Exton, PA 19341. Escutcheon is #L108-065, and butterfly hinge is #H38-C56. Hinge comes with either hand-forged nails or pyramid head screws.

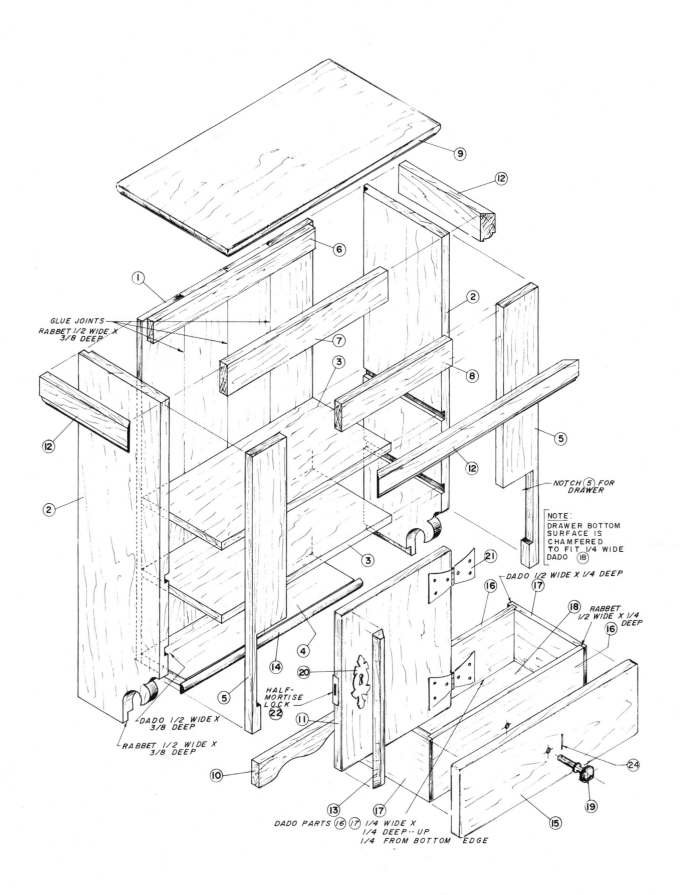

GLUE JOINTS
RABBET 1/2 WIDE X
3/8 DEEP

NOTCH (5) FOR
DRAWER

NOTE:
DRAWER BOTTOM
SURFACE IS
CHAMFERED
TO FIT 1/4 WIDE
DADO (18)

DADO 1/2 WIDE X 1/4 DEEP

RABBET
1/2 WIDE X 1/4
DEEP

HALF-
MORTISE
LOCK

DADO 1/2 WIDE X
3/8 DEEP

RABBET 1/2 WIDE X
3/8 DEEP

DADO PARTS (16)(17) 1/4 WIDE X
1/4 DEEP--UP
1/4 FROM BOTTOM EDGE

WALL CUPBOARD

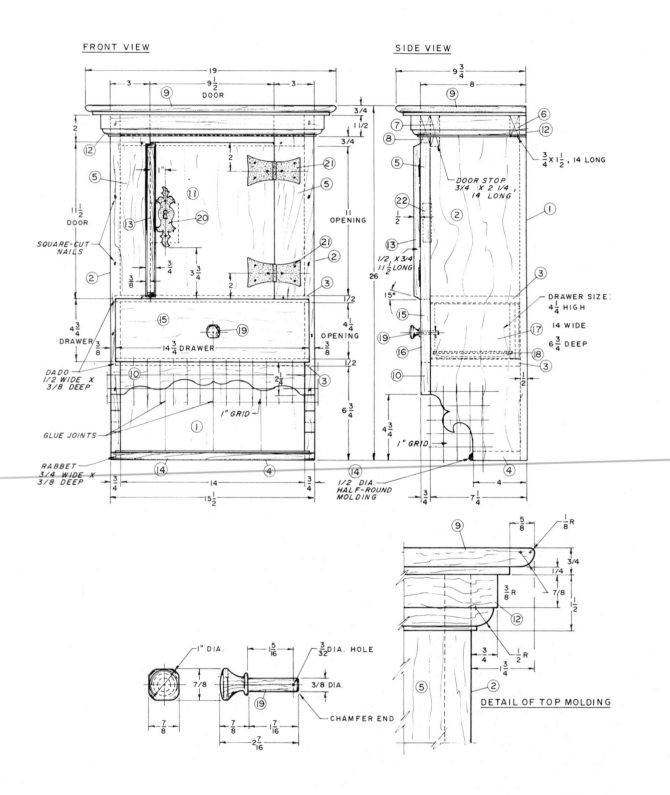

FRONT VIEW

SIDE VIEW

DETAIL OF TOP MOLDING

5. *Cut the door and install the lock.* Cut the door (part 11) to fit the opening. Cut and attach the door pull (part 13). The door pull is beveled approximately 15 degrees on the ends and two sides. It overlaps the edge of the door ⅜ in., as shown, to act as a dust stop.

Mortise the lock (part 22) into the back of the door. Make sure the lock you buy allows a full 1 in. between the door edge and the keyhole; you need the room to install the door pull and escutcheon.

Drill a hole for the door lock in the back of the door and square off the edges with a chisel to match your lock. Attach the lock and make sure it works.

6. *Cut the drawer parts.* To work properly, a drawer must be slightly smaller than the opening provided for it in the case. The best way to do it on this drawer is to cut the dadoes and rabbets in the drawer sides first. Put the sides in place in the cabinet and cut the front and back to give you the proper fit.

This drawer has a raised panel bottom, a practice that was common in the eighteenth and early nineteenth centuries. Some drawers were designed so the panel could slip in from the back. Not this one. The panel is held by grooves in the front, back, and both sides.

Cut the grooves to accept the drawer bottom (part 18). On the table saw, cut a raised panel to fit in the grooves. If you don't feel like making a raised panel, you can simply rabbet the edges to create the properly sized lip.

Dry-fit the drawer together. The bottom should fit snugly in the groove. The grooves should allow ⅛ in. for the bottom to expand and contract across the grain. Make any necessary adjustments.

7. *Assemble the drawer.* Glue and nail the face, front, back, and sides (parts 15, 16, 17, and 18) together with the bottom in place. Don't get any glue on the bottom or in the grooves for the bottom.

Screw or nail the drawer face on the drawer. Turn the drawer pull (part 19) on a lathe to a full 1-in. diameter, then use sandpaper to partially flatten the four sides, as shown in the detail. Pin the knob in place with either a ⅞-in. square-cut headless brad or a small wooden peg.

8. *Finish the cupboard.* You can stain and apply tung oil, or paint the piece to look like the original. To make mine look as old as possible, I painted it off-white, then added a second coat of a traditional shade of blue paint. After the paint dried thoroughly, I carefully sanded through the blue coat here and there to simulate years of use.

9. *Hang the door.* Because the door hangs on "butterfly" hinges (part 21) that are nailed in place, you mount the hinges for the first time after applying finish. Butterfly hinges are nailed in place with "cinched" nails: The nail is driven all the way through and then bent over from the back.

Nail the escutcheon in place.

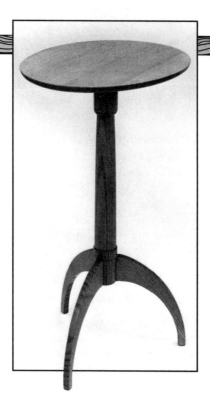

Shaker Table

The Shakers were known for their plain, simple, well-made furniture. Here is a copy of a small Shaker table. The construction is straightforward, although the dovetail cuts at the bottom of the center post can be a bit tricky.

1. *Select the stock and cut the parts.* This project is made out of cherry. Cut the parts to the sizes given in the Materials List.

2. *Make a paper pattern and cut the parts to shape.* Draw a grid with ½-in. squares and enlarge the drawing of the leg onto it. The three legs (part 2) can be cut out at the same time by temporarily joining them with double-faced masking tape. Transfer the pattern to the leg on top of the stack and cut them out as one. Sand the edges before separating them.

Rout six slots, ⅛ in. wide and 1 in. long, in the support (part 3) to receive the screws. The slots are parallel with the long edges of the support. Their exact location isn't important. When the top is attached to the support, the slots will allow it to expand and contract.

Lay out the pattern for the top (part 4) on a ½-in. grid. You might try laying out only a quarter of the ellipse, and using it four times to transfer the shape to the entire top. Cut the top to size. Rout the edge to the profile shown with a ⁷⁄₁₆-in.-radius roundover bit.

3. *Turn the center post.* Turn the center post (part 1) to the profile shown in the side view. Don't forget to include the round, 1-in.-diameter tenon at the top of the post. Note the long, even taper from the top of the post to the collar near the bottom. Sand the post thoroughly while it is turning on the lathe. Turn the lathe off, but leave the post in the lathe to rout the dovetail slots.

To locate the slots, lay out three index marks, spaced equally around the perimeter of the post. Lay out the index marks by wrapping a piece of paper around the bottom of the leg. Cut the paper so the ends just meet, but don't overlap, and then fold it in thirds. Wrap the paper back around the leg. The first index mark is where the two ends meet. The other two are at the folds in the paper. Make index marks on the *end* of the post.

To rout the groove you will need a jig and a fence attachment for your router. The simplest jig is a V-shaped box that slips under the post

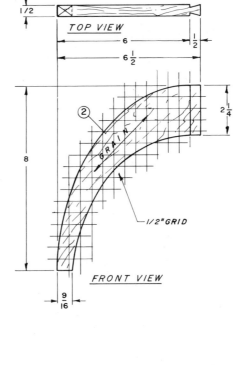

TOP VIEW

FRONT VIEW

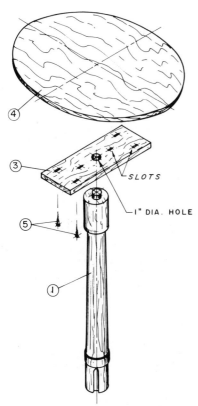

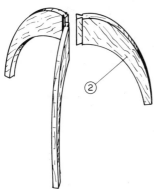

④

③

SLOTS

1" DIA. HOLE

⑤

①

②

EXPLODED VIEW

MATERIALS LIST

Part	Dimensions	Quantity
1. Center post	$1\frac{3}{4}'' \times 1\frac{3}{4}'' \times 18''$	1
2. Legs	$\frac{1}{2}'' \times 6\frac{1}{2}'' \times 8''$	3
3. Support	$\frac{7}{16}'' \times 3'' \times 8''$	1
4. Top	$\frac{7}{16}'' \times 11'' \times 14''$	1
5. Roundhead screws	#6 $\times \frac{3}{4}''$	6

while it is still on the lathe. The router rides on the arms of the V; the router fence rides against an arm to guide the cut.

Build the jig as long as the post. Make the arms long enough to hold the router just above the post when everything is in place.

Clamp the jig directly to the post so the index mark lines up with the corner of the V. Advance the tailstock to keep the post from rotat-

ing further. Put a ½-in dovetail bit in the router and support the router on the ends of the V. Set the router fence against one side of the jig so that the router bit is centered over the post.

Rout the groove. Rotate the post to align the next index mark and rout the second groove. Repeat to rout the third groove.

Rout the pins in the legs with the same dovetail bit in a table-mounted router. Guide the legs against a wooden fence clamped to the table to make the cut. *Do not attempt to make the cut by running the leg between the fence and the cutter.* The safest approach is to have the diameter of the cutter buried almost entirely in the fence. Cut some sample pins in scrap and check the fit in the post. The pins should fit snugly without being forced into place.

Rout the pins in the legs. Saw off the top ½ in. of the pins.

4. *Assemble the table.* Sand the legs and table top thoroughly, except for surfaces involved in the leg joints. Put glue on the top edge of the dovetail pins and slip the pins in the post. Glue the support to the post so that the support is perpendicular to any one of the legs, as shown in the top view. Attach the top to the support with roundhead screws (part 5) only.

5. *Apply finish.* Most Shaker furniture was finished without stains. I suggest a clear penetrating oil.

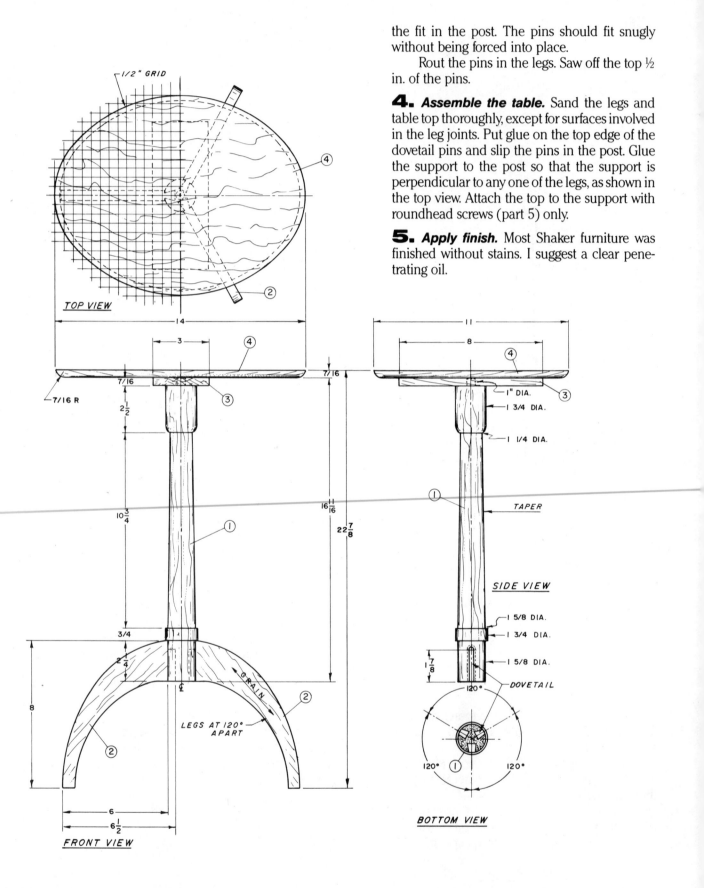

Country Desk

Finding that I needed both a writing surface and book shelves, I came up with the design for this desk. It is fashioned after an old country desk I saw in an antiques' magazine. In the spirit of a traditional secretary desk, this piece has three hidden compartments; secret storage spaces were handy in a day that predated safety deposit boxes. The pigeonhole unit can be slid out of place to get at two hidden compartments, or to provide more desk area when needed. The third compartment is reached through a hidden lid above the top shelf.

This desk is simpler to make than it may appear. Don't let it intimidate you. The project will look more manageable if you think of it as six straightforward assemblies: a base, the drawers, a middle section, the pigeonholes, the top section, and two raised-panel doors. Each assembly is within the abilities of most woodworkers. And the result will be impressive—a project that is certain to be valued by future generations.

1. *Select the stock.* This desk can be made of almost any hard or softwood. If you want yours to look like a country piece, you might want to use pine. Walnut, mahogany, or cherry will make it look more formal. The desk pictured here is made of ash, and I think this wood makes the piece look more contemporary.

Choose well-seasoned, knot-free, straight-grained stock. Order the hardware as soon as possible so that you will not be held up waiting for parts. A mail-order source is given in the Materials List.

2. *Cut the parts.* It's a good idea to build a piece this large as a series of subassemblies, and to cut the parts for each subassembly as you build it. I like to build from the ground up, so let's begin with the base. Cut the legs (part 1) the front, back, and side skirts, (parts 2 and 3) to the dimensions given in the Materials List. Make sure adjoining faces are square to each other.

3. *Mortise the legs.* Each leg has two mortises in it. Mark the outside corner of each leg and lay out the mortises. Double-check the position of the mortises. Orient them so the legs will go together as planned.

You can easily cut these mortises in repeated passes over a table-mounted router. Put a ¼-in.-

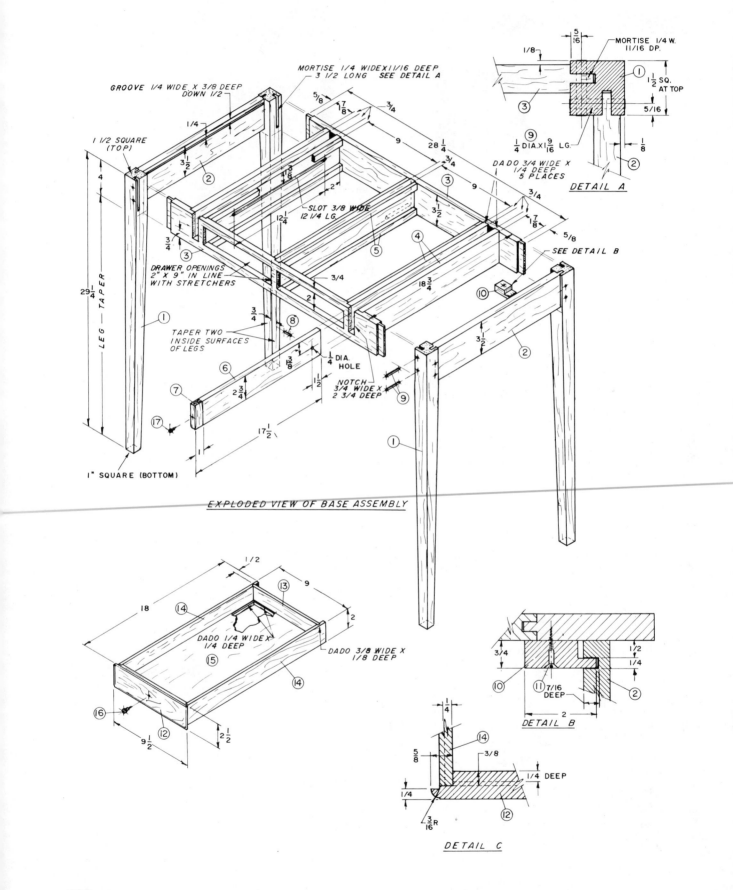

GROOVE 1/4 WIDE X 3/8 DEEP
DOWN 1/2

MORTISE 1/4 WIDEX11/16 DEEP
3 1/2 LONG   SEE DETAIL A

MORTISE 1/4 W.
11/16 DP.

1 1/2 SQ.
AT TOP

5/16

1/4 DIA.X1 9/16 LG.

DETAIL A

1 1/2 SQUARE
(TOP)

DADO 3/4 WIDE X
1/4 DEEP
5 PLACES

SLOT 3/8 WIDE
12 1/4 LG.

DRAWER OPENINGS
2" X 9" IN LINE
WITH STRETCHERS

SEE DETAIL B

29 1/4

LEG — TAPER

TAPER TWO
INSIDE SURFACES
OF LEGS

1/4 DIA.
HOLE

NOTCH
3/4 WIDE X
2 3/4 DEEP

2 3/4

17 1/2

1" SQUARE (BOTTOM)

EXPLODED VIEW OF BASE ASSEMBLY

DADO 1/4 WIDE X
1/4 DEEP

DADO 3/8 WIDE X
1/8 DEEP

9 1/2

2 1/2

DETAIL B

DETAIL C

straight cutting bit in the router. Position a fence on the table so that a leg guided against it will rout the mortise as laid out. Raise the bit about ⅛ in. for each successive cut until you have cut a mortise ¹¹/₁₆ in. deep. Square off the roundover with a chisel.

4. Taper the legs. The inside faces of the legs are tapered. The taper starts 4 in. down from the top and continues to the bottom of the leg, which is 1 in. square. It's easiest to cut the tapers on the table saw using a commercially available tapering jig. You could also bandsaw the legs to shape and then clean up the surfaces on a jointer, with a belt sander, or hand plane.

5. Cut joints on the skirt. Lay out tenons on the ends of the front, and on the back and side skirts, as shown in detail A.

Cut the tenons with a dado blade on the table saw. First, raise the blade to cut away ¼ in. with each pass. Then make a trial tenon on a scrap piece of stock the exact thickness of the skirts. To do this, guide the scrap over the blade with the miter gauge. Then turn the scrap over and make a cut on the other side in the same way.

Test-fit the scrap in the mortise. Adjust the height of the dado blade as necessary. When you cut a successful test joint, cut the joints on the actual stock.

In the side skirts, rout a groove for the top supports (part 10), as shown in detail B.

In the front and back skirts, cut the dadoes that hold the interior stretcher with a router or on the table saw, as shown.

To cut the openings for the drawers, first drill a hole in each corner of each opening. Position the holes carefully: They should be adjacent to, but not on, the cutout lines. Make the cutout with a jigsaw or saber saw.

6. Glue the legs and skirts together. Glue the legs to each of the side skirts. When the glue dries, glue the front and back skirts in place. Make sure everything is square before the glue dries. A small mistake here will have to be repeated throughout construction if all the pieces are to fit correctly.

When the glue has dried, drill holes in the legs for leg pins (part 9), as shown in the exploded view and detail A.

7. Cut and install the interior parts. Cut the interior stretchers (part 4) to fit the base. Rout the slot shown in the exploded view in two of the skirts: These will guide the lid supports later. Glue the stretchers in place. When the glue dries, add the drawer supports (part 5) to the assembly. Glue them in place just above and below the drawer openings, as shown.

Glue a breadboard end (part 7) to the lid support (part 6), as shown. You'll find it's easiest if you glue up one support 6 in. wide, and then rip it on the table saw to form the two supports.

Drill a ¼-in.-diameter hole through both lid supports for a stop pin (part 8). The pin travels in the slots in the interior skirts and makes it impossible to pull the support out by accident. Dry-fit the lid supports to the base assembly with the stops in place and check that they function as they should. Make alterations if needed. Glue the stop pins in place after the desk is completed.

Temporarily install the two support knobs (part 17).

8. Make the drawers. Ideally, drawers should be just a little bit smaller than the openings in which they fit. A total of a ¹/₁₆-in. play, side-to-side, is plenty. The drawers must be assembled in an order that allows you to carefully control the fit.

First, cut all parts to a width of 2½ in., as given in the Materials List. Cut the sides to length. Cut dadoes in the sides and slip the sides in position. Measure the distance between the bottom of the dadoes and cut a back to fit.

Rout the profile on the drawer front (part 12), as shown in detail C. With the drawer backs and drawer sides (parts 13 and 14) temporarily assembled and in place, measure the distance between the inside faces of the drawer sides: This is the distance between the rabbets in the drawer front. Rout the rabbets.

Rout a groove for the drawer bottom, ¼ in. up from the bottom of the drawer. Cut a *plywood* bottom (part 15) to fit in the groove: Solid wood will expand with humidity and might break the drawer apart.

Dry-assemble the drawers. Check that the drawers fit into the opening. Adjust, if necessary, sand or plane to fit. Then assemble all the parts but the bottom with glue; the bottom is left to float in place.

MATERIALS LIST

Part	Dimensions	Quantity	Part	Dimensions	Quantity
Base Assembly			**Pigeonhole Assembly**		
1. Legs	1½″ × 1½″ × 29¼″	4	29. Shelves	¼″ × 7½″ × 27⅞″	3
2. Side skirts	¾″ × 3½″ × 17¼″	2	30. Backs	¼″ × 7¼″ × 27⅞″	2
3. Front/back skirts	¾″ × 3½″ × 28¼″	1 each	31. Ends	¼″ × 7¼″ × 9½″	2
4. Stretchers	¾″ × 3½″ × 17¾″	5	32. Dividers	¼″ × 2¼″ × 7½″	9
5. Drawer supports	½″ × ¾″ × 17¼″	8	33. Spacer	¼″ × 1⅝″ × 7″	1
6. Lid supports	¾″ × 2¾″ × 16¾″	2	34. Bottom	¼″ × 1½″ × 27¾″	1
7. Breadboard ends	¾″ × 1″ × 2¾″	2			
8. Stop pins	¼″ dia. × 1⅜″	2	**Top Assembly**		
9. Leg pins	¼″ dia. × 1⁹⁄₁₆″	16	35. Sides	¾″ × 7½″ × 33½″	2
10. Top supports	¾″ × 1″ × 2″	8	36. Back	½″ × 27″ × 33½″	1
11. Flathead screws	#10 × 1¼″	4	37. Shelves	¾″ × 7″ × 27″	5
			38. Lid	¾″ × 5″ × 19″	1
Drawer Assembly			39. Stile	¾″ × 1¾″ × 33½″	2
12. Drawer fronts	¾″ × 2½″ × 9½″	2	40. Top rail	¾″ × 3″ × 28″	1
13. Drawer backs	⅜″ × 2″ × 8½″	2	41. Bottom rail	¾″ × 1″ × 24½″	1
14. Drawer sides	⅜″ × 2″ × 17⅝″	4	42. Divider	¾″ × 1″ × 29½″	1
15. Drawer bottoms	¼″ × 8½″ × 16¾″	2	43. Side top boards	½″ × 3½″ × 10″	2
16. Drawer pulls*	⅝″ dia.	2	44. Front top board	½″ × 3½″ × 31½″	1
17. Support knobs*	⅜″ dia.	2	45. Side moldings	1¼″ × 1¼″ × 9½″	2
			46. Front molding	1¼″ × 1¼″ × 30½″	1
Middle Assembly			47. Splines	¼″ × ¾″ × 31½″	as needed
18. Writing surface	¾″ × 20″ × 26½″	1			
19. Breadboard ends	¾″ × 2¾″ × 20″	2	**Door Assembly**		
20. Slant front	¾″ × 12⅞″ × 27½″	1	48. Stiles	¾″ × 1¾″ × 29½″	4
21. Breadboard ends	¾″ × 1¾″ × 12⅞″	2	49. Top rails	¾″ × 2¼″ × 9″	2
22. Side boards	¾″ × 8¼″ × 20″	2	50. Bottom rails	¾″ × 2½″ × 9″	2
23. Top board	¾″ × 11″ × 29″	1	51. Panels	½″ × 9″ × 25½″	2
24. Backboard	½″ × 7¾″ × 29¼″	1	52. Door hinges*	2½″ × 1⅜″	4
25. Front molding	¾″ × ¾″ × 29⁵⁄₁₆″	1	53. Door pulls*	¾″ dia.	2
26. Side moldings	¾″ × ¾″ × 9¹⁄₁₆″	2	54. Lid hinges*	2″ × 1³⁄₁₆″	2
27. Hinges*	1½″ × 2⅜″	2	55. Spring catches*		2
28. Finishing nails	6d	as needed	56. Lid pull*	¾″ dia.	1

**Hardware is available from Paxton Hardware, Ltd, 7818 Bradshaw Road, Dept. R.P., Upper Falls, MD 21156. Drawer pulls are #907, support knobs are #905, middle assembly hinges are #4109, door hinges are #4104, lid and door pulls are #908, lid hinges are #4072-19, and spring catches are #4373.*

Temporarily add the drawer pulls (part 16). The base is complete.

9. *Make the slant front desk.* The slant front desk is essentially a box with one sloping side. Build the writing surface first, (part 18) and then the side boards (part 22). Cut the backboard (24), the top board (23), and the slant front (part 20) to fit.

First, install the breadboard ends (parts 19 and 21) on the writing surface and slant front. Cut a groove in each breadboard end. Then cut rabbets on each end of the writing surface to create a tongue that fits in the groove.

Cut two grooves in the assembled writing surface, as shown. The *outer* edges of the dadoes must be exactly 30 in. apart. Cut a rabbet for the back.

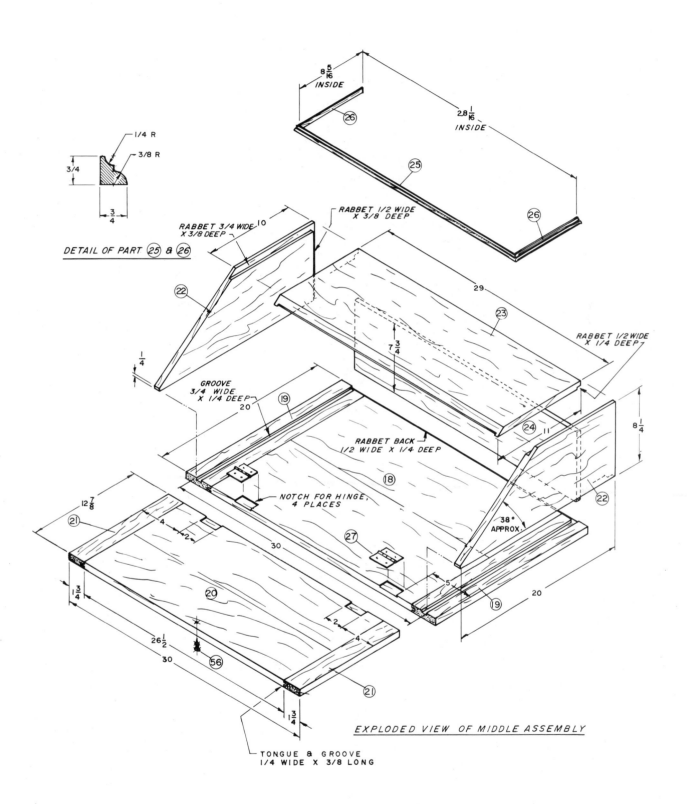

1/4 R
3/8 R
3/4
3/4

DETAIL OF PART (25) & (26)

8 5/16
INSIDE

28 1/16
INSIDE

RABBET 1/2 WIDE
X 3/8 DEEP

RABBET 3/4 WIDE 10
X 3/8 DEEP

29

23

RABBET 1/2 WIDE
X 1/4 DEEP

7 3/4

1/4

GROOVE
3/4 WIDE
X 1/4 DEEP

20

RABBET BACK
1/2 WIDE X 1/4 DEEP

8 1/4

11

NOTCH FOR HINGE,
4 PLACES

12 7/8

4

2

30

27

38°
APPROX.

20

1 3/4

5

2

26 1/2

30

56

2

4

1 3/4

EXPLODED VIEW OF MIDDLE ASSEMBLY

TONGUE & GROOVE
1/4 WIDE X 3/8 LONG

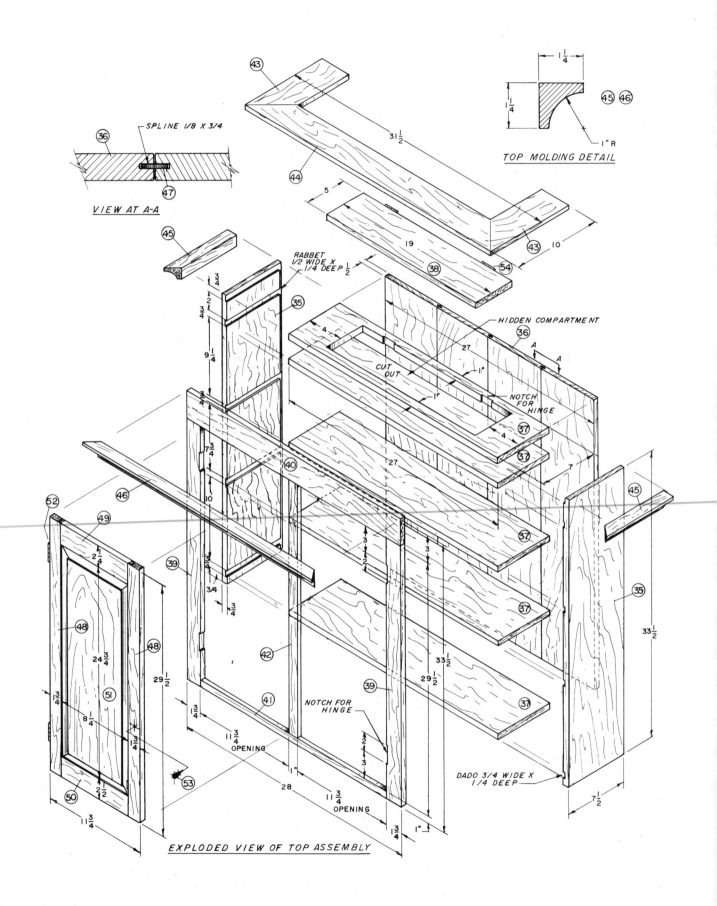

SPLINE 1/8 X 3/4

VIEW AT A-A

TOP MOLDING DETAIL

1" R

RABBET 1/2 WIDE X 1/4 DEEP

HIDDEN COMPARTMENT

CUT OUT

NOTCH FOR HINGE

NOTCH FOR HINGE

DADO 3/4 WIDE X 1/4 DEEP

OPENING

OPENING

EXPLODED VIEW OF TOP ASSEMBLY

212

Cut the sides next. Note that they are not identical: They are mirror images of each other. Label the right and left sides and lay them out carefully. Cut a rabbet for the top and one for the back. Cut the angle on the front edge with a bandsaw and smooth it with a hand plane and sandpaper. To make the angles identical, tack the boards together while sawing and shaping them.

Test-fit the sides in the grooves in the writing surface. Make sure they are square to the writing surface and cut a back to fit the opening.

Rout a rabbet in the back of the top board and test-fit it with the other pieces. Note where the front edge of the top meets the sides and bevel the edge to match. Round-over the sharp edge of the bevel with sandpaper.

Dry-fit the writing surface, side boards, top board, and backboard. Make any adjustments necessary, and then glue the desk together. Make sure everything is square.

Rout mortises for the hinges (part 27) in the slant front and desktop, as shown. Attach the hinges.

Attach the desk to the base with the eight top supports (part 10), as shown in detail B of the base exploded view. The tongue of the top support slips in the groove in the side skirts. Screw the support to the underside of the slant front desk. This arrangement allows the slant front desk to expand and contract with the weather.

Rout moldings (parts 25 and 26) to the profile shown. Set them aside and cut them to fit around the bookcase later.

10. *Make the bookcase.* The bookcase is another box. Cut the sides (part 35), the back, (part 36), and the shelves (part 37) to the dimensions given in the Materials List.

Cut dadoes in the sides for the shelves, as shown in the exploded view of the top assembly. Like the sides of the slant front, the sides of the bookcase are mirror images of each other. Cut a rabbet for the back, as shown.

Pick one of the five shelves (part 37) as a top and make a cutout in it, 5 in. by 19 in., for the lid (part 38).

Cut or rout a groove in the long edges of the back pieces, as shown in the view at A-A. Note that two edges do not get grooves. Cut splines (part 47) to fit. Glue up the back.

Dry-fit the sides, assembled backs, and shelves. The back should fit loosely to allow for expansion and contraction with the weather. Glue the shelves in the sides; check for squareness and let the glue dry. Nail the back in place with 6d finishing nails (part 28).

Cut the stile (part 39), top rail (part 40), bottom rail (part 41), and divider (part 42) to fit. Notch the stile for hinges *before* attaching them to the bookcase. Attach the parts to the assembly with glue and 6d finishing nails.

Cut and attach the top boards (parts 43 and 44) so that they overhang the front and sides by 1¾ in.

Make the moldings (parts 45 and 46) and miter them to fit the bookcase. Nail them in place with 1-in. wire brads.

Position the bookcase on the slant front desk. Miter the molding you made in Step 9 to fit around the bookcase, as shown in the front and side views. Nail the molding to the slant front desk with 1-in. wire brads.

Hang the lid of the secret compartment, as shown.

11. *Make the raised panel doors.* Measure the openings for the doors and adjust the door dimensions to fit.

Rout a ¼-in. groove in the top and bottom door rails and stiles (parts 48, 49, and 50). Cut a tongue in each end of both rails to fit the groove.

Raised panels were once cut by hand with special planes. While router bits that make quick work of cutting the panels are now available, the old reason for making the panels is still valid. Wood expands and contracts with moisture. Allow ⅛-in. play between the long edge of the panels (part 51) and the bottom of the grooves that house it. If humid weather causes the panel to expand, it won't break the door.

Cut the panel to fit and raise the panel on either a router, shaper, or table saw. Assemble the door, and when the glue dries, hang it in its opening.

12. *Make the pigeonholes.* The final bit of woodwork is the pigeonhole assembly. Cut the ends (part 31) to fit in the opening and dado and rabbet them, as shown in the exploded view of the pigeonholes. All pigeonhole dadoes and rabbets are ¼ in. wide by ¹/₁₆ in. deep. Note once again that you aren't making two identical ends.

Cut dadoes in the shelves (part 29) for the dividers. Dado both backs (part 30) for the spacer

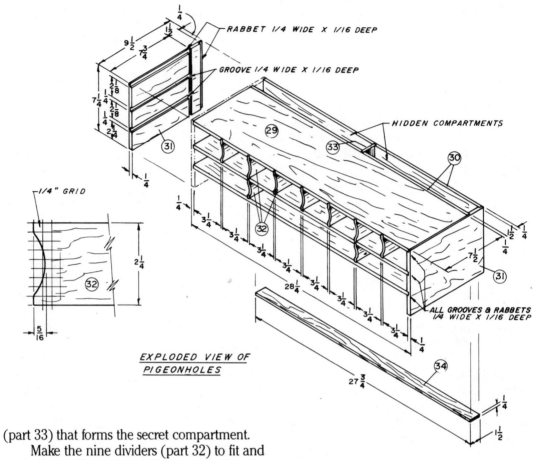

RABBET 1/4 WIDE X 1/16 DEEP

GROOVE 1/4 WIDE X 1/16 DEEP

HIDDEN COMPARTMENTS

1/4" GRID

EXPLODED VIEW OF
PIGEONHOLES

ALL GROOVES & RABBETS
1/4 WIDE X 1/16 DEEP

(part 33) that forms the secret compartment.

Make the nine dividers (part 32) to fit and cut to the profile, as shown. To ensure uniformity, stack and cut several at a time.

Dry-fit the pigeonhole assembly and try sliding it into the middle assembly. You should be able to do so easily. If not, trim as necessary.

Glue up the pigeonhole assembly, checking for squareness.

13. *Apply finish.* Remove all hardware. Apply stain to the wood, if you wish, and then varnish the piece. Reinstall the hardware.

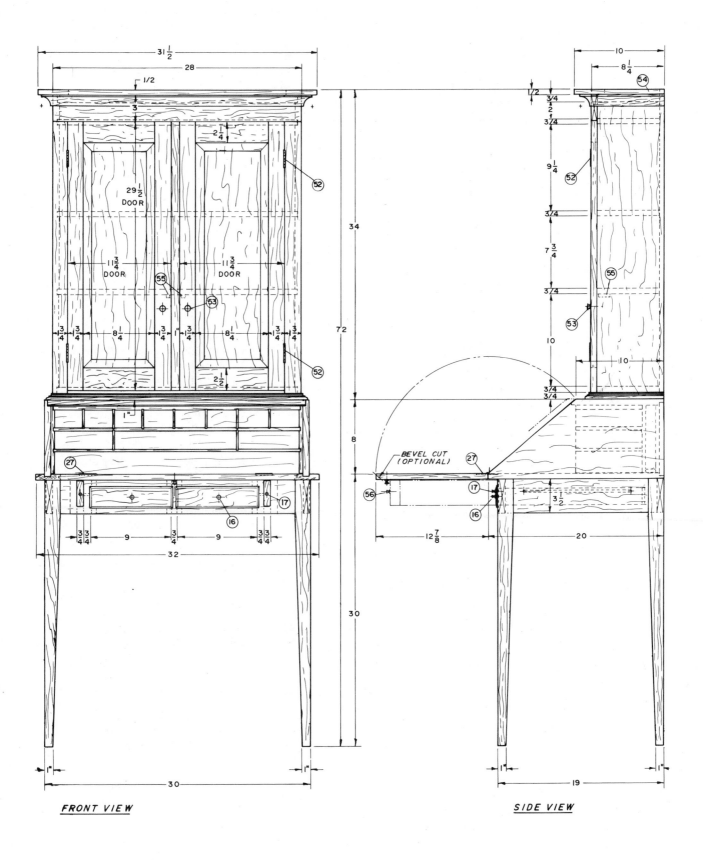

FRONT VIEW

SIDE VIEW

215

Tambour Clock

MATERIALS LIST

Part	Dimensions	Quantity
1. Body	1½″ × 3¼″ × 6½″	1
2. Base	¼″ × 1¹¹/₁₆″ × 6⅞″	1
3. Feet	¹/₁₆″ × ⅝″ × ⅝″	4
4. Movement*		1

Movement is available from Klockit, P.O. Box 636, Lake Geneva, WI 53147; order #15020.

This is the smallest clock project and the easiest to make. It is a scaled-down version of a clock that was popular from 1820 right through the middle of this century. All major clock makers once offered two or three models of the tambour clock. The clock got its name, by the way, from the similarity of its shape to a tambour drum.

1. *Select the wood and cut the parts.* Walnut, oak, and cherry are the more obvious choices of woods for this project. Cut the parts to the sizes given in the Materials List. The movement can be ordered from the source given in the Materials List.

2. *Lay out the clock.* Lay out the pattern on the body (part 1) and locate the center of the hole for the clock face. Drill the hole about ⅝ in. deep. Cut just outside the outline of the body with a jigsaw or band saw, then sand down to the layout line.

Rout the front and sides of the base (part 2) to the profile shown with a ⅛-in.-radius cove bit with a ball-bearing guide.

3. *Assemble the clock.* Locate and glue the body to the base, making sure that the back of the base and body align. Glue the feet (part 3) to the bottom of the base. Sand thoroughly.

4. *Apply finish.* Apply a thin coat of stain, if you wish, and two or three coats of varnish. Let the finish dry and install the movement.

TAMBOUR CLOCK

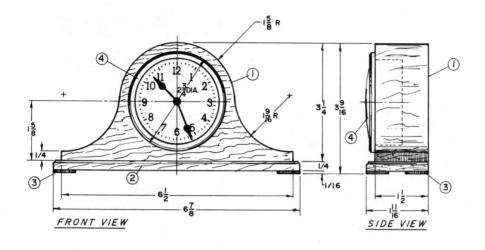

$1\frac{5}{8}$ R

$2\frac{3}{4}$ DIA.

$\frac{9}{16}$ R

$3\frac{1}{4}$

$3\frac{9}{16}$

$1\frac{5}{8}$

1/4

$6\frac{1}{2}$

$6\frac{7}{8}$

1/4

1/16

FRONT VIEW

$1\frac{1}{2}$

$1\frac{11}{16}$

SIDE VIEW

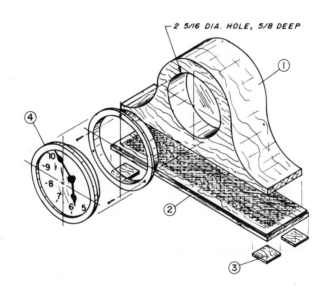

2 5/16 DIA. HOLE, 5/8 DEEP

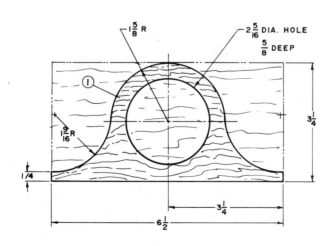

$1\frac{5}{8}$ R

$2\frac{5}{16}$ DIA. HOLE

$\frac{5}{8}$ DEEP

$\frac{9}{16}$ R

1/4

$3\frac{1}{4}$

$3\frac{1}{4}$

$6\frac{1}{2}$

Mission Wall Clock

You don't need much woodworking experience to handle this one. The construction is straightforward; the clock numbers are bought ready-made, and much of your workmanship will be hidden behind the front board. I've scaled the clock down one-quarter of its original size, to suit the lower ceilings of today's homes. This version uses a quartz movement in place of the old eight-day brass works.

1. Select the wood and cut the parts. Most mission style clocks were made of oak. The movement can be ordered from the source given in the Materials List.

Cut the parts to the sizes given in the Materials List and cut the face to shape. Rout a ⅛-in.-radius cove on the edges of the face (part 1) with a bit with a ball-bearing guide. Drill a hole in the center for the movement's hand shaft.

2. Assemble the case. The case mounts on the back of the face, as shown. Rabbet the case sides (part 2) to accept the case top and bottom (part 3). Before assembling the case, cut a 2½ × ⅞ in. notch in the bottom for the pendulum, as shown in the exploded view.

Drill four ⅛-in.-diameter screw holes in the supports.

Glue the case together; then add the supports (part 4), keeping them flush with the *front* edge of the case. When the glue has set, cut the notch for the hanger (part 6) and attach it temporarily.

3. Lay out the clock face. Lightly draw an 8-in.-diameter circle centered on the face. Divide the circumference into 12 equal parts, each 30 degrees apart, to mark the location of each number.

MATERIALS LIST

Part	Dimensions	Quantity
1. Face	½″ × 9½″ × 9½″	1
2. Case sides	½″ × 2″ × 6½″	2
3. Case top/bottom	½″ × 2″ × 6″	1 each
4. Supports	½″ × ⅝″ × 5″	2
5. Roundhead screws	#8 × ⅞″	4
6. Hanger*		1
7. Brads	¾″	2
8. Movement*		1
9. Hands*		1 pair
10. Numbers*	1″ high	1 set

*Hardware is available from Klockit, P.O. Box 636, Lake Geneva, WI 53147. Hanger is #39004, movement is #11907, hands are #66971-H, and numbers are #60045-H.

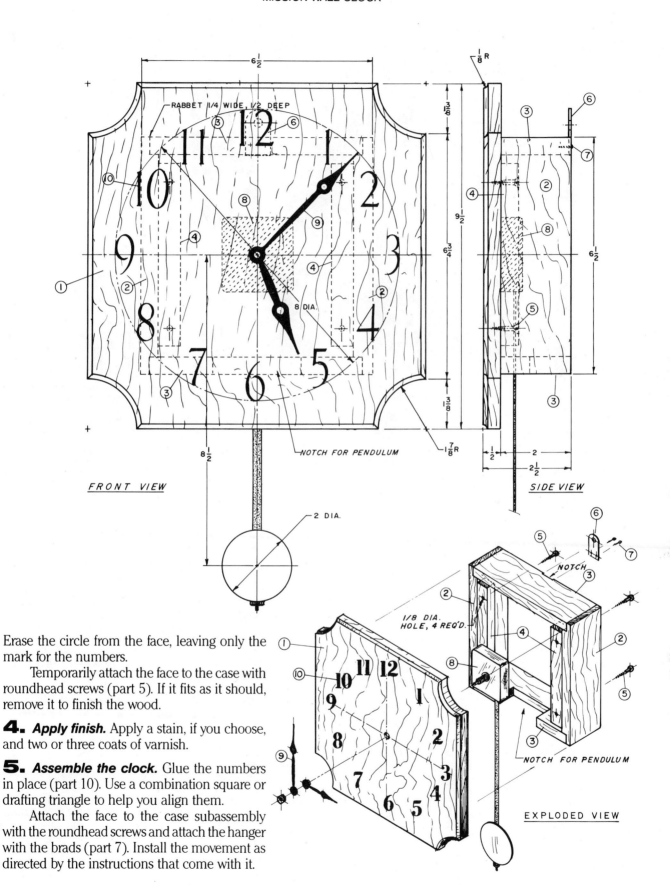

FRONT VIEW

SIDE VIEW

EXPLODED VIEW

RABBET 1/4 WIDE, 1/2 DEEP

NOTCH FOR PENDULUM

8 DIA.

2 DIA.

1/8 DIA.
HOLE, 4 REQ'D.

NOTCH

NOTCH FOR PENDULUM

Erase the circle from the face, leaving only the mark for the numbers.

Temporarily attach the face to the case with roundhead screws (part 5). If it fits as it should, remove it to finish the wood.

4. Apply finish. Apply a stain, if you choose, and two or three coats of varnish.

5. Assemble the clock. Glue the numbers in place (part 10). Use a combination square or drafting triangle to help you align them.

Attach the face to the case subassembly with the roundhead screws and attach the hanger with the brads (part 7). Install the movement as directed by the instructions that come with it.

Square Wall Clock

This clock is based on an early Shaker design. It uses a quartz movement instead of the brass, eight-day pendulum works of the original.

1. Select the stock and make the frame. Make the clock frame out of a hardwood such as cherry or birch. Make the clock face from a matching cabinet-grade plywood.

Cut the profile of the frame (part 1) into a single ½-in.-thick board, 2 in. wide and about 60 in. long, as shown in the end view of part 1. This ensures that the shape of the frame parts will be consistent.

2. Cut the face to size. Make sure the face is perfectly square when you cut it. Cut a 9-in. diameter circle in the center of the face, as shown.

Consult the view at B-B. Round-over the front edge with a router and a ⅛-in.-radius roundover bit with a ball-bearing guide. Rout a rabbet to hold the glass around the inside of the circle, as shown, with a rabbeting bit with a ball-bearing guide.

3. Assemble the clock case. Miter the frame to fit the face board (part 2). Glue the frame around the face board. Cut the insert (part 5) to fit but do not install it yet.

4. Apply finish. Varnish the clock before going on to the final step.

5. Add the glass, dial face, and movement. Have the glass (part 4) cut to size locally. Keep it in place with two glazing points at 6 and 12 o'clock, and putty.

MATERIALS LIST

Part	Dimensions	Quantity
1. Frames	½″ × 2″ × 13″	4
2. Face board	½″ × 12½″ × 12½″	1
3. Support	¼″ × 12⅜″ × 12⅜″	1
4. Glass	³/₃₂″ × 9⅞″ dia.	1
5. Inserts	¼″ × ¼″ × 12½″	4
6. Dial face*	8½″ dia.	1
7. Movement*		1
8. Hands*		1

Hardware is available from Klockit, P.O. Box 636, Lake Geneva, WI 53147. Dial face is #26088-F, movement is #10003, and hands are #66971-H.

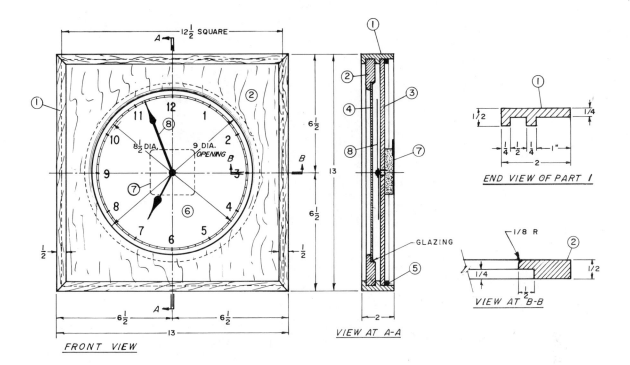

FRONT VIEW

VIEW AT A-A

END VIEW OF PART 1

VIEW AT B-B

GLAZING

Center the dial face (part 6) on the support (part 3) and attach it with rubber cement. Drill a hole as required for the center shaft of the quartz movement. Attach the movement to the support by putting the shaft through the hole and screwing the nut over it, as shown in the exploded view.

Position the dial support in the case. Put the inserts against it and tack them to the side of the case, to hold the support in place.

Add a battery, set the hands (part 8), and mount the clock on the wall.

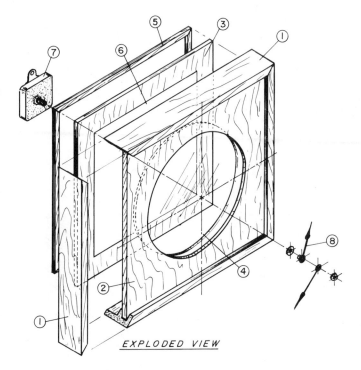

EXPLODED VIEW

221

Child's Clock

MATERIALS LIST

Part	Dimensions	Quantity
1. Body	¾″ × 9½″ × 9½″	1
2. Quartz movement*		1
3. Hands*		1 pair
4. Numbers*		1 set
5. Hanger*		1

Hardware is available from Klockit, P.O. Box 636, Lake Geneva, WI 53147. Quartz movement is #10043-F, hands are #66962-F, numbers are #60006-F, and hanger is #39004. A 3-in.-dia. Forstner bit for construction is #53135-F.

Here again is the elephant you've seen elsewhere in the book. Reuse the pattern found on page 14 if you've made another elephant project.

1. *Select the stock and transfer the pattern.* Pine is a good choice for this project. If you haven't already made a paper pattern, make one now. Draw a grid with ½-in. squares and enlarge the elephant's body onto it. Transfer the pattern to the stock and cut the elephant (part 1) to shape.

The hole for the clock's hand shaft must be centered in the hole for the movement. Locate the center of the hand shaft on the clock and

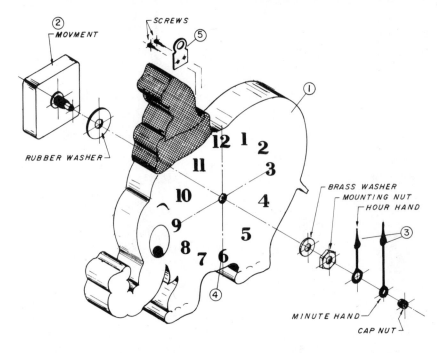

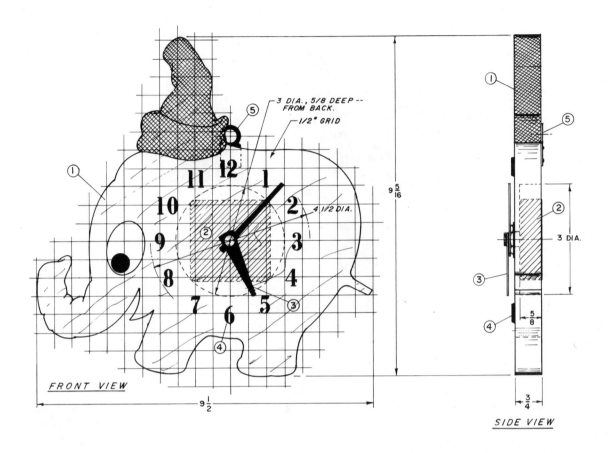

FRONT VIEW

3 DIA., 5/8 DEEP -- FROM BACK.

1/2" GRID

4 1/2 DIA.

9 5/16

9 1/2

SIDE VIEW

3 DIA.

5/8

3/4

drill a 1/16-in.-diameter hole through the body. This establishes the center of both the hand shaft and movement holes. From the back, drill or rout a 5/8-in. × 3-in.-diameter hole centered on this mark.

Drill a 5/16-in.-diameter hole from the front, using the 1/16-in.-diameter hole as a guide.

Sand thoroughly.

2. Apply finish. Paint the clock any colors that appeal to you. Attach the hanger, as shown.

3. Add the numbers. Lay out the numbers (part 4) of the clock so that they all fall within a 4½-in. circle, as shown. Enlarge the dial face template on a photocopier to help you position the numbers. Mark the location of the numbers, remove the template, and glue the numbers just inside the circle. Keep the numbers upright, as shown on the elephant drawings, so that they can be read more easily.

As directed by the instructions that come with the clock movement, install it, put the hands in place, and add the battery.

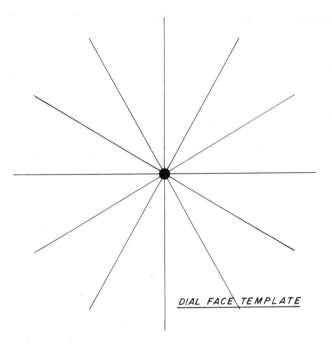

DIAL FACE TEMPLATE

Rooster Wall Clock

Here is a good candidate for a kitchen clock. The shape is scaled down from an antique Massachusetts weather vane.

Before you get underway, you should have the movement on hand so that you'll know what size to make the hole in the center. I used movement #15022-A, available from Klockit, whose address is listed in the appendix.

1. Select the stock. Choose a straight-grained, knot-free piece of hardwood at least 10½ × 14⅝ in. The grain should run the length of the stock. If you can't find a single 10½-in.-wide board (I admit I couldn't), glue up two pieces. If you have a planer, consider gluing up narrow scraps, and then planing and sanding the surfaces smooth.

2. Make a paper pattern and cut the clock to shape. Draw a grid with ½-in. squares and enlarge the rooster onto it. Transfer the pattern to the stock and cut the rooster to shape. Cut just outside the line and sand down to it. Keep all corners sharp.

3. Make the hole for the face. Locate the center of the clock face. The Klockit model I used requires a 2⁵⁄₁₆-in. hole, drilled ½ in. deep. I drilled the hole with a Forstner bit, but depending on the movement you buy, you may be able to cut out a circle with a band saw or jigsaw. With the movement in place, attach a brass hanger, as shown. You may have to adjust its location so that the rooster will hang level.

4. Apply finish. Remove the movement. Paint the rooster's comb and beak bright red, if you wish. Finish with two or three coats of a high-gloss varnish. Add the movement.

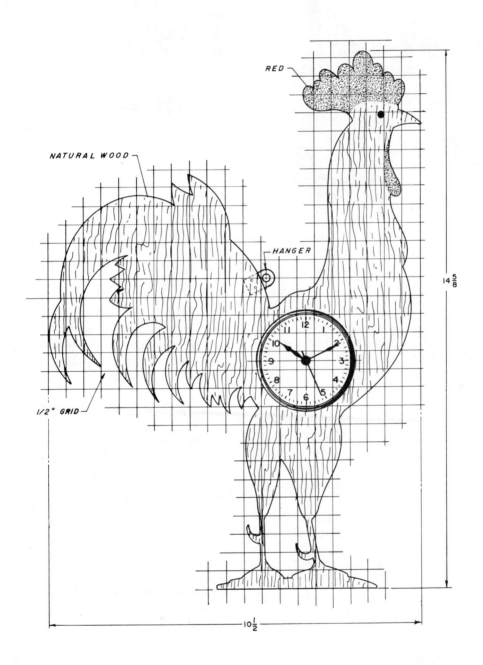

RED

NATURAL WOOD

HANGER

1/2" GRID

14 5/8

10 1/2

Terry Shelf Clock

Ely Terry was an early clock maker and one of the first in the United States to use mass-production methods. Most of his clocks had wooden gears, and many are still in use today.

My research suggests that this small shelf clock was made by Terry around 1860. It caught my eye because the movement has two springs mounted *outside* of the plates rather than between them—a very unusual feature. Could the clock have been one of Terry's prototypes?

This project is taken precisely from the original; note that the nail heads are left showing. You can use a wind-up movement, but the new quartz movements with operating pendulums are very accurate, never need winding, and look old-fashioned once they're in place.

It's a sound practice to read through the steps of any project before getting busy. It's also sound practice to wait until you have the clock movement in hand before building a clock. This clock is no exception to either rule.

1. Select the stock and order the clockwork. The original was made of walnut, but any good grade of hardwood will do. A friend made this clock out of apple wood and the results were beautiful, if less than authentic. The back (part

4) and braces (part 12) can be cut from a less-precious wood than the rest of the case.

Before getting too far under way, order the clock parts from the sources given in the Materials List.

2. Cut the parts. Cut the wooden parts, except for the moldings and skirt, to the sizes given in the Materials List. Lay out the holes for the dial and pendulum in the front (part 3), as shown on the exploded view, and cut them out.

3. Cut the joints. Dado the top and bottom of the side panels (part 1), as shown in detail A. Rabbet the false top and the bottom (part 2) to create a tongue that fits in the dado, as shown in the exploded view. Cut rabbets in the sides to accommodate the back.

4. Make the skirt and moldings. Rout long lengths of the skirt and moldings (parts 9 and 6), and then cut them to make the individual parts (parts 7, 8, 10, 11, and 12). Rout the moldings on the edge of a wide board and then rip the molding from it; a ¼-in.-wide piece of stock is too difficult to work.

5. Assemble the case. Glue the sides to the bottom and false top, keeping everything square.

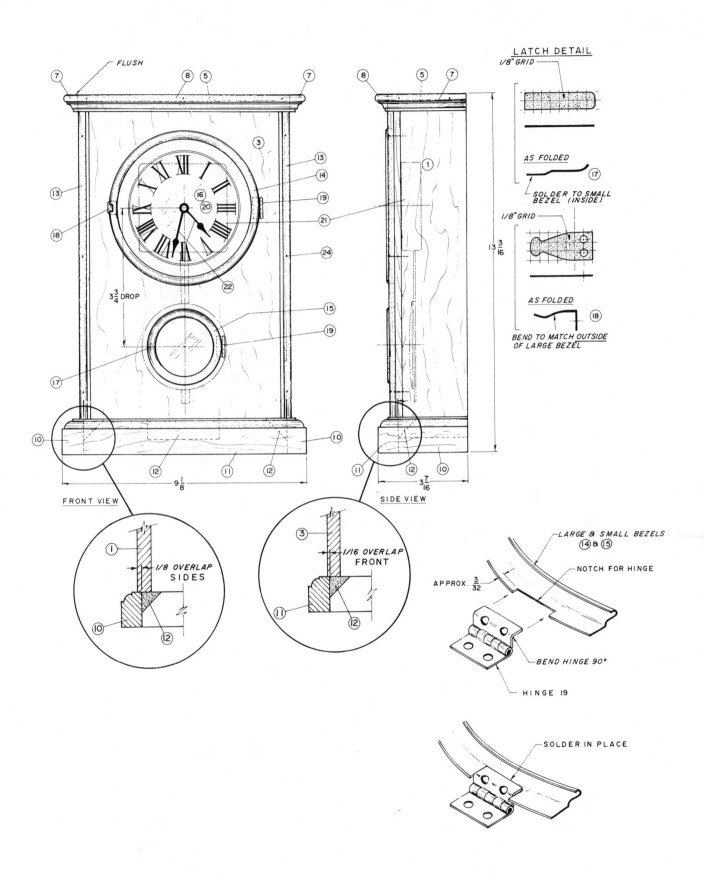

FLUSH

LATCH DETAIL
1/8" GRID

AS FOLDED

SOLDER TO SMALL
BEZEL (INSIDE)

1/8" GRID

AS FOLDED

BEND TO MATCH OUTSIDE
OF LARGE BEZEL

$3\frac{3}{4}$ DROP

$13\frac{3}{16}$

$9\frac{1}{8}$

$3\frac{7}{16}$

FRONT VIEW

SIDE VIEW

1/8 OVERLAP
SIDES

1/16 OVERLAP
FRONT

LARGE & SMALL BEZELS
14 & 15

NOTCH FOR HINGE

APPROX. $\frac{3}{32}$

BEND HINGE 90°

HINGE 19

SOLDER IN PLACE

227

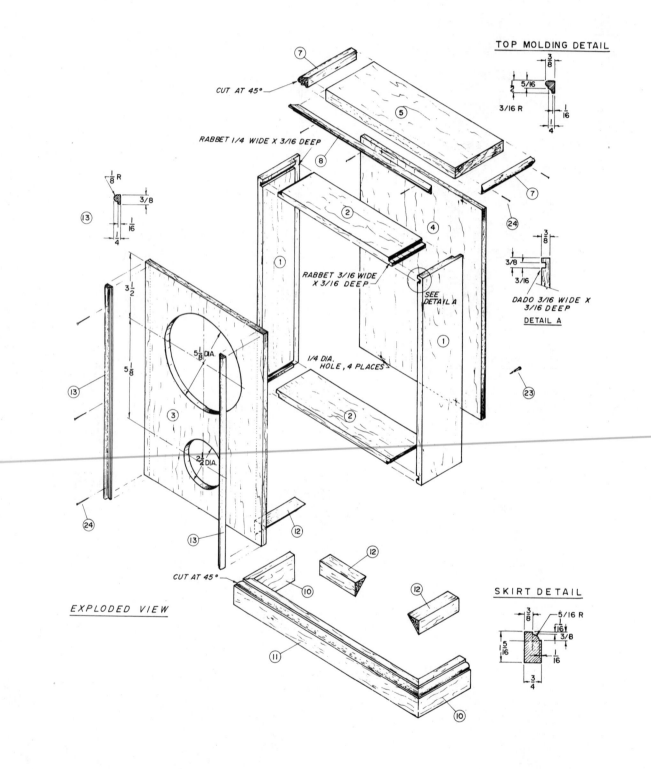

TOP MOLDING DETAIL

CUT AT 45°

RABBET 1/4 WIDE X 3/16 DEEP

3/16 R

1/8 R

3/8

RABBET 3/16 WIDE
X 3/16 DEEP

SEE
DETAIL A

DADO 3/16 WIDE X
3/16 DEEP

DETAIL A

3 1/2

5 1/8 DIA.

5 1/8

1/4 DIA.
HOLE, 4 PLACES

2 1/2 DIA.

CUT AT 45°

EXPLODED VIEW

SKIRT DETAIL

5/16 R

3/4

228

Drill holes slightly larger than the screw shank in the back for the four screws that hold it in place; drill pilot holes slightly smaller than the screw shank in the case. Temporarily screw the back in place.

Glue the face to the assembled case. Glue the false top to the top so that it is flush with the back and overlaps the sides equally.

Miter the top moldings to fit and nail them in place with square-cut headless brads (part 24). Keep the top of the molding flush with the top of the piece.

Glue and nail the two vertical moldings (part 13) to the front of the clock.

Miter and glue up the skirt separately. The clock rests on the skirt, as shown in the detail. Glue the three braces (part 12) in place, as shown.

6. *Prepare the bezels, hinges, and latches.* If you order the parts specified in the Materials List, the hinges and latch come with the bezel when you order it. Before you can mount the bezels, however, you must do some simple metal work. Fortunately, brass is easy to work and can be cut and filed to size and shape.

First, notch the bezels (parts 14 and 15) for the brass hinges (part 19), as illustrated. Bend and solder the hinges to the bezels; be sure to clean the area with 0000 steel wool before soldering. Use a 50/50 acid-core solder.

A metal latch (parts 17 and 18) keeps each bezel from opening. The large latch screws to the case and snaps over the large bezel to keep it closed; the small latch is soldered to the small bezel and snaps against the case. Make the latches from 1/16-in.-thick brass that comes with the bezel. The exact profiles are shown in the latch detail. Solder the small latch to the inner edge of the small bezel. Drill holes in the large latch. You'll screw it to the case later.

Bend both latches to shape after the final assembly in Step 8.

A series of metal tabs solders to the bezel to hold the glass in place. Position the glass and solder the tabs to the bezel. Polish all brass parts and set them aside for final assembly.

7. *Apply finish.* Sand thoroughly. Stain, if you choose to, and varnish.

8. *Install the clockwork.* Cut the dial face (part 20) to size and attach it to the dial pan (part 16) with rubber cement. Be sure the face is

MATERIALS LIST

Part	Dimensions	Quantity
1. Sides	3/8″ × 2½″ × 11¼″	2
2. Bottom/false top	3/8″ × 2¼″ × 7½″	1 each
3. Face	¼″ × 7⅞″ × 11¼″	1
4. Back	¼″ × 7½″ × 11¼″	1
5. Top	5/8″ × 3⅛″ × 8⅜″	1
6. Top molding	¼″ × ½″ × 24″	1
7. Top moldings (side)	Cut from part 6	2
8. Top molding (front)	Cut from part 6	1
9. Skirt	¾″ × 1 5/16″ × 24″	1
10. Side skirts	Cut from part 9—3 7/16″ long	2
11. Front skirt	Cut from part 9—9⅛″ long	1
12. Braces	¾″ × ¾″ × 2 5/8″	3
13. Vertical moldings	¼″ × 3/8″ × 11¼″	2
14. Large bezel*		1
15. Small bezel*		1
16. Dial pan*		1
17. Small latch	1/16″ × ¼″ × 1″	1
18. Large latch	1/16″ × 3/8″ × ⅞″	1
19. Hinges*	¾″ × 5/16″	2
20. Dial face*		1
21. Movement**		1
22. Hands**		1 pair
23. Flathead screws	#2 × 3/8″	10
24. Square-cut headless brads	⅞″	14

*Hardware is available from Merritt Antiques, Inc., R.D. 2, Douglassville, PA 19518. Large bezel is #P-60-I (5⅝″), small bezel is #P-60-A (2¾″), dial pan is #P-61-B, hinge is #P-93, and dial face is #R-400 (4″).

**Hardware is available from Klockit, P.O. Box 636, Lake Geneva, WI 53147. Movement is #11008, and hands are #66992-4.

centered inside the pan. Attach the dial pan to the case with four screws, 90 degrees apart from one another on the rim of the pan. Check that the dial face is centered. Center the large bezel over the dial pan, slide the hinge under the pan, and screw the hinge in place. Slide the latch *under* the dial pan and screw it in place; adjust the latch until it holds the large bezel closed.

Attach the small bezel.

Remove the back and attach the quartz movement (parts 21 and 22) according to the directions that come with it. Cut the pendulum rod so that the pendulum is centered inside its window and swings freely. Attach the pendulum rod and screw the back in place.

Banjo Clock

The banjo clock, named for its distinctive shape, was first made in 1795 by Simon Willard, one of a number of clock makers in the Willard family of Roxbury, Massachusetts. The design was popular with the fast-growing middle class of the early 1800s. This project is a scaled-down version.

1. *Select the stock and cut the parts.* Order the clock movement from the source provided in the Materials List before you begin cutting and alter the clock's dimensions to fit it, if necessary. The case can be made from pine or any wood of your choice. The clock in the photo is birch. Note the thicker-than-usual stock called for in the Materials List, including the head (part 1), the neck (part 2), and the pediment (part 7). Glue up these pieces if necessary.

Cut the parts to the sizes given in the Materials List.

2. *Make the head.* The segments that form the head are cut from a single board so that the grain will flow smoothly from piece to piece. Carefully lay out the cuts, as illustrated. Allow a margin for the width of the saw blade.

Cut the head, as shown in Fig. 2.

Dry-fit the eight pieces, as shown in Fig. 3. If they make a perfect octagon, glue them together. If there are gaps in the seams, glue up two sets of four pieces each. When the glue has set, sand the long flat end of each half until they fit perfectly together. The easiest way to do this is to tape sandpaper to a flat surface and rub the wood across the sandpaper.

With a band saw, jigsaw, or lathe, cut the head to a diameter of 4½ in., as shown in Fig. 4. Sand all edges.

MATERIALS LIST

Part	Dimensions	Quantity
1. Head	1¾″ × 2⅜″ × 9½″	1
2. Neck	1¼″ × 3⅛″ × 7½″	1
3. Bottom, long sides	½″ × 2½″ × 5″	2
4. Bottom, short sides	½″ × 2½″ × 4″	2
5. Back	¼″ × 3½″ × 4½″	1
6. Flathead screws	#6 × 1¼″	2
7. Pediment	2″ × 2″ × 5″	1
8. Glass	³/₃₂″ × 3½″ × 4½″	1
9. Front trim	⅛″ × 2″ × 6½″	1
10. Mount	1¹/₁₆″ × 1¹/₁₆″ × ⅝″	1
11. Hinges*	¾″ × ¾″	2
12. Knob*	⁵/₁₆″ dia.	1
13. Movement*		1
14. Hanger*		1
15. Eagle finial*		1
16. Brads	1″	as needed

Hardware is available from Klockit, P.O. Box 636, Lake Geneva, WI 53147. Hinges are #39090-H, knob is 39047-H, movement is #15004-H, hanger is 39004-H, and eagle finial is #38013-H.

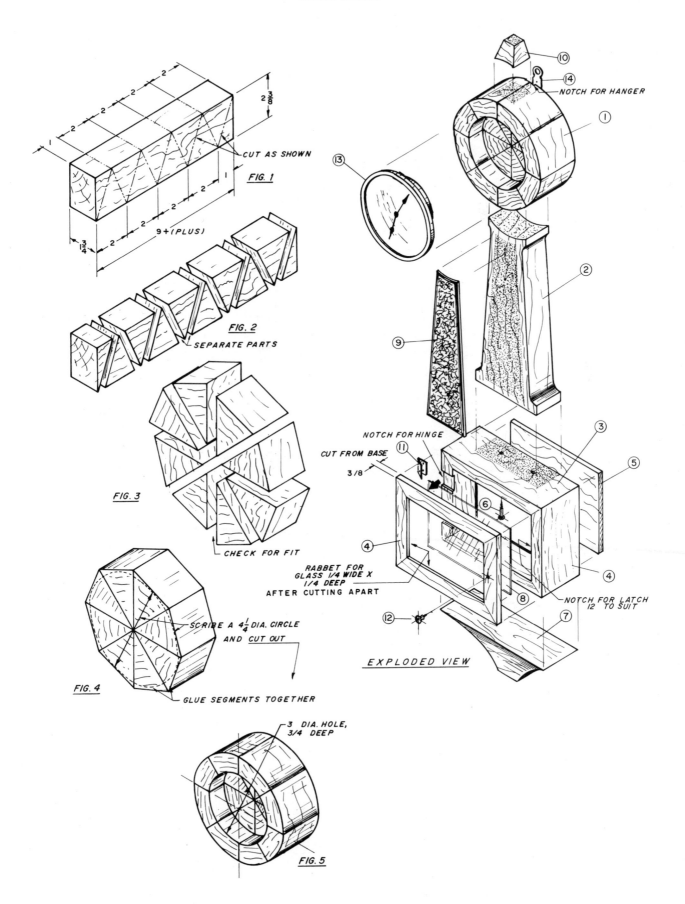

FIG. 1

CUT AS SHOWN

2 3/8

1

2 2 2 2 2

3/4

9 + (PLUS)

2 2 2 2

FIG. 2

SEPARATE PARTS

FIG. 3

CHECK FOR FIT

SCRIBE A 4 1/4 DIA. CIRCLE
AND CUT OUT

FIG. 4

GLUE SEGMENTS TOGETHER

3 DIA. HOLE,
3/4 DEEP

FIG. 5

NOTCH FOR HANGER

NOTCH FOR HINGE

CUT FROM BASE

3/8

RABBET FOR
GLASS 1/4 WIDE X
1/4 DEEP
AFTER CUTTING APART

NOTCH FOR LATCH
12 TO SUIT

EXPLODED VIEW

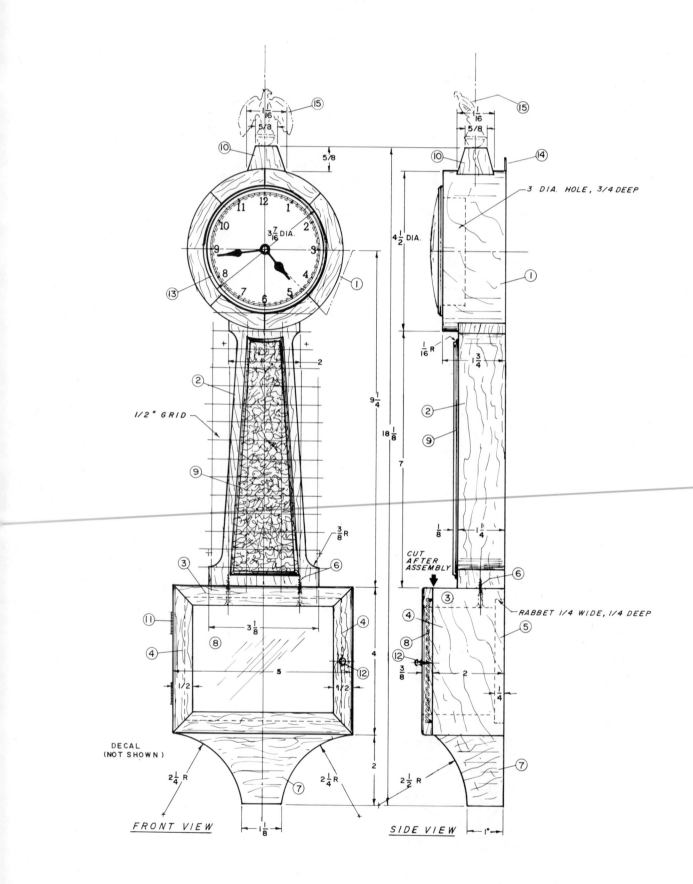

15

16
5/8

10
5/8

12
11   1
10   2
9   3 7/16 DIA.   3
8   4
7   6   5
13   1

1/2" GRID

2

9

3/8 R

3
11
4
8
3 1/8
4
5
1/2   1/2
12

DECAL
(NOT SHOWN)

2 1/4 R   2 1/4 R

7

FRONT VIEW
1 1/8

15
1/16
5/8

10   14

3 DIA. HOLE, 3/4 DEEP

4 1/2 DIA.

1

1/16 R   1 3/4

2

9

9 1/4

18 1/8

7

1/8   1 1/4

CUT
AFTER
ASSEMBLY

RABBET 1/4 WIDE, 1/4 DEEP

3
4   5
8
12
3/8   2   1/4

2

2 1/2 R

7

SIDE VIEW   1"

6

4

6

232

Pick the best face for the front. Drill, rout, or turn a 3-in.-diameter hole in its center, as shown in Fig. 5. Check to see that the movement (part 13) fits this opening.

Notch the back for the hanger (part 14).

3. *Make a paper pattern for the neck.* Draw a grid with ½-in. squares and enlarge the drawing of the neck onto it. Transfer the enlargement to the wood. Band saw to shape and sand thoroughly.

4. *Make the front trim, pediment, and mount.* The front trim (part 9) is a thin, decorative piece glued to the neck. Cut it from wood that has an attractive grain pattern, such as burl, if it is available. Use a router with a $^1/_{16}$-in.-radius core box bit to make the cove cut around the trim. Core box bits do not have a ball-bearing guide: Rout the three straight sides with a fence on your router. Carve the short curved side by hand.

Lay out the shape of the pediment (part 7) and the mount (part 10) on the wood and cut them to shape.

5. *Assemble the bottom box.* Think of the bottom as a box with a glass lid. Like other lidded boxes in this book, you make this one by first building a box deeper than needed. Then you slice off the lid—or in this case, the door.

Before you assemble the box, cut a rabbet for the back in the long and short sides (parts 3 and 4), as shown in the side view. Miter the ends and glue these parts together. Make sure everything is square. When the glue dries, tack the back in its rabbet with 1-in. wire brads. Make sure everything is square.

When the glue has dried, cut a ⅜-in.-thick slab off the front surface to make the door. Cut a rabbet, ¼ in. wide and ¼ in. deep, around the inside of the door's opening to hold the glass.

Make a notch for the two hinges (part 11), ¾ in. from the ends of one of the short sides. Drill a hole for the knob (part 12).

6. *Assemble the clock.* Predrill for screws (part 6) and then glue and screw the bottom subassembly to the neck. Glue the head to the neck, making sure the notch for the hanger will be at the top of the clock. Put glue on the pediment and mount it in place. Glue on the trim. Sand thoroughly.

7. *Apply finish.* Stain and varnish. The grain of the front trim can be emphasized by staining it somewhat darker than the rest of the clock. Install the glass (part 8) with putty and attach the door on its hinges.

Screw the optional eagle finial (part 15) in place. Add the hanger and the knob.

Put a battery in the movement, and place the movement in the case.

Schoolhouse Clock

For many years, schoolchildren looked impatiently at the schoolhouse clock hanging on the wall next to Gilbert Stuart's portrait of George Washington. I hate to date myself, but I remember staring at a schoolhouse clock just like this one, waiting for school to end.

The original schoolhouse clock design is credited to the Ansonia Clock Company of Connecticut. Through the second half of the 1800s and up until around 1910, the clocks were made by manufacturers both here and abroad. Although they are often regarded as prime examples of Americana, many of our antique schoolhouse clocks were actually made in China and Japan.

The clock shown here is a copy of an antique that probably was made overseas around 1895. The original was pine and had a black pinstripe painted on it. The original had a low quality, eight-day brass movement. For accuracy and convenience, I suggest substituting a quartz movement.

1. *Select the stock.* Use either pine or the more traditional oak. You can order the bezel assembly, dial face, brass hinges, hanger, door latch, movement, and hands from the source given in the Materials List.

2. *Lay out and cut the octagon to size.* Take your time when laying out the sectors for the octagon (part 8). To avoid problems, cut a test octagon in scrap and dry-fit it together. If there are gaps, adjust the angle at which you cut and try again. When you have a perfect octagon in scrap, cut the octagon for the clock. Cut the octagon to the *exact* dimensions, or the bezel assembly will not fit.

3. *Assemble the octagon.* Glue up the octagon in two groups of four sectors each.

Masking tape will help you align the pieces and keep them from collapsing when you clamp: Stretch the masking tape along your bench, sticky side up. Line the four sectors along it with their long edges on the tape and their mitered corners touching each other. Put glue in the joints, and with the tape still in place, fold the pieces together. Put the assembly in a band clamp and tighten gently.

Let the glue set thoroughly, then dry-fit the two subassemblies. If the halves do not come together tightly, trim the miters as necessary. Then glue the halves together. After the glue has set, rout ¼-in.-wide, ⅜-in.-deep grooves in the back of the octagon at each of the eight joints and glue in the splines (part 9).

Roundover the outside edge of the octagon after the glue has set. The original profile will require a custom-made bit. The view at A-A shows both the original profile and a simpler profile you can cut with a standard router bit.

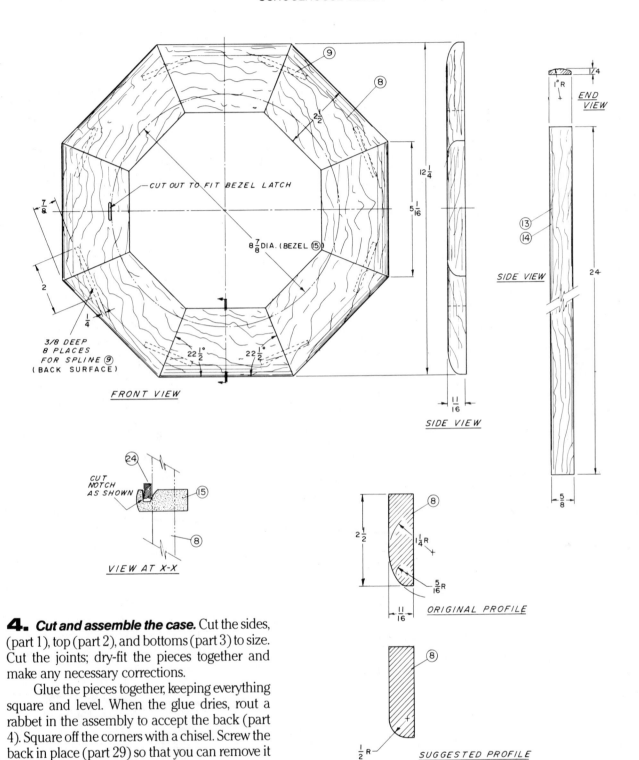

FRONT VIEW

CUT OUT TO FIT BEZEL LATCH

$8\frac{7}{8}$DIA. (BEZEL ⑮)

$\frac{7}{8}$

3/8 DEEP
8 PLACES
FOR SPLINE ⑨
(BACK SURFACE)

$22\frac{1}{2}$° $22\frac{1}{2}$°

$12\frac{1}{4}$

$5\frac{1}{16}$

$2\frac{1}{2}$

$\frac{11}{16}$

SIDE VIEW

END VIEW

$\frac{1}{4}$

1"R

⑬
⑭

SIDE VIEW

24

$\frac{5}{8}$

CUT
NOTCH
AS SHOWN

VIEW AT X-X

$2\frac{1}{2}$

$1\frac{1}{4}$R

$\frac{5}{16}$R

$\frac{11}{16}$

ORIGINAL PROFILE

$\frac{1}{2}$R

SUGGESTED PROFILE

VIEW AT A-A

4. *Cut and assemble the case.* Cut the sides, (part 1), top (part 2), and bottoms (part 3) to size. Cut the joints; dry-fit the pieces together and make any necessary corrections.

Glue the pieces together, keeping everything square and level. When the glue dries, rout a rabbet in the assembly to accept the back (part 4). Square off the corners with a chisel. Screw the back in place (part 29) so that you can remove it later to change the clock batteries.

Cut the top rail (part 5), the stiles (part 6), and the bottom rails (part 7) to fit the case. Glue them in, one at a time. Make sure you cut the notch for the hinges (part 19) in the right hand stile *before* you glue it in place. Keep the rails and stiles flush with the front surface.

MATERIALS LIST

Part	Dimensions	Quantity
1. Sides	½″ × 3¼″ × 14⅝″	2
2. Top	½″ × 3¼″ × 7⅛″	1
3. Bottoms	½″ × 3¼″ × 4⅜″	2
4. Back	¼″ × 7⅛″ × 16⅜″	1
5. Top rail	⅜″ × 1⅜″ × 6⅝″	1
6. Stiles	⅜″ × 1¼″ × 5⅛″	2
7. Bottom rails	⅜″ × 1¼″ × 3¹³⁄₁₆″	2
8. Sectors	¹¹⁄₁₆″ × 2½″ × 5¹⁄₁₆″	8
9. Splines	¼″ × ⅜″ × 2″	8
10. Door top	⅝″ × ⅝″ × 4⅜″	1
11. Door sides	⅝″ × ⅝″ × 3⅜″	2
12. Door bottoms	⅝″ × ⅝″ × 2⁹⁄₁₆″	2
13. Molding sides	¼″ × ⅝″ × 6⅛″	2
14. Molding bottoms	¼″ × ⅝″ × 4⅜″	2
15. Bezel assembly*		1
16. Glass	Cut to size	1
17. Dial face*	7″ dia.	1
18. Hinge blocks	⁵⁄₃₂″ × ½″ × ¾″	2
19. Hinges*		2
20. Glass	Cut to size	1
21. Glass retainer	⅛″ × ¼″ × 20″	1
22. Hanger*		1
23. Door latch*		1
24. Latch lock*	¼″ × ⅜″ × 1″	1
25. Roundhead screw	#6 × ¾″	1
26. Movement*		1
27. Hands*		1 pair
28. Spacer	¾″ × 3″ × 4½″	1
29. Screws	#4 × ¾″	as needed

**Hardware is available from S. LaRose, Inc., 234 Commerce Place, Greensboro, NC 27420. Bezel assembly is #087031, dial face is #74-544, brass hinges are #085187, hanger is #125-8073, door latch lock is #085189, movement is #812121, and hands are #085178.*

Glue the octagonal frame in place, taking care to locate it, as shown.

Cut and fit the side and bottom moldings (parts 13 and 14) and glue them in place. Sand the case.

5. *Make a door to fit in the opening.* The profile of the door is delicate. To avoid injury, cut the molding onto a wide board, and then cut the board to free the molding.

First, rout a roundover on the edge of a board, ⅝ in. thick, 6 in. wide, and 36 in long.

Next, cut a groove to help create one of the steps in the door profile, as seen in the door molding end view. Set your dado blades to cut a groove, ⁵⁄₃₂ in. high and ½ in. wide. Set the saw fence to cut in the groove ¼ in. from the rounded over edge. Cut the groove in one face only. Rout the other step when the door is assembled.

Put a regular blade back in the saw to cut the extra width off the stock. Put the square edge of the stock against the fence and adjust the fence so you can cut a ⅝ in. strip *from the other edge of the board.* This cutoff will be the door stock. At the moment, it only has one rabbet in it. This makes it easier to glue up the door.

Carefully miter the door stock to form the door top, sides, and bottom (parts 10, 11, and 12). Cut the miters so that the rabbet you have already cut will be the one that holds the glass. Glue the door together with masking tape and band clamps.

Rout the second rabbet in the door when the glue has dried. Rout the rabbet with the door flat on the surface of a table-mounted router. Use push sticks to keep your fingers away from the bit.

Check that the door fits into its opening; sand or plane it to fit if necessary. Attach the door with the two hinge blocks and hinges (parts 18 and 19). Attach the door latch (part 23) and see that it locks the door smoothly.

6. *Attach the hardware.* Center the bezel assembly (part 15) on the octagon and lay out a groove to accept the tongue on the bezel, as shown in the exploded view in the octagon. Rout the groove.

Make the latch lock (part 24) and attach it to the back of the clock. File the tongue to fit the latch, as shown in the view X-X.

Attach the dial face (part 17) to the bezel assembly with rubber cement. Apply thin coats to both the bezel and to the back of the dial face. When the cement is dry, set the face in position. Be sure you remember which direction is up on the bezel—it's easy to glue the face on upside down.

Cut the spacer (part 28); drill a hole in it and put the movement's hand shaft through the hole. Put the hand shaft through the hole in the clock and tighten it in place with a nut that comes with the movement. Screw the bezel to

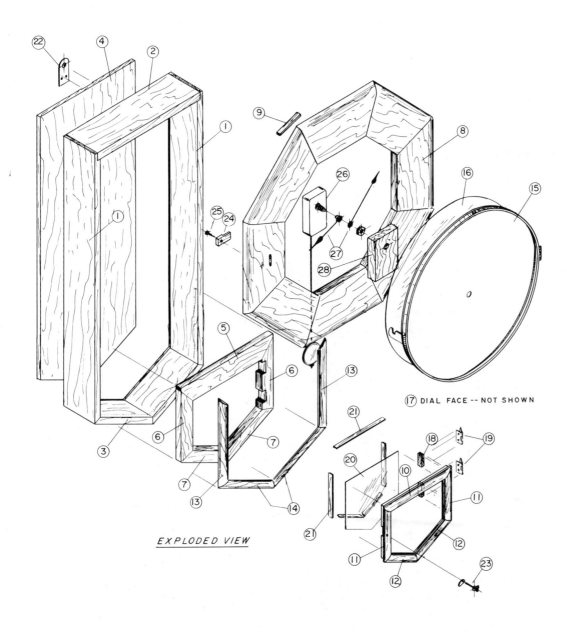

⑰ DIAL FACE -- NOT SHOWN

EXPLODED VIEW

the octagon with #4 × ¾-in. screws (part 29).

The pendulum that comes with the movement is longer than necessary. Cut the pendulum off at about 10 in. so that it is centered in the middle of the lower door.

Notch for and temporarily install the hanger (part 22).

7. Apply finish. Remove the bezel assembly, the door assembly, the hanger, and the hinges.

Sand and apply a stain, if you wish. If you plan to add the pinstripe, apply one coat of shellac or varnish first. Paint the pinstripe with oil-base black paint. When the paint dries, apply two or three more coats of shellac or varnish.

Put the glass (part 16) in the bevel assembly. Small metal tabs come with it to hold the glass in place. Solder the tabs inside the bezel. Put the glass (part 20) in the lower door. Glue the wooden retainer (part 21) in place to hold the glass in the door.

Reassemble the clock, attach the quartz movement (part 26), and put the hands (part 27) in place.

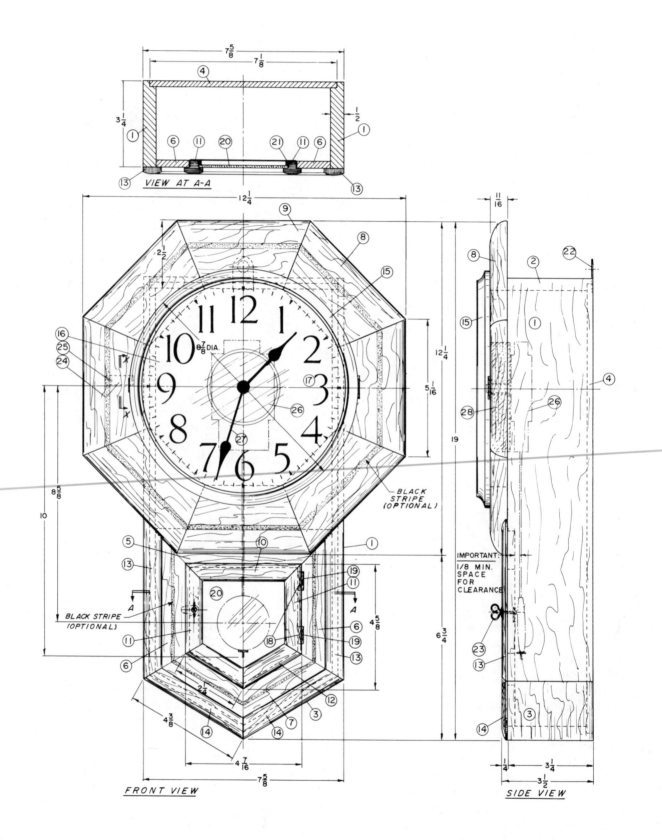

VIEW AT A-A

BLACK STRIPE (OPTIONAL)

BLACK STRIPE (OPTIONAL)

IMPORTANT: 1/8 MIN. SPACE FOR CLEARANCE

FRONT VIEW

SIDE VIEW

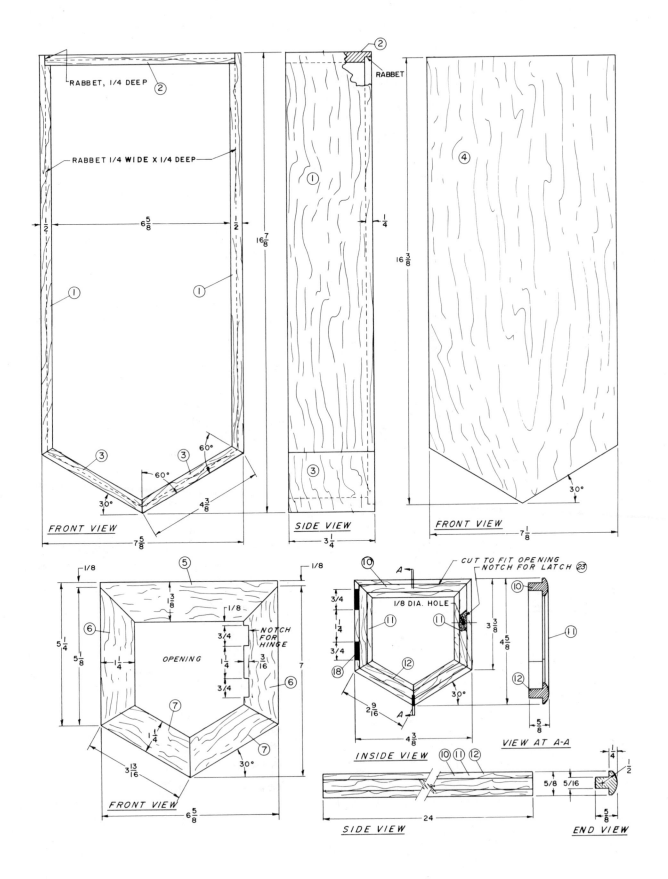

RABBET, 1/4 DEEP ②

RABBET 1/4 WIDE X 1/4 DEEP

② RABBET

①

④

$6\frac{5}{8}$

$\frac{1}{2}$ $\frac{1}{2}$

$16\frac{7}{8}$

$\frac{1}{4}$

$16\frac{3}{8}$

① ①

③ ③ ③

60° 60°

60°

30° 30°

$4\frac{3}{8}$

FRONT VIEW

$7\frac{5}{8}$

SIDE VIEW

$3\frac{1}{4}$

FRONT VIEW

$7\frac{1}{8}$

⑤

1/8 1/8

$1\frac{3}{8}$

1/8

⑥

NOTCH FOR HINGE

3/4

$5\frac{1}{4}$

$5\frac{1}{8}$

$1\frac{1}{4}$

OPENING

$1\frac{1}{4}$

3/16

3/4

7

⑥

⑦

$1\frac{1}{4}$

⑦

⑦

$3\frac{13}{16}$

30°

FRONT VIEW

$6\frac{5}{8}$

⑩ A

CUT TO FIT OPENING
NOTCH FOR LATCH ㉓

3/4

1/8 DIA. HOLE

⑩

$\frac{1}{4}$

⑪ ⑪

3/4

$3\frac{3}{8}$

$4\frac{5}{8}$

⑪

⑱

⑫

30°

⑫

$2\frac{9}{16}$

$\frac{5}{8}$

$4\frac{3}{8}$

A

INSIDE VIEW

VIEW AT A-A

⑩ ⑪ ⑫

⑩ ⑪ ⑫

$\frac{1}{4}$

$\frac{1}{2}$

5/8 5/16

24

$\frac{5}{8}$

SIDE VIEW

END VIEW

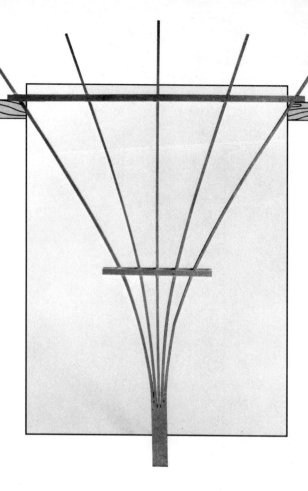

Trellis

This is a copy of a simple trellis that was popular in the late 1930s and early 1940s. It is suited for roses and other climbing plants.

1. Select the stock. It is important to use knot-free, straight-grained wood for this project. Spruce and hemlock are good choices, although nearly any wood should serve.

2. Cut the parts and saw the kerfs. Cut the parts to the sizes given in the Materials List. Locate and draw the position of the four kerfs along the length of the body (part 1). Take the width of the saw blade into consideration when laying out the kerfs. Drill a $^3/_{16}$-in.-diameter hole at what will be the end of each kerf and rip the stock until you reach the hole, as illustrated in detail A. The hole keeps the kerf from splitting the body. If the wood seems likely to split even with this precaution, you can run a $^1/_4$-in.-diameter hex-head bolt through the width of the body, about 2 in. below the ends of the kerfs. Keep the bolt in place with a washer and nut.

3. Spread the fingers. Lay out the position of the top and bottom bars (parts 2 and 3) on the body. Drill a $^1/_{16}$-in.-diameter pilot hole in each finger for the 6d finishing nails (part 4) that attach the bars. Locate and drill pilot holes in the top and bottom bars, 11 in. and 3 in. apart, respectively.

Spread the fingers of the body and nail the bottom bars in place. Spread the fingers further still and nail the top bars in place. Work slowly to avoid splitting the wood.

4. Apply finish. The trellis can be left unfinished. You can also stain and varnish it, or undercoat and paint it. Be sure to use exterior finishes.

MATERIALS LIST

Part	Dimensions	Quantity
1. Body	$1'' \times 3^1/_8'' \times 72''$	1
2. Top board	$^5/_8'' \times 1'' \times 47''$	2
3. Bottom boards	$^5/_8'' \times 1'' \times 18''$	2
4. Finishing nails	6d	20

TRELLIS

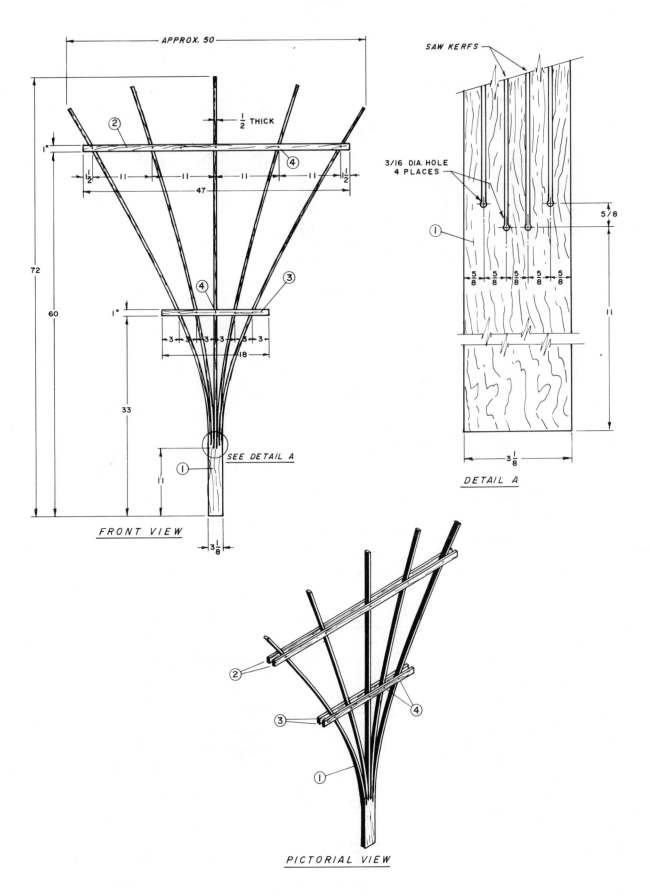

FRONT VIEW

DETAIL A

PICTORIAL VIEW

241

Rail Planter

You can build this project out of scraps. It is designed to fit over the rail of a patio or deck, where it will help keep plants from falling over the edge.

1. *Select the stock.* Use whatever wood you have on hand. The length of the short boards (part 3) depends on how wide the rail happens to be; measure the width of the rail and add 5 in. The drawings give a length of 10½ in. for a planter that will fit over a 2 × 6 rail.

If you will be making the planter from new wood, note that you can rip ten ¾-in. wide pieces from a knot-free 1 × 10. The base board (part 1) is cut from a 2 × 4.

MATERIALS LIST

Part	Dimensions	Quantity
1. Base boards	1½″ × 1½″	2
2. Long boards	¾″ × ¾″	10
3. Short boards	¾″ × ¾″	10
4. Spacers	¾″ × ¾″ × 1½″	8
5. Finishing nails	4d	48

2. *Cut the parts.* Rip your scraps to ¾ in. × ¾ in. Get the long boards out of the longer scraps, and the short boards from the leftovers. Cut the eight spacers (part 4). Cut the base boards and chamfer, as shown. Sand all parts.

3. *Assemble the planter.* The planter will hold together well enough with finishing nails (part 5), but for greater durability you may want to use a waterproof glue as well or even screw the parts together.

Put the base boards on the bench with the chamfer down and nail a long board into them flush with the top and ends. Space the base boards as far apart as the width of the rail. Nail the first two short boards in place. They should overhang the long boards by ¼ at each end. Keep everything square. Before going on, make sure the piece will fit over the rail without binding. Then continue stacking long boards and short boards, nailing them in place and using spacers, as indicated in the drawings. Check for squareness as you build.

4. *Apply finish.* Stain or paint the planter if you wish. Be sure to use products intended for exterior use. Screw the planter to the rails.

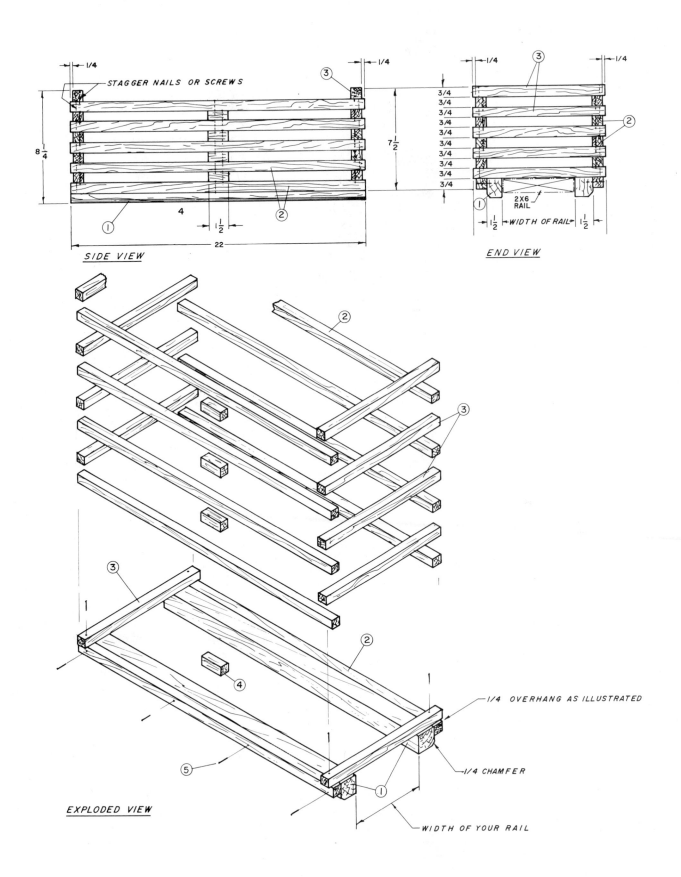

STAGGER NAILS OR SCREWS

1/4

8 1/4

4

1 1/2

22

SIDE VIEW

3

1/4

7 1/2

2

END VIEW

1/4

3

1/4

3/4
3/4
3/4
3/4
3/4
3/4
3/4
3/4
3/4

2

1

2 X 6 RAIL

1 1/2

WIDTH OF RAIL

1 1/2

2

3

3

2

4

3

2

1

5

1/4 OVERHANG AS ILLUSTRATED

1/4 CHAMFER

WIDTH OF YOUR RAIL

EXPLODED VIEW

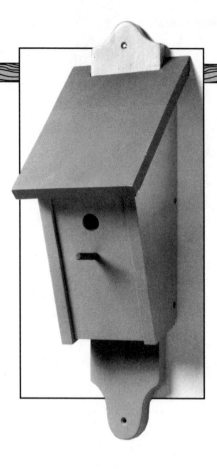

Bluebird Nesting Box

The bluebird was once a common sight in eastern North America, but its numbers have been diminished by some 90 percent over the past half-century. The reasons include irresponsible use of pesticides, loss of habitat, and competition with sparrows and starlings.

You can give bluebirds an edge by building a nesting box designed especially for them. The back is attached with screws so that it can be removed for cleaning.

Bluebirds are particular about their nesting sites, and you can increase your chances of attracting them by hanging the boxes a certain way. Place them on posts or trees in clearings, no more than 4 or 5 feet above the ground.

1. *Select the stock and cut the parts.* You can use any sort of wood for this project. You might be able to make several boxes out of the ¾-in.-thick scraps in your workshop.

Cut out the parts to the sizes given in the Materials List.

2. *Make a paper pattern and cut the back to shape.* Draw a grid with ½-in. squares and enlarge the back (part 1) onto it. Transfer the enlargement to the wood and cut out the back. Locate and drill the two ¼-in.-diameter hanging holes in the back.

The two sides (part 2) can be cut to shape and drilled at the same time. Place one on top of the other, attaching them with rubber cement.

MATERIALS LIST

Part	Dimensions	Quantity
1. Back	¾" × 4½" × 24"	1
2. Sides	¾" × 6¼" × 15¹/₁₆"	2
3. Front	¾" × 4½" × 9¾"	1
4. Bottom	¾" × 4½" × 2"	1
5. Top	¾" × 7½" × 11"	1
6. Perch	¼" dia. × 2½"	1
7. Flathead screws	#8 × 1½"	6

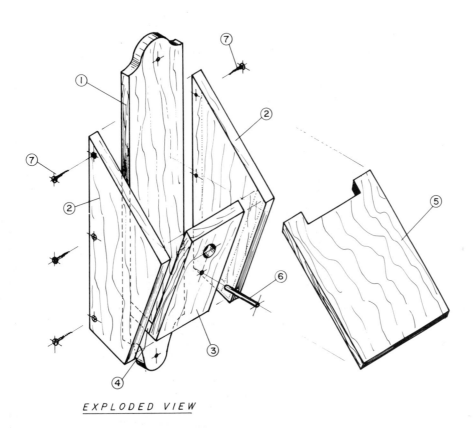

EXPLODED VIEW

Lay out the shape on the top piece, as shown in the side view of part 2. *Maintain the 90 degree angle between the front and bottom.* Cut the sides to shape on the band saw. While the pieces are still together, drill the ⅛-in.-diameter screw holes and countersink them on both sides for a #8 flathead screw (part 7). Sand the edges and take the sides apart.

Cut the front (part 3) and bottom (part 4) to shape, as shown in the details for those parts. Note the bevel on each. Locate and drill holes for the entrance and the perch in the front. The 1½-in.-diameter entrance may seem small, but it discourages other species from taking up residence. Note that the perch hole is drilled at a 25-degree angle so that the perch will project horizontally from the assembled birdhouse.

Cut the top (part 5) to shape, beveling both

the edge and the back of the notch at 45 degrees, as shown. I cut the bevels with a band saw, but a saber saw set at 45 degrees also would work.

3. *Assemble the nesting boxes.* Screw the sides to the back—do not use glue. Glue the front, bottom, top, and sides together. Note that the sides overhang the front and bottom by ⅛ in., as shown in the side and exploded views. Do not glue any of these parts to the back, or you won't be able to take the nesting box apart for cleaning.

Glue the perch (part 6) in place.

4. *Apply finish.* Remove the back from the sides, brush on an oil-base primer, and then an oil-base exterior paint inside and out. The example in the photograph has a two-tone paint job. When dry, put the box together with the six flathead screws.

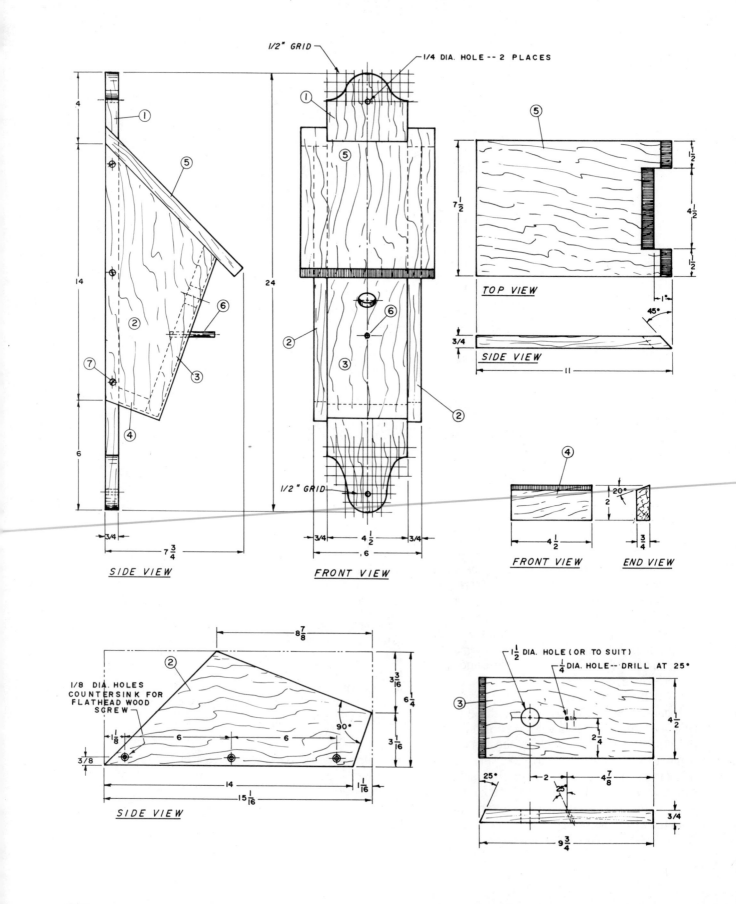

1/2" GRID

1/4 DIA. HOLE -- 2 PLACES

TOP VIEW

SIDE VIEW

SIDE VIEW

FRONT VIEW

FRONT VIEW

END VIEW

1/8 DIA. HOLES
COUNTERSINK FOR
FLATHEAD WOOD
SCREW

SIDE VIEW

1 1/2 DIA. HOLE (OR TO SUIT)
1/4 DIA. HOLE-- DRILL AT 25°

246

Artist's Easel

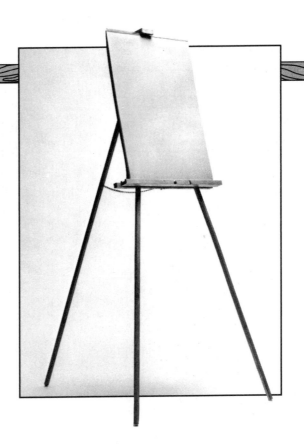

My wife, Joyce, took up painting a few years ago and insisted that she have an easel. That meant either driving 60 miles to the nearest art supply store or walking to the workshop.

I took the latter option. This easel doesn't take long to make, although you do have to be particular when selecting wood for the legs.

1. *Select the stock and cut the parts.* Because the legs are so long and thin, they should be made out of completely knot-free stock. I made-do with flawed pieces I had on hand and ended up replacing several broken legs.

Cut the parts to the sizes given in the Materials List.

2. *Cut the parts to shape.* Study the drawings and then lay out the shape on the block you've cut for the head. Locate the holes, the notch, and the rabbet. I cut the head (part 1) with a band saw. First, cut the $^{13}/_{16} \times 1^{11}/_{16}$-in. notch shown in the front view. Then cut the rabbet, $^3/_4$ in. wide and $1^5/_{16}$ in. deep shown in the side view.

Drill two $^1/_4$-in.-diameter holes in the head, as shown in the front view, for the bolts that hold the front legs.

Drill the hole for the bolt that fastens the rear leg in two steps: First, drill a $^1/_4$-in.-diameter hole all the way through the head, as shown in the side view. Then redrill the hole on the right side to a $^1/_2$-in. diameter, using the first hole as a guide as shown in the pictorial view.

The four corners of the legs (part 2) can be left square or shaped with a router, as shown. Drill a hole in each for the bolt that attaches it to the head.

Drill the $^1/_4$-in.-diameter holes in the support shelf (part 3) and brace (part 4). Cut or rout the groove, $^1/_2$ in. wide and $^3/_{16}$ in. deep, in the support shelf.

Drill two $^1/_8$-in.-diameter screw holes in the upper support (part 5) for the mounting screws (part 11). Put the support in place over the head and transfer the location of the screw holes to the head. Drill $^1/_{16}$-in. pilot holes in the head at these locations.

MATERIALS LIST

Part	Dimensions	Quantity
1. Head	$1\frac{5}{8}'' \times 2\frac{9}{16}'' \times 3''$	1
2. Legs	$\frac{3}{4}'' \times \frac{3}{4}'' \times 60''$	3
3. Support shelf	$\frac{3}{4}'' \times 1\frac{1}{4}'' \times 21''$	1
4. Brace	$\frac{3}{4}'' \times \frac{3}{4}'' \times 21''$	1
5. Upper support	$\frac{3}{4}'' \times 2\frac{1}{2}'' \times 2\frac{9}{16}''$	1
6. Carriage bolt	$\frac{3}{16}'' \times 2\frac{1}{4}''$	1
7. Carriage bolts	$\frac{3}{16}'' \times 2''$	2
8. Carriage bolt	$\frac{3}{16}'' \times 3\frac{1}{4}''$	1
9. Flat washers	$\frac{3}{16}''$	4
10. Wing nuts	$\frac{3}{16}''$	4
11. Roundhead screws	#8 × $\frac{3}{4}''$	2
12. Rubber feet	$\frac{1}{2}''$ dia.	3
13. Roundhead screws	#4 × $\frac{3}{4}''$	3
14. Eye screws		2
15. Chain	16"-18"	1

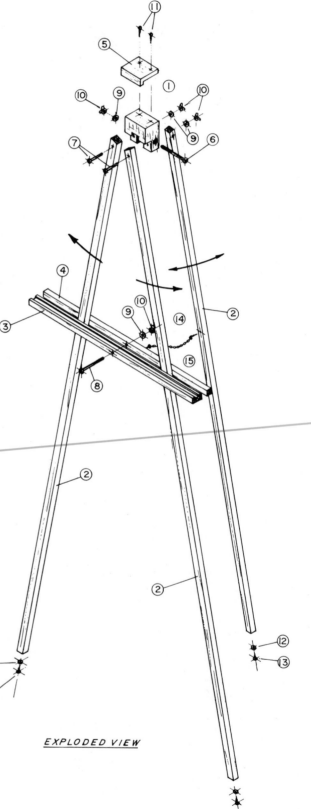

EXPLODED VIEW

3. *Apply finish.* Sand thoroughly. Stain the easel if you wish, and apply a coat of varnish.

4. *Assemble the easel.* The exploded view shows how the pieces come together. The center leg is held in the center slot of the head with the 2¼-in. carriage bolt (part 6). The head of the bolt rests in the ½-in.-diameter hole. Attach the other legs to the head with 2-in. carriage bolts (part 7). Attach the support shelf and brace with the 3¼-in. carriage bolt (part 8).

Attach the rubber feet (part 12) to the bottom of the legs. The chain (part 15) prevents the back leg from opening so far that it will threaten the stability of the easel. Attach it with eye screws (part 14) in the brace and back leg.

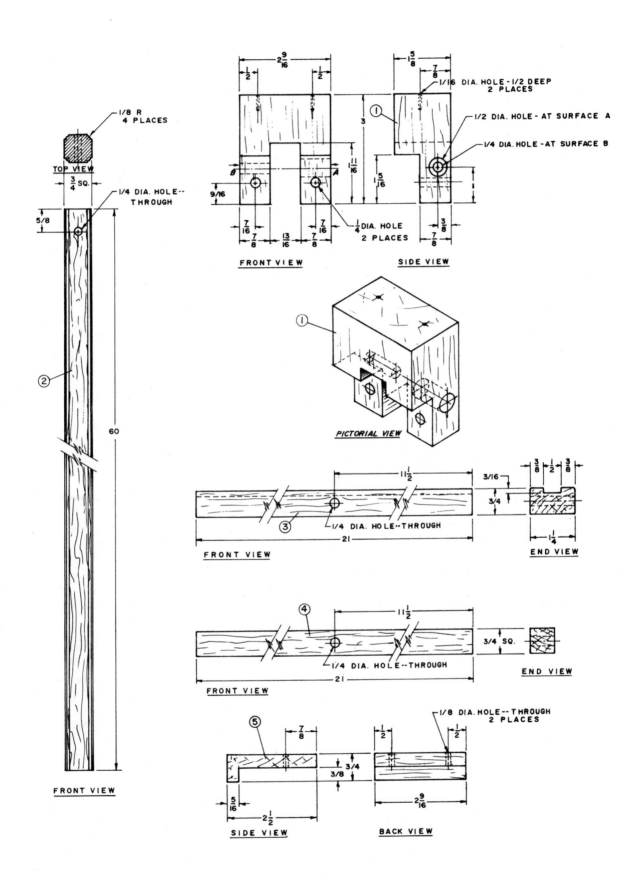

1/8 R
4 PLACES

TOP VIEW

3/4 SQ.

1/4 DIA. HOLE--
THROUGH

5/8

②

60

FRONT VIEW

2 9/16

1/2   1/2

B   A

9/16

7/8   13/16   7/8

7/16   7/16

FRONT VIEW

1/4 DIA. HOLE
2 PLACES

1 5/8

7/8

1/16 DIA. HOLE - 1/2 DEEP
2 PLACES

①

3

1 5/16

3/8

7/8

SIDE VIEW

1/2 DIA. HOLE - AT SURFACE A

1/4 DIA. HOLE - AT SURFACE B

①

PICTORIAL VIEW

11 1/2

3/16

3/4

③

1/4 DIA. HOLE--THROUGH

21

FRONT VIEW

3/8 1/2 3/8

1/4

END VIEW

④

11 1/2

3/4 SQ.

1/4 DIA. HOLE--THROUGH

21

FRONT VIEW

END VIEW

1/8 DIA. HOLE-- THROUGH
2 PLACES

⑤

7/8

1/2   1/2

3/4

3/8

5/16

2 1/2

SIDE VIEW

2 9/16

BACK VIEW

249

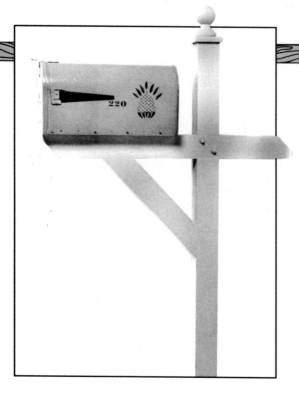

Mailbox Post

A while ago I had to replace my mailbox post. I looked through all of my woodworking magazines and books and couldn't come up with a single plan. Wooden posts can be bought at hardware stores, but somehow they seem incomplete. Because the mailbox post is such a visible part of a home, I think it should reflect something of the people who live there. So, I sat down and designed this one.

The finial is a fairly standard item from woodworker's supply companies, so you can buy one if you don't have a lathe.

1. Select the stock. You can use pressure-treated 4 × 4s for the post (part 1), but if you plan to paint the post, make sure you've bought kiln-dried wood stamped "dry." You also can choose between cedar, white oak, locust, and other rot-resistant woods. The support (part 4) is cut from exterior plywood.

2. Cut the parts. Cut the parts to the sizes given in the Materials List. The plywood support is designed to fit snugly into the base of the mailbox. Cut the plywood support (part 4) to fit the base on your mailbox.

Cut the half-lap joints necessary for assembling the post and rail (part 2), as shown in the detail drawings. Make the joints $1/32$ in. undersized to ensure a tight fit. Cut the ends of the rail at 45 degrees and cut tenons into them, as shown. Dry-assemble the post and rail. Make sure the post and rail are at exactly 90 degrees to one another and lay the brace over them to lay out the notches for it. Cut notches in the rail.

MATERIALS LIST

Part	Dimensions	Quantity
1. Post	$3\frac{1}{2}'' \times 3\frac{1}{2}'' \times 96''$	1
2. Rail	$3\frac{1}{2}'' \times 3\frac{1}{2}'' \times 40''$	1
3. Brace	$3\frac{1}{2}'' \times 3\frac{1}{2}'' \times 23\frac{7}{8}''$	1
4. Support (plywood)*	$\frac{3}{4}'' \times 8\frac{1}{2}'' \times 4\frac{1}{4}''$	1
5. Top board	$\frac{3}{4}'' \times 4\frac{1}{4}'' \times 4\frac{1}{4}''$	1
6. Finial**	$3\frac{1}{8}''$ dia.	1
7. Hex bolts, nuts, washers	$\frac{1}{4}'' \times 4''$	2 each
8. Flathead screws	#8 × $1\frac{3}{4}''$	6
9. Sheet metal screws	#8 × $\frac{3}{4}''$	8
10. Hanger bolt	$\frac{1}{4}'' \times 3''$	1
11. Finishing nails	4d	4

*Before sawing, check the size of your mailbox.
**Finial is available from Constantine, 2050 Eastchester Road, Bronx, NY 10461; order #WF-33.

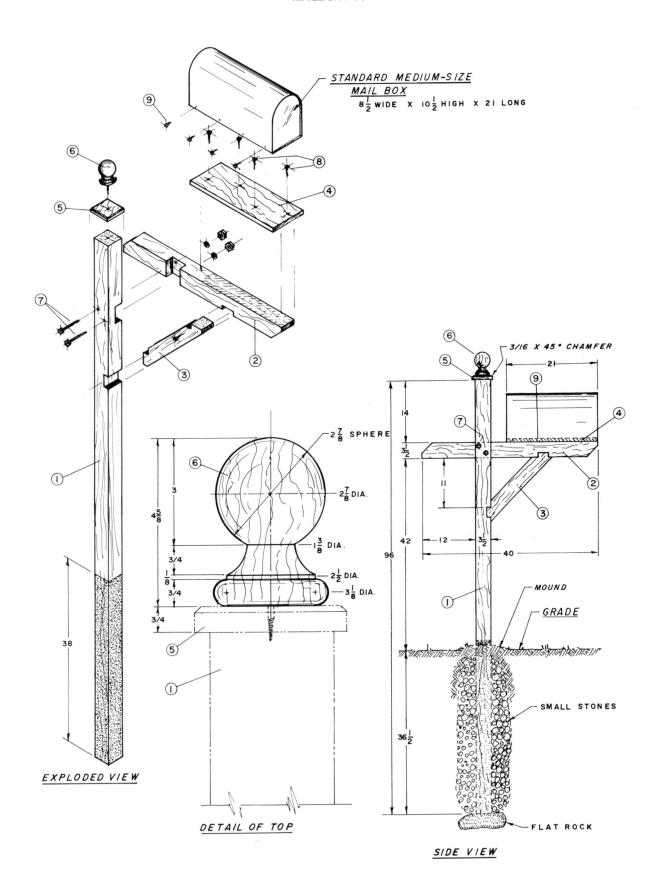

STANDARD MEDIUM-SIZE
MAIL BOX
$8\frac{1}{2}$ WIDE X $10\frac{1}{2}$ HIGH X 21 LONG

$2\frac{7}{8}$ SPHERE

$2\frac{7}{8}$ DIA.

$1\frac{3}{8}$ DIA.

$2\frac{1}{2}$ DIA.

$3\frac{1}{8}$ DIA.

EXPLODED VIEW

DETAIL OF TOP

3/16 X 45° CHAMFER

MOUND

GRADE

SMALL STONES

FLAT ROCK

SIDE VIEW

251

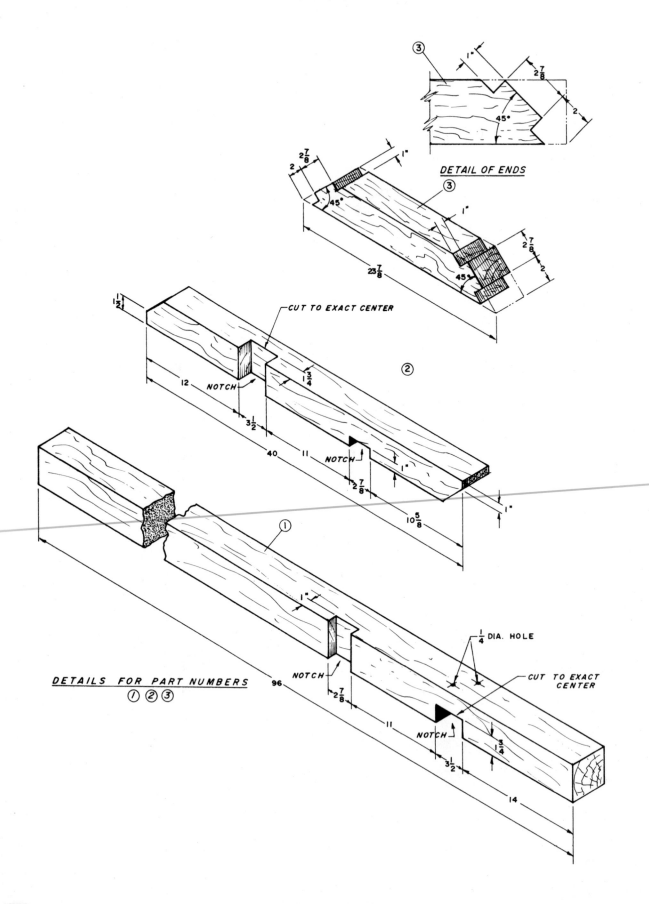

DETAIL OF ENDS

CUT TO EXACT CENTER

NOTCH

NOTCH

¼ DIA. HOLE

CUT TO EXACT CENTER

DETAILS FOR PART NUMBERS
① ② ③

3. *Assemble the post.* Using waterproof resorcinol glue, assemble the post, rail, and brace (part 3). After the glue has set, locate and drill two ¼-in.-diameter holes in the post where the post and rail cross. Add the two hex head bolts with washers (part 7).

Screw and glue the plywood support to the top of the rail with a flathead screw (part 8) but don't attach the mailbox yet. First, chamfer the top board (part 5), as shown in the drawing. Glue and nail it to the top of the post top with 4d finishing nails (part 11).

Turn the finial (part 6) to the given dimensions or buy one. Drill a pilot hole through the top board and into the post for the hanger bolt (part 10). Attach the finial.

If you will be painting the post a different color than the mailbox, you may want to attach the mailbox after the painting is completed. Otherwise, attach the mailbox by driving eight sheet metal screws (part 9) into the support.

4. *Apply finish.* Finish with an exterior primer and two coats of exterior paint; apply a coat of tar or other waterproof material to the end grain and the bottom 38 in. or so of the post.

5. *Install the mailbox.* Dig a hole about 40 in. deep and put a flat stone at the bottom. Put the post in the hole and surround it with small pea stones or sand. Mound the filled hole with topsoil so that rainwater will be diverted from the post.

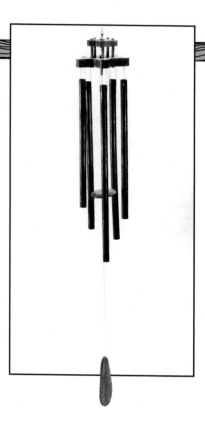

Wind Chimes

With this project, you can turn your workshop scraps and the wind into music.

1. Select the stock and cut the parts. Almost any wood will do, although especially weather-proof choices include redwood, cedar, and teak. I used leftover ash. Make the metal chimes from either ⅝-in.-diameter copper pipe or electrical conduit.

Cut the wooden parts—the supports, spacers, and clanger (parts 1, 2, 3, and 11)—to their overall sizes, as given in the Materials List. Turn the clanger to the profile shown or leave it unadorned. Drill a ¹⁄₁₆-in.-diameter hole in the exact center.

Cut out the sail (part 13) from any scrap metal or wood, following the pattern shown in the detail.

Cut the chimes (parts 6, 7, 8, 9, and 10) with a pipe cutter or hack saw to get five different tones: 11½ in., 12½ in., 13½ in., 14½ in., and 15½ in. (The tones will be close to a pentatonic scale, and you can further tune a chime to your liking by grinding it to raise the pitch.)

Drill ⅛-in.-diameter holes ⅜ in. down from the top of the chimes and the sail. Lightly sand the sharp edges of the metal parts.

2. Make a paper pattern and cut the supports to shape. Draw a grid with ½-in. squares, and enlarge the main support and the top support onto it. Transfer the enlargement to the wood. Locate and drill the holes, as shown. Cut the parts to shape. Sand thoroughly.

3. Add the spacers. Glue the five spacers (part 3) in the holes in the main and top supports,

MATERIALS LIST

Part	Dimensions	Quantity
1. Main support	¾" × 6" × 6"	1
2. Top support	½" × 3" × 3"	1
3. Spacers	¼" dia. × 2½"	5
4. Eyebolts	⅛" dia. × 1"	2
5. Hex nuts	For eyebolts	2
6. Chime	⅝" dia. × 15½"	1
7. Chime	⅝" dia. × 14½"	1
8. Chime	⅝" dia. × 13½"	1
9. Chime	⅝" dia. × 12½"	1
10. Chime	⅝" dia. × 11½"	1
11. Clanger	½" × 2½" dia.	1
12. Beads	To suit	2
13. Sail	¹⁄₁₆" × 2½" × 3½"	1
14. Fish line	60"	1

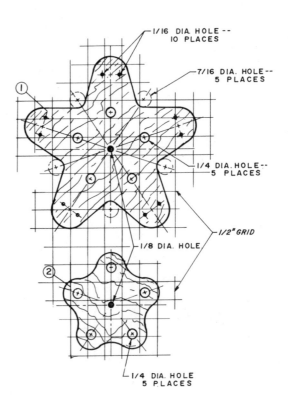

1/16 DIA. HOLE --
10 PLACES

7/16 DIA. HOLE --
5 PLACES

1/4 DIA. HOLE --
5 PLACES

1/2" GRID

1/8 DIA. HOLE

1/4 DIA. HOLE
5 PLACES

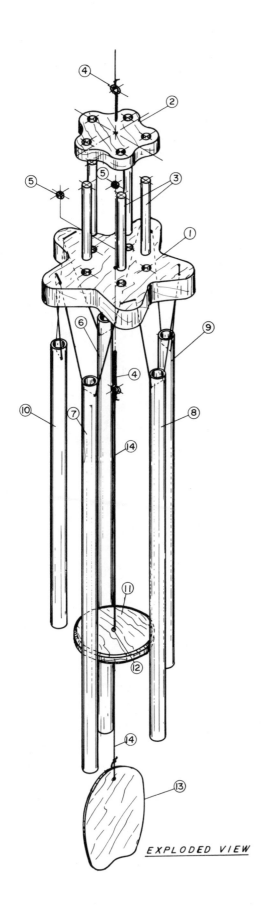

EXPLODED VIEW

leaving a space of 1 in. between the supports. Unless you have used teak, brush two or three coats of an exterior sealer on this subassembly and on the clanger.

4. *Assemble the chimes.* Study the top and exploded views to see how the chimes are put together. Thread a continuous length of fish line (part 14) through the pipes and supports, as shown in the exploded view. The chimes should be about 1½ in. below the main support. Once you've gotten back to the starting point, tie a square knot in the end of the line and put a dab of glue on the knot to secure it.

Install the eyebolts (part 4) in the main support. Tie a new piece of fish line to it, then run the line through a small wooden bead (part 12) and the clanger. Feed the line through the second bead, and then bring it back up and through the bead a second time to hold the clanger in place. The clanger should be about 7¼ in. from the main support. Thread the fish line through the hole in the sail and knot it. Place a bit of epoxy glue on the knots and at both beads.

To hang up the chimes, place the eyebolt in the top support and attach fish line to it.

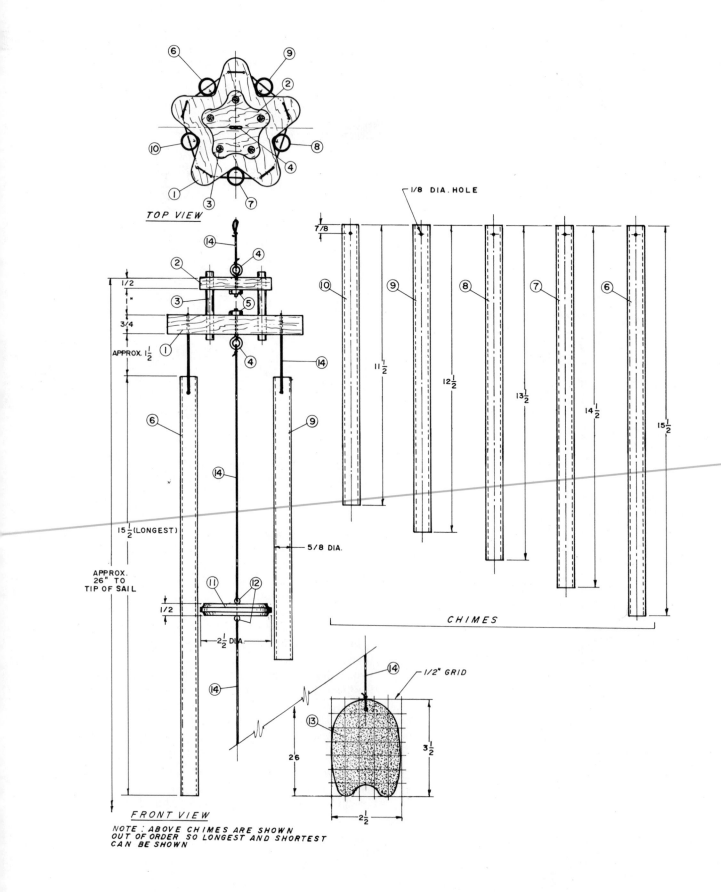

TOP VIEW

FRONT VIEW

NOTE: ABOVE CHIMES ARE SHOWN
OUT OF ORDER SO LONGEST AND SHORTEST
CAN BE SHOWN

CHIMES

1/8 DIA. HOLE

256

Whirligig

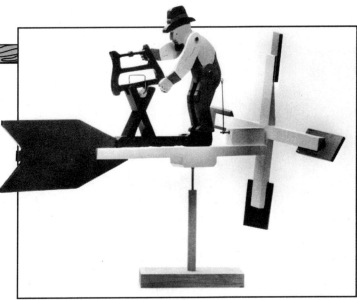

Whirligigs are wind-driven works of folk art. This one is based on an old, battered whirligig I found near Keene, New Hampshire. I've specified commercial brass parts so that you don't have to make your own. The trickiest task remaining to you is making the propeller.

1. Select the stock and cut the parts. You can make this project out of scraps, but sort through them for straight-grained, knot-free hardwood. Cut the parts to their overall sizes, as given in the Materials List.

2. Transfer the patterns and cut the parts to shape. Draw a grid with ½-in.-squares. Enlarge the patterns of the crossbuck (part 2), the legs (part 4), the body (part 6), the arms (part 7), and the screw (part 8) on to it. Transfer the patterns to the wood. To make it easier to negotiate the tight corner cuts in the saw, drill the holes illustrated in the detail for that part. To save time, cut the two arms and two legs together, joining the pairs with rubber cement. Sand the edges while the parts are still together.

After cutting all the parts to shape, drill the holes, as shown, and sand all over. Lay out and cut the back end of the crossbuck to receive the tail fin (part 16), as shown in the drawing of the crossbuck. Cut a dado in the shaft housing (part 18), as shown in the detail for part 18.

Cut the base (part 1), the bottom board

(part 13), and the tail fin to the profiles shown in the side view.

3. Make the propeller. This propeller is a copy of the one on the original whirligig. It is somewhat more complicated than the propellers used on most whirligigs today.

To make the blade supports (part 26), first locate and cut 1-in.-wide, ⅜-in.-deep notches, as shown in the detail drawings of part 26. Note that the notch is in the top of one support and in the bottom of the other.

Lay out the pattern on the top and side surfaces of the supports with a sharp pencil. Note the ⅛-in. shoulder located 2 in. from either end. Cut away the shaded areas with a band saw or a coping saw. Try to make the four cuts as nearly the same as you can.

Temporarily fit the two blade supports together and drill a hole through both; the hole should be sized to make a snug fit for the propeller tube (part 25). Take the supports apart and sand the supports. Glue the four blades (part 27) on the supports, centering them and placing them flush against the shoulder. To help keep the blades in place, drive ½-in. tacks (part 14) through them and into the supports.

Glue the two supports together and insert the tube.

4. Assemble the whirligig. To add strength to the glued joints called for here, you can drive

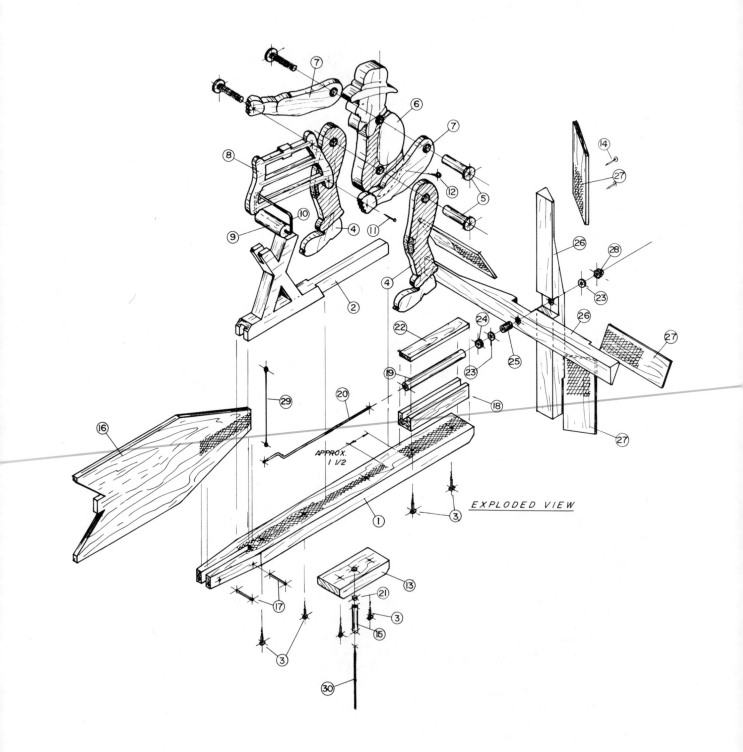

APPROX.
1 1/2

EXPLODED VIEW

⅜-in. tacks (part 11) through them before the glue has set.

Attach the tail fin to the base with glue and dowel pins (part 17). Attach the bottom board and the shaft housing to the base with glue and screws.

Add the drive shaft tube and glue the top shaft housing (part 22) in place.

Locate the exact center of the bottom board and drill a hole sized to take the pivot bearing (part 21); drill the hole from the bottom until it's about 1¼ in. deep. Place the bearing in the hole and drive the pivot tube (part 15) in after it. The pivot tube will hold the bearing in place.

Temporarily add the driveshaft (part 20), washers (part 23), and hex nut (part 24). Attach the propeller assembly with the acorn nut (part 28) and check that everything functions correctly.

Attach the arms and legs to the body, using the self-locking post (part 5). With the arms and legs in place, glue the feet to the crossbuck and the hands to the saw. Position the hands as shown in the side view of the project.

Drill ¹⁄₁₆-in.-diameter, ½-in.-deep holes in the center of the ends of the log (part 9) to hold the support wire (part 10). The support wire holds the saw in place; make it from a coat hanger. Glue the log to the crossbuck and temporarily add the support wire, as shown in the exploded view. Put it in place permanently after painting the whirligig. Check that the assembly moves freely and adjust it if necessary before the glue sets.

Attach the crossbuck and the body assembly to the base and bottom board with glue and flathead screws (part 3).

Cut the tie wire (part 29) to length and bend a loop in each end. Attach the tie wire to the drive shaft and position it to see where on the man the eye screw should be. Mark the spot and put the eye screw in the man. Attach the tie wire to the eye screw.

Check that everything functions correctly. Move the eye screw slightly higher or lower, if necessary. Adjust the other parts as needed so that they function with as little friction as possible; the point is to enable the whirligig to turn in a modest wind as well as in a gale. It is better for the parts to fit loosely than tightly.

5. *Apply finish.* Disassemble all moving parts and any others that aren't glued in place. Paint

MATERIALS LIST

Part	Dimensions	Quantity
1. Base	¾″ × 1½″ × 17″	1
2. Crossbuck	¾″ × 4⁵⁄₁₆″ × 9½″	1
3. Flathead screws	#6 × 1¼″	7
4. Legs	¼″ × 3″ × 6″	2
5. Self-locking post*		2
6. Body	½″ × 4″ × 7½″	1
7. Arms	¼″ × 2″ × 5½″	2
8. Saw	¼″ × 3¾″ × 5½″	1
9. Log	½″ dia. × 1⅜″	1
10. Support wire	¹⁄₁₆″ dia. × 4″	1
11. Tacks	⅜″	as needed
12. Eye screw*		1
13. Bottom board	¾″ × 1½″ × 3¼″	1
14. Tacks	½″	8
15. Pivot tube*		1
16. Tail fin		1
17. Dowel pins	⅛″ dia. × 1½″	2
18. Shaft housing	¾″ × 1″ × 3¾″	1
19. Driveshaft tube*		1
20. Driveshaft wire*		1
21. Pivot bearing*		1
22. Top shaft housing	¼″ × ¾″ × 3¾″	1
23. Washers*		2
24. Hex nut*		1
25. Propeller tube*		1
26. Blade supports	¾″ × 1″ × 12″	2
27. Blades	¼″ × 2¼″ × 4″	4
28. Acorn nut*		1
29. Tie wire*		1
30. Pivot nail*		1

Hardware is available from Cherry Tree Toys, Inc., P.O. Box 369, Belmont, OH 43718. Self-locking post is #908, eye screw is #914, pivot tube is #916, driveshaft tube is #917, drive shaft wire is #921, pivot bearing is #909, washer is #910, hex nut is #912, propeller tube is #915, acorn nut is #913, tie wire is #920, and pivot nail is #918.

the project as you wish. I've suggested colors in the drawings but don't feel restricted to them. I highlighted various parts with black paint, using a thin brush. Relax and have fun. The whirligig will operate a little more smoothly if you apply a coat of paste wax after the paint has dried.

Reassemble the project and make adjustments if necessary to restore free movement. Put sewing machine oil on the moving metal parts. Mount the whirligig on a post that has a nail (part 30) driven into it.

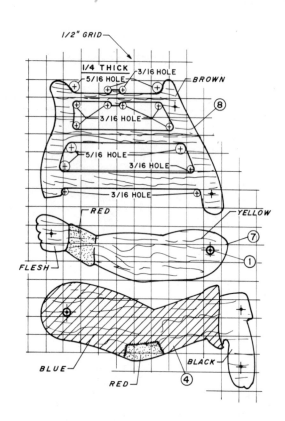

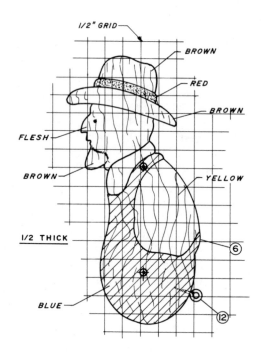

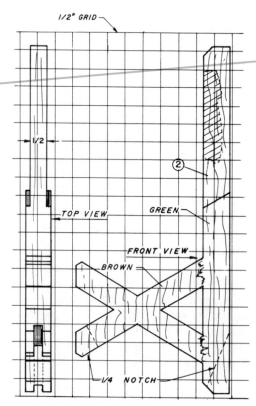

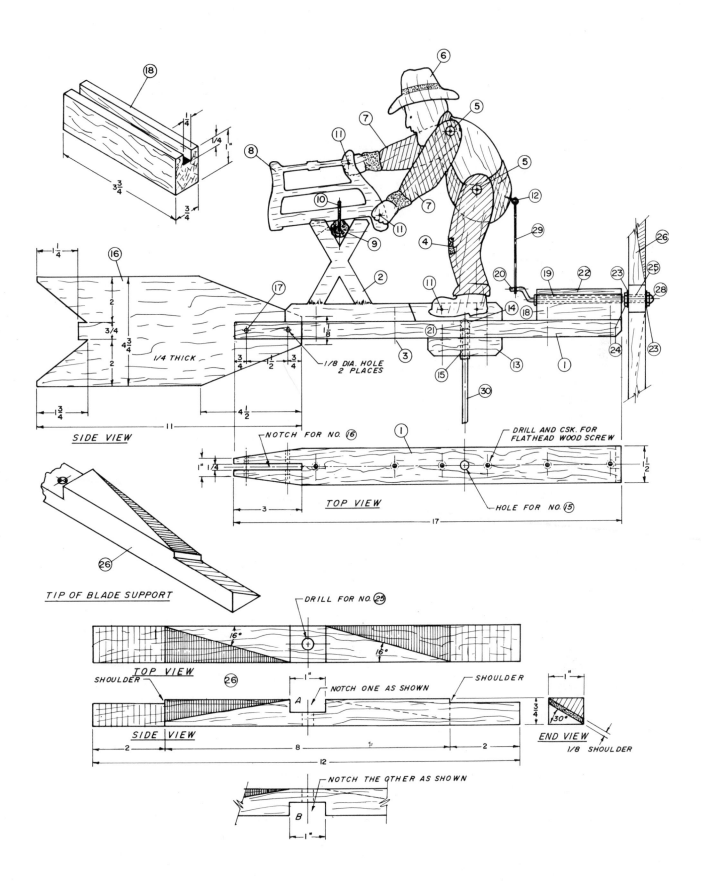

SIDE VIEW

TIP OF BLADE SUPPORT

1/4 THICK

1/8 DIA. HOLE
2 PLACES

NOTCH FOR NO. 16

TOP VIEW

DRILL AND CSK. FOR
FLATHEAD WOOD SCREW

HOLE FOR NO. 15

DRILL FOR NO. 25

TOP VIEW

SHOULDER

SHOULDER

NOTCH ONE AS SHOWN

SIDE VIEW

END VIEW

1/8 SHOULDER

NOTCH THE OTHER AS SHOWN

Coasting Sled

Until the first half of the 1800s, most sleds were built by the father or grandfather of the family, a local woodworker or cabinetmaker, or the local blacksmith. These early sleds were not used as toys but for the practical purpose of hauling supplies over the snow. As attitudes toward children's play changed over the years, the sled evolved into something on which to slide down hills. By the mid 1800s, at least 12 companies were manufacturing sleds in the United States.

These early sleds were gaily decorated with bright colors and gold stripes to catch the consumer's eye. It took a lot of body English to steer these sleds because the one-piece runners didn't flex like those on today's sleds. This project is an exact copy of an early coasting sled I found in Rhode Island.

1. Select the stock and cut the parts. The old sleds were extremely sturdy and usually made from a hardwood such as oak or rock maple. But the choice of wood is up to you. You may find it necessary to glue up boards to make the top. The iron for the runners can be bought at metal supply firms.

Cut the parts to their overall sizes given in the Materials List.

2. Make a paper pattern and cut the parts to size. Draw a grid with 1-in. squares and enlarge the top (part 1) and rails (part 2) onto it. Transfer the pattern to the stock. Include the outline of the heart in the top. To save time, trace the pattern onto just one rail and join the two

rails temporarily by tacking them with two finishing nails where they won't interfere with the cut. Cut out the rails and the top with a saber saw, jigsaw, or coping saw.

To cut the heart-shaped hole in the top, drill a hole within the traced outline and start to saw from there. Locate and drill a ¾-in.-diameter hole in the rails for the handle (part 4).

Cut the braces (part 3) and the handle to size. Sand all cut edges. To ensure strong glue joints, avoid rounding off edges where the pieces will meet.

3. Make the runners. It's a simple matter to bend the runners (part 5) to shape as you attach them. Before you attach them, however, flatten the ends to the profile shown in the runner detail.

Each runner is attached to its rail with nine #8 flathead screws (part 6). Mark the location of the holes on each runner by dimpling the metal with an awl or center punch. The dimple keeps the bit from wandering as you drill the hole. Select a bit that will just allow the full width of the screw shank to pass through, and then drill the holes. Counterbore the holes so that the mounting screws will be slightly recessed.

4. Attach the runners. Put one end of the still unbent rail in position on the runner. Mark the location of the end hole on the rail and drill a pilot hole to make it easier to drive the screw.

After driving the first screw, press the runner to conform with the rail. Then mark, drill, and

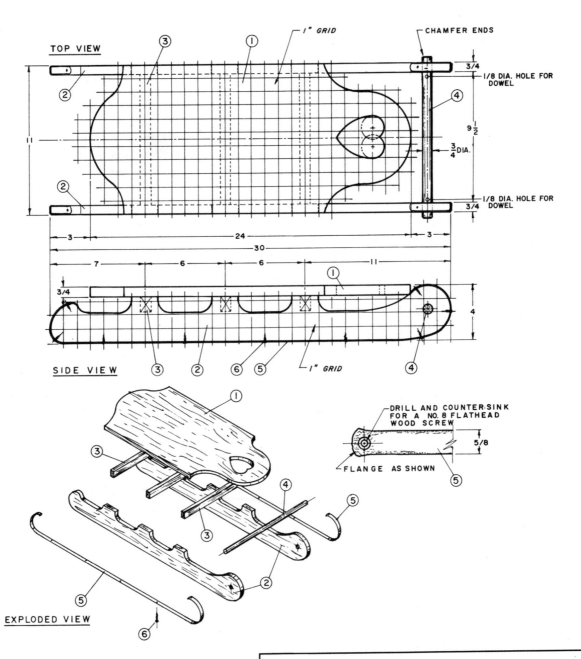

TOP VIEW

1" GRID

CHAMFER ENDS

3/4

1/8 DIA. HOLE FOR DOWEL

9 1/2

3/4 DIA.

1/8 DIA. HOLE FOR DOWEL

3/4

11

3 — 24 — 3

30

7 — 6 — 6 — 11

3/4

4

SIDE VIEW

1" GRID

EXPLODED VIEW

DRILL AND COUNTER-SINK FOR A NO. 8 FLATHEAD WOOD SCREW

5/8

FLANGE AS SHOWN

MATERIALS LIST

Part	Dimensions	Quantity
1. Top	1" × 11" × 24"	1
2. Rails	1" × 4" × 30"	2
3. Braces	1" × 2" × 10"	3
4. Handle	¾" dia. × 12"	1
5. Runners	⅛" × ⅝" × 38"	2
6. Flathead screws	#8 × ¾"	18
7. Square-cut nails		as needed

drive the screw in the second hole. Continue until all nine screws are in place. You'll find that the runners can be bent easily by hand. Repeat the process on the second rail.

5. *Assemble the sled.* Test-fit all parts and make any adjustments necessary. Nail the sled together with square-cut nails (part 7). First, nail the braces to the top. Before you nail the top to the rails, align them by temporarily slipping the handle through the holes in the rails. Then nail the top to the rails and remove the handle.

Put glue into the hole for the handle, slip the handle in place, and wipe off any excess glue with a damp rag. Further secure the handle with ⅛-in. dowels driven through holes in the handle shown in the top view.

6. *Finish the sled.* If you've used an attractive wood, consider applying a clear weather-resistant finish. I chose to paint my sled bright blue with yellow pinstriping. I used oil-base exterior enamel for the base coat. When it dried, I added pinstripes with thinned enamel.

Don't be afraid to try your hand at pinstriping; the job on the antique sled itself was not perfect by any means. The trick is to use a long pinstriping brush, available at art supply stores. Practice on a piece of scrap wood until you get the hang of it. You can make a straighter line if you clamp a strip of wood to the top of the sled and run your hand along it. Clean up any mistakes with a rag or cotton swab dampened with paint thinner.

Child's Sleigh

This is an exact copy of a sleigh from the 1800s. Its construction is a little unusual—the grain direction of the legs and rails seems to be an invitation to breakage. Common practice is to steam-bend such pieces for greater strength, but the original has held up for more than a century.

If you live in a part of the country that rarely sees snow, you can use this sleigh as a planter.

1. Select the stock and cut the parts. Any wood will do if the sleigh will carry nothing more stressful than plants, but make the runners from hardwood if children will be playing with it.

Cut the parts to the sizes given in the Materials List. Make sure the grain direction is as shown in the drawings.

2. Make a paper pattern for the sides and cut the body to shape. Draw a grid with ½-in. squares on a piece of paper and enlarge the sides (part 1) onto it. Transfer the enlargements to the stock and cut the parts to shape. Lay out the back (part 2), front (part 3), and bottom (part 4) directly on the wood. Pay particular attention to the arcs on the back and front and to the beveled edges, as shown in the front view of these parts. Cut the parts to shape.

3. Assemble the body of the sleigh. Dry-fit the sides, front, back, and bottom and make any necessary adjustment. When they come together correctly, assemble them with glue and nails. Use a waterproof glue for this project.

4. Turn the handle. Turn the handle (part 10) on a lathe to the profile shown in the handle front view. Drill two ½-in.-diameter holes in it for the handles, as shown.

5. Lay out the handle supports and cut them to shape. Draw a pattern for the handle support on a ½-in. grid and transfer it to the wood. Lay out the pattern of the handle supports and cut them out. Round the supports with a rasp to the profile shown in the view at A-A. Leave the area where the handle supports meet the back of the sleigh flat, as shown in the exploded view. With a backsaw cut square tenons on the top of the handle supports and then round them to fit the holes drilled for them in the handle. Sand smooth the surfaces that will be visible.

Drill two $^{11}/_{64}$-in.-diameter screw holes in each support, as shown.

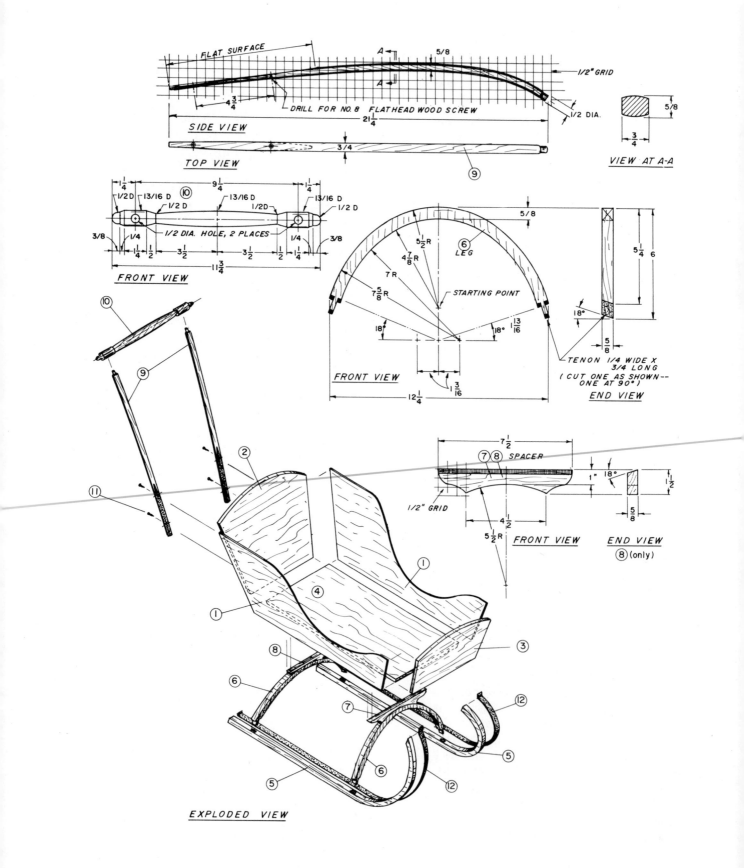

FLAT SURFACE

A

5/8

1/2" GRID

4 3/4

DRILL FOR NO. 8 FLATHEAD WOOD SCREW

A

1/2 DIA.

21 1/4

SIDE VIEW

5/8

3/4

3/4

VIEW AT A-A

3/4

TOP VIEW

9

1/4

9 1/4

1/4

10

1/2 D

13/16 D

13/16 D

13/16 D

1/2 D

1/2 D

1/2 D

3/8

1/4

1/2 DIA. HOLE, 2 PLACES

1/4

3/8

1/4 1/2

3 1/2

3 1/2

1/2 1/4

11 3/4

FRONT VIEW

5/8

5 1/2 R

6

LEG

4 7/8 R

7 R

STARTING POINT

7 5/8 R

18°

18°

13/16

5 1/4

6

18°

TENON 1/4 WIDE X
3/4 LONG
(CUT ONE AS SHOWN --
ONE AT 90°)

5/8

FRONT VIEW

12 1/4

1 3/16

END VIEW

10

9

7 1/2

7 8 SPACER

1" 18°

2

1 1/2

1/2" GRID

11

5/8

4 1/2

5 1/2 R

FRONT VIEW

END VIEW
8 (only)

1

4

3

8

6

7

12

5

5

6

12

EXPLODED VIEW

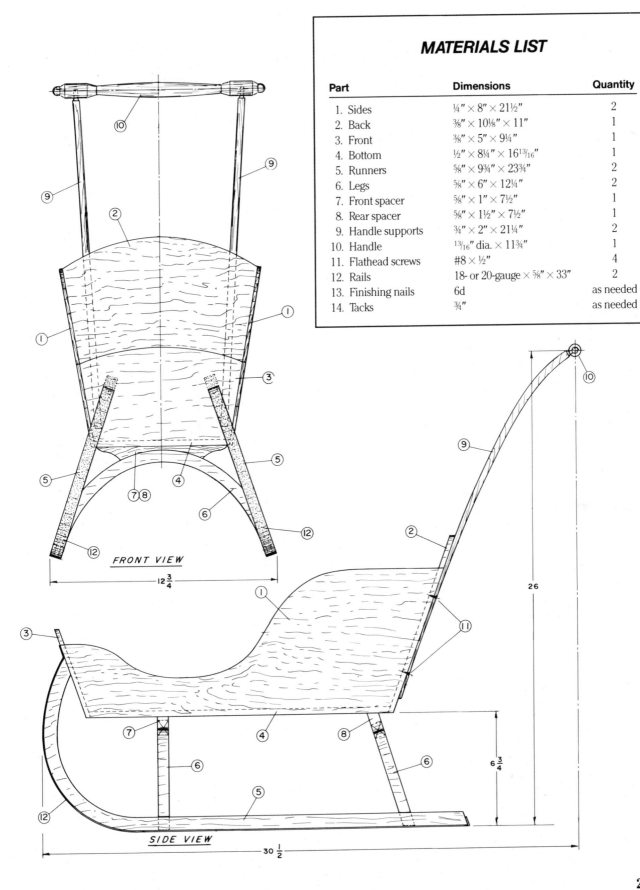

MATERIALS LIST

Part	Dimensions	Quantity
1. Sides	$\frac{1}{4}'' \times 8'' \times 21\frac{1}{2}''$	2
2. Back	$\frac{3}{8}'' \times 10\frac{1}{8}'' \times 11''$	1
3. Front	$\frac{3}{8}'' \times 5'' \times 9\frac{1}{4}''$	1
4. Bottom	$\frac{1}{2}'' \times 8\frac{1}{4}'' \times 16\frac{13}{16}''$	1
5. Runners	$\frac{5}{8}'' \times 9\frac{3}{4}'' \times 23\frac{3}{4}''$	2
6. Legs	$\frac{5}{8}'' \times 6'' \times 12\frac{1}{4}''$	2
7. Front spacer	$\frac{5}{8}'' \times 1'' \times 7\frac{1}{2}''$	1
8. Rear spacer	$\frac{5}{8}'' \times 1\frac{1}{2}'' \times 7\frac{1}{2}''$	1
9. Handle supports	$\frac{3}{4}'' \times 2'' \times 21\frac{1}{4}''$	2
10. Handle	$\frac{13}{16}''$ dia. $\times 11\frac{3}{4}''$	1
11. Flathead screws	#8 $\times \frac{1}{2}''$	4
12. Rails	18- or 20-gauge $\times \frac{5}{8}'' \times 33''$	2
13. Finishing nails	6d	as needed
14. Tacks	$\frac{3}{4}''$	as needed

FRONT VIEW

$12\frac{3}{4}$

SIDE VIEW

$30\frac{1}{2}$

26

$6\frac{3}{4}$

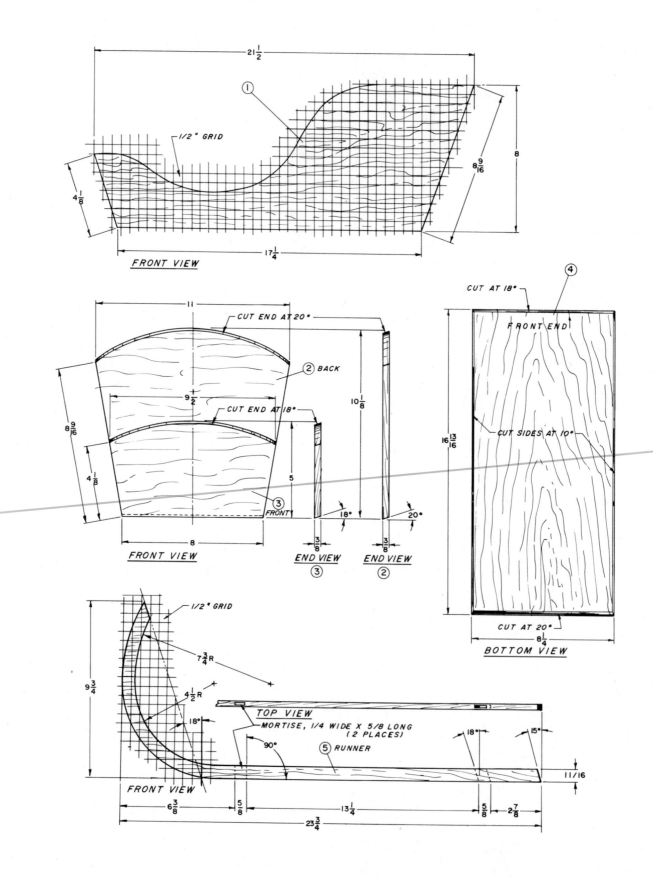

21 1/2

① 1/2" GRID

8 9/16

8

4 1/8

17 1/4

FRONT VIEW

11

CUT END AT 20°

② BACK

9 1/2

CUT END AT 18°

10 1/8

8 9/16

4 1/8

5

③

18°

20°

③ FRONT

8

3/8

3/8

FRONT VIEW

END VIEW
③

END VIEW
②

CUT AT 18°

④

FRONT END

16 13/16

CUT SIDES AT 10°

CUT AT 20°

8 1/4

BOTTOM VIEW

1/2" GRID

9 3/4

7 3/4 R

4 1/2 R

18°

TOP VIEW

MORTISE, 1/4 WIDE X 5/8 LONG
(2 PLACES)

90°

⑤ RUNNER

18°

15°

11/16

FRONT VIEW

6 3/8

5/8

13 1/4

5/8

2 7/8

23 3/4

6. *Transfer the runner pattern and cut the runners to shape.* Draw the runner pattern on a ½-in. grid and transfer it to the wood. Include the location of the through mortises. Note that the rear mortise in each is cut at an 18-degree angle. Cut out the runners (part 5). To cut the mortises, drill a series of adjoining ¼-in. holes through the runner. Square off the holes with a sharp chisel. You may find it easiest to drill a very short mortise in the rear and create its sloping surfaces entirely with the chisel.

7. *Lay out the legs.* Each of the legs (part 6) is formed by drawing a series of overlapping arcs.

Lay out the arcs directly on the wood. Lay out the tenons, too, but note that the front and back tenons differ. The shoulders of the rear tenons slope because of the slope of the rear legs. See the side view of the assembled sleigh. Cut the legs on a band saw; cut the tenons with a backsaw.

The spacers join the sleigh to the runners. Lay out the front and rear spacers (parts 7 and 8) on the wood. They differ too: The rear spacer is wider and beveled to accommodate the slope of the legs. The top of the front spacer is square to the sides. Cut the spacers on a band saw.

8. *Assemble the sleigh.* Glue the legs in the runners. Put the spacers on top of the legs and glue them in place.

Attach the runner subassembly to the body by placing glue on the top surface of the spacers. When the glue dries, drill pilot holes for 6d nails through the sleigh and into the supports. Nail the parts together with 6d finishing nails (part 13) to reinforce the joint.

Glue the handle supports in the handle and then screw the supports to the back of the body with #8 × ½-flathead wood screws (part 11).

9. *Apply finish.* Sand the sleigh all over. Use exterior paint if the sleigh will see outdoor service. The original was painted barn red.

10. *Attach the rails (optional).* If the sleigh will be used in the snow, you may want to add metal rails (part 12). Those on the original sleigh appear to be made out of scavenged strips of tin. You can tack ⅝-in.-wide strips of 18- or 20-gauge steel to the runners with carpet tacks. Drill pilot holes through the steel, and dimple them with a punch so that the tack heads (part 14) will be flush. Note that the rails extend somewhat beyond the bottom of the runners at either end.

Adirondack Chair and Child's Adirondack Chair

MATERIALS LIST

Part	Dimensions	Quantity
Adult's chair		
1. Front legs	¾″ × 3½″ × 20″	2
2. Seat rails	¾″ × 3½″ × 30½″	2
3. Back support	¾″ × 1½″ × 19″	1
4. Front brace	¾″ × 3½″ × 20½″	1
5. Seat slats	¾″ × 2½″ × 19″	5
6. Arm braces	¾″ × 3″ × 6½″	2
7. Lower cross brace	¾″ × 1¾″ × 22″	1
8. Arms	¾″ × 4¾″ × 24″	2
9. Upper cross brace	¾″ × 1″ × 15¼″	1
10. Back slats	½″ × 2½″ × 30″	4
11. Finishing nails	6d and 8d	as needed
12. Flathead screws	#6 × 1″ and #8 × 1½″	as needed
Child's chair		
1. Front legs	⁹⁄₁₆″ × 2⅝″ × 15″	2
2. Seat rails	⁹⁄₁₆″ × 2⅝″ × 22½″	2
3. Back support	⁹⁄₁₆″ × 1⅛″ × 14¼″	1
4. Front brace	⁹⁄₁₆″ × 2⅝″ × 15⅜″	1
5. Seat slats	⁹⁄₁₆″ × 1⅞″ × 14¼″	5
6. Arm braces	⁹⁄₁₆″ × 2¼″ × 4⅞″	2
7. Lower cross brace	⁹⁄₁₆″ × 1¼″ × 22½″	1
8. Arms	⁹⁄₁₆″ × 3½″ × 18″	2
9. Upper cross brace	⁹⁄₁₆″ × ¾″ × 11½″	1
10. Back slats	⅜″ × 1⅞″ × 22½″	4
11. Finishing nails	6d and 8d	as needed
12. Flathead nails	#6 × 1″ and #8 × 1½″	as needed

The design for the original Adirondack chair is credited to H. C. Bunnel. He received a patent for his straight, boxy version in 1905. The chair was named for the region in upstate New York where it was designed and first used.

Over the years, Bunnel's design has been modified by others to make it more accommodating to the body. Backs have been rounded, and the seats contoured. But the chair you see here stays quite close to the early chairs. It is an exact copy of one made by my grandfather around 1918, when he was living in the Adirondacks. As a very young woodworker, I copied one of my grandfather's rotted chairs in 1949. You can see that the design is unpretentious—no frills, no curved back or seat. And yet it is quite comfortable. The chair is roomy enough for you to prop yourself on a pillow or two. You can lay a book or a drink on the wide arms.

On becoming a grandfather myself, I made a child's version, scaled down about a quarter. Either it or the full-size chair can be made with these plans and instructions. The Materials List gives two sets of overall dimensions. Note that even the thickness of the stock has been reduced for the child's chair—⁹⁄₁₆ in., rather than ¾ in.

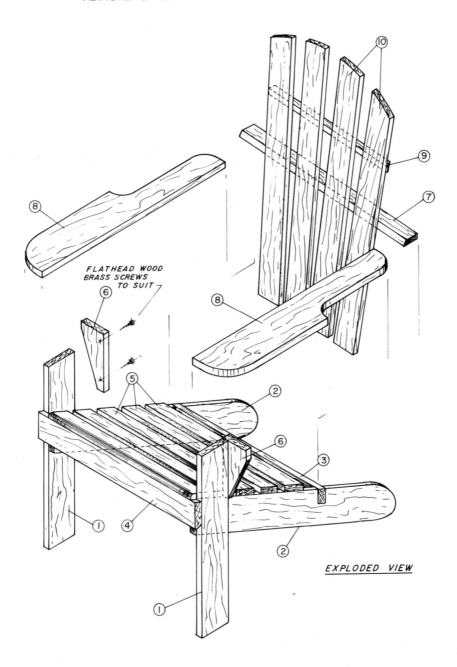

FLATHEAD WOOD
BRASS SCREWS
TO SUIT

EXPLODED VIEW

The chair can be put together with either brass-plated flathead screws or waterproof glue and finishing nails. You may want to countersink the screws 3/16 in. or so and cover them with plugs cut from dowels; nails should be set and puttied.

1. *Select the stock and cut the parts.* Here in New England, knot-free pine or spruce are common choices for making lawn furniture. If primed and kept painted, the wood should last 20 years or more. Woods especially suited for outdoor furniture include Honduras mahogany, oak, redwood, and teak.

Decide which chair model you are going to make. Cut the parts to the thickness and width given in the Materials List, but leave pieces with curved or angled ends an inch or so long.

2. *Make the seat.* An Adirondack chair begins with the seat. You can save time when cutting details in the seat rail and other paired parts by joining the pieces temporarily with double-sided tape. Lay out the details on one board, and then cut both boards at once.

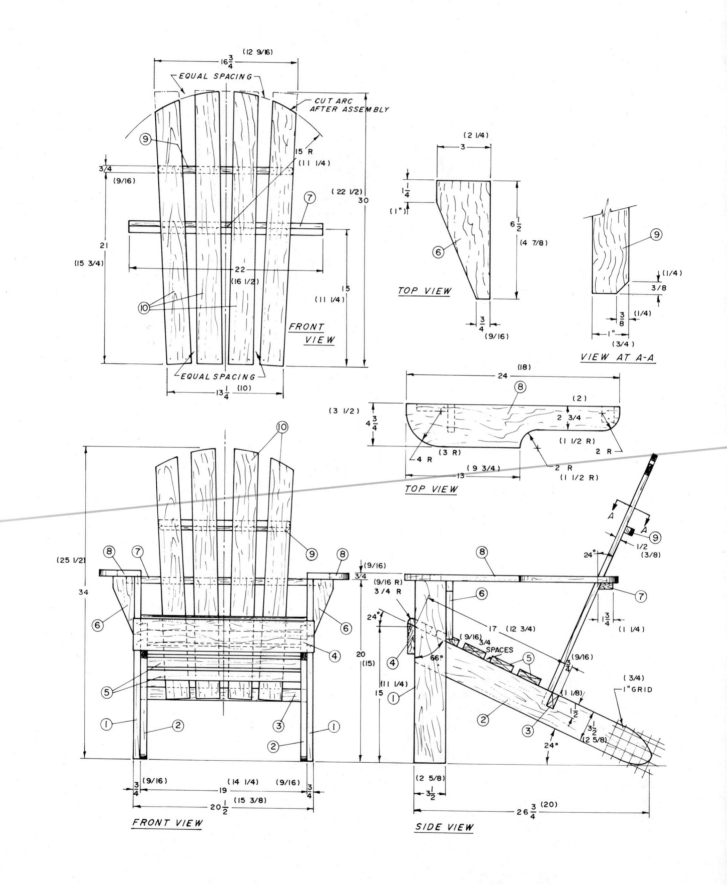

Cut a notch in each seat rail (part 2) to accept the back support (part 3). Round-over one end of the seat rail, following the pattern given and cut the other end at a 66-degree angle, as shown. Cut the seat rail to the proper length in the process.

After you've cut the seat rails to the proper profile, nail or screw the slats (part 5) to them. Attach the back support. Rip a 24-degree bevel on one edge of the front brace (part 4) and nail or screw it in place.

Round-over the front slat, as shown, with a router and the appropriately sized roundover bit.

3. *Make the back subassembly.* I found that the best way to assemble the back is to lay it out on a full-size pattern drawn on a large sheet of paper.

Draw a box 30 in. high and 16¾ in. wide on the paper. Lay out in pencil the location of the parts, as shown in the front view of the back.

Carefully position the back slats (part 10) on the drawing.

Rip a 24-degree bevel on the lower cross base (part 7) and chamfer the corner of the upper cross brace (part 9), as shown in the view at A-A. Position the upper and lower cross braces on the back slats. Check that the cross braces are parallel to the bottom of the box and then attach the slats to them with screws or nails and glue.

To lay out the cut for the curved top of the back, draw a 15-in.-radius arc from the center of the upper cross brace. Cut the curve with a saber saw and sand the cut edges.

Clamp the assembled back to the back support and glue or nail it in place. The back will be somewhat flimsy until you attach the arms, so treat it with respect.

4. *Attach the legs and arms.* Attach the legs (part 1) to the seat rail, as shown in the side view. Cut the arm braces (part 6) to the profile shown in the top view of part 6, and attach the braces to the legs so the top surfaces are flush with each other. Cut the arms (part 8) to the profile shown. Position the arms so the front extends about 1 in. beyond the legs. The arms' inner edges should be parallel to each other and flush with the inner face of the legs. Nail or screw them to the leg and arm brace. Clamp the back end of the arm to the upper cross brace and nail or screw the two together. Nail or screw the back slats to the lower brace.

5. *Apply finish.* If you've used nails, set them all over the chair, then putty and sand the holes. If you decided to countersink the screws, glue the plugs in place now.

Sand the chair all over. If you used a weather-resistant wood, your work is done. For added protection, you might add a coat or two of marine spar varnish. Other woods should be primed and finished with two coats of exterior paint. Don't forget to cover the bottom surfaces of the legs. You can expect to apply another coat of paint every two or three years.

Victorian Garden Bench

Gardeners have always taken time out to sit back and admire their work. That explains the popularity of the garden bench over the years. Here is a copy of a bench found in New Hampshire, bearing the patent date of December 12, 1893. This project substitutes fixed wooden braces for the iron castings on the original.

MATERIALS LIST

Part	Dimensions	Quantity
1. Legs	1″ × 14¾″ × 18″	2
2. Center battens	1″ × 3″ × 16″	2
3. End battens	1″ × 2″ × 16″	2
4. Seat	1″ × 16″ × 72″ (length variable)	1
5. Braces	1″ × 4⅝″ × 14½″	2
6. Stove bolts, washers, nuts	¼″ × 3½″	4 each
7. Flathead screws	#10 × 1¾″	16

1. Select the stock. Before shopping for lumber, keep in mind that you can either shorten or lengthen the bench as you wish. You might want to make a short bench for use as a coffee table.

The bench is made of stock that measures a full 1 in. thick. The original was of poplar. Pick a hardwood for outdoor use; pine will do if your bench is to serve as a coffee table.

2. Cut the battens and seat. Cut the center battens (part 2), end battens (part 3), and seat (part 4) as specified. Cut a 15-degree chamfer on the ends of the four battens.

Locate and cut the mortises in each center batten. Each mortise is 1 in. wide, 2¼ in. long, and spaced 1¾ in. from the ends; the inner edges of each pair of mortises should be 8 in. apart. Drill a series of 1-in. holes along the center line of the mortise to remove most of the waste. Cut to the edge of the mortise with a chisel.

3. Make a paper pattern for the legs and braces. Draw a grid with 1-in. squares, and enlarge the legs (part 1) and the braces (part 5) onto it. Transfer the patterns to the wood. Cut out

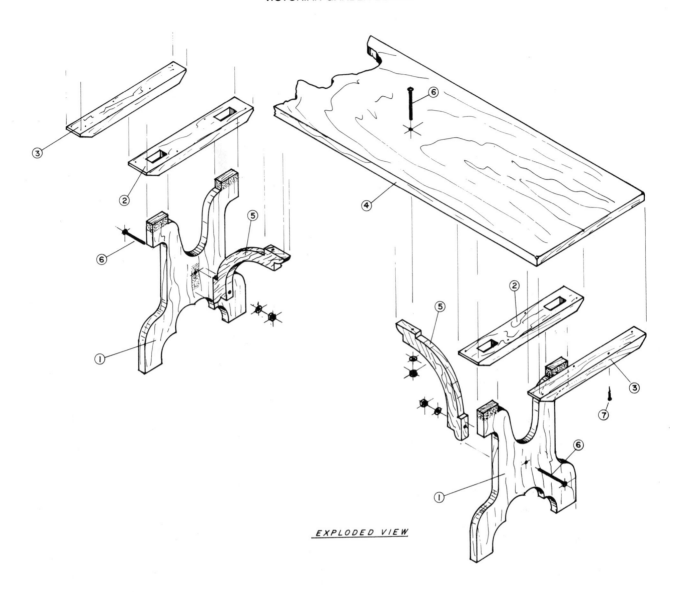

EXPLODED VIEW

the pieces, leaving the tenons slightly oversized. Trim the tenons to fit the mortises.

4. Assemble the bench. Glue the legs to the center battens. When the glue dries, screw the legs and battens to the seat bottom, staggering the screws (part 7), as shown in the drawings. Screw the two end battens to the seat with the eight remaining screws.

Attach the two braces to this assembly with stove bolts (part 6). Drill ¼-in.-diameter holes for the four stove bolts (bolts with slot heads) through the braces, legs, and seat. Be sure to keep the legs exactly perpendicular to the bench.

5. Apply Finish. Sand all surfaces and round the top edges of the seat. The original bench was painted powder blue and then, at some point in its history, repainted red. Over the years the red coat has worn away to show the blue—an attractive effect that you can duplicate. First, paint the bench a light shade of blue, repaint it red when dry, and go over the dry top coat with fine sandpaper or 0000 steel wool. Simulate wear by rubbing through the red paint here and there. Don't be afraid to sand right down to bare wood in a few spots. Apply a top coat of dark stain, allow it to soak into corners and edges, and wipe away the excess with a rag and turpentine.

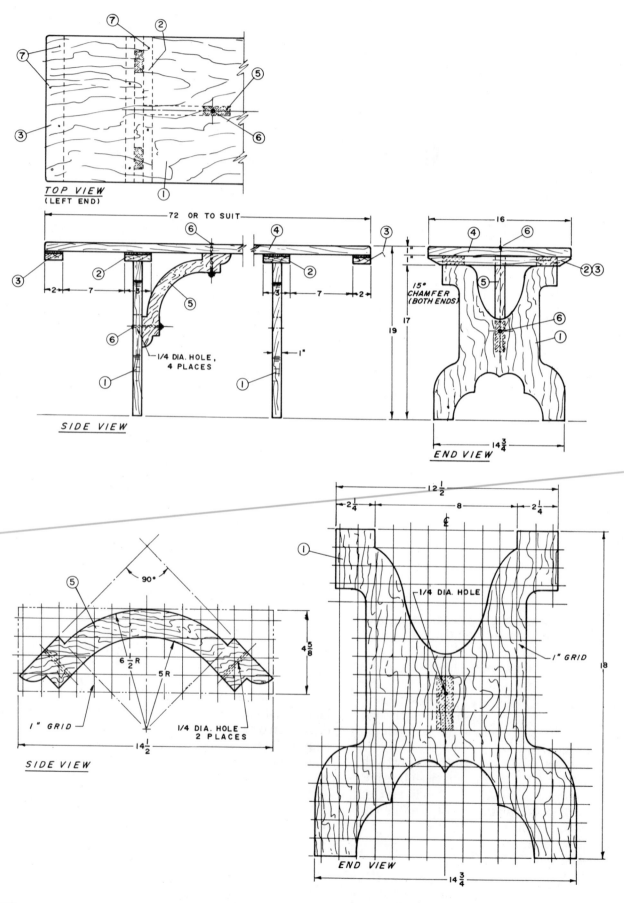

TOP VIEW
(LEFT END)

72 OR TO SUIT

SIDE VIEW

1/4 DIA. HOLE,
4 PLACES

END VIEW

16

15°
CHAMFER
(BOTH ENDS)

17

19

14 3/4

90°

5R

6 1/2 R

4 5/8

1" GRID

1/4 DIA. HOLE
2 PLACES

14 1/2

SIDE VIEW

12 1/2

2 1/4

8

2 1/4

1/4 DIA. HOLE

1" GRID

18

14 3/4

END VIEW

Card Holder

Here is a handy place to store the recipe cards that tend to end up in the back of kitchen drawers.

1. Select the stock and cut the parts. You can use almost any kind of wood for this project. I made the holder shown here out of pieces of ¼-in. mahogany from my scrap pile. The holder is made entirely with simple butt joints.

Cut the parts to the sizes given in the Materials List.

2. Make a paper pattern and cut the parts to shape. Draw a grid with ½-in. squares and enlarge the back (part 1) and a side (part 2) onto it. Transfer the enlargements to the wood. Lay out the outline of the lid (part 5), establishing the curve in the front edge by drawing the ⅝-in. radius.

Cut the pieces to shape. You can save time and ensure accuracy by cutting the two sides out together. Note the 20-degree cuts on the lid, front (part 3), and stop (part 6), as shown.

Drill the ¼-in.-diameter hole in the back.

3. Assemble the holder. Using the 4d finishing nails (part 7), nail the sides to the back and front, aligning their bottom edges on a flat surface. Sand the bottom edges of this subassembly as necessary so that it will sit flat.

Turn the assembly upside down. Hold the lid in place and scribe a line on it to locate the front edge of the stop. Glue the stop in place.

Nail the bottom (part 4) in place, keeping it centered and flush with the back, as shown.

4. Apply finish. Sand thoroughly, rounding the edges slightly. Apply clear varnish.

MATERIALS LIST

Part	Dimensions	Quantity
1. Back	¼" × 7½" × 6"	1
2. Sides	¼" × 3¾" × 5¾"	2
3. Front	¼" × 3¼" × 5⅛"	1
4. Bottom	¼" × 3¹⁵/₁₆" × 6"	1
5. Lid	¼" × 4½" × 5¹/₁₆"	1
6. Stop	¼" × ¼" × 5¹/₁₆"	1
7. Finishing nails	4d	16

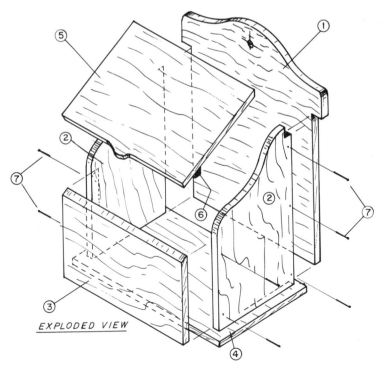

EXPLODED VIEW

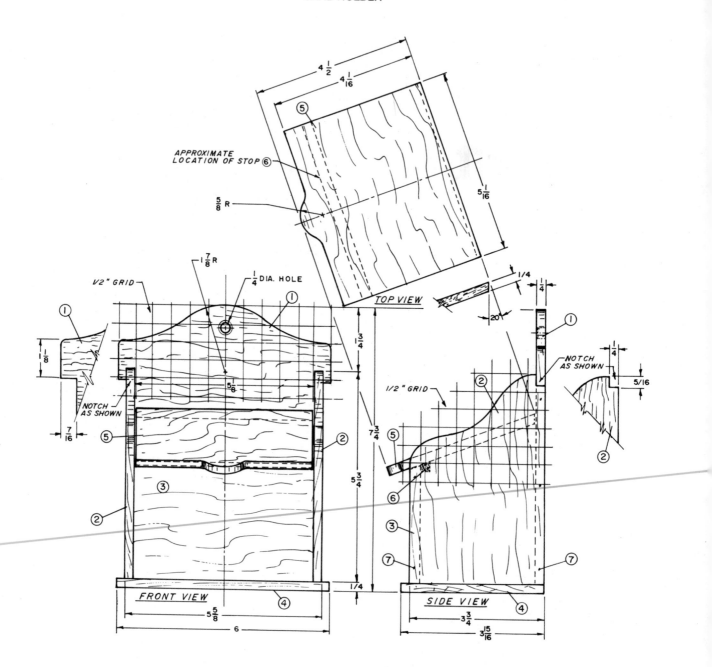

APPROXIMATE
LOCATION OF STOP ⑥

5/8 R

TOP VIEW

4 1/2

4 1/16

⑤

5 1/16

1/4

1/4

20°

1 7/8 R

1/4 DIA. HOLE

1/2" GRID

①

1 1/8

NOTCH
AS SHOWN

7/16

⑤

5 5/8

②

3 4

7 3/4

5 3/4

1/4

NOTCH
AS SHOWN

1/4

5/16

②

①

1/2" GRID

②

⑤

⑥

③

⑦

⑦

③

②

FRONT VIEW

④

5 5/8

6

SIDE VIEW

④

3 3/4

3 15/16

Child's Wheelbarrow

This project is a scaled-down copy of an antique wheelbarrow, made around 1850, which I found in Maine. The original was a little larger, and its wheel had true spokes rather than the cutouts in the wheel of this design.

You can use this scaled-down version as a magazine rack, a container for kindling, or a plant stand. Outdoors, you may want to place the wheelbarrow in the flower garden as an ornament, or you can press it into service for its intended use. Children will love to pile lawn clippings and leaves in it.

As you read through these instructions, note that the project is broken down into three parts: the wheel assembly, the frame assembly, and the box assembly. Study the drawings, including the detail views, before getting started.

1. Select the stock. The wheelbarrow in the photo is oak with a pine box assembly. While I'd recommend a hardwood frame, almost any combination of woods will work. The wheel can be hardwood or 1-in. exterior plywood. The axle is a ¾-in.-diameter hardwood dowel.

2. Lay out the wheel pattern. The *simplest* way to make the wheel is to cut it out of 1-in.-thick exterior plywood. I took a more time-consuming approach: I cut 21 pieces of ¾ × 1¼ × 20-in. oak and glued them up into a 1¼-in.-thick panel, measuring 16 × 20 in. I planed the panel down to 1 in. and made the eight cutouts that define the spokes.

Lay out the pattern of the wheel on paper. Locate the center. From that spot, swing diameters of 15 in. (representing the outside of the wheel), 11 in., and 7 in.

To lay out the heart-shaped cutouts, draw lines to divide the circle into eight equal pie-shaped pieces. Each intersection of a line with the seven-in. circle is the center of a circle that defines the bottom of the heart. Draw the circle, as shown in the front view of the wheel.

Now lay out and draw the circles that define the top of the heart. The center of these circles are along the 11-in. circle, ¹³/₁₆-in. either side of where it intersects each of the radii you drew. There are 16 such points; draw a circle from each of them.

Lay out the spokes by connecting the circles, as shown. The spokes should be about ¹¹/₁₆ in. wide. If you are off by much, or if the spokes are inconsistent in width, redraw the pattern.

Put a light coat of rubber cement on the back of the pattern. When the cement is dry, center the pattern on the board. Using an awl or a pointed nail set, punch the centers of all the circles through the paper into the wood. Each prick marks the center of a hole you will drill in the next step.

3. Cut out the wheel assembly. Carefully cut out the diameter of the wheel (part 12), staying just outside the 15-in. line. Sand it down to the line.

Drill the axle hole.

Begin the heart cutouts by drilling 24 2-in.-diameter holes on the marks you made in the last step. Drill the holes with a 2-in. Forstner bit. If the wood tears out on the back of the board, drill until the tip of the bit just pokes through, then turn the wheel over and finish drilling from that side.

Now cut along the lines connecting the circles with a jigsaw or coping saw. Sand the inner surfaces of the cutouts with a sanding drum mounted in the drill press. Sand the two sides of the wheel and fill any defects with putty.

MATERIALS LIST

Part	Dimensions	Quantity
1. Handles	$1'' \times 3'' \times 48''$	2
2. Front brace	$\frac{3}{4}'' \times 1\frac{1}{2}'' \times 8''$	1
3. Rear brace	$\frac{3}{4}'' \times 1\frac{1}{2}'' \times 13\frac{7}{8}''$	1
4. Bottom board	$\frac{3}{4}'' \times 14\frac{5}{8}'' \times 21\frac{1}{2}''$	1
5. Side boards	$\frac{3}{4}'' \times 9\frac{1}{2}'' \times 22\frac{3}{8}''$	2
6. Front supports	$\frac{3}{4}'' \times 1'' \times 9\frac{5}{8}''$	2
7. Rear supports	$\frac{3}{4}'' \times 1'' \times 11\frac{1}{2}''$	2
8. Vertical supports	$1'' \times 2\frac{1}{2}'' \times 11\frac{1}{2}''$	2
9. Front board	$\frac{3}{4}'' \times 9\frac{9}{16}'' \times 11\frac{3}{8}''$	1
10. Legs	$1'' \times 2\frac{1}{2}'' \times 12''$	2
11. Leg braces	$\frac{3}{4}'' \times 5'' \times 22''$	2
12. Wheel	$1'' \times 15'' \times 15''$	1
13. Inner hubs	$1'' \times 3'' \times 3''$	2
14. Outer hubs	$1'' \times 2\frac{1}{2}'' \times 2\frac{1}{2}''$	2
15. Axle	$\frac{3}{4}''$ dia. $\times 7\frac{1}{2}''$	1
16. Rim	$\frac{1}{8}'' \times \frac{5}{8}'' \times 47\frac{1}{4}''$	1
17. Flathead screws	#8 × ¾″	9
18. Roundhead screws	#8 × 1¾″	as needed
19. Roundhead screws	#8 × 1½″	as needed
20. Flathead screws	#8 × 1½″	as needed
21. Roundhead screws	#8 × 1″	as needed
22. Finishing nails	6d	as needed

Rout a ⅛-in.-radius cove in the cutouts, as shown in the detail at *A-A*. This is not necessary to the function of the wheelbarrow, but it will make the wheel look better.

Next, cut the wheel hubs (parts 13 and 14) on the band saw. Note the 15-degree taper, as shown in the end views of both parts. Tilt the table of your band saw to the appropriate angle to make the cuts. Drill ¾-in.-diameter axle holes through the center of each hub.

Sand the edges smooth and glue the hubs to the wheel. Slide the axle—a ¾-in.-diameter hardwood dowel—in place to align the centers of the hubs. To keep the dowel from being glued fast, rub it with a bar of soap. The soap also will act as a lubricant to make the wheel turn more easily.

With the completion of a bit of metal work, the wheel is finished. Cut the rim (part 16) from a strip of soft iron, available at metal supply firms. Drill and countersink the holes, as shown. Cut or file the ends at the angle shown in the detail for part 16, to make a tight, smooth joint. Attach the rim to the wheel with #8 × ¾-in.

flathead screws, starting at either end and progressing one screw at a time. Drill the pilot holes as you go, to avoid splitting the wheel. Before you drive the last screws, check how closely the ends meet and file them, if necessary, to make a smooth joint.

4. *Build the frame assembly.* The frame assembly includes the handles, front and rear braces, vertical supports, legs and leg braces, and axle (parts 1, 2, 3, 8, 10, 11, and 15). The front board (part 9) will be dealt with later. Cut each, as shown in the detail drawings. Be sure to make a right-hand and a left-hand handle: They are not identical. Shape the handle ends, as shown in the pattern in the drawing for part 1, and round them to a radius with a spokeshave.

Drill ¾-in.-diameter holes for the axle in front of the handles carefully. The holes are drilled at an 8-degree angle, as shown, to compensate for the splayed handles. If you drill the holes square to the handle, the axle won't align in the assembled frame.

Check to make sure the frame will go together correctly. Put the parts on a flat surface. Put the front brace 20¾ in. from the handle ends and the rear brace 16 in. from the handle ends, as shown in the exploded view. Check the distance between handles. As shown in the top view, the handles should be 18¼ in. apart at the ends and *exactly* 5¹/₁₆ in. apart at the front. Adjust as necessary to establish these last dimensions.

When all is in order, temporarily slide the axle in place to align the frame.

Screw the handles to the braces with roundhead screws (part 18). Before you drive any screws in this or any other project, drill pilot and clearance holes. The pilot hole should be slightly smaller than the shank, and in this case, it's drilled in the handle. The clearance hole, in the brace, is slightly larger than the screw shank. Countersink the clearance holes for flathead screws. Most hardware stores sell an inexpensive bit that will do all three at once.

Screw the vertical support to the frame assembly with #8 × 1¾-in. screws (part 18). As the final step in building the frame, attach the legs. Position the legs, as shown, and screw the legs to the handles with roundhead screws. Attach the leg braces to the handles next with roundhead screws (part 19) and to the bottom of the legs with two flathead screws (part 20).

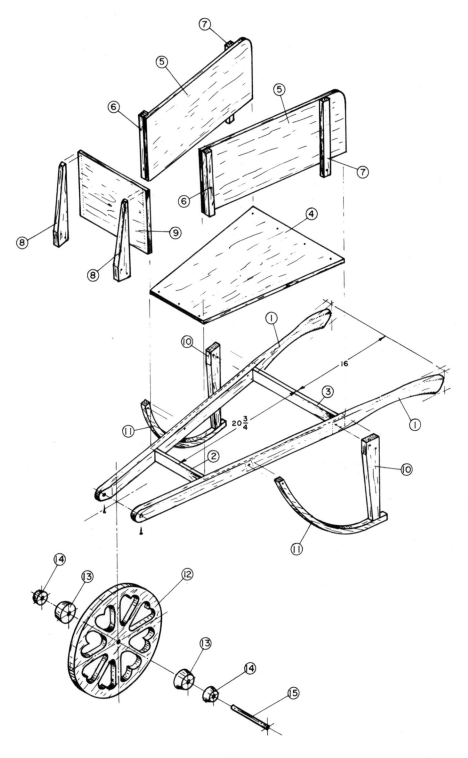

EXPLODED VIEW

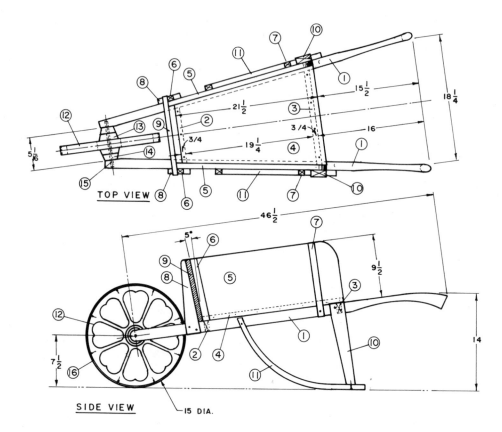

TOP VIEW

SIDE VIEW — 15 DIA.

5. **Build the box assembly.** The box is made of the bottom board, side boards, front and rear supports, and vertical supports (parts 4, 5, 6, 7, and 8). In construction, the actual size tends to vary from the drawings, so use the dimensions in the Materials List as a guide. Cut the actual parts to fit the actual frame.

First, lay out bottom. Here's how: Draw a line ¾ in. from the outer edge of each handle, shown as a dotted line in the exploded view. This line marks the edge of the bottom. Make a mark on each line 15½ in. from the handle ends, as shown, to mark the back corners of the bottom. Make a mark where the lines cross the *front* of the front brace, to mark the front corners of the bottom. Measure the distance and angles from corner to corner, and lay out the bottom board from them. Attach the bottom board with seven #8 × 1½-in. flathead screws.

Cut the side boards, front supports, and rear supports to fit the bottom. Nail and glue the sides to the bottom with 6d finishing nails (part 22); then screw each rear support to the handle with #8 × 1¾-in. roundhead screws (part 18). Cut the front board, noting the bevels shown in the edge view for part 9. Glue and nail it in place with 6d finishing nails. Check that everything is square.

6. **Assemble the wheelbarrow.** Screw the two vertical supports (part 8) tightly against the box assembly with two #8 × 1¾-in. roundhead screws.

Attach the wheel assembly to the axle and put the axle in place. Drill ⅛-in.-diameter holes from the bottom of the handles and halfway into the axle; drive #8 × 1-in. roundhead screws (part 21) into the axle to secure it. Trim the ends of the axle to make them flush with the sides of the handles.

7. **Apply finish.** Disassemble the wheelbarrow and stain and varnish the frame and wheel. If the wheelbarrow is to be used outside, use a water-proof finish.

Prime the box assembly and paint it the color of your choice. The original was barn red with a green pinstripe. I'm not a very good pinstriper, but even my poor job adds a lot to the appearance of the wheelbarrow. So, don't be afraid to try your hand at this detail.

After the finish has dried thoroughly, reassemble the wheelbarrow.

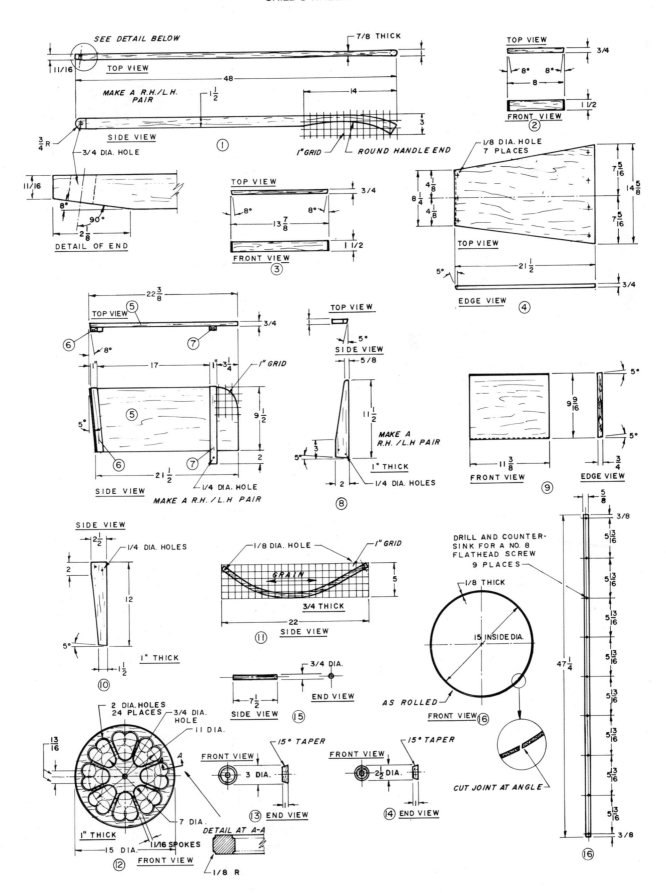

Four-Tiered Plant Stand

This is an exact copy of a plant stand made in the mid-1800s. It is simpler to make than you might guess from the drawings. Don't let the spindles discourage you; you can purchase a well-made set of them from the source given in the Materials List. They are available in almost any kind of wood, but I suggest either maple or beech. I've included a detail drawing of the turnings, in case you choose to make your own, or have them made by a local turner.

1. Select the stock and cut the parts. Use a softwood for the shelves. Note that the four semi-circular shelves (parts 2, 3, 4, and 5) are cut out of a single glued-up board measuring ¾ in. × 23 in. × 46 in. Cut the parts to their overall sizes. Purchase or turn the spindles (part 7).

2. Make a paper pattern for the legs. Draw a grid with 1-in. squares and enlarge the drawing of the legs (part 1) onto it. Be precise in measuring off the steps in the leg. Your accuracy here will ensure that the turnings fit properly.

3. Cut out the legs. Make a stack of the three pieces of wood from which you'll cut the legs and tape them together with double-sided tape. Drive the nails (part 9) within the final shape so that the parts won't fall apart as you cut them. Transfer the leg pattern to the top piece and cut all three legs at once. Sand the edges while the legs are together and sand the surfaces once you separate the legs.

MATERIALS LIST

Part	Dimensions	Quantity
1. Legs	¾" × 5½" × 45"	3
2. Shelf		
3. Shelf	One ¾" × 23" × 46" board	
4. Shelf	yields all shelves.	
5. Shelf		
6. Braces	¾" × ¾" × 7½"	2
7. Spindles*	1" dia. × 8½"	12
8. Flathead screws	#8 × 1¹/₁₂"	12
9. Finishing nails	4d	as needed

*Turnings are available from River Bend Turnings, R.D. 1, P.O. Box 364, Wellsville, NY 14895; order set #EAL-8.

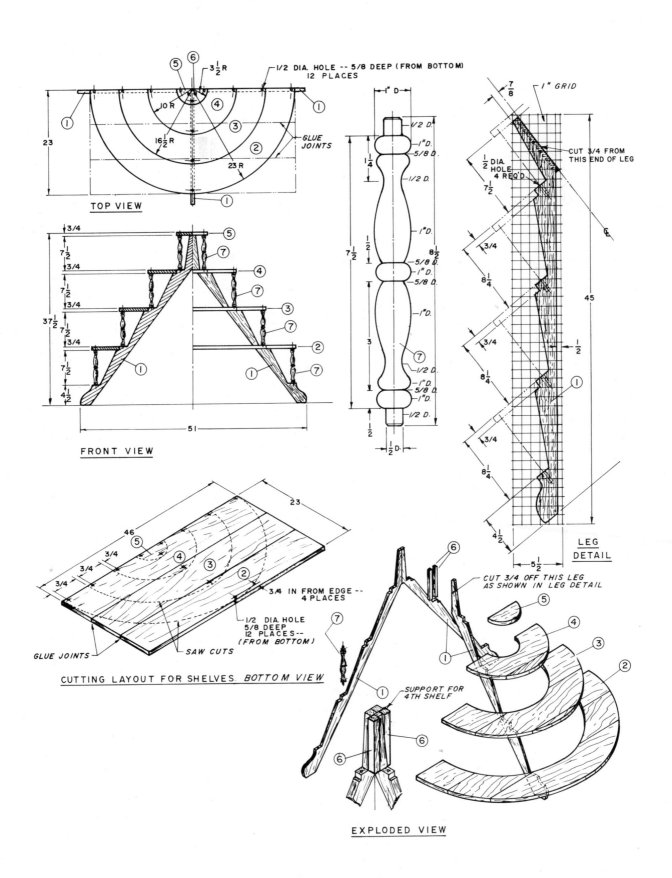

TOP VIEW

1/2 DIA. HOLE -- 5/8 DEEP (FROM BOTTOM) 12 PLACES

GLUE JOINTS

FRONT VIEW

LEG DETAIL

1" GRID

CUT 3/4 FROM THIS END OF LEG

1/2 DIA HOLE 4 REQ'D

CUT 3/4 OFF THIS LEG AS SHOWN IN LEG DETAIL

CUTTING LAYOUT FOR SHELVES. *BOTTOM VIEW*

GLUE JOINTS

SAW CUTS

3/4 IN FROM EDGE -- 4 PLACES

1/2 DIA HOLE 5/8 DEEP 12 PLACES -- (FROM BOTTOM)

SUPPORT FOR 4TH SHELF

EXPLODED VIEW

The three legs go together, as shown in the exploded view. First, however, you must trim the front leg, as shown in the leg detail, so that it projects the same distance from the center of the stand as the two side legs.

Lay out and drill ½-in.-diameter holes, 1 in. deep, in the steps of each leg, as shown in the leg detail. Try to keep the holes parallel to one another. Locate the center of each hole ¾ in. from the outside edge of its step and centered in the thickness of the stock.

4. Cut out the shelves. Draw four arcs to lay out the shelves, as shown in the top view.

Before you cut out the shelves, lay out and drill holes for the spindles, as shown. The center of each hole is ¾ in. from one of the arcs.

Cut out the four arcs, following the layout lines closely. Sand the surfaces and edges.

5. Assemble the stand. Glue the two identical legs to one another. When the glue dries, glue and nail the front leg in place. Glue the braces (part 6) in place, as shown in the exploded view. Make sure the legs stand evenly on the floor.

Glue the spindles in the legs, and glue the shelves to the spindles. Screw the lower shelves to the legs; first, drill a pilot hole, slightly smaller than the screw shank in the legs, and a clearance hole slightly larger than the shank in the shelf. Countersink the shelf for the flathead screws. Hardware stores sell an inexpensive bit that will cut all three in one pass.

6. Apply finish. The original plant stand was painted a dark, drab green and showed plenty of wear. Use any color that suits your room.

Picnic Table

Over the years, I've become a connoisseur of picnic tables. I've look at picnic tables at state parks and roadside stands from Maine to California. I've looked at plans from dozens of books going back to the 1920s and 1930s. For years, my favorite design was the one used in public picnic spots in Vermont. Recently, I came across this design at a Pennsylvania state park. It has quickly become my favorite.

1. Select the stock. Your choice of woods will depend on where you live. The Pennsylvania picnic table is made of oak. Here in the Northeast, straight-grain fir is often used. You can shop around for woods that are resistant to decay, such as redwood, cedar, and cypress. You also can work with pressure-treated lumber. If you do, buy wood that is stamped "dry," so you can paint it if you wish. In any event, I suggest you avoid chemically treated wood for the top to avoid the chance of contaminating food.

Unlike lumberyard 2 × 4s, which measure 1½ in. × 3½ in., the stock on the Pennsylvania picnic table is what I call full dimensioned: A 2 × 4 measures a full 2 × 4 inches. I've drawn the table with full-dimensioned stock. Feel free to use the more commonly available 2 bys, but adjust dimensions accordingly.

2. Cut the parts to size. Cut everything but the cross braces and the trestle (parts 5 and 6) to the sizes given in the Materials List. Trim the legs (part 1) and the seat braces (part 2) to the angles shown in the end view.

3. Assemble the ends. Using the dimensions given in the end view, lay out the legs, seat braces, and top braces (part 3) for each end. Make sure that the seat and top braces are parallel to each other and to the floor, and that they are spaced correctly. Nail them together with a few 10d nails (part 11) but don't drive the nails home so that you can remove them, if necessary. Stand the ends upright on a flat floor, side by side, and check to see that their angles and overall dimensions are exactly alike.

Adjust as needed, and once everything is as it should be, drive the nails home. Drill eight holes for carriage bolts, positioned as shown in the end view. Bolt the seat brace to the legs with carriage bolts (part 10), as shown in the exploded view.

4. Assemble the table. Put the top pieces (parts 7 and 8) face down on the floor, and nail the top supports (part 4) to them, as shown. Put the assembled ends in place next to the top supports and nail the supports and ends together.

Make sure the ends are square to the top and cut the cross braces (part 5) to fit. Nail the braces in place. Cut the trestle (part 6) to fit and nail it in place.

Turn the table right side up and nail the seats (part 9) in place.

5. Finish the table. If you used pressure-treated wood, allow the table to weather outdoors for two months or so before applying a coat of exterior oil stain. The weathered wood will have lost much of its characteristic green color by then, and the stain will be able to penetrate better.

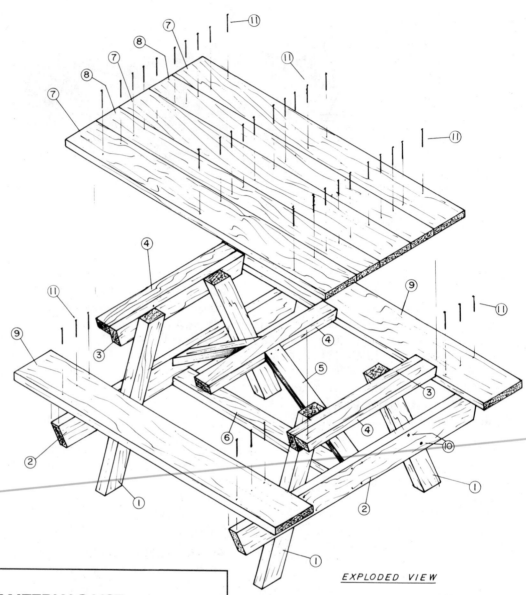

EXPLODED VIEW

MATERIALS LIST

Part	Dimensions	Quantity
1. Legs	$3'' \times 4'' \times 35\frac{1}{2}''$	4
2. Seat braces	$2'' \times 6'' \times 63\frac{1}{2}''$	2
3. Top braces	$2'' \times 4'' \times 34''$	2
4. Top supports	$2'' \times 4'' \times 34''$	3
5. Cross braces	$2'' \times 4'' \times 27''$	2
6. Trestle	$2'' \times 4'' \times 49''$	1
7. Wide tops	$2'' \times 8'' \times 71''$	3
8. Narrow tops	$2'' \times 6'' \times 71''$	2
9. Seat	$2'' \times 10'' \times 71''$	2
10. Carriage bolts	$\frac{3}{8}''$ dia. $\times 5''$ long	8
11. Nails	10d common	as needed

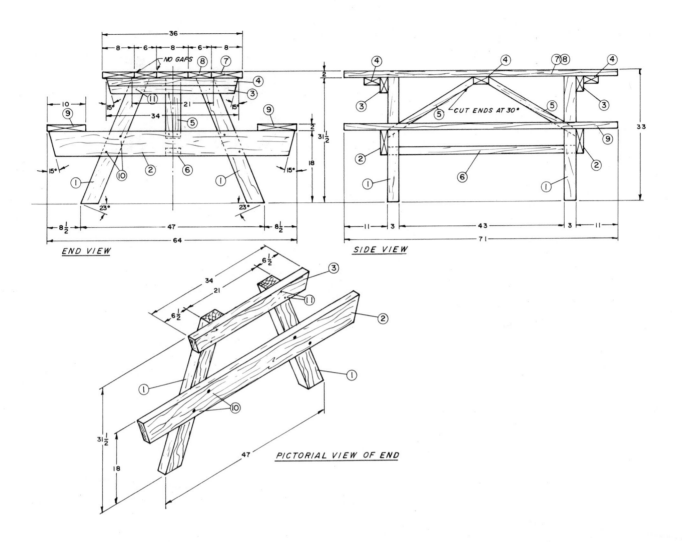

END VIEW

SIDE VIEW

NO GAPS

CUT ENDS AT 30°

PICTORIAL VIEW OF END

Appendix: Suppliers

I've found that buying high-quality hardware and finishes adds relatively little to the overall cost of a project. With that bit of advice shared, here is a list of mail-order sources for better-than-average supplies.

Brasses

Anglo-American Brass Co.
P.O. Box 9487
San Jose, CA 95157

Ball and Ball
463 W. Lincoln Hwy.
Exton, PA 19341

The Brass Tree
308 N. Main St.
St. Charles, MO 63301

Heirloom Enterprises
P.O. Box 146
Dundas, MN 55019

Horton Brasses
P.O. Box 95
Nooks Hill Rd.
Cromwell, CT 06416

Imported European Hardware
4320 West Bell Dr.
Las Vegas, NV 89103

Paxton Hardware Ltd.
Dept. R.P.
7818 Bradshaw Rd.
Upper Falls, MD 21156

The Renovators' Supply
Millers Falls, MA 01349

Ritter and Son Hardware
Gualala, CA 95445

The Shop, Inc.
R.D. 1, Box 207A
Oley, PA 19547

Garrett Wade Co., Inc.
161 Avenue of the Americas
New York, NY 10013

Clock Accessories

Barap Specialties
835 Bellows Ave.
Frankfort, MI 49635

Selva Borel
347 13th St.
Oakland, CA 94604

Craft Products Co.
2200 Dean St.
St. Charles, IL 60176

Craftsman Wood Service Co.
1735 W. Cortland Ct.
Addison, IL 60101

H. De Covnick and Son
P.O. Box 68
Alamo, CA 94507

Emperor Clock Co.
Emperor Industrial Park
Fairhope, AL 36532

Empire Clock, Inc.
1295 Rice St.
St. Paul, MN 55117

Klockit
P.O. Box 636
Lake Geneva, WI 53147

Kuempel Chime Clock Works
21195 Monnetonka Blvd.
Excelsior, MN 55331

S. LaRose, Inc.
234 Commerce Pl.
Greensborough, NC 27420

Mason and Sullivan Co.
586 Higgins Crowell Rd.
West Yarmouth, MA 02673

Merritt Antiques, Inc.
R.D. 2
Douglassville, PA 19518

Newport Enterprises, Inc.
2313 W. Burbank Blvd.
Burbank, CA 91506

Pacific Time Co.
138 W. 7th St.
Eureka, CA 95501

Precision Movements
2024 Chestnut St.
Box 689
Emmaus, PA 18049

M. L. Shipley and Co.
Rt. 2, Box 161
Cassville, MO 65625

Southwest Clock Supply, Inc.
2442 Walnut Ridge
Dallas, TX 75229

T.E.C. Specialties
P.O. Box 909
Smyrna, GA 30081

Turncraft Clock Imports Co.
Golden Valley, MN 55427

Viking Clock Co.
Box 490
Foley Industrial Park
Foley, AL 36536

Westwood Clock 'N Kits
2850 B E. 29th St.
Long Beach, CA 90806

General Catalogs

Brookstone Co.
Vose Farm Rd.
Peterborough, NH 03458

Cherry Tree Toys, Inc.
P.O. Box 369
Belmont, OH 43718

Constantine
2050 Eastchester Rd.
Bronx, NY 10461

Cryder Creek Wood Shoppe, Inc.
Box 19
101 Commercial Ave.
Whitesville, NY 14897

The Fine Tool Shops
P.O. Box 1262
20 Backus Ave.
Danbury, CT 06810

Leichtung, Inc.
4944 Commerce Pkwy.
Cleveland, OH 44128

Meisel Hardware Specialties
P.O. Box 70
Mound, MN 55364

River Bend Turnings
R.D. 1, P.O. Box 364
Wellsville, NY 14895

Silvo Hardware Co.
2205 Richmond St.
Philadelphia, PA 19125

Trendlines
375 Beacham St.
Chelsea, MA 02150

Woodcraft Supply Corp.
P.O. Box 4000
41 Atlantic Ave.
Woburn, MA 01888

The Woodworkers' Store
21801 Industrial Blvd.
Rogers, MN 55374

Woodworker's Supply of New Mexico
5604 Alameda Pl. NE
Albuquerque, NM 87113

Lathe Turnings
River Bend Turnings
R.D. 1, P.O. Box 364
Wellsville, NY 14895

Old-Fashioned Nails, Brass Screws
Equality Screw Co., Inc.
P.O. Box 1645
El Cajon, CA 92022

Horton Brasses
P.O. Box 95
Nooks Hill Rd.
Cromwell, CT 06416

Tremont Nail Co.
P.O. Box 111
21 Elm St.
Wareham, MA 02571

Paint, Stain, Tung Oil
Cohassett Colonials
38 Parker Ave.
Cohassett, MA 02025

Deft, Inc.
17451 Von Karman Ave.
Irvine, CA 92714

Formby's, Inc.
825 Crossover Ln.
Suite 240
Memphis, TN 38117

Stulb Paint and Chemical Co., Inc.
P.O. Box 297
Norristown, PA 19404

Watco–Dennis Corp.
Michigan Ave. & 22nd St.
Santa Monica, CA 90404

Painters of Reverse Glass and Dials
Linda Abrams
26 Chestnut Ave.
Burlington, MA 01803

Judith W. Akey
173 Harbourton Rd.
Pennington, NJ 08534

Marianne Picazio
P.O. Box 1523
Buzzards Bay, MA 02532

Linda Rivard
27 Spur Ln.
Newington, CT 06111

Astrid Thomas
21 Mast Hill Rd.
Hingham, MA 02043

Veneering
Bob Morgan Woodworking Supplies
1123 Bardstown Rd.
Louisville, KY 40204

Wood
Croffwood Mills
R.D. 1, Box 14
Driftwood, PA 15832

Wooden Finials
Boland V. Tapp Imports
13525 Alondra Blvd.
Santa Fe Springs, CA 09670

Rodale Press, Inc., publishes AMERICAN WOODWORKER™, the magazine for the serious woodworking hobbyist. For information on how to order your subscription. write to AMERICAN WOODWORKER™, Emmaus, PA 18098.